POSTDEVELOPMENT IN PRACTICE

Postdevelopment in Practice critically engages with recent trends in postdevelopment and critical development studies that have destabilised the concept of development, challenging its assumptions and exposing areas where it has failed in its objectives, whilst also pushing beyond theory to uncover alternatives in practice.

This book reflects a rich and diverse range of experiences in postdevelopment work, bringing together emerging and established contributors from across Latin America, South Asia, Europe, Australia and elsewhere, and it brings to light the multiple and innovative examples of postdevelopment practice already underway. The complexity of postdevelopment alternatives are revealed throughout the chapters, encompassing research on economy and care, art and design, pluriversality and *buen vivir*, the state and social movements, among others. Drawing on feminisms and political economy, postcolonial theory and critical design studies, the 'diverse economies' and 'world of the third' approaches, and discussions on ontology and interdisciplinary fields such as science and technology studies, the chapters reveal how the practice of postdevelopment is already being carried out by actors in and out of development.

Students, scholars and practitioners in critical development studies and those seeking to engage with postdevelopment will find this book an important guide to applying theory to practice.

Elise Klein is Senior Lecturer of Development Studies in the School of Social and Political Sciences at the University of Melbourne, Australia.

Carlos Eduardo Morreo teaches Development Studies and International Political Economy in the School of Politics and International Relations at the Australian National University.

ROUTLEDGE CRITICAL DEVELOPMENT STUDIES

Series Editors

Henry Veltmeyer is co-chair of the Critical Development Studies (CDS) network, Research Professor at Universidad Autónoma de Zacatecas, Mexico, and Professor Emeritus at Saint Mary's University, Canada.

Paul Bowles is Professor of Economics and International Studies at UNBC, Canada.

Elisa van Wayenberge is Lecturer in Economics at SOAS, University of London, UK.

The global crisis, coming at the end of three decades of uneven capitalist development and neoliberal globalization that have devastated the economies and societies of people across the world, especially in the developing societies of the global south, cries out for a more critical, proactive approach to the study of international development. The challenge of creating and disseminating such an approach, to provide the study of international development with a critical edge, is the project of a global network of activist development scholars concerned and engaged in using their research and writings to help effect transformative social change that might lead to a better world.

This series will provide a forum and outlet for the publication of books in the broad interdisciplinary field of critical development studies—to generate new knowledge that can be used to promote transformative change and alternative development.

The editors of the series welcome the submission of original manuscripts that focus on issues of concern to the growing worldwide community of activist scholars in this field.

To submit proposals, please contact the Development Studies Editor, Helena Hurd (Helena.Hurd@tandf.co.uk).

Neoextractivism and Capitalist Development
Dennis C. Canterbury

The Rise and Fall of Global Microcredit
Development, Debt and Disillusion
Edited by Milford Bateman, Stephanie Blankenburg and Richard Kozul-Wright

Postdevelopment in Practice
Alternatives, Economies, Ontologies
Edited by Elise Klein and Carlos Eduardo Morreo

For more information about this series, please visit: www.routledge.com/Routledge-Critical-Development-Studies/book-series/RCDS

POSTDEVELOPMENT IN PRACTICE

Alternatives, Economies, Ontologies

Edited by Elise Klein and
Carlos Eduardo Morreo

Routledge
Taylor & Francis Group
LONDON AND NEW YORK

First published 2019
by Routledge
2 Park Square, Milton Park, Abingdon, Oxon OX14 4RN

and by Routledge
52 Vanderbilt Avenue, New York, NY 10017

Routledge is an imprint of the Taylor & Francis Group, an informa business

© 2019 selection and editorial matter, Elise Klein and Carlos Eduardo Morreo; individual chapters, the contributors

The right of Elise Klein and Carlos Eduardo Morreo to be identified as the authors of the editorial material, and of the authors for their individual chapters, has been asserted in accordance with sections 77 and 78 of the Copyright, Designs and Patents Act 1988.

All rights reserved. No part of this book may be reprinted or reproduced or utilised in any form or by any electronic, mechanical, or other means, now known or hereafter invented, including photocopying and recording, or in any information storage or retrieval system, without permission in writing from the publishers.

Trademark notice: Product or corporate names may be trademarks or registered trademarks, and are used only for identification and explanation without intent to infringe.

British Library Cataloguing-in-Publication Data
A catalogue record for this book is available from the British Library

Library of Congress Cataloging-in-Publication Data
Names: Klein, Elise, 1983- editor. | Morreo, Carlos Eduardo, editor.
Title: Postdevelopment in practice : alternatives, economies, ontologies / edited by Elise Klein & Carlos Eduardo Morreo.
Description: Abingdon, Oxon ; New York, NY : Routledge is an imprint of the Taylor & Francis Group, an Informa Business, 2019. | Series: Routledge critical development studies | Includes index.
Identifiers: LCCN 2018052667 (print) | LCCN 2019004013 (ebook) | ISBN 9780429492136 (Master) | ISBN 9781138588653 (hardback) | ISBN 9781138588677 (pbk.) | ISBN 9780429492136 (ebook)
Subjects: LCSH: Economic development–Developing countries. | Capitalism–Developing countries.
Classification: LCC HC59.7 (ebook) | LCC HC59.7 .P624 2019 (print) | DDC 338.9009172/4–dc23LC record available at https://lccn.loc.gov/2018052667

ISBN: 978-1-138-58865-3 (hbk)
ISBN: 978-1-138-58867-7 (pbk)
ISBN: 978-0-429-49213-6 (ebk)

Typeset in Bembo
by Swales & Willis, Exeter, Devon, UK

Printed and bound in Great Britain by
TJ International Ltd, Padstow, Cornwall

CONTENTS

List of figures viii
List of tables x
List of contributors xi

Introduction 1
Elise Klein and Carlos Eduardo Morreo

PART I
Theorising a practice of postdevelopment 19

1 Postdevelopment @ 25: on 'being stuck' and moving forward, sideways, backward and otherwise 21
   Gustavo Esteva and Arturo Escobar

2 Postdevelopment in Japan: revisiting Yoshirou Tamanoi's theory of regionalism 37
   Yoshihiro Nakano

3 Postdevelopment's forgotten 'other roots' in the Spanish and Latin American history of development thought 52
   Sara Caria and Rafael Domínguez

4 Revisiting Transition 66
   S. Charusheela

5 Praxis in world of the third contexts: beyond third worldism and development studies   84
Anup Dhar and Anjan Chakrabarti

6 Crisis as opportunity: finding pluriversal paths   100
Ashish Kothari, Ariel Salleh, Arturo Escobar, Federico Demaria, and Alberto Acosta

PART II
Siting postdevelopment practice   117

7 Beyond development: postcapitalist and feminist praxis in *adivasi* contexts   119
Bhavya Chitranshi

8 Postdevelopment alternatives in the North   133
Daniel Bendix, Franziska Müller, and Aram Ziai

9 Who wants a 'development' that doesn't recognise alternatives?: Working with and against postdevelopment in Jagatsinghpur, India   149
Sandeep Pattnaik and Samantha Balaton-Chrimes

10 Economic hybridity in remote Indigenous Australia as development alterity   163
Katherine Curchin

11 Plurinationality as a strategy: transforming local state institutions toward *buen vivir*   176
Miriam Lang

12 Surviving well together: postdevelopment, maternity care, and the politics of ontological pluralism   190
Katharine McKinnon, Stephen Healy, and Kelly Dombroski

13 State-funded services delivery as cosmopolitical work: opportunities for postdevelopment in practice in northern Australia?   203
Michaela Spencer

14 Myths of development: democratic dividends and gendered
   subsidies of land and social reproduction in Uganda   217
   Lyn Ossome

15 Green and anti-green revolutions in East Timor and Peru:
   seeds, lies and applied anthropology   231
   Christopher J. Shepherd

16 Body Politics and Postdevelopment   247
   Wendy Harcourt

17 Manoeuvring political realms: alternatives to development
   in Haiti   263
   Julia Schöneberg

18 Technoaffective Reinscriptions: networks of care and critique
   'inside' and 'outside' of Europe in the age of precarity   276
   Anyely Marín Cisneros and Rebecca Close

19 Design futuring in a borderland of postdevelopment   294
   Tony Fry

20 Is Contemporary Art Postdevelopmental?: A study of
   'art as NGO'   306
   Verónica Tello

Concluding remarks and an invitation   321
Elise Klein and Carlos Eduardo Morreo

Index   *325*

FIGURES

15.1 A *campesino* family of the Q'enqomayo Valley, Paucartambo Province, Cusco, in their potato fields observing a ritual tradition at harvest time   234
15.2 The director of CESA, Luís Revilla, emphasises the importance of agrobiodiversity conservation in an information session with prospective 'conservationists'   236
15.3 Recuperated diversity. Forty varieties of potato make up this pile. This is about nurturing – not simply cultivating – diversity, which is the patrimony of the family, the community and the Andean cosmos   236
15.4 Each variety has a name, a distinctive taste, a personality and even a story in this all-animate Andean cosmos   237
15.5 A Seeds of Lies research assistant takes data on plant growth at an on-farm demonstration plot while the peasant farmer dreamily looks on   239
18.1 *Radio Europe*, performance, Rennes, April 2015. Gabrielle Leroux, Johanna Renard and Anyely Marín Cisneros reading the performance script   279
18.2 *How to Write a Tropical Disease/How to Write a Manifesto*, performance, 2016. Scan of a page of the performance script   282
18.3 *How to Write a Tropical Disease/How to Write a Manifesto*, performance, Guayaquil, 9 September 2016. María Auxiliadora Balladares and Francisco Santana reading a text of various fragments of manifestos and archival documents   283
18.4 *Llamando al mago*, video performance, 2017   284
18.5 *Llamando al mago*, video performance, 2017   285
18.6 *Llamando al mago*, video performance, 'Selfcare is Warfare', Bar Ocaña Barcelona, 2017   285

18.7	*Llamando al mago*, video performance, 2017. Film still of extract from Pratibha Parmar's *Reframing Aids* (1989), which uses an extract of Isaac Julien's *This is Not An AIDS Advertisement* (1987)	286
18.8	*Fuga Caníbal*, video, 2017. Film still	287
18.9	'Diagram of the causes of mortality in the army in the East' by Florence Nightingale was published in *Notes on Matters Affecting the Health, Efficiency and Hospital Administration of the British Army*, sent to Queen Victoria in 1858	289
18.10	Chromolithographs (produced in Catalonia during the 1872 yellow fever epidemic)	290
18.11	Photo taken during the workshop 'Reinscripciones', part of the 'Escuelita' public programme at CA2M, Madrid, curated by Julia Morandeira. Here, a group of participants named and ordered a corpus of images from the history of data visualisation (from maps to phylogenetic trees) on a timeline and connected them to keywords	290
20.1	*Institute for Human Activities*, Critical Curriculum programme, initiated by Renzo Martens	308
20.2	Daniela Ortiz, *97 empleadas domésticas (97 House Maids)*, 2016	314

TABLES

5.1 Class process and modes of appropriation 93
5.2 Class sets and world of the third 95

CONTRIBUTORS

Alberto Acosta is an Ecuadorian economist and former Minister of Mines and Energy, President of the Constituent Assembly (2007–2008) and a candidate for the Republic's presidency in 2013. He is a professor and researcher at FLACSO-Ecuador and the author of several books, including *El Buen Vivir* (2013).

Daniel Bendix is a postdoctoral researcher and Lecturer in Development and Postcolonial Studies at the University of Kassel, Germany. He is the author of *Global Development and Colonial Power: German Development Policy at Home and Abroad* (2018).

Sara Caria is faculty member of the Department of Public Economics at the Instituto de Altos Estudios Nacionales (IAEN), Ecuador. Her recent research and academic activities are in the field of development studies, with emphasis on structural transformation and international trade.

Anjan Chakrabarti is Professor of Economics at the University of Calcutta. His present area of interest is Marxian theory and political philosophy. His latest co-authored book is *The Indian Economy in Transition: Globalization, Capitalism and Development* (2015). He was awarded the VKRV Rao Prize in Economics in 2008.

S. Charusheela is Professor at the School of Interdisciplinary Arts and Sciences (IAS), University of Washington, Bothell. Selected publications include 'Response: History, historiography, and subjectivity' and 'Engendering feudalism: Modes of production debates revisited' in the journal *Rethinking Marxism*.

Bhavya Chitranshi has her master's in Gender Studies and an MPhil in Development Practice and is currently Fellow in Action Research at the Centre for

Development Practice, Ambedkar University, Delhi. She has been working on the question of 'singleness' among indigenous women and co-founded the Single Women's Collective in the Rayagada district of Odisha, India.

Samantha Balaton-Chrimes is Lecturer in International Studies at Deakin University. Her research is concerned with enduring political questions about how difference is negotiated in contexts of power asymmetries. Her work is interdisciplinary in nature, engaging political theory, anthropology and development studies. She works in India with people's movements, and in Kenya with the Nubian community.

Katherine Curchin is a non-Indigenous Australian and Lecturer in Social Policy at the Australian National University. She was a Research Fellow at the Centre for Aboriginal Economic Policy Research from 2013 to 2018. Her current Australian Research Council fellowship project explores rival visions of Indigenous development in remote Australia.

Critical Días is an arts research platform coordinated by **Anyely Marín Cisneros** and **Rebecca Close**, who have worked together since 2013, when they cofounded the collective Diásporas críticas. *Critical Días* uses feminist pedagogy techniques in projects that often combine elements of archival research, the writing of poetic-political texts and collective performance.

Federico Demaria is an ecological economist at the Autonomous University of Barcelona and at Research & Degrowth. He is the co-editor of *Degrowth: A Vocabulary for a New Era* (Routledge, 2014), which has been translated into ten languages.

Anup Dhar is Professor of Philosophy and Director of the Centre for Development Practice in Ambedkar University, Delhi. His co-authored books include *Dislocation and Resettlement in Development: From Third World to World of the Third* (Routledge, 2009) and *The Indian Economy in Transition: Globalization, Capitalism and Development* (2015). He also co-edited *Psychoanalysis in Indian Terroir: Emerging Themes in Culture, Family, and Childhood* (2018).

Kelly Dombroski is Senior Lecturer in Human Geography at the University of Canterbury Te Whare Wānanga o Waitaha. She works on the theory and practice of care and social transformation through feminist, postdevelopment, cultural geography and community economies perspectives. Her fieldwork has been in the areas of infant care and mothering in different cultural groups in northwest China and Australasia, as well as care and wellbeing in postdisaster contexts.

Rafael Domínguez is Professor of Economic History and Institutions at the University of Cantabria, Spain, Lecturer in the PhD programme in Social

Sciences at the University of Salamanca and Visiting Professor at several universities in Colombia, Ecuador and Mexico. He chairs the Research Group in Human Development and International Cooperation.

Gustavo Esteva is a grassroots activist and a public intellectual. He works independently and in conjunction with Mexican, Latin American and international grassroots organisations. He was an advisor to the Zapatistas in their negotiations with the government of Mexico. He has authored, co-authored and edited many books and essays.

Arturo Escobar is Professor of Anthropology at the University of North Carolina, Chapel Hill and Research Associate with the Culture, Memory, and Nation group at Universidad del Valle, Cali.

Tony Fry is a design and cultural theorist and an award-winning designer, writer and educator. He is Adjunct Professor at the Creative Exchange Institute at the University of Tasmania and Visiting Professor at the University of Ibagué in Colombia. Tony is the author of twelve books, his latest being *Remaking Cities* (2017).

Wendy Harcourt is Professor and Chair of Gender, Diversity and Sustainable Development and Westerdijk Professor at the International Institute of Social Studies of the Erasmus University (ISS/EUR) in The Hague, the Netherlands. At ISS/EUR she is Coordinator of the EU H2020-MSCA-ITN-2017 Marie Skłodowska-Curie Innovative Training Network (ITN), WEGO (Well-being, Ecology, Gender, and Community) and Chair of the ISS Institute Council.

Stephen Healy is an economic geographer and Senior Research Fellow at the Institute for Culture and Society, Western Sydney University. He is co-author of *Take Back the Economy* (2013) with J.K. Gibson-Graham and Jenny Cameron, and his research features community-based efforts to enact alternative economies, including commoning practices.

Ashish Kothari is a founding member of Kalpavriksh, an Indian environmental action group (an early ICCA Consortium member), a member of the ACKnowl-EJ network (Academic-Activist Co-Produced Knowledge for Environmental Justice), and coordinates the global Radical Ecological Democracy network.

Miriam Lang is Associate Professor for Social and Global Studies at Universidad Andina Simón Bolívar, Ecuador. She collaborates with the Permanent Working Group on Alternatives to Development and various social movements. Her co-edited book *Beyond Development: Alternative Visions from Latin America* (2013) has been translated into seven languages.

Katharine McKinnon is a human geographer whose work engages with community economies, gender, development and care. Her work in Australia and the Asia-Pacific region focuses on women's economic empowerment measures, social enterprises and the wellbeing economy, and community economies of maternity care.

Franziska Müller coordinates a research group on governance and the political economy of African energy transitions. Her research focuses on critical international relations theories and environmental governance in postcolonial contexts.

Yoshihiro Nakano is Junior Researcher at Waseda University, Japan. His area of specialisation is social philosophy, especially global intellectual history of anti-productivist social theories. Dr Nakano is an instigator of degrowth and convivialism in Japan and publishes Japanese translations of French, Spanish and Italian literature on alternative economies.

Lyn Ossome is Senior Research Fellow at the Makerere Institute of Social Research, Uganda. She writes broadly within the fields of feminist political economy and feminist political theory. Her new book is titled *Gender, Ethnicity and Violence in Kenya's Transitions to Democracy: States of Violence* (2018).

Sandeep Kumar Pattnaik works as a consultant at the National Center for Advocacy Studies (NCAS), in Pune, India. He is involved in undertaking research on the rights of tribals, *dalits* and women to natural resources. He also provides support to people's movements and highlights their cause to foster international solidarity.

Ariel Salleh is a scholar and activist and the author of *Ecofeminism as Politics: Nature, Marx, and the Postmodern* (1997), *Eco-Sufficiency and Global Justice* (2009) and some 200 articles on radical alternatives.

Christopher J. Shepherd conducts historical and ethnographic research on development, agriculture and mining in Peru and East Timor, following anthropological and science studies perspectives. He has published *Development and Environmental Politics Unmasked: Authority, participation and equity in East Timor* (Routledge, 2013) and numerous articles and book chapters.

Julia Schöneberg studied and taught sociology, peace and development studies at the universities of Hamburg, Lancaster, Bonn (ZEF), Rhine-Waal and Salzburg. She is currently Research Fellow at the University of Kassel. Her research interests focus on practical postdevelopment, social movements and resistances, as well as decolonial approaches to knowledge production and pedagogy.

Michaela Spencer is a postdoctoral Fellow with the Northern Institute at Charles Darwin University in Australia. She is involved in ethnographic and policy-design research that draws on STS sensitivities and frequently involves collaborative work with Indigenous Elders and knowledge authorities, as well as government and non-government organisations.

Verónica Tello is a Chilean-Australian theorist and historian of contemporary art. Her work focuses on aesthetics and technologies of counter-memory/history, bio- and necro-politics and border politics. She is currently Lecturer at UNSW Art & Design and Research Fellow (Arts of Global South research cluster) at Rhodes University, South Africa.

Aram Ziai is Professor of Development and Postcolonial Studies at the University of Kassel, Germany and has published widely on postdevelopment. He is the author of *Development Discourse and Global History: From Colonialism to the Sustainable Development Goals* (Routledge 2016).

INTRODUCTION

Elise Klein and Carlos Eduardo Morreo

Whilst the global development industry emerged from the colonial period in the mid-twentieth century (Kothari 2005), its colonial links continue (Kothari 2005; Mignolo 2011) alongside narratives of freedom and improvement. Though development is an 'amoeba concept' reflecting its high malleability and resilience to adapt (Demaria & Kothari 2017: 2588), it nonetheless continues to promote ideas of improvement for populations in the Global South rehearsed through the teleologies of capitalism and liberalism (Escobar 1995, 2015). The array of developmental improvements is based on the lessons of Western modernity and is commonly legitimised through expert knowledge that tends to define peoples and societies around the world as 'less developed' (Ziai 2013). Yet, the failures of development are recognised both in the Global South and increasingly within the Global North. A paradox emerges; the institutions and practices that development has promoted to better the world, have, in fact, contributed to growing inequality and poverty. Perhaps the ultimate failures of development are most starkly seen through the persistence of poverty despite over fifty years of aid and intervention, in the recognition of anthropogenic climate change and biodiversity loss (Sachs 2017) and in the realisation that millions of people continue to find their labour, environments and lives surplus to the requirements of 'variegated capitalism' (Peck & Theodore 2007).

Still, prominent scholars and authorities within development point to the numbers that international technocracies and local bureaucracies regularly produce to highlight the success of their projects – the many who have been 'lifted from poverty', treated for AIDS or malaria, the number of children in schooling, those that have had their life expectancy extended or maternal health improved. Yet, scholarship has shown that there is a perverse politics inherent to the production of these reassuring indices and statistical indicators as relations of power are distorted and the complexity gets obscured (Engle-Merry 2011; Reddy & Lahoti

2016). One only needs to scratch the surface of these measures to uncover a darker side to achieving development (Nandy 2002; Weber 2010).

Over a decade ago, Barbara Harriss-White (2006) showed the links between economic precarity and capitalism in India, not only through ongoing accumulation by dispossession and the pauperising of petty commodity production, but also through climate change and insecurity-producing disaster events. The latter have arisen from the need for greater energy inputs and through the production of waste driving productivity in the so-called formal economy. In his analysis of capitalism in India and China, Anthony D'Costa (2014) illustrates how the dispossession and displacement of rural communities from their land by national and international capital is integral to economic production, forcing these people into what over a century ago Engels had termed 'petty commodity production'. Livelihoods have been ruined through loss of biodiversity, degradation of water and soils and through climate change (Lohmann 2011; Martínez-Alier 2012). Whilst formal employment has been created in these economies, it is nowhere near at a rate high enough to absorb the people being dispossessed (D'Costa 2014). Here we come to see the importance of recognising 'the decisive shift since the 1980s from the "developmental state" to neoliberal "accumulation by dispossession" in the global south' (Wilson 2017: 2688).

The 'inconvenient truth' remains that the development celebrated by North Atlantic institutions and tethered to GDP charts and rates is the same model that continues to subjugate and dispossess. Whilst gains can always be located, the global rise in inequality continues at pace, and race, patriarchy and coloniality endure. Through the homogenising impacts of development, cultural and social relations have been disrupted (Connell 2007), 'gender' and kin unsettled (Walsh 2016; Lugones 2016), and bodies scarred (Kapur 2005). In the name of development and human rights, imperial wars have been staged (Douzinas 2000) and racialised borders have been erected (Bakewell 2008). Indigenous peoples have been pushed off their land, imprisoned or institutionalised for resisting assimilation (Watson 2009; Altman 2010; Coulthard 2014), while precarious lives in 'developed' societies and 'advanced' economies are sustained by punishing pharmacologies, where people are willing to take their own lives because labour cannot be an institution of self-realisation, equality or freedom (Ehrenreich 2010; Mills 2014).[1] Furthermore, the political economy ills of 'financialisation' and 'neoliberalism', both largely programmes and measures taken to address the ongoing crises or outright failures of 'developed' economies, have recently brought about the events of conservative populism in the USA and European disintegration, while condoning the extraordinary concentration of wealth in the hands of an ever-shrinking global elite. Contemporarily, an undifferentiated humanity is held responsible for climate change's unsalvageable pace, exposing the fundamental flaw of capitalism's and neoliberalism's economic rationalities (Klein 2015; Santelices Spikin & Rojas Hernández 2016).

The development industry has adapted its project of continued improvement and progress through 'participatory regimes', 'empowerment', 'sustainability' and 'inclusive growth' (Cooke & Kothari 2001; Batiwala 2007; Li 2007). The Sustainable Development Goals (SDGs) advance the Millennium Development Goals (MDGs) through refocusing projects of improvement to include the Global North. Yet, as Sachs (2017) points out, there are contradictions in these goals; poverty reduction often comes at the price of increasing inequality and environmental degradation. Likewise, the SDGs still centre contemporary capitalism as a mechanism to deal with persistent poverty, growing inequality and ecological ruin, yet 'inclusive growth driven by the financial markets is an impossibility' (Sachs 2017: 2578). Amartya Sen and capability scholars equally face similar critiques with their view of development as expanding capabilities (Sen 1999, 2009; Nussbaum 2001). While these ideas have significantly moved debates away from development as reducible to economic development and towards a multi-dimensional approach to understanding human flourishing, this shift takes place within an unacknowledged framework bundling neoclassical economic science and liberalism's political commitments, the upshot being new tools for the development industry to keep reproducing itself through deploying new and improved expertise (Mignolo 2011).

In the meantime, as these conceptual alterations to development rekindle development, millions around the world whose lives intersect in all manner of ways with global capitalism are encouraged to wait patiently, seized by development's promise that things will get better. Development as catch up and as doubling down on capitalism has been futile for so many. This is not to overlook the creativity, politics and forms of resistance populations have mounted amid the forms of subalternity, or to disregard the developmental hybrids that have emerged as people adapt, survive and persist (Long 2001). Indeed, the thrust behind this volume is to pay homage to these agencies, to engage them and put them up for discussion. It is also necessary to acknowledge the work of the many who have hitched their livelihoods to neoliberal globalisation hoping to benefit, captivated by the shine of capital's promise, contemporary entrepreneurial philosophies, or the appealing idea that near enough might just be reasonable. Neither is this engagement with development necessarily linear; a person or group may reject some development initiatives while welcoming others (Matthews 2017). Development has not been the emancipatory project its early manifestos promised it to be. So, what then are the alternatives? Which cracks and edges are actors already turning to? Within the pages of this book, we build upon a genealogy of critical scholarship from the North and South, and across the humanities and social sciences, which has interrogated the promises of development, pointing beyond its disappointing experience. However, this project goes further; we will specifically examine already existing practices, or what we are calling postdevelopment in practice.

Postdevelopment

Postdevelopment emerged in the 1980s drawing on poststructuralist legacies in order to destabilise the discourse or apparatus of development as a hegemonic principle organising social life (Esteva & Escobar 2017). Postdevelopment scholars and activists provided a cutting critique of the global development assemblage. First, development was questioned for measuring diverse socialities by Western models of progress where an individualised subject and capitalism were taken as central. This system classified many populations and non-capitalist practices and ways of being around the world as subordinate and inferior, all the while conveniently overlooking and silencing the darker side of modernity in which colonisation, accumulation by dispossession and exploitation had been integral (Mignolo 2011). Second, postdevelopment scholars identified in development discourse a project strongly privileging European and Anglo-American expertise and technocracy, systematically obscuring or masking coloniality, patriarchy and other relations of power marshalling the 'will to improve' (Escobar 1995; Li 2007; Ziai 2007). Third, development, whilst delivering Western prescriptions, had overlooked and marginalised 'pluriversality', the diverse ontologies and ecologies of knowledge, rendering them 'traditional', regressive and non-credible (Dussel 2002; de Sousa Santos 2009).

Today postdevelopment is not only concerned with the Global South, but equally addresses the North. The work of postdevelopment includes staking out a position about northern theory that is conscious of the intricacies of hegemony in its own perspectives (such as the series of cultural and epistemic hierarchies within institutions of 'global' knowledge production). Postdevelopment has sought to displace the universalisation and globalisation of modernity, insisting instead on the need for what Gustavo Esteva has described by paraphrasing the Zapatista motto, as 'a world in which many worlds can be embraced' (Esteva & Escobar 2017: 4). In the early years of postdevelopment's critique, Rahnema (1997) stated that postdevelopment would not be the end of the search for justice, but rather should only mean that the 'binary, the mechanistic, the reductionist, the inhuman and the ultimately self-destructive approach to change is over' (Rahnema 1997: 391). Similarly, Colombian scholar Arturo Escobar, a major contributor to the debates on postdevelopment, announced over two decades ago that, '[w]e are not looking for development alternatives but alternatives to development' (1995: 215). For Escobar, postdevelopment critically examines a set of key principles: the support of pluralistic grassroots movements while tempering localised relations of power, and upholding a critical stance towards established scientific discourses and development expertise often refracted through the postcolonial state. Postdevelopment also encompasses the promotion of different conceptions of economy, taking into account solidarity, reciprocity and other forms of valuation as opposed to the axioms of *homo oeconomicus*. Therefore, postdevelopment references not only alternatives to development, but by doing so works to overcome the dualisms that have hidden the ongoing and contemporary making of worlds (explained below).

Postdevelopment and theoretical links

Beyond the well-known link with poststructuralist theory, postdevelopment has cultivated a dialogue with other theoretical discourses. For instance, postcolonial theory shares many of the critical concerns of postdevelopment, where both are troubled by the 'ongoing relationship between colonial forms of rule and governance and the purpose and practice of development' (Kothari 2005: 118) and 'capital's ability to assimilate all forms of life that oppose its aspirations' (Gidwani 2008: 217). Similarly, like postdevelopment, postcolonial critique has also challenged the construction of the 'Other'; however, it has done so by 'conceptualising the historical and social context of these constructions, revealing the distinct notions of race, ethnicity, gender and class in their constitution, and by replacing them with alternative ones' (Kayatekin 2009: 1114). In essence, postcolonial critique has demanded that scholars rethink the ontological and epistemological positioning of research – the sites of knowledge production and circulation. In addition, if the 'vocation of postcolonial discourse', as Harry Harootunian comments, has been 'to presen[t] the voiceless as capable of enunciating tactics of resistance and negotiation, elevating them as subjects worthy of study and inclusion' (2012, 9), it is postdevelopment rather than the subject of postcolonial critique that would both affirm such a vocation and be transformed by this demand. The encounter between development's Southern critics and postcolonialism has profoundly shaped the project of postdevelopment.

Critical feminist approaches have also been crucial to postdevelopment in making visible relations of power linked to modernity/coloniality such as economic exploitation, race, heterosexuality and gender. For example, María Lugones (2016) has examined the 'coloniality of gender' and how eurocentric, biologised, binary and hierarchical constructions of gender have attempted to write over and write out diverse erotics. For Lugones, simply put, 'gender is a colonial construction' (Walsh 2016: 37). Critical feminist approaches have been crucial in pointing to the plurality of feminisms (and patriarchies) shaping politics in the South and North. This diversity of feminisms, with specific histories and ontologies, matters. Therefore, the question articulated by Catherine Walsh (2016) has much to say to postdevelopment; what might it mean to 'think with and from postures, perspectives and experiences that transgress, interrupt and [that] break with the universalism, dualism and hegemonic pretensions that these categories [of imperial reason] announce and construct?' (Walsh 2016: 44). In this light, the significant work of feminists such as Wendy Harcourt has bought attention to the embodiment of cultural, economic and social relations (Harcourt 2009). Harcourt points to how postdevelopment can contribute to unmaking the ways bodies are shaped and to build on 'multiple resistances and rebellions expressed in feminist and queer struggles for the bodily integrity of the many "Others"' (Harcourt, Chapter 16 in this volume). In addition, if relationality is a central and guiding concept in critical feminist thought, relationality to the human and non-human world has become equally significant for postdevelopment, thereby challenging the extractivist, controlling and exploitative relationship Western patriarchal modernity has to other ecologies (Harcourt & Nelson 2015). Indeed, as Harding states, 'modernization and its development theories, policies, and practices, […] have always been masculinized' (Harding 2016: 1072). The possibility for diverse ways of being in the world that respond to and value the affects, connectedness, sacredness and the complex and ongoing collaborations between humans and nonhumans represents a significant challenge (Escobar 2018).

The turn to an ontological politics in contemporary scholarship is yet another concern shaped by debates with postdevelopment (Blaser 2009, 2013; Escobar 2018). Political ontology here refers to

> the power-laden practices involved in bringing into being a particular world or ontology; [and] to a field of study that focuses on the interrelations among worlds, including the conflicts that ensue as different ontologies strive to sustain their own existence in their interaction with other worlds.
>
> *(Escobar 2018: 66)*

The aim of detailing ontology results from a concern with everyday practices and the worlds they sustain, and the discordant or conflicting relations between these coeval worlds. A key aim here is to make visible those 'heterogeneous assemblages of life that enable non-dualist, relational worlds' (Escobar 2018: 66). An important theoretical resource, animating the ontological turn has been the earlier and prominent work of Bruno Latour and others associated with actor-network theory (ANT) and the interdisciplinary field of science and technology studies (STS). Scholars engaging with ANT and the work of Latour or John Law, among others, have sought to examine the plurality of practice at the level of ontology, challenging the anthropocentrism of the modern, and the possibility of setting 'society' apart from 'nature'. In documenting a multiplicity of practices enrolling humans and non-humans, ANT has shifted the focus of development, opening up a plurality of conceptions of change, but also a plurality of ways of being 'modern' (Donovan 2014).

More broadly, a key STS insight in its actor-network theory variant has been to alert us to the ongoing and necessary work in the making of realities. 'Reality' is an achievement, an effect of sanctioned or unofficial ontological practices, not a space-box within which different epistemological perspectives battle it out (Latour 2005; Law & Singleton 2013; Law 2015). Therefore, as John Law puts it, 'in a multiple world of different enactments, if we participate in a *fractiverse*, then there will be, there can be, no overarching logic or liberal institutions, diplomatic or otherwise, to mediate between the different realities' (Law 2015: 127; our emphasis). Nevertheless, as postcolonial STS scholar Katayoun Shafiee has argued, the field of STS has generally been marked by a preference or 'bias toward the investigation of small-scale economic and scientific experiments, technical systems and laboratories', such as eye-catching electric cars or northern financial products, and has not often traced 'other connections to politics by moving from the laboratory or the market to think of the broader socio-technical processes at work in [...] large-scale political project [s]' such as development interventions (Shafiee 2012: 588). It has been critical development scholarship and postdevelopment critique rather than STS that has firmly focused on 'relations between countries of the Global North and Global South' (Shafiee 2012: 588). Still, the turn to ontology in STS, which is taken further in Escobar's own recent scholarship, has highlighted the need to attend to both 'pluriversality' and 'ontological design'. With the latter what is at stake is an 'ethics of deep coalitions, rather than modern/colonial agonistics' (Tlostanova 2017: 58). This shift within postdevelopment approaches hails the pluriversal as the need to recognise and work with different ways of imagining, embracing and enacting ontological diversity as other modes of existence (Escobar 2011).

Postdevelopment apart from post-neoliberalism

While there are some links with postdevelopment and other theoretical projects, it is important to also map out projects that sit apart from postdevelopment, although often mistaken as co-constitutive. Within Latin America and over the last decade-and-a-half, what came to be known as 'post-neoliberalism' is one such example. The establishment of 'left-turn' governments starting in 1999 with the electoral victory of president Hugo Chávez in Venezuela paved the way for post-neoliberal approaches, or what were originally conceived as development alternatives for the region. If for close to two decades the '10-point' Washington Consensus had defined the parameters of mainstream development and its economic imaginary, by the mid-2000s, with the shift in the political and economic landscape of Latin America, an ongoing transformation had taken place rendering neoliberalism politically and economically defunct. Aided by social movements and the irruption of Indigenous mobilisation in national politics, the left turn's post-neoliberalism would encompass the return of statist political economies, a renationalisation of 'the economy', new regional and South-South trade initiatives and the rebranding of social spending as 'social investment' (Ruckert, Macdonald & Proulx 2017). The series of political events, policies and programmes encompassed by the left turn raise important questions. After the Latin American experience of the left turn, whose hopes may have come to an end as the demise of the Washington Consensus settled on what Argentinean sociologist Maristella Svampa has termed the 'commodities consensus' (Svampa 2015), what can be said regarding the relations between the post-neoliberal programme and postdevelopment?

Svampa has argued that 'developmentalist neo-extractivism', characterised by large-scale export-oriented monocultures and the deepening of resource extraction, has come to fully represent the darker side of a post-neoliberal present in the region. In this regard, Svampa concurs with the work of Uruguayan political ecologist Eduardo Gudynas and Ecuadorean environmentalist and political economist Alberto Acosta. Svampa argues that 'the commodities consensus [has] deepen[ed] the dynamic of dispossession'; 'the dispossession and accumulation of land, resources, and territories, principally by large corporations, in multiscalar alliances with different governments' (Svampa 2015: 66). Unexpectedly, the promises of cornucopianism are common to both the Left's post-neoliberalism and the earlier Washington-focused neoliberal project (Holst 2016: 201). In turn, post-neoliberal 'progressive' social policies have been bundled through left governance with regressive economic policies. In parallel, the recent mobilisations of previously disenfranchised populations and late-twentieth-century forms of Latin American subalternity – Indigenous political parties and '*sin techo*' urban dwellers among others – have found repressive rejoinders when questioning the paradoxical policy assemblage. That a sharp divide between economic and environmental policy is seen as tenable should be questioned. That such a splitting of postcolonial realities into 'environmental' and 'economic' policy is seen as defensible is something that postdevelopment indeed does challenge. Postdevelopment would interrogate the ease within which the 'post-neoliberal' programme and governmental discourse has become an enabling condition for a regressive economic orientation summed up in Svampa's 'commodities consensus' and its export-oriented thrust. There are specific discontinuities between the experience of post-neoliberalism and the practice of postdevelopment.

Postdevelopment in practice

It is the aim of this volume to critically engage with postdevelopment ideas. Though it is not a project of theoretical works *per se*, instead we seek to offer a review of postdevelopment practice already underway. There are many such initiatives with which to begin. For instance, the recovery of Indigenous and hybrid economies (Altman 2010, 2016), the reclaiming of radical subjectivities against capitalism and patriarchy (Hook 2012) and the meticulous documenting of diverse and community economies by researchers following the work of Katherine Gibson and Julie Graham (2006, 2008, 2013, 2014) all point to sites where postdevelopment is in practice. Likewise, the recent work of Kelly Dombroski (2015), investigating 'hygiene assemblages' in northwestern China, takes up postdevelopment to guard the health of families, challenging prevalent notions of sanitation and health. The de-commodification of nature and wellbeing mobilised through *sumak kawsay* in the Andean region has also offered possibilities for postdevelopment in practice, often accompanied by intricate and contested negotiations with the post-neoliberal state (Gudynas & Acosta 2011; Caria & Domínguez 2016).[2] Postdevelopment in practice begins with the insistence that an enduring diversity of socialities, a multiplicity of southern knowledges and nature/culture assemblages and postcolonial political economies reveals already existing alternatives.

Our claim is that there have been ongoing and diverse forms of doing postdevelopment, yet paradoxically little acknowledgement of postdevelopment in practice. We are thus motivated by the need to render visible this diversity, to consider its futures and to offer some hope-full pathways. Our own preference for 'postdevelopment' without the hyphen (rather than 'post-development') is meant to purposefully denote the ongoing tension in demanding a temporal break with development, an 'after' development. In contrast, the alternatives in practice are occurring alongside, interspersed with and counter to development and not awaiting some complete break with development in order to begin. This difference between 'post-development' and 'postdevelopment' has not been explicitly theorised in our reading of the literature. In contrast, in the allied field of postcolonial studies and critique, the 'hyphen' has been explicitly theorised. 'Postcolonialism' there refers to a 'condition, to a project and form of critique, while the hyphen is used primarily as a temporal marker, and thus to emphasise an after of official colonialism' (Mishra & Hodge 1991: 407). To speak of 'postcolonialism' is then to reject that there is a clear after; indeed, we are still marked by the 'coloniality of power' (Quijano 2000). Similarly, Venezuelan anthropologist Fernando Coronil has stated that 'the apparently simple grammatical juxtaposition [...] serves as a sign to address the murky entanglement of knowledge and power' (Coronil 2013). The 'post' as suffix, Coronil argues, 'functions both as a temporal marker to refer to the problem of classifying societies in historical time and as an epistemological sign to evoke the problem of producing knowledge of history and society in the context of imperial relations' (Coronil 2013). Postdevelopment in practice is therefore marked by the diversity and complications of a postcolonial present where other contemporaneous worlds may be remade.

These collected works on postdevelopment in practice do not ignore what Gidwani (2008) has called 'capital's hegemonising operations' (217), referring to capital's ability to assimilate forms of life opposing its aspirations. The resiliency of capitalism is real, and in part due to its alluring qualities – what Marx identified as commodity fetishism, what Lordon (2014), drawing on Spinoza, has identified as our willingness to be slaves of capitalism, or what Kapoor (2017) identifies as unconscious libidinal attachments such as desire and enjoyment (*jouissance*) whose nature is reshaped through capitalism. Yet at the same time, one cannot overlook the ways peoples around the world are already living through and beyond the confines of 'development'. Following Dhar and Chakrabarti (2012), there is a *world of the third* – lives that are neither capitalist nor pre-capitalist, but non-capitalist, peoples that are neither within the circuits of global capital nor at the margins of global capitalism. To deny a third space outside, fully contemporaneous and exterior to 'empire-nation exchange' (Spivak 1990: 90), by reductively defining such realities as 'postmodern' or without material foundation, is indeed an imperial project in itself. Further, J.K. Gibson-Graham (2006) have meticulously documented the diverse nature of economy, beyond one of capitalist productivity, accumulation of capital and surplus labour, outlining a necessary rupture in critical discourses' commitment to 'capitalocentrism'. In advancing both a critique and an ethnographically oriented research programme, they have identified three sets of often ignored but common economic relations for sustaining and generating life. First, transactions of goods and services, which can include fair trade markets, co-op exchange, gleaning, Indigenous exchange, gift giving, informal markets and alternative credits. Second, the performance and modes of remuneration of labour such as in-kind, family-care, neighbourhood work, reproductive labour and volunteering. Third, the production, appropriation and distribution of surplus within different kinds of enterprise, such as nonprofit enterprises, communal, feudal, green capitalism and state enterprise (Gibson-Graham 2006).

Whilst postdevelopment in practice is about holding space for alternative assemblages, at the same time, it cannot overlook the pervasive nature of capital. There is a need for a kind of transition scholarship to go beyond the conventional remit of 'modern' research and rationality. Esteva and Escobar call for a serious exploration of the hypothesis

> that we will not have modern solutions to modern problems because modernity itself already collapsed. We are in the transition to another era (which is not postmodernism), with the uncertainty created by the fact that old rationalities and sensibilities are obsolete and the new ones are not yet clearly identified.
>
> *(2017: 7)*

Within the Latin American context, such an exploration had led political philosopher Enrique Dussel, whose writings have been central to the work carried out by Escobar and others collected in the modernity/coloniality critique, to speak of 'trans-modernity' as both an epoch and practice (2000).

Postdevelopment in practice is not a matter of 'dreaming up alternatives'; this collection of essays entails examinations of events, lives, practices and knowledges that are different to development. Contributions mark out this third space and the efforts to construct these realities. The authors of this volume have launched their analyses from actually existing postdevelopment, cases that may address in all manner of ways the complex challenges of alternative futures and the diversity of postdevelopment. Therefore, these chapters engage with a range of literatures and theoretical approaches traversing what we have termed 'postdevelopment in practice'.

The chapters

The first section of this volume outlines theoretical contributions to postdevelopment in practice. We begin with the exchange between Gustavo Esteva and Arturo Escobar reflecting on the continuities and ruptures, but also the continued possibilities and practice of postdevelopment twenty-five years on from the publication of the *Development Dictionary*. S. Charusheela shows that whilst J.K. Gibson Graham's diverse economies is important to loosen the grip of orientalism and modernism, there is a need for a postcolonial feminist lens to explore how vocabularies of race, modernity and gender are built into – and thus performatively express – our organisation of the different modes of production and relations of power within economy. Yoshihiro Nakano illustrates how Yoshirou Tamanoi's theory of regionalism is a precursor to the Japanese school of postdevelopment. Similarly, Sara Caria and Rafael Domínguez draw on the works of Spanish and Chilean economists Sampedro and Max Neef to further illuminate Ecuador's *buen vivir* and explore the Latin American genealogies of postdevelopment. Anup Dhar and Anjan Chakrabarti outline their world of the third approach. They argue that postdevelopmental understanding of the 'third world' and the 'local' as a world of the third creates conditions for a reconstructive praxis that is not developmental. The first section of the collection concludes with the exploration of the pluriversal illustrated within the recent *Post-development Dictionary* published by Ashish Kothari, Ariel Salleh, Arturo Escobar, Federico Demaria and Alberto Acosta.

The second section then focuses in on siting postdevelopment – outlining the ways people negotiate and resist development at the fringes and within, but also how they refuse development and already live alternatives. Bhavya Chitranshi describes shifts in 'single women' subjectivities as an important feminist and postcapitalist project for Adivasi women. Chitranshi documents the becoming of a collective of single women farmers who worked towards a radical postcapitalist and feminist future, a future beyond dictated developmental agendas. Daniel Bendix, Franziska Müller and Aram Ziai illustrate how postdevelopment is not a Global South project, but is also located in the Global North. Their work is a vital reminder of the importance of Northern ruptures and alternatives. Samantha Balaton-Chrimes and Sandeep Pattnaik explore ways in which community aspirations and agencies in the Indian state of Odisha align and depart from a postdevelopment vision. While Katherine Curchin reflects on Altman's notion of hybridity in Indigenous communities in Northern Australia. She traces how the conceptualisation of the hybrid economy includes livelihoods of the informal, non-market or customary and the potential advantages of plural or hybrid economies over the market-dependent and ecologically unsustainable status quo.

Postdevelopment in practice and the state are also considered by several authors in the collection. Miriam Lang shows that whilst integration of the concept of *buen vivir* into governance has been bridled by the modern development paradigm, there continue to be localised zones of depatriarchalisation, decolonialisation and redefinition of social relations with nature. Katharine McKinnon, Stephen Healy and Kelly Dombroski outline a feminist postdevelopment research practice to move beyond a monoculture of knowledge and practice. They outline examples of strategies to recognise multiple ontologies involving gender in Melanesia, breastfeeding practices in China and the politics of postdevelopment scholarship more broadly. Michaela Spencer explores points of rupture in settler-colonial policy making through cosmopolitical diplomacy, reflecting on her experience of working with Indigenous communities in Australia's Northern Territory. Lyn Ossome traces Ugandan women's land struggles and resistance to land dispossession and how their practices of resistance function both as a feminist critique of development and as a praxis *beyond* capitalism. Christopher Shepherd further explores resistance to the Green Revolution in both Peru and East Timor, contrasting twentieth-century agro-biotechnology projects and local and Indigenous knowledges in both experiences. Shepherd's analysis also highlights the tensions and challenges faced by researchers challenging the status quo.

Wendy Harcourt reveals body politics as a critical site of postdevelopment; bodies are considered sites of cultural and political resistance to dominant understandings of the 'normal' body as White, male, Western and heterosexual. Harcourt shows how body politics have been central not only to the politics of collective action in its queer and feminist iterations but have been key to postdevelopment itself. Julia Schöneberg examines examples of solidarity groups and social movements in Haiti to explore spaces for alternatives to development. She specifically observes possible shifts in North-South relationships from apolitical development projects towards interactions as a form of 'development-as-politics', in which local social movements and international NGOs jointly engage in resistance struggles. Anyely Marín Cisneros and Rebecca Close, decolonial curators working in Barcelona and Guayaquil, examine the role of art practice as a space of experimentation and invention capable of interrupting narratives of financial capitalism and its logic of 'progress' through context-specific tactics of critique. Tony Fry outlines how design is ontologically prefigurative of futuring worlds, and as such has specific links to postdevelopment and decoloniality. Verónica Tello explores the tensions and complementarities of postdevelopment in artistic practice. Postdevelopment as art can offer a promising site for the practice of postdevelopment, although Tello reminds us the risks of not getting it right and becoming the usual *modus operandi* of art history and practice.

Our book seeks to engage with these invigorating approaches and to canvas alternative horizons. We are concerned, specifically, with the already existing approaches that are up to the challenge of retrieving and appraising the knowledges and practices underway in these diverse sites of postdevelopment. To put forward postdevelopment in practice is a rejoinder to the ongoing disavowal of theoretical critique via appeals to empirical applicability and further intervention. Our book may thus serve as a collection of contemporary approaches, underscoring the theoretical and political moves undertaken to encompass the diversity of alternatives already underway.

Notes

1 Nikolas Rose (2003) examines the sharp increase in the sales of psychiatric drugs around the world. Between the period of 1990–2000, sales increased in Europe by 125% and 600% in the USA.
2 As discussed earlier, post-neoliberalism is both an attempt to do away with neoliberalism in the early and mid-2000s together with the paradoxical turn to expanding extractive industries, greater foreign investment and the reliance on the 'commodities boom'. Whilst some have seen *buen vivir* or 'good living' as part of the post-neoliberal moment, and part of the post-neoliberal project insofar as it became official discourse in Ecuador and Bolivia, and briefly though to a lesser extent in Venezuela, we do not see *buen vivir* and its more strongly Indigenous appellations in Quechua *sumak kawsay* and Aymara *sumaq qamaña* as reducible to the post-neoliberal policies of these governments' executive branches. The point is that *buen vivir*, and not its being coupled with extractivism by left-turn governments, represents a novel postdevelopment discourse and resource for practice.

References

Altman, J. (2010) 'What future for remote Indigenous Australia?: Economic Hybridity and the neoliberal turn'. In Altman, J. & Hinkson, M. (eds.), *Culture Crisis: Anthropology and Politics in Aboriginal Australia*. Sydney: UNSW Press, pp 259–280.

Altman, J. (2016) 'Basic income for remote Indigenous Australia: Prospects for a livelihoods approach in neoliberal times'. In Mays, J., Marston, G. & Tomlinson, J. (eds.), *Basic Income in Australia and New Zealand: Perspectives from Neoliberal Frontiers*. Basingstoke: Palgrave Macmillan.

Anderson, W. (2009) 'From subjugated knowledge to conjugated subjects: Science and globalisation, or postcolonial studies of science?' *Postcolonial Studies*, vol 12, no 4, pp 389–400.

Bakewell, O. (2008) '"Keeping Them in Their Place": The Ambivalent Relationship between Development and Migration in Africa'. *Third World Quarterly*, vol 29, no. 7, pp 1341–1358.

Batiwala, S. (2007) 'Taking the power out of empowerment – Experiential account'. *Development in Practice*, vol 17, no 4, pp 557–565.

Blaser, M. (2009) 'The political ontology of a sustainable hunting program'. *American Anthropologist*, vol 111, no 1, pp 12–20.

Blaser, M. (2013) 'Ontological conflicts and the stories of peoples in spite of Europe: Towards a conversation on political ontology'. *Current Anthropology*, vol 54, no 5, pp 547–568.

Caria, S. & Domínguez, R. (2016) 'Ecuador's buen vivir: A new ideology for development'. *Latin American Perspectives*, vol 43, no 1, pp 18–33.

Chakrabarti, A. & Dhar, A. (2012) 'Gravel in the shoe: Nationalism and world of the third'. *Rethinking Marxism*, vol 24, no 1, pp 106–123.

Connell, R. (2007) *Southern Theory: The Global Dynamics of Knowledge in Social Science*. Sydney: Allen & Unwin.

Cooke, B. & Kothari, U. (2001) *Participation: The New Tyranny?* London and New York: Zed Books.

Coronil, F. (2013) 'Latin American postcolonial studies and global decolonisation'. *Worlds & Knowledges Otherwise*, vol 3, dossier 3, Spring.

Coulthard, G. (2014) *Red Skin, White Masks: Rejecting the Colonial Politics of Recognition*. Minneapolis, MN: University of Minnesota Press.

D'Costa, A.P. (2014) 'Compressed capitalism and development'. *Critical Asian Studies*, vol 46, no 2, pp 317–344.

Demaria, F. & Kothari, A. (2017) 'The post-development dictionary agenda: Paths to the pluriverse'. *Third World Quarterly*, vol 38, no 12, pp 2588–2599.

de Sousa Santos, B. (2009). 'A non-Occidentalist West?: Learned ignorance and ecology of knowledge'. *Theory, Culture & Society*, vol 26, no 7–8, pp 103–125.

Dhar, A. & Chakrabarti, A. (2013) 'The world of the third', conference paper, pp 1–18.

Dombroski, K. (2015) 'Multiplying possibilities: A postdevelopment approach to hygiene and sanitation in Northwest China'. *Asia Pacific Viewpoint*, vol 56, no 3, pp 321–334.

Donovan, K.P. (2014)'"Development" as if we have never been modern: Fragments of a Latourian development studies'. *Development and Change*, vol 45, no 5, pp 869–894.

Douzinas, C. (2000) *The End of Human Rights: Critical Legal Thought at the Turn of the Century*. Oxford: Hart Publishing.

Dussel, E. (2002). 'World-System and "trans"-modernity'. *Nepantla: Views from South*, vol 3, no 2, pp 221–244.

Ehrenreich, B. (2010) *Nickel and Dimed: On (Not) Getting By in America*. New York: Metropolitan Books.

Engle-Merry, S. (2011) 'Measuring the world indicators, human rights, and global governance'. *Current Anthropology*, vol 52, Supplement 3, pp S83–S95.

Escobar, A. (1995) *Encountering Development: The Making and Unmaking of the Third World*. Princeton, NJ: Princeton University Press.

Escobar, A. (2011) 'Sustainability: Design for the pluriverse'. *Development*, vol 54, no 2, pp 137–140.

Escobar, A. (2015) 'Degrowth, postdevelopment, and transitions: A preliminary conversation'. *Sustainability Science*, vol 10, no 3, pp 451–462.

Escobar, A. (2018) *Designs for the Pluriverse: Radical Interdependecne, Autonomy, and the Making of Worlds*. Durham, NC: Duke University Press.

Esteva, G. & Escobar, A. (2017) 'Post-development @ 25: On "being stuck" and moving forward, sideways, backward and otherwise'. *Third World Quarterly*, vol 38, pp. 2559–2572.

Ferguson, J. (1994) *The Anti-politics Machine: Development, Depoliticisation, and Bureaucratic Power in Lesotho*. Cambridge: Cambridge University Press.

Gibson-Graham, J.K. (2006) *A Postcapitalist Politics*. Minneapolis and London: University of Minnesota Press.

Gibson-Graham, J.K. (2008) 'Diverse economies: Performative practices for other worlds'. *Progress in Human Geography*, vol 32, no 5, pp 613–632.

Gibson-Graham, J.K. (2013) 'Being the revolution, or, how to live in a "more-than-capitalist" world threatened with extinction'. *Rethinking Marxism*, vol 26, no 1, pp 76–94.

Gibson-Graham, J.K. (2014) 'Rethinking the economy with thick description and weak theory'. *Current Anthropology*, vol 55, Supplement 9, pp S147–S153.

Gidwani, V. (2008) *Captial Interrupted: Agrarian Development and the Politics of Work in India*. Minneapolis, MN: University of Minnesota Press.

Gudynas, E. & Acosta, A. (2011) 'La renovación de la crítica al desarrollo y el buen vivir como alternativa'. *Utopía Y Praxis Latinoamericana*, vol 16, no 53, pp 71–83.

Harcourt, W. (2009) *Body Politics in Development: Critical Debates in Gender and Development*. London: Zed Books.

Harcourt, W. & Nelson, I. (2015) *Practising Feminist Political Ecologies: Moving Beyond the Green Economy*. London: Zed Books.

Harding, S. (2011) *The Postcolonial Science and Technology Studies Reader*. Durham, NC: Duke University Press.

Harding, S. (2016) 'Latin American decolonial social studies of scientific knowledge'. *Science, Technology, & Human Values*, vol 41, no 6, pp 1063–1087.

Harootunian, H. (2012) '"Memories of underdevelopment" after area studies'. *Positions: East Asia Cultures Critique*, vol 20, no 1, pp 7–35.

Harriss-White, B. (2006) 'Poverty and capitalism'. *Economic and Political Weekly*, vol 41, no 13, pp 1–14.

Holst, J. (2016). 'Colonial histories and decolonial dreams in the Ecuadorean Amazon: Natural resources and the politics of post-neoliberalism'. *Latin American Perspectives*, vol 43, no 1, pp 200–220.

Hook, D. (2012) *A Critical Psychology of the Post-colonial: The Mind of Apartheid*. London and New York: Routledge.

Kapoor, I. (2017) 'Cold critique, faint passion, bleak future: Post development's surrender to global capitalism'. *Third World Quarterly*, vol 38, pp 2664–2683.
Kapur, R. (2005) *Erotic Justice: Law and the New Politics of Postcolonialism*. London: The Glass House Press.
Kaul, N. (2007) *Imagining Economics Otherwise: Encounters with Identity/Difference*. London: Routledge.
Kayatekin, S.A. (2009) 'Between political economy and postcolonial theory: First encounters'. *Cambridge Journal of Economics*, vol 33, no 6, pp 1113–1118.
Klein, N. (2015) *This Changes Everything: Capitalism vs. The Climate*. New York: Simon & Schuster.
Kothari, U. (2005) *A Radical History of Development Studies: Individuals, Institutions and Ideologies*. London: Zed Books.
Latouche, S. (1993) *In the Wake of an Affluent Society: An Exploration of Post-development*, trans. Arnoux, M.O.C.a.R. London: Zed Books.
Latour, B. (2005) *Reassembling the Social: An Introduction to Actor-network Theory*. Oxford: Oxford University Press.
Law, J. (2015) 'What's wrong with a one-world world?' *Distinktion: Journal of Social Theory*, vol 16, no 1, pp 126–139.
Law, J. & Singleton, V. (2013) 'ANT and politics: Working in and on the world'. *Qualitative Sociology*, vol 36, no 4, pp 485–502.
Li, T. (2007) *The Will to Improve: Governmentality, Development and the Practice of Politics*. Durham, NC: Duke University Press.
Lie, J.H.S. (2007) 'Post-development and discourse-agency interface'. In Ziai, A. (ed.), *Exploring Post-development: Theory and Practice, Problems and Perspectives*, pp 47–62. Abington: Routledge.
Lohmann, L. (2011) 'Capital and climate change'. *Development and Change*, vol 42, no 2, pp 649–668.
Long, N. (2001) *Development Sociology: Actor Perspectives*. London: Routledge.
Lordon, F. (2014) *Willing Slaves of Capital: Spinoza and Marx on Desire*. London: Verso Books.
Lugones, M. (2016) 'The coloniality of gender'. In Harcourt, W. (ed.), *The Palgrave Handbook of Gender and Development Critical Engagements in Feminist Theory and Practice*, pp 13–33. Basingstoke: Palgrave Macmillan.
Maldonado-Torres, N. (2007) 'On the coloniality of being'. *Cultural Studies*, vol 21, no 2, pp 240–270.
Martínez-Alier, J. (2012) 'Environmental justice and economic degrowth: An alliance between two movements'. *Capitalism Nature Socialism*, vol 23, no 1, pp 51–73.
Matthews, S. (2017) 'Colonised minds? Post-development theory and the desirability of development in Africa'. *Third World Quarterly*, vol 38, no 12, pp 2650–2663.
McFarlane, C. (2006) 'Transnational development networks: Bringing development and postcolonial approaches into dialogue'. *Geographical Journal*, vol 172, no 1, pp 35–49.
Mezzadra, S., Reid, J. & Samaddar, R. (2013) *The Biopolitics of Development: Reading Michel Foucault in the Postcolonial Present*. New Delhi: Springer.
Mignolo, W. (2011) *The Darker Side of Western Modernity: Global Futures, Decolonial Options*. Durham, NC: Duke University Press.
Mills, C. (2014) *Decolonizing Global Mental Health: The Psychiatrization of the Majority World*. New York: Routledge.

Mishra, V. & Hodge, B. (1991) 'What is post(-)colonialism?' *Textual Practice*, vol 5, no 3, pp 399–414.

Mitchell, T. (2002) *Rule of Experts: Egypt, Techno-Politics, Modernity*. Berkeley, CA: University of California Press.

Mohanty, C. (2003) '"Under Western eyes" revisited: Feminist solidarity through anticapitalist struggles'. *Signs*, vol 28, no 2, pp 499–535.

Mosse, D. (2013) 'The anthropology of international development'. *Annual Review of Anthropology*, vol 42, no 1, pp 227–246.

Nakano, Y. (2007) 'On the singular name of post-development: Serge Latouche's Destrucktion of development and the possiblity of emancipation'. In Ziai, A. (ed.), *Exploring Post-development: Theory and Practice, Problems and Perspectives*, pp 63–80. Abington: Routledge.

Nandy, A. (2002) 'The beautiful, expanding future of poverty: Popular economics as a psychological defense'. *International Studies Review*, vol 4, no 2, pp 107–121.

Nussbaum, M. (2001) *Women and Human Development: The Capabilities Approach*. Cambridge: Cambridge University Press.

Peck, J. & Theodore, N. (2007) 'Variegated capitalism'. *Progress in Human Geography*, vol 31, no 6, pp 731–772.

Quijano, A. (2000) 'Coloniality of power and eurocentrism in Latin America'. *International Sociology*, vol 15, no 2, pp 215–232.

Rahnema, M. (1997) 'Towards post-development: Searching for signposts, a new language and new paradigm'. In Rahnema, M. & Bawtree, V. (eds.), *The Post-development Reader*, pp 377–404. London: Zed Books.

Rajão, R. & Duque, R.B. (2014) 'Between purity and hybridity: Technoscientific and ethnic myths of Brazil'. *Science, Technology, & Human Values*, vol 39, no 6, pp 844–874.

Reddy, S. & Lahoti, R. (2016) '$1.90 a day: What does it say? The new international poverty line'. *New Left Review*, 97. https://newleftreview.org/II/97/sanjay-reddy-rahul-lahoti-1-90-a-day-what-does-it-say.

Rose, N. (2003) 'Neurochemical selves'. *Society*, vol 41, no 4, pp 46–59.

Ruckert, A., Macdonald, L. & Proulx, K.R. (2017) 'Post-neoliberalism in Latin America: A conceptual review'. *Third World Quarterly*, vol 38, no 7, pp 1583–1602.

Sachs, W. (2017) 'The sustainable development goals and Laudato si': Varieties of post-development?'. *Third World Quarterly*, vol 38, no 12, pp 2573–2587.

Santelices Spikin, A. & Rojas Hernández, J. (2016) 'Climate change in Latin America: Inequality, conflict, and social movements of adaptation'. *Latin American Perspectives*, vol 43, no 4, pp 4–11.

Sen, A. (1999) *Development as Freedom*. Oxford: Oxford University Press.

Sen, A. (2009) *The Idea of Justice*. New York: Penguin Books.

Shafiee, K. (2012) 'A petro-formula and its world: Calculating profits, labour and production in the assembling of Anglo-Iranian oil'. *Economy and Society*, vol 41, no 4, pp 585–614.

Spivak, G. (1990) 'Gayatri Spivak on the politics of the subaltern'. *Socialist Review*, vol 3, pp 81–97.

Svampa, M. (2015) 'Commodities consensus: Neoextractivism and enclosure of the commons in Latin America'. *South Atlantic Quarterly*, vol 114, no 1, pp 65–82.

Tlostanova, M. (2017) 'On decolonizing design'. *Design Philosophy Papers*, vol 15, no 1, pp 51–61.

Walsh, C. (2016) 'On gedner and its "otherwise"'. In Harcourt, W. (ed.), *The Palgrave Handbook of Gender and Development: Critical Engagements in Feminist Theory and Practice*, pp 34–47. Basingstoke: Palgrave Macmillan.

Watson, I. (2009) 'Aboriginality and the violence of colonialism'. *Borderlands*, vol 8, no 1, pp 1–8.

Weber, H. (2010) 'Politics of global social relations: Organising "everyday lived experiences" of development and destitution'. *Australian Journal of International Affairs*, vol 64, no 1, pp 105–122.

Wilson, K. (2017) 'Worlds beyond the political? Post-development approaches in practices of transnational solidarity activism'. *Third World Quarterly*, vol 38, no 12, pp 2684–2702.

Zein-Elabdin, E.O. (2009) 'Economics, postcolonial theory and the problem of culture: Institutional analysis and hybridity'. *Cambridge Journal of Economics*, vol 33, no 6, pp 1153–1167.

Zein-Elabdin, E.O. & Charusheela, S. (2004) *Postcolonialism Meets Economics* (Vol. 24). London: Routledge.

Ziai, A. (2007) *Exploring Post-development: Theory and Practice, Problems and Perspectives*. Abingdon: Routledge.

Ziai, A. (2013) 'The discourse of "development" and why the concept should be abandoned'. *Development in Practice*, vol 23, no 1, pp 123–136.

PART I
Theorising a practice of postdevelopment

The chapters that follow all ask, in one way or another, what is postdevelopment? Some also seek to rewrite postdevelopment's history and therefore can be seen as asking, where has postdevelopment come from? Similarly, there are contributions that look to the future of postdevelopment, asking, what can postdevelopment be?

The six contributions making up this first part of the volume tackle such questions. The chapters address not only the critique of development advanced by postdevelopment over the last twenty-five years, but also present us with its other possible genealogies and histories. This series of theoretical contributions all shape the concept and call for 'postdevelopment in practice'. The contributions either extend current theoretical insights or consider new theoretical work in relation to the practice of postdevelopment, relating the latter to broader debates in critical development studies. In pursuing these discussions, the contributions show the diverse paths leading to postdevelopment critique and postdevelopment practice.

1

POSTDEVELOPMENT @ 25

On 'being stuck' and moving forward, sideways, backward and otherwise[1]

Gustavo Esteva and Arturo Escobar

Arturo

It's been almost 30 years since that memorable week of September 1988, when we sat around the convivial table at Ivan Illich's house on Foster Avenue in University Park (where Penn State University is located), summoned by Wolfgang Sachs and Ivan. Out of the intense and enjoyable discussions of those days there emerged the task of writing our respective chapters for what a few years later would emerge as *The Development Dictionary*. The book made a 'splash' of sorts when it made its debut in print. For some, the splash has been enduring and one of the most essential elements behind what came to be known as the postdevelopment school. Other, less generous, retrospective analyses of the *Dictionary* (and postdevelopment) argue that it was interesting but ineffective and that, in any way, it is superseded by now since development has certainly not died, as the *Dictionary* appeared to prognosticate. Many mainstream scholars and development practitioners, harsher in their appraisal, consider it to have been a terribly misguided endeavour and a disservice to the poor.

Aram Ziai's invitation comes at an auspicious time to take stock of what has gone 'under the bridge' of the *Dictionary* and postdevelopment waters in the intervening years, and to renew our understanding and critique. You were not only one of the pioneers of the critique but your position regarding development has, if anything, become even more radical than in 1992 – at least that's how I read your most recent texts on the subject (Esteva, Babones & Babcicky 2013). To remain for now on a historical register, I would like to ask you, to start this conversation: how do you see now the intellectual-political ferment of those early days, when the radical problematisation of development was first launched, as compared with the conditions that exist today for radical critiques? Is there something you think that our group could have done differently? Where do you hear echoes from those conversations in current debates?

Gustavo

'Development' is no longer an unquestionable category. At the grassroots, I have seen in recent years open resistance and opposition to development itself, not only to certain forms of development – and some have a long history. Such opposition is now fully incorporated in people's discourses, something they did not dare to do before. In my contribution to the *Dictionary*, I celebrated the emergence of new commons, which I saw as an alternative to development. *The Ecologist* described such emergence that very year. And the commons movement is today in full swing, everywhere, in what we can legitimately call a post-economic society, not only beyond development.

Salvatore Babones' classification of the current development panorama is very effective. He associates it with three Sachses (Esteva, Babones & Babcicky 2013: 22–23).

The 'Goldman Sachs' approach expresses a pretty general consensus that dominates in governments and international institutions. It defines development through their commodities trading desks, their infrastructure projects and their exploration units. It means an oil platform located 10 km offshore, safe from harassment by local indigenous militants.

The 'Jeffrey Sachs' approach blindly believes in development and capitalism but is concerned with massive hunger and misery, which they see not as consequences but as insuf- ficiencies of both. Well-meaning people like Sachs, Gates and major US and European NGOs focus on the alleviation of obvious suffering – they stand for a chicken in every pot, a mosquito net over every bed and a condom on every penis.

The 'Wolfgang Sachs' approach circulates in critical development studies circles and departments and among indigenous leaders, independent intellectuals and a motley group of people basically ignored by academia and the 1%. In my view, this approach corresponds today to the awareness and experience, not necessarily the discourse, of millions, perhaps billions, of ordinary men and women around the world who are increasingly 'beyond' development.

The adventure of the *Dictionary* started for me a few months before that meeting in Foster Avenue. Ivan invited us to his house in Ocotepec, Cuernavaca, Mexico to talk about 'After development, what?' Majid Rahnema, Jean Robert and Wolfgang were there. One of the things that I remember very well of that meeting was that we abandoned the expression 'after development', with an implicit periodisation that Wolfgang retained. We knew that the developers were still around and would continue their devastating enterprise. We wanted to explore how *to be* beyond development.

As you know, I am not a scholar. I read a lot, but my ideas, my words, my vocabulary, my inspiration, come from my experience at the grassroots, in my world of *campesinos, indios* and urban marginals. Ivan knew that. At one point in the conversation, he asked me: 'Gustavo, if you had only one word to express what is to be beyond development, which is the word you will use?' My immediate answer was 'hospitality'. Development is radically inhospitable: it imposes a universal definition of the good life and excludes all others. We need to hospitably embrace the thousand different ways of thinking, being, living and experiencing the world that characterise reality.

This was not an occurrence: it came from my experience. In the early 1980s those classified as 'underdeveloped' were frustrated and enraged with always being at the end of the line. We knew by then that 'development' as the universalisation of the American Way of Life was impossible; that we would not catch up with the developed, as Truman promised; that we would be permanently left behind. For many of us such awareness became a revelation; we still had our own notions of what is to live well and they were feasible. Instead of continuing the foolish race to nowhere, we should reorient our effort. In my experience, it was not dissident vanguards attempting development 'alternatives' or alternatives to development, but many grassroots groups reaffirming themselves in their own path, in many cases for sheer survival in the dramatic 1980s, what was later called 'the lost decade' in Latin America. For me, they were already beyond development.

I bought into underdevelopment when I was 13 years old. That implied that I fully assumed my 'lacks': I wanted development for me, for my family and for my country, in order to satisfy all the 'needs' suddenly created. Let me clarify this. When I was a child the word 'need' had only one practical application: shitting. It was used when my mother told us: 'Once you arrive at your uncle's house, ask him where you can make your needs'. We *made* the 'needs'; we did not *have* them. This way of talking applied to everything: our 'needs' were defined by our own capacity, our tools and the way we used them, and were strictly personal, imponderable and incommensurable. It was in the course of my lifetime that all current 'needs' were created and we were transmogrified into needy, measured and controlled people. Professionals defined the needs and we were classified according to them.

When I was a child, people were talking to me. Words were symbols, not representations or categories, and only one of every ten of them addressed me as an undifferentiated member of a crowd. As I grew, words became categories and I was addressed as a member of a class of people: children, skinny, underdeveloped… according to our 'needs': education, nutrition, development.

As you know very well, in the early 1970s, the recognition that the development enterprise was causing hunger and misery everywhere produced the Basic Needs Approach. The goal became to satisfy a package of 'basic needs'. There was no consensus about the definition of those needs, but such orientation still characterises most development efforts… and shaped the UN Millennium Goals and the Sustainable Development Goals (SDGs) today.

In 1976, I was in the immediate danger of becoming a minister in the new administration of the Mexican Government, after my success as a high officer for more than ten years in conceiving and implementing great development programmes. I quit. I started to work autonomously with people at the grassroots. By then I knew that instead of 'development' the people looked for autonomy, as expressed in the name of an independent organisation I created with some friends (*Autonomía, Descentralismo y Gestión*). I also knew that the 'State' was a mechanism for control and domination, useless for emancipation. After observing the damages done by professionals, as the transmission belts for the creation of 'needs' and dependence, I began the complex process of deprofessionalising myself.

In the early 1980s, there was increasing awareness of the failures of the development enterprise and the foolishness of adopting a universal definition of the good life. The idea of postdevelopment started to circulate; people were reclaiming their own, feasible, ways of living well. In the 1985 conference of the Society for International Development in Rome, invited by Wolfgang to discuss the future of development studies, I suggested it lay in archaeology: only an archaeological eye could explore the ruins left by development. I was seeing development in my past, not in my present and even less in my future. I was exploring those ruins in my own world and already looking for hospitality for our ways of being… the ways captured in the expression *buen vivir* now coming from your area of the world.

A few years ago, when Salvatore Babones approached me with a proposal to write a book about development, he observed that 'we' in the postdevelopment school don't use statistics. He was right; we hate them. Salvatore is a quantitative sociologist, well acquainted with development statistics. He wanted to incorporate them to our analysis. He also observed that people studying development are often concerned with the real problems of the world, interested in making a difference. But we closed the door on them by proclaiming a firm 'No' to development. Can we open a decent door to them? He was right. And he appeared at a time when I was adopting, with many others, the position of 'One No and Many Yeses', following the Zapatista suggestion to create a world in which many worlds can be embraced. Yes, I agreed, we can share a common 'No' to development but be open to a thousand 'Yeses': the many paths people are following around the world beyond development; people studying development can accompany and support them. That is why we wrote and published *The Future of Development: A Radical Manifesto*.

Arturo

There are so many interesting dimensions to your answer, Gustavo. I would like to explore a few, and perhaps provide a counterpoint on some of them (as in the musical counterpoint, where a theme is developed in various directions). But first there is something I remembered as I read your comment on 'needs', something I heard Ivan saying once, I am not sure whether it was at Penn State or perhaps at Berkeley in the early 1980s when he came to do his then controversial lectures on *Gender*. *Homo faber*, he said, had given way to *homo miserabilis* (the 'man of needs') which eventually gave rise to *homo oeconomicus*. The history of needs was one of Ivan's long-term interests, and it still has to be worked on, for instance, in today's digital age and given the expansion of middle classes in many world regions, for whom 'needs' have seemingly skyrocketed. How do we treat needs 'postdevelopmentally'?

Here I arrive at my first substantive question. It is a question often asked of me, so I thought we ought to give it our best answer. I think it is a significant obstacle in getting many people to embrace the thinking of postdevelopment. And it is: You speak about the grassroots as the space par excellence to explore how *to be* beyond development. In doing so, are we not romanticising the grassroots (in your case) or ethnic communities and social movements (in mine)? Are they not also, now and increasingly, the subject of needs and desires, including those that 'development' and capitalist modernity promise and eventually delivers (though in limited ways: cheap cell phones, more consumer goods, second-rate overcrowded schools and health services)? Let me give you my answer to this issue, and then I would like to hear yours. The first part of my answer is a simple reversal: faced with the social and ecological devastation brought about by patriarchal capitalist modernity, coupled with the fact that things are not getting better (skyrocketing inequality, climate change), isn't it more romantic to think that 'more of the same', in whatever guise (new World Bank recipes, green economy, SDGs or the new 'Green Revolution for Africa' advocated by J. Sachs), is going to lead to lasting improvement? In this context, more genuinely realist and less romantic are the alternatives emerging at the grassroots and with social movements. I would rather bet on them than on the world bankers and mainstream NGOs.

This links up with the historical dimension of my reply to the 'romanticism' charge. I was remembering Walter Benjamin's injunction: 'To articulate the past historically [...] means to seize it as it flashes up at a moment of danger'. He associates this moment with 'the politicians' stubborn faith in progress' (Benjamin 1968). Are we not going through one of these moments again, with technology promising humans anything they wish, from unlimited information and immediate communication to eternal life, a 'life beyond biology'? At the same time, we are, as Boaventura de Sousa Santos puts it, at a juncture where we are facing modern problems for which there are no longer modern solutions. And yet the slogan of the moment seems to be: 'Everything for the corporations! Everything for the super-rich!' What is the danger, then? That of an even more profound ontological occupation of people's territories and lives. Land grabbing and extractivism are the ugliest heads of it, but they also include growing consumerism and individualism. It is not romantic, in my mind, to be on the side of those who oppose these tendencies, especially when Earth itself is 'on our side', considering the warnings she is giving as we wound her ever more deeply and extensively.

Finally, on the theoretical side, I am pondering the question of how to understand 'really existing communities' without falling into the trap of endorsing or re-enacting modernist traps. Here I find the recent debates on autonomy and the communal (or 'communalitarian', as you would say) that have emerged in Chiapas, Oaxaca and the Norte del Cauca in Colombia's southwest new and hopeful. Both of us have written about this recently (though largely in Spanish) (Escobar 2014). Here we might also locate the intense South American debates on *buen vivir* of the last decade. This is not the place to even try to summarise these currents of thought and action. But I'd like to refer, however briefly, to recent works that conceptualise communities in all of their entanglement with global forms of capital and modern technology without reducing them to the terms of capitalism or modernity. I am referring to the recent work by Silvia Rivera Cusicanqui and Verónica Gago (Gago 2014; Rivera Cusicanqui 2014). As they show, communities are also the site of intense forms of capitalist exploitation, patriarchal domination and consumerism. They are significantly affected by globalisation and yet they are not completely determined by it. Rivera Cusicanqui points at this feature of many of today's indigenous and popular communities by referring to their capacity to define their own forms of modernity, more convivial than the dominant ones precisely because they also find nourishment in their own histories, intricately weaving indigenous and local practices with those which are not and resulting in worlds made up of different cultural strands without nevertheless fusing into one. They find sustenance in the complementarities among diverse worlds without overlooking the antagonisms, articulating with market economies while anchored in indigenous knowledge and technologies; she says (emphasis added):

> There is no 'post' nor 'pre' in this vision of history which is not linear nor teleological but rather moves in spirals and cycles, that always traces a path but never fails to return to the same point. *The indigenous world does not conceive of history as linear; the past-future are contained in the present.*
> (Rivera Cusicanqui 2014: 57)

I would say that social groups in struggle, at their best, move in several directions at once: adding to and strengthening their long-standing practices, while engaging selectively and effectively with the 'modern world' and its practices and technologies. This ability is crucial for deepening the autonomous and communalitarian foundations of social life. I suspect you'll have much to add in this regard.

The second aspect of your reply that caught my attention was the idea of 'opening a door' to those genuinely concerned with the world's problems. You go on to state that what you mean is one No to 'development' and many Yeses to 'the many paths people are following around the world beyond development; people studying development can accompany and support them'. Are you here suggesting opening a door to those working with progressive development organisations? Could you please clarify? I want to offer a reflection that came to mind recently as I was responding to an interview on 'development cooperation' in Barcelona. I came up with three paths for thinking about cooperation, as follows: (1) *Cooperation as development aid*: this is the standard form of cooperation, practiced by institutions such as USAID, the World Bank and mainstream NGOs. It takes for granted the dominant world (in terms of markets, individual actions, productivity etc.). Cooperation under this rubric might lead to some improvements for some people but it can only reinforce colonialist understandings of development and, so, dispossession. To this I'd say: let's keep the doors tightly closed on them; (2) *cooperation as, or for, social justice*: this is the kind of cooperation practiced with the intention of fostering greater social justice and environmental sustainability; it embraces human rights (including gender and ethnic diversity), environmental justice, the reduction of inequality, direct support for grassroots groups and so forth. Oxfam might serve as a paradigm for this second trajectory. In this case I'd say: let's keep the door open, while applying pressure on them to move towards the third trajectory; (3) could go under several names, such as *cooperation for civilisational transitions* or *cooperation for autonomy*: those practicing this option would be, in my view, radical postdevelopment's natural allies. What is interesting is that this form would go beyond the binary of 'us' (who have) and 'them' (who need), and embrace all sides in the same, though diverse, movement for civilisational transitions and inter-autonomy, that is, coalitions and meshworks of autonomous collectives and communities from both the Global North and the Global South. There are no ready-available models for this third kind of solidarity cooperation, but there are groups here and there that approach it (like a few I know in Catalunya).

Do you see any value in this distinction? Is it helpful to raise the question of 'allies' for the project of moving beyond development?

Gustavo

My hope, Arturo, is that some readers may enjoy our conversation as much as I am enjoying it!

You are right, of course: we still have a lot of work to do about 'needs'. A good starting point is the chapter on 'Needs' by Ivan Illich for the *Dictionary*. He clarifies how, for thousands of years, 'human' implied communal submission to the rule of necessity in a particular place and time. He explains the transition to prescribed universal needs, to the needy addict, and tells the story of *homo miserabilis*.

We must remember that in classical political economy, for Malthus, Ricardo or Marx, a vague 'standard of living' alluded to an acceptable subsistence income, the cost of the reproduction of labour force. That notion, however, was transmogrified into a *desired* form of living presented as a condition to reach, and finally a normalised definition of a *necessary* standard defined by basic needs. In that process, the idea of the good became a quantity. The very different ways of the art of living vanished and were substituted by standards that homogenised individual searches. Serge Latouche, also in the *Dictionary*, urges us to view with scepticism this fetishistic object 'standard of living', and to rediscover the multidimensionality of life.

To discuss 'needs' today requires acknowledging that more than ever they are created through dispossession, in the classical tradition of the enclosure of the commons that marked the beginning of capitalism. The commoners, dispossessed of their means of subsistence, became people in need of jobs, shelter, food, everything. As Illich explained in the *Dictionary*, development changed the human condition by transmogrifying necessities and desires into prescribed 'needs'. For the dominant mind it is difficult to understand that the commoners, before the enclosures, were eating, learning, healing, settling... within the limits imposed by nature and their culture to their desires and necessities.

We should also explore questions like those examined by Agnes Heller in her critical analysis of the notion of 'needs' in Marx. What she and others observed in the Soviet Union as the dictatorship of needs (Feher, Heller & Markus 1986) can be applied today to the functioning of contemporary societies, through other means, like compulsory schooling, marginalisation of alternative ways of healing, repression of the art of dwelling, elimination of self-mobility in a world organised to create dependency of the automobile and other vehicles and so forth.

In exploring what grassroots people are doing we must carefully draw a line between market- and state-imposed needs and people's own uses of technology. Around the year 2000, more than half of people on Earth had never made a phone call. Even when phone booths came to their villages, many people never used them because they did not have anybody to call; their family and friends had no phones. Today the situation is entirely different. Even the poorest people have access to a cellular phone and use them intensely. Yes, as we all know, many young people are now pathologically plugged into this technology and alienated from their communities. But there are people of all ages that are effectively using it for their own purposes in their own way. In a conversation with David Cayley, Ivan Illich observed that the change he anticipated took finally the form of millions of people 'misusing' or tweaking for their own purposes the failing counter-productive institutions as well as the market (Cayley 2005).

Of course, we must resist any romanticisation of the people at the grassroots. 'Don't idealise us', insists the Zapatista Subcomandante Moisés all the time. All kinds of horrors happen at the grassroots. If women are taking the lead in many communities, in a very radical post-patriarchal attitude, it is because for them the combination of traditional patriarchy and modern sexism has become a kind of hell.

At the same time, we must acknowledge that these communities, particularly the indigenous communities, are today a source of inspiration for all of us. They have been struggling for centuries with the predicaments we are facing today; they have the experience. They know well how to deal with 'modernity'. Many of them successfully resisted modernisation and were able to protect their own traditional ways. We need to seriously explore the hypothesis that we will not have modern solutions to modern problems... because modernity itself already collapsed. We are in the transition to another era (which is not postmodernism), with the uncertainty created by the fact that old rationalities and sensibilities are obsolete and the new ones are not yet clearly identified. Using the experience of similar periods in the past, we must turn to the artists – who often smell the new era and produce their creations not with the old logic but with new insights.

The communities were never isolated; this was an invention of British anthropology. We can find all the global forces affecting and infecting the communities and *barrios* everywhere. But what we also observe is the creative construction of a contemporary art of living. The Zapatistas are amazingly autonomous and self-sufficient. They don't get any funds from the government. They don't need the market or the state to live their lives. If a total siege were suddenly imposed on them, their way of life would basically remain the same. But they have X-rays and ultrasound equipment in their health clinics and they buy in the market equipment for their community radios, mobile phones, computers, bikes, vehicles and so on, but they know how to use those technologies instead of being used by them.

An increasing number of people are resisting old and new enclosures, thus preventing the creation of new needs. Yes, they are exposed to all kind of pressures and many times surrender to old or new dependencies. But what I am increasingly observing at the grassroots is how people dismantle the 'need' for state apparatuses or the goods and services offered by the market. Many people are producing their own food (small farmers, mainly women, feed 70% of the people on Earth); learning in freedom (beyond the school system, escaping from education); 'healing from health' (trusting again their own healers and their own notions and traditions of how to be sane or heal… with a little help from modern technologies); recovering the art of dwelling (building by themselves their houses and buildings) and so forth. This is, in my view, to live beyond development. It is not going back to the Stone Age, but saying no, for sheer survival or in the name of old ideals, to a tragic path destroying Mother Earth, dissolving the social fabric and dooming millions to hunger, misery and homelessness… even in prosperous societies like the US.

Silvia is right, of course. If you live among indigenous people, sometimes you don't know if what they are talking about is happening now, happened yesterday or a thousand years ago or will happen tomorrow. Time is not real for them. They pack into the present as much past and future as they can. They live in cycles, natural and social cycles, and the image of the spiral of the Zapatista *caracoles* may represent changes in which they come back to the same place but at a different level.

I agree with all your reflections on aid and cooperation. In 1994 and 1995 there was a flow of people and goods coming to help the Zapatistas. At one point, the famous subcomandante Marcos produced a communiqué in which he stated that he was now forced to carry in his backpack a red high heel, just to remember what was happening. In one of the many boxes with charity for the communities came that red high heel, just one, not the pair, for the jungle. It was for him a symbol of what was happening.

> If you want to offer help to these poor Indians, struggling against a bad government, thanks… but no thanks. We don't want or need your help. However, if you think that our struggle is also your struggle, please come. There are plenty of things we need to talk about […] and to do together.

Yes, we need more than ever alliances and coalitions. There are many things that we can do together with people that want to make a difference in this tragic world in which we all live today, people that also want to resist the horror, the destruction of Mother Earth and culture and social fabric and hunger and misery. We can join forces with them.

After the US election on 8 November 2016, it seems evident that very diverse groups in the US should join forces and find new forms of articulation. Instead of issue struggles – for the environment in the face of climate change, against racism or racist police violence, against all forms of *machismo* and sexual discrimination, against chronic debt, unemployment or homelessness – what is needed is to struggle together: to resist the horror – to resist specific measures, policies, decisions, behaviour, offensive language; to construct a better society, more humane and sensible. This is the time to come together, to hold each other tight, both inside every country and between people of different countries.

I don't see a lot of conventional developers around me these days. Public developers no longer have large enough budgets. Private developers are increasingly concentrated on grabbing and dispossession, not really on development. The rich are accumulating more money than ever, but that money is not transformed into capitalist social relations, into hiring workers. Many of us are increasingly becoming, as the Zapatistas warned, disposable human beings. What we are calling *extractivismo* in Latin America (mining, urban, financial *extractivismo* but also labor and services *extractivismo*) cannot be described as development… with any notion of that concept of monumental emptiness, as Wolfgang used to say.

The long agony of development as a myth and as an enterprise is clearly ending. Do we really think that the American Dream is intact? That the American Way of Life is still the universal definition of the good life?

In my view, development is no longer a myth, a taboo, a promise or a threat. It is an obsession, an addiction, a pathological mania that some people suffer, in their minds, their emotions or their behaviour… and also a tool of domination and control. I don't see people mobilised to get development in all its masks and shapes as they were in the past. Of course, we still have capitalism. But can we really call capitalism this society in which we have many zombies – capitalist enterprises blaming anyone for falling profits, whether the banks, the state, immigrants or what have you – controlled and mined by a group, a very small group, of vampires, sucking from them and from all of us the blood of profit, income, goods, everything? As everybody knows, the vampires are not only devastating the planet to the point of endangering the survival of the human species. They are also killing the goose of the golden eggs… by accumulating through extraction and speculation, instead of production; by reducing both salaries and employment and exhausting resources, thus preventing or limiting the reproduction of the very system in which they thrive.

We are no longer in the time of TINA (There Is No Alternative). There are now thousands of alternatives and a new one emerges every day; many of them, perhaps most of them, are alternatives to development or express conditions beyond development, in spite of the ominous march of vampires and do-gooders in governments, international institutions, NGOs and academia still threatening or harassing the social majorities and the planet itself.

Arturo

Your answers pose many challenges, Gustavo. I shall take two of them only, for the sake of space: the idea that modernity has already collapsed, and what you so insightfully refer to as 'the creative construction of a contemporary art of living' by many communities resisting capitalism and development. They are inter-related, and there is a reason why I want to take on the question of modernity here, and this is the angst that the 'death of modernity' causes among so many friends and potential allies, particularly otherwise critical academics in both the North and the South.

I have found the following paraphrase to be true: that it is easier to imagine the end of the world than the end of modernity. I would like to attempt two displacements of modernity's centrism, starting with Ashis Nandy's telling reversal that the pathologies of science-driven modernity have already proven to be more lethal than the pathologies of tradition (Nandy 1987: 51). And yet we seem utterly unwilling to consider the creative retrieval of traditions' history making potentiality, a task that Nandy's 'critical traditionalism' embraces. Beyond a handful of philosophical treatises, critical academics rarely entertain seriously the end of modernity; most scholars react disdainfully against such proposition, disqualifying it as utopian or even reactionary. It is, however, implicit (though rarely stated out loud) in most discourses that speak of the need for civilisational transitions. The revered Buddhist teacher Thich Nhat Hanh has spoken openly about it in his critique of consumerism (he could well be referring to development as addiction): '[T]his civilisation of ours will have to end one day. But we have a huge role to play in determining when it ends and how quickly… Global warming may be an early symptom of that death' (Nath Hanh 2008: 43, 44). He goes further, inviting us to actively accept the end of our civilisation by meditating on this thought: 'Breathing in, I know that this civilization is going to die. Breathing out, this civilization cannot escape dying' (Nath Hanh 2008: 55). He is calling us to move beyond a civilisation that has become antithetical to the ontology and ethics of interexistence.[2]

For us moderns (I include myself here), actively facing the ontological challenges posed by the idea of the end of modernity – of a world significantly different than the current one – is not easy; it induces a type of fright that is deeply unsettling. How do we articulate this civilisational anxiety in effective ways? After all, most other worlds have had to exist (still do) with the fright and, not infrequently, the reality of their vanishing.

I have found two responses among European and Latin American academic friends. First, that what they perceive as a condemnation of modernity is not fair because the West itself is plural, inhabited by dissenting voices and plural modernities. This is an important corrective to the tendency, in our critiques, to homogenise the West/modern. We need to acknowledge the many non-dominant, peripheral and alternative forms of modernity, the non-dominant Wests that exist within the West. At the same time – I say to these colleagues – we need to do it decolonially and postdevelopmentally, in other words, without disavowing the privileges accorded to all things European (especially white European), and without reinforcing Western modernity as the de facto (naturalised) site of reason, progress, civility and so forth in contrast to the alleged barbarism or unviability of other worlds. And, in my view, the best way to do so is to see clearly how we are all in this together, that is, that the Liberation of Mother Earth (as the indigenous *Nasa* people of Colombia put it) and the defence of the pluriverse ('a world where many worlds can be embraced', in the Zapatista dictum) is a project we should all embrace, from wherever we are, whether in the Lacandon forest or in the heart of Europe or Cali or Mexico City.

Our critique is not really 'anti-European' or 'anti-West', but in pro of the Liberation of Modern Earth and the pluriverse, and the Earth and the pluriverse are all of us, not just 'indigenous peoples'. These concepts have not been created by indigenous and ethnic movements just for them, but for all. They apply to all. It is incumbent upon those of us 'in the belly of the beast' who would like to defend those other non-dominant modernities to set into motion *effectively* their differences with the dominant West, thus joining forces with those opposing the assemblages of patriarchal, Eurocentric and racist capitalist modernity from the peripheries of the Global South, those struggling daily to construct territories for re-existence in mutually enriching ways with the planet. This is the meaning, for me, of inhabiting ethically and politically the civilisational crossroads in which we are enmeshed at present. And this means that we all need to make serious efforts at *vivir entre mundos*, to live in-between, with and from multiple worlds, as we attempt the re-communalisation of our daily existence.

Said differently, we need to resist endowing 'modernity' with the ability to fully and naturally occupy the entire field of the social, making invisible or secondary other ways of instituting it, including what have been called 'traditions'. This brings me to the second aspect of your answer I want to comment on, that of constructing other forms of re-existence. This would include the question of how we might cultivate ourselves as subjects who desire non-capitalist, non-liberal and non-modern forms of life – more autonomous, convivial and communal. In the field of transition visions and narratives, re-localisation (of food, energy, transportation, health etc.) and the re-communalisation of social life (reconnecting with other humans and non-humans, including the spiritual worlds) are emerging as two principal criteria for moving in this direction; these are the *sine qua non* conditions for living beyond development. *Autonomía* is the name given by Latin American grassroots struggles to this attempt at creating conditions for re-existence and a thoroughly contemporary art of living. Again, this concept is not just for those in the peripheries, but for all. How do we think about autonomous living and communities everywhere, and perhaps particularly in the densest and most consumption-oriented liberal worlds, namely, those of today's middle classes worldwide? This is one of today's greatest challenges, and debates on degrowth and postdevelopment have lots to contribute to making it tangible and realisable.

Gustavo

The end of modernity, in my view, comes first in the form of disillusionment, as Wolfgang Dietrich brilliantly describes in his *Call for Many Peaces* (Dietrich & Sützl 1997). Modern people increasingly doubt the universal truth of the modern paradigm – a societal project characterised by Newtonian physics, Cartesian reductionism, the nation-state of Thomas Hobbes and the capitalist world system. This doubting comes from everyday experience. The subsequent scholarly reflection has not been very productive. As a consequence, we have confusion, a loss of values and orientation, or the insight of a pluriverse; instead of dissolving plurality, the idea is to celebrate it, to demand respect for and coexistence with difference, as expressed in the Zapatista dictum you already mentioned – a world in which many worlds can be embraced.

Many academics and universities are already engaged in the search for a new unitary system of reference, as a substitute for the exhausted modern paradigm. But such a search is becoming something like the old definition of metaphysics: the search in a dark room for a black cat that does not exist. As Einstein observed, we cannot find a solution for a problem within the frame that created it. Some of us are beginning to believe that the new paradigm already exists, not in academic rooms but in reality – in the form of an alternative practice that is in itself a theory. The Zapatistas are the best example, but many groups are engaged in the same path. It is not the impossible attempt of going back in history or of discarding everything that modernity has brought about. It is the autonomous construction of a contemporary art of living. Instead of cutting a head off the capitalist hydra, only to see how it regenerates other heads, people are drying up the soil on which the hydra can grow, that is, escaping from the habit of 'needs' and thus dissolving their dependence on the market and the state.

That is the very nature of autonomy for many in Latin America. And this is the attitude, by the way, that the so-called 'progressive governments' in Latin America don't want to understand.

Indigenous peoples have a long experience in dealing with modernity and they are a source of inspiration for those imagining its end. I see again a very creative alliance with those inside modern thinking looking for alternatives. Foucault, for example, talked repeatedly about the insurrection of the great diversity of subjugated knowledges, when erudite knowledge is juxtaposed with empirical knowledge to generate historical knowledges of struggle. Similarly, the commons movement is today everywhere, not only in the so-called Global South. Everywhere, people exposed to hyper-individualism, consumerism, exploitation and climate change seem to have had enough. They are rescuing old terms to give them new meanings to name their contemporary social constructions – even if often in contradictory ways – which in my view are clearly beyond development … and the conventional, modern, capitalist paradigms.

A recent UN report, prepared for the Quito Conference Habitat III in October 2016, called *Urbanisation and Development: Emerging Futures* has some pertinent gems, buried in the mass of bureaucratic jargon. It mentions the failure of urban policies that can be translated as the failure of development policies – entirely visible and of devastating consequences. For the report, prosperity was described as a tide raising all vessels and boats… but it is clear now that it raises only the yachts. I can adopt without reservation that kind of obituary for development. I don't think we said in the *Dictionary* (nor today) that developers are dead; they continue their destructive enterprise. What is dead is its promise. We can no longer argue seriously that development may bring justice, sustainability, dignity or a good life, or that it eliminates hunger and misery – that it is a tide raising all vessels.

Of course, we must continue exploring the conditions that shaped the desire to be led and to have others legislate life, which generates a herd instinct, massively displayed in the 1930s and still at work today. Foucault made these observations 50 years ago, in his preface of the *Anti-Oedipus* of Deleuze and Guattari (Foucault 1983). They are today more pertinent and urgent than ever, given the increasingly destructive ethos of the dominant economic and political system we now suffer. We need to resist the current horror, and the best way to resist is to construct a new society, in the many shapes it will take in our pluralist world.

Arturo

Unfortunately, Gustavo, we must bring this conversation to an end… for now. To conclude, could you summarise succinctly how your views on development have changed over the past 25 years?

Gustavo

Have I changed my views about 'development' in the last 25 years? Yes, and no.

Today, I am insisting in my call to public debate and action to stop the current madness still packaged as 'development' or 'progress'. Today, like 25 years ago, I denounce the cynicism of those still promoting 'development', even when they pose as 'do-gooders' and pretend to help the poor.

But there is a change. Twenty-five years ago we were not explicit enough in showing how 'development' was just the slogan used by capital to facilitate the implementation of a neocolonial enterprise. We all know well that capitalism has permeated the whole society through every pore.

I am fully aware that today there are still many millions whose desires are shaped by the belief that 'development' defines a universal norm of the good life. Many people still believe in the Western or American Way of Life, no matter how much they experience its consequences: the immense price to be paid by adopting it in terms of decency, joy, freedom and humanity; the radical impossibility of extending it to all people on Earth; the measure in which it endangers the survival of life on the planet.

I am also aware that the current ecological, economic, social and political limits to that irresponsible race are stimulating violent and blind reactions, of a fundamentalist character. We are living in a moment of extreme danger that was not so clear 25 years ago.

Yet today, most of all, I am enjoying the surge of a new hope. I wrote, 25 years ago, that it was 'time to recover a sense of reality, time to walk with one's own feet, on one's own path, in order to dream one's own dreams, not the borrowed ones of development'. Millions, perhaps billions, are following that path and experiencing what is to be beyond development. Capitalism is not an almighty and omnipresent monolith. The current wave of violence and destruction is fostering struggles against capital, which involve the heart, the head and the hands of people increasingly discontent with the situation. A new social force, transforming rebellion and indignation into a political revolution, is thus beginning to take shape.

There is no place for optimism, in this tragic circumstance of the world, in this transition to a new era. Many of those millions are struggling for sheer necessity and everywhere the struggle requires lots of courage and lucidity. But there is room for hope, the opposite to the expectations defining the economic society, 'development' and capitalism; hope is not the conviction that something will happen in a certain way, but the conviction that something makes sense, whatever happens. What makes sense today, like always, is to reclaim our human condition and decency.

Notes

1 This chapter was originally published as Esteva, G. & Escobar, A. (2017) 'Post-development @ 25: on "being stuck" and moving forward, sideways, backward and otherwise', *Third World Quarterly*, vol 38, no 12, pp 2559–2572.
2 This idea has found a recent lucid expression in the domain of insurrectionary politics: 'The biggest problem we face is a philosophical one: understanding that this civilization is *already dead* [...] [its end] has been clinically established for a century'; Invisible Committee, *To Our Friends*, 29. For this group, it is the West that is the catastrophe – nobody is out to 'destroy the West', it is destroying itself.

References

Benjamin, W. (1968) *Illuminations*. New York: Schocken Books.
Cayley, D. (2005) *The Rivers North of the Future: The Testament of Ivan Illich*. Toronto: House of Anansi Press.
Dietrich, W. & Sützl, W. (1997) *A Call for Many Peaces*. Peace Centre Burg Schlaining, November 1997. www.friedensburg.at/uploads/files/wp7_97.pdf.
Escobar, A. (2014) *Sentipensar con la Tierra* [*Thinking-Feeling with the Earth*]. Medellín: UNAULA.
Esteva, G. (2015). 'Para sentipensar la comunalidad' ['To think-feel the communal']. *Bajo el Volcán*, vol 16, no 23, pp 171–186.
Esteva, G., Babones, S. & Babcicky, P. (2013) *The Future of Development: A Radical Manifesto*. Chicago: Policy Press.
Feher, F., Heller, A. & Markus, G. (1986) *Dictatorship over Needs*. Oxford: Blackwell.
Foucault, M. (1983) 'Preface'. In Deleuze, G. & Guattari, F. (eds.), *Anti-Oedipus, Capitalism and Squizophrenia* pp xi–xiv. Minneapolis: University of Minnesota Press.
Gago, V. (2014) *La razón neoliberal* [*On Neoliberal Reason*]. Buenos Aires: Tinta Limón.
Invisible Committee (2015) *To Our Friends*. Cambridge, MA: MIT Press.
Nandy, A. (1987) *Traditions, Tyrannies, and Utopias*. New Delhi: Oxford University Press.
Nath Hanh, T. (2008) *The World We Have*. Berkeley, CA: Parallax Books.
Rivera Cusicanqui, S. (2014). *Hambre de Huelga* [*Hunger for the Strike*]. Querétaro: La Mirada Salvaje.

2
POSTDEVELOPMENT IN JAPAN

Revisiting Yoshirou Tamanoi's theory of regionalism

Yoshihiro Nakano

Introduction

The early twenty-first century is marked by the proliferation of counterproductivity in industrial societies. From global warming and the 2008 financial crises to the Fukushima nuclear disaster, the multiple crises that undermine the survival of humanity originate in the Global North, and this fact urges us to question the liveability of the productivist model of development.

The new global situation brings a new research agenda in the academic discourse of postdevelopment. In the 1990s, postdevelopment theory emerged as a radical critique of development projects in the Global South (Escobar 1995; Latouche 1991; Rahnema with Batwree 1997; Sachs 1992; Shiva 1991). However, today, postdevelopment must also tackle the problems of overdevelopment in the Global North. The developed world has an urgent need for a sustainability project and this concern is hotly discussed among Southern European theorists who promote the project of degrowth (Ariès 2009; Cacciari 2006; D'Alisa, Demaria & Kallis 2014; Latouche 2006, 2010).

In this context, the Japanese theory of regionalism also makes a fresh contribution to the international debate on postdevelopment and degrowth. As early as the 1970s, Yoshirou Tamanoi (1918–1985), a pioneer of ecological economics in Japan, instigated the debate on alternatives to development in the name of regionalism (*Chiikishugi*), exploring a scenario of sustainable transition for Japanese society that is reminiscent of degrowth.

In what follows, I will examine Tamanoi's theory of regionalism, illuminating its key theoretical categories. The chapter begins with the introduction of the historical background of regionalism. I then explain the objectives of regionalism and its impact on academic research and civil society. The third section discusses the new vision of community as conceptualised by Tamanoi. I will examine four theoretical pillars that constitute his concept of community, namely, (1) a politics of the common good, (2) an economics of the commons, (3) an aesthetics of a human-scale lifeworld, and (4) an ethics of future. In the fourth section, I will analyse the debate on epistemologies of the South that took place between Tamanoi and philosopher Yujirou Nakamura (1925–2017). This is a relatively unexplored topic in the postwar Japanese intellectual history and I will discuss its actuality by reference to Boaventura de Sousa Santos' work. In the concluding section, I will propose a new research project, which reexamines regionalism in global intellectual history.

Regionalism as a project of postdevelopment in Japan

Regionalism is arguably the most original socio-intellectual movement in postwar Japan exploring alternatives to development. This unique social experiment illustrates how the theoretical discourse of postdevelopment can be applied to concrete practices of Japanese civil society. On 25 October 1976, Tamanoi and his colleagues founded the Regionalism Study Group and started public debate on this newly emerging idea. The objectives of the study group were twofold: (1) to provide critical reflections on the historical experiences of economic development in modern Japan, especially the social and ecological damages produced by centralised industrial development projects; and (2) to conceptualise an alternative vision of economy and society in ways which could avoid a catastrophic scenario of industrial overgrowth. The concept of regionalism was thus introduced to denote a 'possible economic regime' (Tamanoi 1979).

The idea is iconoclastic as it questions the legitimacy of the development paradigm that runs through Japanese modernity. Since the Meiji Restoration (1868),[1] modern Japan blindly pursued the ideology of productivism, imitating the Western model of industrial development. For most of Japan, the history of industrialisation and the postwar experience of high economic growth are conceived of as a symbol of success. However, Tamanoi demystifies such a narrative of modernisation and defines the ongoing model of development as disempowering local societies and hence unsustainable in the long run.

> The centralised nature of Japanese society since the Meiji era has been further reinforced in the decade of high economic growth after the Second World War. Most Japanese are concentrating their energies on the urban centre and have become indifferent to their communities. Against this background, regionalism aims to enhance the autonomy of local societies.
>
> *(Tamanoi 1978a: 5)[2]*

The exigency for the revival of local autonomy comes from the necessity of delimiting the aberrant path of economic centralisation. Regionalism thus challenges the entire paradigm of modernist development projects in Japan and proposes a possible alternative. As Tamanoi states, 'regionalism means that residents in a given region identify themselves with local communities, surrounded by their unique natural and cultural climate and pursue political and administrative autonomy and cultural identity' (Tamanoi 1990a [1977]: 29).

It should be noted that, in this passage, Tamanoi deconstructs the prevailing notion of region in two aspects. First, since the late nineteenth century, the national government in Japan treated the regional or the local as a satellite of urban metropoles. Centralised development projects were implemented by subordinating the local to the national, with the economic and political autonomy of local communities being severely restricted. As opposed to such a bureaucratic perspective, regionalism redefines the regional or the local as an autonomous living space in which each local community or region is entitled to irreducible political autonomy. Second, regionalism also challenges a widespread economism in local development discourses, relativising the GDP-centred perspective of wealth and highlighting non-economic dimensions of local realities. Tamanoi depicts the regional or the local as a multi-dimensional space in which historical heritage of local culture and the natural environment cultivate a unique ambience of community life.

Once it was introduced, regionalism provoked controversy in the world of academy. Both the modernist liberals and the left-wing Marxists disapproved the idea. Regionalism was not recognised as a serious research topic for modern economic sciences. However, regionalism attracted a group of heterodox economists as well as the interests of historians, linguists, sociologists, political theorists, and ethnologists; it paved the way for new research programs that buttressed the search for alternatives.

Three research programs were proposed by scholars attracted for regionalism. The first research program is the study of local history. Regionalism brought to light the diversity of historical experiences of each local area, omitted by the discursive space of modern nation-state. It investigated the role that local geography, cultural climates, traditional customs, and vernacular language played in the sustainable reproduction of local livelihood and commons. In the epistemology of regionalism, the local or the regional is no longer a homogeneous economic entity whose wealth is measured by GDP alone.

The second research program is the economy of the living system or the living economy. In *Economy and Ecology: Towards a Broad Concept of Economy* (1978b), Tamanoi draws on Nicholas Georgescu-Roegen's 'bioeconomics' and establishes an original theory of ecological economics, which he termed the 'economy of the living system'. The economy of the living system offers a theoretical framework which analyses effects of industrial activities on the metabolism of biosphere.

As early as the 1970s, Tamanoi anticipated a catastrophic result of the globalisation of industrial societies. He warns that the proliferation of nuclear energy and industrial production would cause a situation of high entropy making sustainable reproduction of life impossible. To prevent the catastrophe, he argues, that industrial entropy must be reduced drastically. In his theory, entropy is introduced as a key to the paradigm change of modern economics, deeply rooted in Newtonian physics and ignorant of the negative effects of production outside market exchange. In 1983, Tamanoi founded *The Association for Entropy* with his colleagues and paved the way for the Japanese School of Circular Economy, whose researches were comparable to their international counterparts (Bonaiuti 2001; Ekins 1986; Martinez-Alier 1987).

The third research program is the study of organic farming. The study of the living system led Tamanoi to reevaluate the role of water and soil in the reduction of redundant entropy. From this vantage, he started a study of traditional farming methods, i.e., organic farming, as a concrete foundation of the living economy. In 1984, Tamanoi and his collegues published a book entitled *The Logic of Living and Farming: Beyond Urbanisation and Industrialisation* (Tamanoi, Sakamoto & Nakamura 1984). This is one of the earliest attempts at mainstreaming organic farming in Japan. For Tamanoi, organic farming could be a catalyst bringing about a systemic transformation of high-entropy urban life to low-entropy sustainable life. As opposed to modernisation theory, which devalues the agricultural sector vis-à-vis industrial and service sectors, regionalism centres its value on agriculture as the latter plays a significant role in the reproduction of the living system.

Apart from these academic progressivisms, regionalism also stimulated ordinary citizens' participation. Since its instigation, Tamanoi held a series of meetings and seminars across Japan, discussing social realities with local people. The regionalism meetings took place in Tokyo (September 1976), Kyoto (November 1976), Kumamoto (March 1977), Aomori (October 1977), Matsumoto in Nagano Prefecture (August 1978), and Bihoku in Hiroshima Prefecture (September 1979). In every meeting, Tamanoi invited local practitioners interested in regionalism and created a space of open dialogue between academics and citizens.

These local participants, varied from municipal public servants and local bank officers to medical doctors and poets, brought to light the diversity of local experiments such as a local medical system, local education programs, community banking and organic farming. Alternatives to development were explored through the action-research of citizens, which amounted to the publication of a monograph comprising research articles written by academics and ordinary citizens (Tamanoi, Kiyonari & Nakamura 1978).

As a theorist, Tamanoi concentrated himself on the construction of a theoretical framework of regionalism. Much of key ideas in his work were not immediately translated into concrete practices during his lifetime. However, he played an indispensable role in networking diverse academics and citizens and promoted their collaboration. One of the fruitful results is the Shitara School of Farming in Aichi Prefecture, founded in 1983 by a citizen who participated Tamanoi's research project of organic farming. In addition, the study of community banking paved the way for the diffusion of NPO banks and local complementary currencies during the 1990s.

Reconstructing the common

Regionalism established a transdisciplinary space of academic research that produced a unique articulation between the human, social and natural sciences. Such an experiment ultimately aims at the construction of a new vision of community, as Tamanoi argues.

> What is at stake here is to explore the concept of the common (i.e. community), which is reducible to neither the public (i.e. the state) nor the private (i.e. the market). [...] Probably, the construction of the common is possible in a sphere in which human beings develop their livelihood with a full realization of their personhood. [...] The biggest challenge of regionalism lies in the construction of such a sphere
>
> *(Tamanoi 1978a: 17)*

The tripartite of the common, the public and the private draws on Polanyi's reflections on three principles of the livelihood of man: reciprocity, redistribution and market exchange (Polanyi 1977). As Polanyi delineates, the history of the modern West is conceived of as the evolution of 'market society'. The political construction of free market economy introduced commodity relationship in every sphere of social life to the extent in which subsistence of community was transformed to fictive commodities (Polanyi 2001 [1944]).

Inspired by Polanyi's work, Ivan Illich observed the decline of the commons in the wake of market society. In *Shadow Work* (1981), *Gender* (1982) and *H2O and the Waters of Forgetfulness* (1985), Illich identified a historical moment in which people's vernacular autonomy (i.e., subsistence), maintained by multidimensional cultural ethos such as language, gender, bodily senses and imagination, was destroyed by the heteronomy of industrial system. For this reason, Illich reckons that the history of development in the modern West is nothing other than the history of a war against subsistence (Illich, 1981: 139).

Japanese modernity is no exception. Modern Japan followed the Western model of development under the centralised bureaucratic regime and waged the war against subsistence in the name of wealth creation. The process was accelerated after World War II, especially during the 1960s. The high economic growth in Japan went hand in hand with the denigration and destruction of the commons in the rural areas, hitherto maintained by traditional methods of farming and fishery. The decline of the commons allowed the infiltration of the logic of the market and the industrial system everywhere. The social life of modern Japan was thus uprooted from local culture and ecosystem and captured by the universe of modern economic sciences in which every individual was condemned to play the drama of rational economic man. Disastrous public pollutions such as Minamata disease occurred in this way.

Following Polanyi and Illich, Tamanoi observes that the problem of Japanese modernity lies in the decline of community, that is, an autonomous sphere in which people cultivate their livelihood without recourse to the state and the market. Regionalism, it was argued, must contribute to the reconstruction of such a sphere. The 'common' is thus introduced to denote various non-market and non-state relationships of human existence, conventionally described as community or the commons.

It should be noted that, by community or the common, Tamanoi never romanticises a previous golden era nor does he claim that what is needed is a return to traditional communal life. As early as the 1970s, he was aware of growing new social movements in and outside Japan, such as ecology, feminism, organic farming, community development, and alternative technologies movements. He expected Japanese civil society to reconstruct their local communities through networking the diversity of civic associations. As political theorist Masao Kikuchi (2007) rightly points out, the regionalist vision of community is comparable to Michael Sandel's and Charles Taylor's leftist communitarianism. It also resonates with the ideal of civic associationism and the democratisation of economy widely discussed today in the name of social and solidarity economy (Biolighini 2007; Laville 2010), civil economy (Bruni & Zamagni 2004, 2015) and diverse economy (Gibson-Graham 1996, 2006).

Four theoretical pillars of the common

In Tamanoi's theory, a new vision of community is explored in four theoretical pillars: (1) a politics of the common good; (2) an economics of the commons; (3) an aesthetics of a human-scale lifeworld; (4) an ethics of future. Basic ideas were developed during his stay in Okinawa (1978–1985). This is a period in which his study of regionalism flourished through his dialogue with local people as well as his intellectual exchange with Ivan Illich.[3]

First, the *politics of the common good* aims to enhance local capacity of self-governance. Since the late nineteenth century, Japanese politics has been developing a centralised political system that subordinates local municipalities to the central government. The autonomy of local governments has been strictly limited, with their status being reduced to a satellite of state administration. As opposed to this tendency, Tamanoi argues that the rights of self-government derive from unique histories of each local society; it should not be violated by the arbitrary state power. He proposes that each local government must be able to adopt its own local 'constitution' to protect the common good and to implement self-governance of society (Tamanoi 1990b [1979]).

In 1981, Tamanoi organised a study group for local constitution with local scholars and citizens and wrote the *Okinawa Self-Governance Constitution* (Tamanoi 1990c). The manuscript, published posthumously, consists of a preamble and eighteen articles, which prescribe the rights of self-governance and political participation, basic social rights, the rights to protect cultural heritage and nature against rampant development projects, and the rights to live in peace without fear of war. Unfortunately, the manuscript failed to create a broad consensus and was not adopted by the local governments. However, it reflects Okinawa's social atmosphere at that time, in which local citizens and scholars hotly discussed the possibility of economic and political autonomies against mainland Japan.

Second, the *economics of the commons* puts the economy of the living system into practice. As already discussed, the economy of the living system aims at the construction of a low-entropy economy, which is today also called a circular economy. The consideration of entropy law led Tamanoi to reject the blind pursuit of big science and advanced technology such as nuclear power and to follow the path of alternative technologies. Moreover, his theory positively reevaluates the role that nature's economy, especially the circular system of water and soil, plays in the reduction of redundant entropy. In this context, Tamanoi comes to focus on traditional livelihood practiced by local villagers in Okinawa.

One of his final works was to reevaluate the sea of Okinawa as the commons for local islanders. In the posthumously published article *Sea as the Commons* (1995), Tamanoi sheds lights on vernacular language and customs of local villagers living in seaside areas of Okinawa. These villagers, he remarks, maintain their local customs for generations, collectively managing local marine resources (e.g., sea weeds) available in coral reef seas and utilising them to fertilise their farm land. He started his research on the seas as the commons in 1985, but was interrupted by his untimely death and succeeded by his colleagues such as Hisashi Nakamura and Masahiro Tabeta.

The third theoretical pillar is an *aesthetics of a human-scale lifeworld*. This concept was coined in the last stage of Tamanoi's life through the reading of Illich's 1982 book *Gender*.[4] Tamanoi interprets Illich's historical study of the loss of 'vernacular gender' as an attempt at identifying an autonomous sphere of *reproduction* of human life, which is made invisible in industrial society. He argues that Illich's reflections on vernacular gender bring to light the world of 'contrasting complementarities' between women and men, which are irreducible to market relations; such a perspective of vernacular gender leads us to further investigate diverse perceptions of bodily senses and their modalities of social recognition (Tamanoi 1990d [1984]: 229). From this vantage, Tamanoi introduced a new concept of a 'human-scale lifeworld' as a basic unit of community which regionalism must explore:

> For a long time, I have been thinking that there is an appropriate scale of living space for human beings and such a space can be called the 'region'. [...] The reproduction of life is possible in that space. Therefore, when we speak about peace in a region, that kind of peace must protect the reproduction of life.
>
> *(Tamanoi 1985a:105)*

His reflections on life and peace challenge basic assumptions of modern political theory. Modern political theory, as established by Hobbes and developed by political liberalism, is based on an ontology of atomistic individualism. It depicts the state of nature as a situation of war of all against all and conceptualises peace as that which is achieved through a 'social contract' between isolated individuals. At the heart of modern political theory lies the fear of others and the fear of death; there is no positive ontological connection between human lives, let alone that between the lives of human and non-humans.

In contrast, Tamanoi adopts a biocentric ontology; human existence is sustained in a web of life, which is cultivated in a living economy. Peace is realised so long as this flow of life is protected and reproduced for generations. In his thinking, major actors for the protection of life are neither abstract individuals nor rational economic man, still less the state institutions; they are the living people (*Seikatsusha*), women and men constituting a world of vernacular gender (Tamanoi 1985a: 60).

Fourth, and finally, reflections on a human-scale lifeworld lead to an *ethics of future*. In *The Loads of Scientific Civilisation* (1985a), his main posthumous work, Tamanoi denounces gender discrimination and sexism inherent in the ideology of productivism and seeks to transcend the logic of the industrial system which instrumentalises human life for masculine principles such as profit-making and efficiency. Here, he introduces a notion of *identification* and conceptualises a human-scale lifeworld as an ontological ground from which a post-Cartesian biocentric subjectivity emerges:

> For people living in a human-scale lifeworld, the most important principle is *identification*. A human-scale lifeworld is not the world dominated by the masculine principles that instrumentalise life for the sake of profit-making, efficiency and violent revolution. It is the world of living things in which goal and means become one. Since Galileo and Descartes, modern philosophy has created a world that transforms living things to lifeless objects. Philosophy is still evolving in that direction even today. The paradigm of modern philosophy makes it extremely difficult to find the world of living things. For my part, I have deepened my thought through the concept of the 'living system' and reached a conclusion that this is the only world with which human beings can identify themselves. For exploring the world of the living system, is there any more positive expression than *identifying ourselves with the flow of life, including future generations*?
>
> (*Tamanoi 1985a: 41, my emphasis*)

Since Descartes, the modern scientific rationalism introduced a separation of the human mind (*cogito*) from the world of objects (*res extensa*). It is on the basis of this distinction that the modern world expanded technological and economic domination of the world of life. As opposed to the Cartesian paradigm, Tamanoi seeks to re-embed human subjectivity in the web of life, which is reproduced from generation to generation. The position of a human being in the world is decentred and subjectivity is reconceptualised as a responsibility for sustaining the flow of life in the generational time-scale.

Moreover, the notion of *identification* also introduces a different mode of subjectivity in contrast with what, say, Kantian moral philosophy might posit. In Tamanoi's theory, responsibility for the future generation does not stem from the faculty of reason, disconnected from the world of life. Rather, it emerges from an awareness of the deep ontological connection between diverse living things, in which human life, its mind and body, is embedded. Such an ethics of future is possible because of the concept of the living system. A theory of the living system establishes an original philosophy of life. It introduces a relational ontology and makes it possible to examine consequences of human action in a broad web of life.

In the last stage of his life, Tamanoi developed a biocentric vision of community with a strong sustainability imperative. His vision not only resonates with Vandana Shiva's concept of 'earth democracy' (Shiva 2005) but also suggests a possible theoretical ground for postdevelopment subjectivities.

Unfinished debate: epistemologies of the South

Regionalism made an original contribution to the Japanese debate on alternatives to development in both theory and practice. It opened a space in which academics and citizens meet and discuss economic alternatives, reevaluating diverse non-market community-based economic activities. However, its theoretical discourse gradually lost influence in Japanese society after Tamanoi's untimely death in 1985. Unprecedented economic booms in the late 1980s created a situation serious enough to obliterate the socio-ecological crisis that had affected Japanese society. The whole nation was immersed in the culture of high consumerism. The argument in favour of regionalism was marginalised in the collective narrative of Japanese society.

Regrettably, important theoretical agendas in regionalism remain undeveloped. Although a group of ecological economists such as Takeshi Murota, Masahiro Tabeta and Makoto Maruyama continue to study the theory of the living system, their research remains within the field of economic sciences and has not contributed to the development of transdisciplinary research articulating politics, economics, aesthetics and ethics, as the late work of Tamanoi did.

As I have discussed elsewhere (Nakano 2016), one of the most unexplored topics in regionalism is its relationship with the *epistemologies of the South*. This topic was originally put forward by philosopher Yujirou Nakamura and produced a short period of intellectual exchange with Tamanoi in the early 1980s. If the discussion had continued between the two, it may have provided a great opportunity to deepen the research program of regionalism, especially that associated with an aesthetics of a human-scale lifeworld. I will briefly summarise the debate.

Since the late 1960s, Nakamura investigated alternative traditions of knowledge that could counteract the reckless expansion of industrial societies and their negative effects on the natural environment. As he observes, historically the development of industrial societies goes hand in hand with the rise of scientific rationalism, which is nothing other than a product of a specific geographical setting: Northwestern Europe (Nakamura 1993b [1986]).

After a decade-long research period on the Aristotelian concept of *sensus communis* and its geographical influence in the history of Western philosophy, Nakamura discovered the lasting tradition of non-Cartesian knowledge in Southern Europe (1993a [1982], 2000 [1979]). In Southern European epistemologies, he remarks, the Aristotelian concept of *sensus communis* historically played a central role until the period of Giambattista Vico. It provided a holistic understanding of human being, illuminating the interaction between bodily senses and the mind, between human action and the surrounding world. In contradistinction to modern scientific rationalism, the philosophical tradition of Southern Europe permits us to understand the dimensions of performance and symbolic action in the constitution of human society.

Nakamura argues that, in a situation in which industrial societies are losing a sense of limits, it is imperative for human beings to reactivate their bodily senses and communion with the environment. In other words, human beings need be able to coordinate the faculty of reason with the faculty of senses, so that they can comprehend their position in the world as well as the consequences of their action in a holistic way. The epistemologies of Southern Europe hint at such an alternative ground.

According to Nakamura, the possibility of post-Cartesian knowledge can also be found in the Global South (Nakamura 1993b [1986]). In fact, the Global South and Southern Europe in some cases share epistemological traits; historically, both areas are cultivating diverse cosmological visions of human society, which he refers to as *place-based knowledge*. In this tradition, the perception of the human world is gleaned from the communion of bodily senses with the environment.

Nakamura states that these diverse knowledges in the South are marginalised in the discursive space of Western modernity but nevertheless have a potential to develop an alternative epistemological ground that transforms underlying principles of industrial societies. What is at stake is to establish a global research project to reevaluate these rich epistemological traditions. It is for this reason that he introduced the concept of 'epistemologies of the South' (*Minamigata No Chi*) as a common denominator for alternative knowledges in Southern Europe and the Global South (Nakamura 1993b [1986]).

In the early 1980s, Nakamura focused on Tamanoi's work and suggested the development of regionalism within the framework of epistemologies of the South (Nakamura, 2001 [1982]). A short period of intellectual exchange took place between the two. Both agreed on the importance of epistemologies of the South in Japan. However, their conclusions diverged due to the difference of research methodologies and approaches. Whereas Nakamura proposed structuralist and semiotic analysis in regionalism, Tamanoi stressed historical analysis, arguing that epistemologies of the South must be gleaned from the voices of ordinary peoples in the Global South. The debate did not produce a constructive intellectual convergence and has been obliterated in Japanese social sciences until today.

This is a great point missed in the postwar intellectual history of Japan. On the one hand, Nakamura's proposal is conceived of as an attempt at deepening aesthetic and cosmological dimensions of regionalism. This research topic certainly became the object of concern for late Tamanoi's work as he introduced the concept of a human-scale life space. However, he was not convinced by Nakamura's structuralist/semiotic approach. This is partly because Tamanoi followed Illich's critique of structural anthropology in *Gender* (1982) and considered that structuralism, especially its method of binary oppositions, did not contribute to the understanding of complex historical reality.

On the other hand, Tamanoi maintained his commitment to the historical reality of the Global South, especially that experienced by the ordinary people who suffered colonialism and developmentalism. In a letter to Nakamura (Tamanoi 1985b), he defined the history of the Global South as a 'history of sorrow', contending that epistemologies of the South must emerge as challenges of the Global South to the paradigm of the Global North. Tamanoi envisioned epistemologies of the South as knowledge promoting the liberation of ordinary people in the Global South, including people in Okinawa. This kind of historical perspective is missing in Nakamura's approach.

Are their approaches destined to diverge? Certainly not. The recent debate on epistemologies of the South in Southern Europe and Latin America suggests that there is a possibility for constructive convergence between the two. Boaventura de Sousa Santos's recent project of epistemologies of the South is a promising example (de Sousa Santos 2016).[5] For his part, de Sousa Santos points out the lasting influence of cognitive injustice in the modern world-system. He argues that European colonialism and the subsequent development of capitalism not only engendered economic and political subordination of Asia, Africa and Latin America, but also introduced cognitive injustice through the universalism of the modern sciences. In the modern world-system, vernacular knowledges in the non-Western world are denigrated and reduced to non-existence. A 'monoculture of knowledge' prevails on a global scale (de Sousa Santos 2016: 252–257).

His project of epistemologies of the South challenges this historically constructed cognitive injustice. As opposed to the monoculture of knowledge, he proposes an 'ecology of knowledges', which means the recognition of the diversity of local knowledges and cosmologies and their necessary interdependence (de Sousa Santos 2016: 257–266). More importantly, he uses the concept of 'the South' in a symbolic manner. In his theory, the South refers to not only the geographical area of the Global South but also a multitude of peoples marginalised and excluded in the modern world-system, for example, precarious workers, women, Indigenous peoples and various sexual and religious minorities. His project of epistemologies of the South aims at the liberation of these denigrated peoples, establishing cognitive justice.

De Sousa Santos' work suggests that there is no contradiction between Nakamura's vision and Tamanoi's, in fact, the two are mutually reinforcing. Epistemologies of the South must reevaluate diverse local knowledges and cosmologies in the Global South. This approach paves the way for an ecology of knowledges, which serves as the condition for cognitive justice, promoting the liberation of denigrated peoples in the modern world-system. De Sousa Santos clearly shows how Nakamura's approach converges with Tamanoi's. The potential of regionalism can be further explored in this direction, contextualising it into the global intellectual history of epistemologies of the South.

Concluding remark

This chapter examined Tamanoi's theory of regionalism as a project of alternatives to development in Japan. It discussed its vision of community (i.e., the common) and its relationship with epistemologies of the South.

Regionalism still holds relevant. After three decades of marginalisation, its theoretical agendas are becoming much more pertinent, as demand for sustainable community grows in an unprecedented way. It remains an unfinished project of postdevelopment in Japan, being a matrix of problems and perspectives. Key ideas of regionalism can be further explored in the recent studies of degrowth, solidarity economy and post-capitalist community economy in and outside of Japan. In particular, the concept of a human-scale lifeworld has a possibility of further development in line with epistemologies of the South.

One of the challenges for Japanese social sciences would be to re-elaborate Tamanoi's theoretical reflections in the global intellectual history of alternatives to development. This chapter presented such a possibility in the context of de Sousa Santos's project of epistemologies of the South. The proposed new research program not only helps to examine the Japanese debate on postdevelopment in a global context but also promotes intercultural dialogue between different linguistic and philosophical universes. The international debate on postdevelopment contributes to cultivating the conditions for ecology of knowledges in this way. The future of postdevelopment theory and the future of Japanese society will be gleaned from such an intellectual landscape.

Notes

1 The Meiji Restoration is a political event that marks the end of feudalism and the construction of the modern nation-state in Japan.
2 All the citations from Tamanoi's work are my translation.
3 Ivan Illich was an intellectual whom Tamanoi acknowledged as a 'true friend' during his lifetime. Illich visited Okinawa to meet Tamanoi and their intellectual exchange lasted until the latter's death. More importantly, Tamanoi read Illich's *Shadow Work* (1981) and *Gender* (1982) by contextualising them into the historical situation of Okinawa. This permitted him a highly original and constructive interpretation of Illich.
4 Tamanoi translated Illich's *Gender*. The Japanese translation published in 1984 is not only based on the English text but also reflects the French and German texts, which contain extended discussions on the relationships between vernacular gender, the perceptions of space and time, and everyday practices of dwelling.

5 As far as I investigated Nakamura's writings in Japanese, there occurred no explicit dialogue between him and de Sousa Santos. Nakamura confesses that he discussed his idea of epistemologies of the South with Paul Ricoeur in the late 1970s.

References

Ariès, P. (2009) *La décroissance: un nouveau projet politique*. Villeurbanne Cedex: Editions Golias.
Biolghini, D. (2007) 'Reti locali di economia solidale: Possibili cantieri della decrescita?' In Bonaiuti, M. (ed.), *Obiettivo Decrescita*. Bologna: Editrice Missionaria Italiana, pp 161–178.
Bonaiuti, M. (2001) *La teoria bioeconomica: la "nuova economia" di Nicholas Georgescu-Roegen*. Roma: Carocci Editore.
Bruni, L. & Zamagni, S. (2004) *Economia civile: Efficenza, equità, felicità pubbilica*. Bologna: il Mulino.
Bruni, L. & Zamagni, S. (2015) *L'economia civile*. Bologna: il Mulino.
Cacciari, P. (2006) *Pensare la decrescita: Sostenibilità ed equità*. Napoli: Edizioni Intra Moenia.
D'Alisa, G., Demaria, F. & Kallis, G. (eds.) (2014) *Degrowth: A Vocabulary for a New Era*. London: Zed Books.
Ekins, P. (ed.) (1986) *The Living Economy: New Economics in the Making*. London: Routledge and Kegan Paul.
Escobar, A. (1995) *Encountering Development: Making and Unmaking the Third World*. Princeton, NJ: Princeton University Press.
Gibson-Graham, J.K. (1996) *The End of Capitalism as We Know It: A Feminist Critique of Political Economy*. Minneapolis: The University of Minnesota Press.
Gibson-Graham, J.K. (2006) *A Post-capitalist Politics*. Minneapolis: The University of Minnesota Press.
Illich, I. (1981) *Shadow Work*. Boston and London: Marion Boyars.
Illich, I. (1982) *Gender*. New York: Pantheon Books.
Illich, I. (1985) *H2O and the Water of Forgetfulness*. Boston and London: Marion Boyars.
Kikuchi, M. (2007) *Nihon O Yomigaeraseru Seiji Shisou: Gendai Komyunitarianismu Nyumon* [Political Thought that Revives Japanese Society: An Introduction to the Contemporary Communitarianism]. Tokyo: Kodansha Publishers.
Latouche, S. (1991) *La planète des naufragés: Essai sur l'après-développement*. Paris: La Découverte.
Latouche, S. (2006) *Le pari de la décroissance*. Paris: Fayard.
Latouche, S. (2010) *Sortir de la société de consommation*. Paris: Les liens qui libèrent.
Laville, J.L. (2010) *Politique de l'association*. Paris: Le Seuil.
Martinez-Alier, J. (1987) *Ecological Economics: Energy, Environment, and Society*. Oxford: Blackwell.
Nakamura, Y. (1993a [1982]) 'Kyotsuu kankaku teki ningenzou no tenkai' ['The history of the anthropology of sensus communis']. In *Nakamura Yujirou Chosakushuu V* [*The Collected Works of Nakamura Yujirou V*]. Tokyo: Iwanami Shoten Publishers, pp 319–348.
Nakamura, Y. (1993b [1986]) 'Minamigata no chi to kindai sangyou shakai' ['Epistemologies of the South and the modern industrial societies']. In *Nakamura Yujirou Essai Shusei 3* [*The Collected Essays of Nakamura Yujirou 3*]. Tokyo: Seidosha Publishers, pp 111–128.
Nakamura, Y. (2000 [1979]) *Kyotsuu Kankaku Ron* [*On Sensus Communis*]. Tokyo: Iwanami Shoten Publishers.

Nakamura, Y. (2001 [1982]) 'Minamigata no chi no kanousei: Tamanoi Yoshirou eno tegami' ['Possibilities of the espitemologies of the South: A letter to Tamanoi Yoshirou']. In *Yorokobashiki Poiesis* [*Joyful Poiesis*]. Tokyo: Seidosha Publishers, pp 245–251.

Nakano, Y. (2016) 'Minamigata no chi toshiteno chiikishugi: Komonzu ron to kyotsukankaku ron ga deau basho de' ['Regionalism as an epistemology of the South: In search of the dialogue between the commons and sensus communis']. In Nakano, Y., Laville, J.L. & Coraggio, J.L. (eds.), *21 Seiki No Yutakasa: Keizai Wo Kae Shin No Minshushugi O Tsukuru Tame Ni* [*Reinventing the Commons in the Twenty-first Century: Alter-economy, Alter-democracy*].Tokyo: The Commons Publishers, pp 381–412.

Polanyi, K. (1977) *The Livelihood of Man*. New York: Academic Press.

Polanyi, K. (2001 [1944]) *The Great Transformation: The Political and Economic Origins of Our Time*. Boston: Beacon Press.

Rahnema, M. & Bawtree, V. (eds.) (1997) *The Post-development Reader*. London: Zed Books.

Sachs, W. (ed.) (1992) *The Development Dictionary: A Guide to Knowledge as Power*. London: Zed Books.

Shiva, V. (1991) *The Violence of the Green Revolution: Third World Agriculture, Ecology, and Politics*. London: Zed Books.

Shiva, V. (2005) *Earth Democracy: Justice, Sustainability, and Peace*. London: Zed Books.

Sousa Santos, B. de (2016) *Epistémologies du Sud: Mouvements citoyens et polémique sur la science*. Paris: Desclée de Brouwer.

Tamanoi, Y. (1978a) 'Chiikishugi no tameni' ['For Regionalism']. In Tamanoi, Y., Kiyonari, T. & Nakamura, H. (eds.), *Chiikishugi: Atarashii Shichou Eno Riron To Jissen No Kokoromi* [*Regionalism: Theoretical and Practical Experiments toward the New Idea*]. Tokyo: Gakuyoshobo Publishers, pp 3–17.

Tamanoi, Y. (1978b) *Economie To Ecologie: Kougino Keizaigaku Eno Michi* [*Economy and Ecology: Towards a Broad Concept of Economy*]. Tokyo: Misuzushobo Publishers.

Tamanoi, Y. (1979) *Chiikishugi No Shisou* [*The Philosophy of Regionalism*]. Tokyo: Nousan Gyoson Bunka Kyokai.

Tamanoi, Y. (1985a) *Kagakubunmei No Fuka: Toshindai No Seikatsusekai No Hakken* [*The Loads of Scientific Civilization: The Discovery of Human-scale Life World*]. Tokyo: Ronsousha Publishers.

Tamanoi, Y. (1985b) 'Rekishi to riaritie no minaoshi no nakade: Nakamura Yujirou eno hensyo' ['In the middle of rethinking history and reality: A reply to Nakamura Yujirou']. In *Kagakubunmei No Fuka: Toshindai No Seikatsusekai No Hakken* [*The Loads of Scientific Civilization: The Discovery of Human-scale Life World*]. Tokyo: Ronsousha Publishers, pp 126–134.

Tamanoi, Y. (1990a [1977]) 'Chiikibunken no konnicitekiigi' ['Actuality of decentralization']. In Tsurumi, K. & Arasaki, M. (eds.), *Tamanoi Yoshirou Chosakushu 3* [*The Complete Works of Yoshirou Tamanoi Vol. 3*]. Tokyo: Gakuyoshobo Publishers, pp 24–33.

Tamanoi, Y. (1990b [1979]) 'Chiikishugi to jichitai kenpou' ['Regionalism and local constitutions']. In Tsurumi, K. & Arasaki, M. (eds.), *Tamanoi Yoshirou Chosakushu 3* [*The Complete Works of Yoshirou Tamanoi Vol. 3*]. Tokyo: Gakuyoshobo Publishers, pp 82–109.

Tamanoi, Y. (1990c) 'Heiwa to seizon o konkan tosuru Okinawa jichi kenshou' ['Okinawa self-governance constitution for peace and survival']. In Tsurumi, K. & Arasaki, M. (eds.), *Tamanoi Yoshirou Chosakushu 3* [*The Complete Works of Yoshirou Tamanoi Vol. 3*]. Tokyo: Gakuyoshobo Publishers, pp 248–255.

Tamanoi, Y. (1990d [1984]) 'Ecologie to chiikishugi to seikatsu kuukan' ['Ecology, regionalism, and life space']. In Nakamura, H. & Kabayama, K. (eds.), *Tamanoi Yoshirou*

Chosakushu 4 [*The Complete Works of Yoshirou Tamanoi Vol. 4*]. Tokyo: Gakuyoshobo Publishers, pp 222–230.

Tamanoi, Y., Kiyonari, T. & Nakamura, H. (ed.) (1978) *Chiikishugi: Atarashii Shichou Eno Riron To Jissen No Kokoromi* [*Regionalism: Theoretical and Practical Experiments toward the New Idea*]. Tokyo: Gakuyoshobo Publishers.

Tamanoi, Y., Sakamoto, K. & Nakamura, H. (eds.) (1984) *Inochi to 'Nou' No Ronri: Toshika To Sangyouka O Koete* [*The Logic of Living and Farming: Beyond Urbanisation and Industrialisation*]. Tokyo: Gakuyoshobo Publishers.

Tamanoi, Y. (1995) 'Komonzu toshiteno umi' ['Sea as the commons']. In Nakamura, H. & Tsurumi, Y. (eds.), *Komonzu No Umi: Kouryu No Michi, Kyouyu No Chikara* [*Sea as the Commons: The Path of Exchange, The Power of Commoning*]. Tokyo: Gakuyoshobo Publishers, pp 1–10.

3
POSTDEVELOPMENT'S FORGOTTEN 'OTHER ROOTS' IN THE SPANISH AND LATIN AMERICAN HISTORY OF DEVELOPMENT THOUGHT

Sara Caria and Rafael Domínguez

Introduction

This chapter aims at re-discovering a piece of the Spanish and Latin American contribution to the history of ideas that influenced the theoretical construction of postdevelopment prior to Escobar's conceptualisation during the 1990s (Escobar 1995). The theoretical and methodological framework for this work derives from the history of ideas and the importance of ideas in history, as described in Hegel's dialectic and Marx's sociology of knowledge, and reinterpreted later by Weber, Manheim and Lovejoy. The basic pillar of this approach is that 'ideas are a driving force in human progress. This is not to deny the role of power and material interests but to highlight the role of ideas in helping to shape interests and constrain the exercise of raw power' (Emmerij, Jolly & Weiss 2005: 212). Following Emmerij, Jolly and Weiss (2005: 214) we understand that ideas are 'normative or causal beliefs held by individuals or adopted by institutions that influence their attitudes and actions'; under this assumption, it would seem relevant to trace an historical reconstruction of ideas about development in Latin America in the last century, in order to identify a connection with today's concept of postdevelopment, specifically Ecuador's *buen vivir*, often considered a postdevelopmental experiment and an alternative to the traditional concept of development (Gudynas 2014).

Economic growth and the strengthening of national productive capacity has been at the heart of the notion of development since it became an international issue in the middle of the twentieth century, where a whole set of institutions were devoted to its theoretical and practical concretion. Then, from the 1990s, international development priorities shifted to goal-oriented agendas whose main focus was poverty reduction. To such a degree, in fact, that Chang (2010) defined the Millennium Development Goals agenda (MDGs) as 'Hamlet without the Prince of Denmark', to stress how understandings of development at the beginning of the twenty-first century have moved away from their original core. The MDGs, for instance, did not contemplate any goal related to production increase or structural change of the economy.[1]

Nevertheless, gross domestic product (GDP) as a predominant measure of development had already been questioned. Early in 1969, after the United Nations' First Development Decade failed to achieve a convergence between developed and developing countries, Dudley Seers published his famous essay on 'the meaning of development', arguing that GDP-per-capita growth alone could not be considered an achievement in terms of development; the goal had to be reformulated as 'the realisation of the potential of human personality' (Seers 1969: 3). In the pursuit of that goal, the issues to be addressed were poverty (satisfaction of basic needs, or 'physical necessities' such as food, clothing, and shelter), employment ('without a job a personality cannot develop') equality ('which should [...] be considered an objective in its own rights') and 'much that cannot be specified in purely economic terms' (Seers 1969: 4–5).

Seers's essay inaugurated a new era (Arndt 1989: 99), and from this initial debate the meaning of development was going to acquire progressively wider connotations. Growing objections were raised to a GDP-based understanding of development, basically due to its Western, anthropocentric and economistic universality, which disregarded any historical, ethnic, cultural, geographic or natural specificity.[2] In the 1990s such criticism converged into postdevelopment theorisation (Escobar 1995).

However, different trends appeared during the 1970s and 1980s in the field of development studies, which dissented with the mainstream idea of development as economic growth and structural change, anticipating some of the core issues at the heart of postdevelopment approaches. Two approaches have been selected for analysis in this chapter, due to their similarity with the conceptualisation of *buen vivir*: the concept of human and ecological development theorised by Spanish economist José Luis Sampedro (1979, 1982a, 1982b, 1982c) and human-scale development by Max-Neef (Max-Neef, Elizalde & Hopenhayn 1986). Both reject development as a quantitative concept, based on a GDP-per-capita measure, and put emphasis on other dimensions of human life. On the one hand, Sampedro (1980), a humanist structuralist, argues for the need to humanise the concept of development, emphasising the existence of physical and psychological limits to development, understood in its traditional meaning of economic growth with structural change. In a similar perspective, Max-Neef, an Chilean economist and international consultant, and his colleagues (Max-Neef, Elizalde & Hopenhayn 1986) stress the importance of living in harmony with the environment, the community and oneself. These authors, less known than other postdevelopment pioneers, suggest public policy orientations for practical implementation, based on the revalorisation of local knowledge and practices, the emphasis on traditional communities and the role of civil society in participatory democracy.

Our hypothesis is that there is a connection between their thought and what Hidalgo-Capitán & Cubillo-Guevara (2014: 27–28) defined as the ecologist and Indigenous interpretation of Ecuador's *buen vivir*.[3] Their early postdevelopment-like theorisation contributed to the shaping of the *buen vivir* ideal, reflected in Ecuador's 2008 political constitution and national planning between 2008 and 2016. The tension between such an ideal and the more pragmatic and developmentalist tendency, eventually adopted by the government, can provide valuable lessons about the possibility of putting postdevelopment into practice.

The chapter is structured as follows: the first part contains a characterisation of human and ecological development and human-scale development, theorised by Sampedro (1979, 1982a, 1982b, 1982c) and Max-Neef, Elizalde and Hopenhayn (1986), respectively. The second part will analyse *buen vivir* as a 'new pact of coexistance' in Ecuador's 2008 political constitution and as a 'basic principle of policy formulation' in the two national development plans issued between the enforcing of the new constitution and 2016, the last year of President Correa's mandate, PNBV 2009–2013 and PNBV 2013–2017. The chapter closes with some final considerations about the effective influence of *buen vivir* on the government's orientation during the Citizens' Revolution, a brief state of the art about *buen vivir* in the current Ecuadorian development debate and by drawing some lessons that can be useful for further experiments of postdevelopment in practice.

Human and ecological development and human-scale development: psychological limits and harmonies

Across the first three United Nations Development Decades, the focus of development changed according to different priorities. The first Decade, the 1960s, centred on social issues, while during the second Decade, the 1970s, the main debate was about ecological concerns; the Third Development Decade saw the irruption of subjective perspectives (Domínguez & Caria 2018). José Luis Sampedro (1983), a Spanish pioneer in development studies (Domínguez 2013), was the first to speculate about the existence of a psychological limit to development. A third limit[4] referred to how 'the sense of identity deteriorates, reflected day by day in so many manifestations of bewilderment and requests for support', described as a consequence of giving greater importance to 'having' than to 'being' (Sampedro 1983: 1666). Sampedro himself had argued that 'development was being sought at the expense of man's inner life […] leaving a sense of emptiness driving to anxiety and aberrations' (Sampedro 1980: 362). He had also pointed out the contradiction between 'being conscious that the planet is the first scarce good' and a 'conventional [economic] theory that makes of scarcity its identifying category as science' and that, nonetheless, ignores this fact (Sampedro 1980: 362). The author goes behind the physical and political limits, considering development to be a 'technocracy that threatens nature, other cultures and inner life' leading to 'progressive human degradation' (Sampedro 1983: 1667–1668). Development is 'cancer' (Sampedro 1982b: 335) and developmentalism, with its false ideal of perpetual growth, is a pathological dimension of Western culture (Sampedro 1982c: 352).

The way out of this discomfort is to be found in 'the adoption of another development' that breaks with the 'atrophy of goals and the hypertrophy of means': an economy that is concerned with poverty from a humanised perspective and that can correct 'the basic imbalance of industrialisation; the preference for things over people' (Sampedro 1982b: 341–345). The way out from the 'crisis of development' demands a change in values, so as to permit its 'humanisation' (Sampedro 1982b: 347). To transform the development paradigm and adopt a new perspective, a mental decolonisation is required, a 'cultural revolution' inspired by a new meta-economic approach, a 'field that goes beyond the economy' and that the author identifies with 'ecodevelopment' (Sampedro 1983: 1655, 1660, 1663, 1667). Sampedro questioned the utilitarian paradigm, arguing, like Amartya Sen would later, that 'liberty can only be conquered, for it is not a good to be consumed but to be exerted. It is produced by exerting it, which is the way it can be enjoyed' (Sampedro 1978: 92). In 1980 he would affirm 'the necessity for a new human and ecological development' based on solidarity: 'Why not imagine a new culture for the 21st century founded on "solidarity" as an approximation to fraternity? Solidarity with our fellow citizens, solidarity among peoples, with the environment [...] and welding our exterior and inner life' (Sampedro 1982a: 254). The similarity with *buen vivir*'s three harmonies, with oneself, with the community and with the environment is striking (see Section 2).

Sampedro's idea of a psychological limit to development influenced profoundly the conceptualisation of 'barefoot economics' by Chilean Manfred Max-Neef ([1982] 1986).[5] Max-Neef, like Sampedro, was concerned with the dehumanisation of economics; both considered that at the beginning of the 1980s this discipline was undergoing a 'total crisis' caused by the attempt to subdue nature. The concept of development, based on GDP increase, that's to say, measured through the increase in market activities, regardless of their productive, non-productive or destructive effect, was a clear reflection of this 'crisis' (Max-Neef [1982] 1986: 40, 42–43, 51).

From this premise, Max-Neef derives the proposal of a new 'quantifier', which he called '*econson*', or a 'reasonable use of resources that a person needs, to have an acceptable quality of life', that's to say, to satisfy 'energy, nutrition, clothing and housing needs' (Max-Neef [1982] 1986: 61). This quantifier measures the 'desirable development' (the 'development we seek and in which we believe'), defined as an 'integral ecological humanism', whose roots Max-Neef attributes to 'humanist eco-anarchism' (Max-Neef [1982] 1986: 48, 62–63, 72).

This is where Max-Neef takes distance from the previous development tradition and approaches of socialist inspiration, forging what he eventually would call human-scale development.[6] Max-Neef affirmed, 'I don't believe in "national solutions" anymore, or in "national styles" [...] I believe, as a barefoot economist, in local action and in small dimensions' (Max-Neef [1982] 1986: 136). This proposal of interdependence, identity and integration between human beings and nature, along with the local organisation of power and small-scale production, will connect with the ecologist and Indigenous understanding of *buen vivir*.

Max-Neef adopts the same point of view as Seer's basic needs, although Seers does not appear among the references in Max-Neef's text, nor that of the Bariloche Foundation – an Argentinian development think tank well-known for its critique of the neo-Malthusian approach of the *limits of growth*, where Max-Neef worked for some years after Pinochet's *golpe*. However, like Sen, Max-Neef goes well beyond the materialist approach of commodity fetishism (Stewart 2006), guided by the disappointment of real socialism, the loss of efficacy of Keynesian policies and the discrediting of neoliberal measures (Espinoza 1988). He accepts that needs are finite and introduces the distinction between 'needs' and 'satisfiers' in an early work written in 1978 for the Bariloche Foundation (Espinoza 1988). Needs are not hierarchically ordered, they are interconnected by a matrix organised according to existential categories, 'to be, to have, to do, and to stay' and axiological categories, 'subsistence, protection, affection, understanding, idleness, creation, identity, and liberty'. Human needs are the same across cultures and historical periods, while satisfiers, the means and the way in which they are used to satisfy needs, change (Max-Neef [1982] 1986: 237–238; Max-Neef, Elizalde & Hopenhayn 1986, 25–27). Each social and political system adopts different styles for the satisfaction of the same fundamental human needs; therefore, poverty can only be defined according to different existential or axiological dimensions (Max-Neef [1982] 1986: 239–240; Max-Neef, Elizalde & Hopenhayn 1986: 27–29, 41–42). Starting from this epistemological premise, the author and his colleagues try to recover what is 'possible or desirable'; their vision of 'desirable' differs remarkably from CEPAL's developmentalism as well as from monetarist neoliberalism, since they considered both economic approaches to be mechanical and not inclusive (Max-Neef, Elizalde & Hopenhayn 1986: 10–13, 72).

These considerations led Max-Neef to propose, in 1986, a model of human-scale development, based on the satisfaction of basic human needs, increased auto-dependence and on four organic relations: human being-nature; local-global; individual-society; civil society-state. The goal is to give real protagonism to persons, setting the priority on the 'diversity and autonomy of the environment where this protagonism is possible' and 'to achieve the transformation of the person-object into person-subject of development'. As Max-Neef states, 'to the fetishism of numbers we must oppose the development of persons' (Max-Neef, Elizalde & Hopenhayn 1986: 14–15).

It is to be noted that human-scale development represents, in some respects, a step backwards in the socialist agenda of 'another development' due to its disregard of the state's role. It renounces the demand for a New International Economic Order (NIEO) and embraces a methodological commitment to 'localism'.[7] Human-scale development proposes for the state the role of stimulating and strengthening grassroots processes, based on each one's efforts, capacities and resources, instead of providing 'exogenous satisfiers' (nutrition, health and housing programmes) (Max-Neef, Elizalde & Hopenhayn 1986: 62). This vision of the state, supported by social capital theory and complemented by international cooperation financing, conforms to the traditional understanding that neoliberalism has of human development. Human-scale development is not concerned with structural change nor with any strengthening of the economy in terms of national production upgrading (Max-Neef, Elizalde & Hopenhayn 1986: 77), as it relies entirely on local capacities. As a matter of fact, there is no full consensus regarding the role of the state in *buen vivir* orientations (see Section 2) and this represents an ambiguous issue.

While in barefoot economics Max-Neef advocates for an 'ecological humanism able to replace or at least correct the anthropocentrism prevailing among us' (Max-Neef [1982] 1986: 52), in the Human-Scale Development Report he denounces the 'anthropocentric cosmovision that puts human being above nature' and that is typical of traditional styles of development (Max-Neef, Elizalde & Hopenhayn 1986: 57). *Buen vivir* has been understood from three different perspectives that emphasise some aspects over others: an Indigenous stream focuses on the relevance of Indigenous tradition, a socialist approach gives predominance to equality among the people and in the ecologist stream the need to protect the environment and to promote harmony with nature prevails (Hidalgo-Capitán & Cubillo-Guevara 2014: 27–28). Max-Neef's approach, while refuting the 'anthropocentric cosmovision' anticipates the ecological *buen vivir* 'biocentric' vision (see Section 2).

Ecuador's *buen vivir* as the central goal of public policy

'The Government of the Citizen's Revolution, accepting the proposals of Andean-Amazonian peoples, establishes the notion of *Buen Vivir* as a central goal of public policy' states PNBV 2013–2017 (SENPLADES 2013: 23), the second official national development plan issued after the approval of the new political constitution in 2008, and also the second one to bear the name of the 'National Plan for *Buen Vivir*'.

The preamble to Ecuador's constitution, approved by referendum in 2008, describes the task of the constituency in charge of drafting it as 'to build a new form of citizens' co-existence, in diversity and harmony, to achieve *Buen Vivir* or "*sumak kawsay*"' (ANC 2008: 1).[8] *Buen vivir* is also described as a 'new social pact' or 'new pact of coexistence' (Ramírez 2010b: 55, 60, 62, 63, 64) and supposes a vision of human beings as a whole, recognising both material and spiritual aspects of wellbeing. René Ramírez (2010a: 139), the former National Secretary of Planning, affirms that 'by *Buen Vivir* we understand the satisfaction of needs, the achievement of an appropriate quality of life and death, to love and be loved, the healthy flourishing of everyone, in peace and harmony with nature' (Ramírez 2010a: 139). Here we can find analogies with Sampedro's claiming that human wellbeing can't be achieved at nature's expense and that psychological elements have to be taken into account.

The constitution dedicates an entire chapter to the rights of *buen vivir*, which include the rights to water and food, to a healthy environment, education, health, culture, employment and social security; that's to say, all basic human needs, such as Max-Neef had recommended. As far as the development model is concerned, Title VII is dedicated to the *buen vivir* 'regime' and to the treatment of social inclusion and equity (chapter 1), and biodiversity and natural resources (chapter 2). Ecuador's constitution was the first one to establish that nature has rights on its own, regardless of its usefulness to human needs satisfaction. Again, a connection with Sampedro's idea that human wellbeing could not be achieved at nature's expense. This represents an important historical precedent, whatever the judgement about its character of transcendent innovation or legal rhetoric may be (Campaña 2013).

Despite the different interpretations of *buen vivir* that have been proposed (Hidalgo-Capitán & Cubillo-Guevara 2014: 27–28; Macas 2010: 10; Correa & Falconí 2012: 267), some common elements can be found in all *buen vivir* understandings: harmony with nature, appreciation of ancestral peoples' values, satisfaction of basic needs, social justice and equality, and democracy. Furthermore, *buen vivir* is also seen as presenting a critique of the modernity paradigm and its occidental, anthropocentric, capitalist and economist characterisation (Caria & Domínguez 2014). An insight into each one of these characteristics can be useful to make the connection with Sampedro's and Max-Neef's thought clearer.

Harmony with nature

Respect for nature, symbolised by *Pachamama*, or Mother Earth in the *Kichwa* language, is perhaps the basic element of *buen vivir* and the one that gathers greatest consensus among its different interpretations. Ecuador's constitution, in its chapter devoted to the 'Rights of *Buen Vivir*', states:

> The people have the right to live in a healthy and ecologically balanced environment, where sustainability and *Buen Vivir, Sumak Kawsay*, can be granted. Environment and ecosystems preservation is declared a matter of public interest, as well as biodiversity, the integrity of genetic heritage, the prevention of environmental damage and the recovery of damaged natural areas.
>
> *(ANC 2008: 32)*

Buen vivir means that people have a relationship of belonging to nature, not of domination or exploitation. It reflects a 'biocentric' way of understanding life, as opposed to a Western anthropocentric vision of the world; it claims that 'intergenerational justice is to be pursued not only for humans but also with other living species' (Ramírez 2010b: 62). The biocentric perspective is so essential to *buen vivir* that the constitution dedicates a whole chapter and four articles to the 'Rights of Nature' (ANC 2008 65). As a consequence, *buen vivir* can't be achieved through an economic model that destroys the environment; Ramírez (2010b: 68) argues that 'the new social pact that Ecuadorian society has signed can't coexist with a primary exporter economy [...] This model was always doomed to fail'.

Recognition of ancestral principles and values

Reference to the tradition of Indigenous peoples becomes explicit when *buen vivir* is identified with *sumak kawsay*: 'Ecuador, as an Andean country, builds up economic, social, cultural and environmental rights on a vision of the world born in the ancient societies of the Andes: Buen Vivir is *sumac kawsay*' (SENPLADES 2013: 16). Diversity is conceived as richness, while interculturality is important for the construction of a society of *buen vivir*, which is 'based on the ideals of solidarity and wealth distribution' that come from Indigenous people's traditions (SENPLADES 2013: 16). The constitution, in chapter 4, seeks to protect the rights of communities, peoples and nationalities, as well as the integrity of their territories (ANC 2008: 41–43). Both PNBV 2009–2013 (titled 'Building a Plurinational and Intercultural State') and 2013–2017 settle specific goals for the promotion and strengthening of the multiple identities that shape a diverse and multicultural Ecuadorian society. Take, as an example, goal 8 in PNBV 2009–2013, which seeks to 'Affirm and strengthen [...], the diverse identities, plurinationality and interculturality' (a very similar text describes goal 5 in PNBV 2013–2017). This approach resembles the one proposed by Max-Neef, who argued that solutions to development had to be found at the local level and based on people's potentialities and initiative.

Satisfaction of basic needs

The constitution names as a 'right' what in development jargon is usually defined as a 'need'. Among the fundamental duties of the state it includes a guarantee to the right to 'education, healthcare, nutrition, social security and water' (ANC 2008: 25). On this point we find the stress on basic needs that characterised Max-Neef's approach. The notion of basic needs reappears in PNBV 2009–2013: 'in a society characterised by many unsatisfied needs, it is vital to create economic possibilities, other than the export of commodities' (SENPLADES 2009: 55). That's to say, it is vital to achieve a structural change towards higher-productivity sectors and income generating activities to promote employment. To achieve this purpose a new strategy of accumulation and distribution must be put in place in the long run: 'an endogenous and sustainable strategy for the satisfaction of basic needs' (SENPLADES 2009: 56–58). Such a strategy was to be implemented through a four-stage pathway leading to an economy based on bio-knowledge and tourism services (SENPLADES 2009: 57). The PNBV 2013–2017 reaffirmed this option (SENPLADES 2013: 63), stressing the need for a structural transformation of the economy that would 'provide a solution to issues such as unemployment, poverty and inequality' (SENPLADES 2013: 73). It is to be noted that the way needs are satisfied, according to national planning, differs from Max-Neef's arguments; while he advocates for the strengthening of local systems, here the emphasis is on the macroeconomic level, specifically on structural change, an issue Max-Neef wasn't concerned at all with.

Social justice and equality as state responsibilities

Buen vivir is related to the defence of common goods and collective interests (Falconí 2013: 13). 'To promote the common wellbeing and put the general interest before individuals, according to *Buen Vivir*' is one of the duties that the constitution assigns to the citizenry (ANC 2008: 74). To refer to *buen vivir*, a new term has been coined: '*Sumak Kawsay* Socialism' or 'Socialism of the 21st Century' (Patiño 2010), to emphasise that social justice and equality have to be a major concern of the public sector (Ramírez 2010a: 136). The state becomes again a fundamental stakeholder, 'the main agent of collective action' (SENPLADES 2013: 85), and national planning is conceived as 'one of the basic instruments of the political engine' (SENPLADES 2013: 16) within the framework of a 'decentralised and participatory planning system' (SENPLADES 2013: 55). From the point of view of political praxis, *buen vivir* represented the return of the state and a massive programme of public social and productive investments. The balance of this policy differs among the different *buen vivir* approaches; the indigenist *buen bivir* – and to some extent the ecological strand – claims that local communities have the right to govern themselves and their resources autonomously, while socialist *buen vivir* advocates for a strong state and intervention to reduce inequality and guarantee equal opportunities for all (Hidalgo-Capitán & Cubillo-Guevara 2014: 28).

Democracy

'The socialism of *Buen Vivir* supposes a deep democracy with ongoing participation in politics. It can't be implemented without the continued and active commitment of peoples and citizens' (SENPLADES 2013: 24).

Final considerations and future perspectives

From this brief description of *buen vivir* as the guiding principle of Ecuador's social and political reorganisation during the government of the Citizens' Revolution, many elements of similarity with human and ecological development and human-scale development emerge. The most relevant are the need to consider inner elements as part of people's general wellbeing and the conception of human beings not as individuals, but as part of social communities and the environment. Perhaps the most astonishing rupture with politics as usual is the introduction in the public scene of dimensions that had always been reserved to the private inner sphere; 'to love and be loved', 'to have time for contemplation' (SENPLADES 2009: 6), 'the project of life that is going to give us happiness, dignity, fulfilment' (SENPLADES 2013: 22). The latter are principles established as part of an overall framework in Ecuadorian national planning between 2009 and 2017 and connect with Sampedro's argument that human inner life is just as important as material wellbeing. This undoubtedly represents an innovation in the official concept of development and shows a connection with the critique of Western economic notions of development and progress. From this perspective, the recognition of the values and wisdom of ancient Andean people reflects the will to grant equal dignity to a culture that has been marginalised and derided during centuries, and the right of people to decide their own way to wellbeing, which can be considered the heart of the human-scale development approach. Similarly, the recognition of the rights of nature (beyond the debate about their effectiveness) expresses the need to balance the troubled relationship with the environment resulting in so many consequences for human life (Houtart 2011: 62), just like Sampedro had pointed out.

Buen vivir has represented an ideal that gathered a great consensus among Ecuadorian society; Ecuador's constitution was approved with a majority of 64% of voters. Nevertheless, *buen vivir* has also been considered a 'political proposal' and, although it has had a remarkable influence in Ecuador's official planning (Hidalgo-Capitán & Cubillo-Guevara 2018: 38), public policy during the years of the Citizens' Revolution has followed an ambiguous pattern. On the one hand, the great enthusiasm for a new type of development, a humanised and environmentally friendly one, has generated strong and widespread social policy, high investments in health and education, a remarkable effort to satisfy basic needs and a substantial improvement in poverty and inequality reduction (Domínguez & Caria 2016). It also generated innovative and renowned proposals, the most famous of which was the Yasuní-ITT Initiative – a proposal to leave oil underground and make the global community responsible for the conservation of the Yasuní National Park – eventually included into a wider scheme, aiming at avoiding CO_2 emissions.[9] Unfortunately, this initiative was abandoned in mid-2013, after obtaining poor international support.

On the other hand, the general orientation of the government, especially in what concerns the economy, has been much more in line with a neo-developmentalist approach, defined as a process of socio-economic endogenous transformation led by public policy (Cypher & Alfaro 2016: 38). This transformation, in the case of Ecuador during the period of Correa's government, was meant to be based on three pillars: the promotion of a national project, a strong emphasis on industrial policy for a structural change of the economy and the attempt to build a national system of innovation. The main source of financing was oil exports during the commodities boom, and an increase in mining activities (Cypher & Alfaro 2016) – not the best example of harmony with nature.

Some scholars (Altmann 2017) have also highlighted the gap between a local *buen vivir*, used by communities as an instrument of decolonisation, and the national state-centric *buen vivir*, which ended up concealing territorial and cultural diversity and imposing the same development strategy for the whole country. This contradiction reflects the ambiguity that different *buen vivir* approaches maintain with respect to the role of the state.

Whatever the balance of the Citizens' Revolution, the concept of *buen vivir* has aroused great interest within and beyond the Andean countries from which it emerged (see, among others, Vanhulst & Beling 2013; Waldmüller 2014), and has been proposed as a global model, or 'global *buen vivir*'.[10] Meanwhile, it has almost disappeared from official discourse in Ecuador since the election of President Moreno in April 2017. As a matter of fact, the new national development plan doesn't mention *buen vivir* in its title and the references to *buen vivir* across the text are very limited (Hidalgo-Capitán & Cubillo-Guevara 2018).

The end of high prices for commodities places at the centre of debate the urgent need to sustain the social improvements obtained during the last decade while at the same time social innovation has become a secondary issue in Ecuador. So, what is going to be the fate of *buen vivir*? In their work on the ideas in action that were generated through the United Nation's Development Decades, Jolly, Emmerij, Ghai and Lapeyre (2009: 298) argue that 'ideas are like inventions': they remain latent, keep themselves hidden, until favourable conditions – political, social and economic – arise, and someone tries to put them into practice as 'old ideas with a new disguise'. Ideas are influential, but follow tortuous pathways. That has been the past of *buen vivir* and will possibly be its future; it may retreat to its subaltern origins (Domínguez, Caria & León 2017) until the conditions are propitious for it to resurge, perhaps with a new disguise appropriate for new times. Meanwhile, it is important to keep on nurturing the idea with new reflections without forgetting where it came from, how it emerged and the different sources that fostered it. Every experience and every experiment is an opportunity for ideas to face reality and the lessons that they generate add a piece that can contribute to making the next postdevelopment proposal stronger. That is why it is important to keep track of the history of ideas.

The Ecuadorian attempt to put *buen vivir* into practice represents an important social experiment, seeking to reorient a country's pathway to development. The tension generated between the ideal and the praxis shows where the weak parts of the ideal are shedding light on the next research field. The relationship between local and national perspectives, the contradiction between satisfying people's needs – in a developing country in transition between 'lower-middle income' and 'upper-middle income' – and protecting the environment are issues that require greater analysis. And they also need much more widespread public debate in order to understand the context in which ideas are born, their current validity and the possibility to adjust them to specific contexts.

Notes

1 Sustainable Development Goals (SDGs) do include economic development: SDG No. 8 'Decent work and economic growth' and SDG No. 9 'Industry innovation, and infrastructure'. See: www.un.org/sustainabledevelopment/sustainable-development-goals/.
2 For a thorough and complete historical reconstruction of development theories and practice see Currie-Alder, Kanbur, Malone and Medhora (2014).
3 For a wider analysis of *buen vivir*'s intellectual precedents see Domínguez & Caria (2018).
4 The first limit refers to the social improvement associated with economic growth (inner constraints), while the second one depends on external ecological constrains.
5 The term 'barefoot economics' alludes to the method of participant observation that leads the researcher to 'live and share the invisible reality' (Max-Neef [1982] 1986: 41) and proposes a new kind of expert, the 'barefoot expert' that needs to 'subordinate his values, his own knowledge to those of the community he seeks to serve' (Tinbergen 1977: 170–171). Max-Neef was deeply influenced by grassroots movements inspired by the doctrine of Gandhi, through the thought of Fritz Schumacher and his claiming of the good life (Chick 2013). Max-Neef's approach was the result of a personal option; he began working for the Shell Company, then turned to the academy and subsequently he worked as consultant for FAO and ILO. In the early 1970s he worked for ILO Andean Mission (Max-Neef [1982] 1986: 22, 131; Abrahamsen 2005: 171; Goodman 2012: 97).
6 The term itself is not used in the book on barefoot economics; the author only mentions 'human-scale economics' and 'human-scale social dimension' (Max-Neef [1982] 1986: 25, 152).
7 '[N]o new Economic International order, will be relevant if it's not based on a structural reform of a dense network of New Local Economic Orders' (Max-Neef, Elizalde & Hopenhayn 1986: 23).
8 Buen vivir in *Kichwa*, the main Indigenous language of the country.
9 This proposal was presented to the Ad Hoc Working Group on Long-Term Cooperative Action under the United Nations Framework Convention on Climate Change in February 2011. See https://unfccc.int/files/meetings/ad_hoc_working_groups/lca/application/pdf/ecuador_submission_various_approaches.pdf
10 See monographic edition of the *Iberoamerican Journal of Development Studies* (IJDS), Hidalgo-Capitán, A.L. & García-Alvarez, S. (eds.) (2018) 'Los objetivos del *Buen Vivir* como propuesta alternativa a los ODS'. *RIED*, forthcoming.

References

Abrahamsen, R. (2005) 'Manfred Max-Neef (1932–)'. In Simon, D. (ed.), *Fifty Key Thinkers on Development*. New York: Routledge, pp 171–176.
Altmann, F. (2017) 'Sumak Kawsay as an element of local decolonization in Ecuador'. *Latin American Research Review*, vol 52, no 5, pp 749–759.
ANC. (2008) *Constitución de la República de Ecuador*. Asamblea Nacional Constituyente, Quito.
Arndt, H. (1989) *Economic Development. The History of an Idea*. Chicago: University of Chicago Press.
Campaña, F.S. (2013) 'Derechos de la naturaleza: ¿innovación trascendental, retórica jurídica o proyecto político?' *Juris Dictio. Revista de derecho*, vol 13, no 15, pp 9–38.
Caria, S. & Domínguez, R. (2014) 'El porvenir de una ilusión: la ideología del Buen Vivir'. *América Latina Hoy*, vol 67, pp 139–162.

Chang, J.H. (2010) 'Hamlet without the Prince of Denmark: How development has disappeared from today's "development" discourse'. In Khan, S. & Christiansen, J. (eds.), *Towards New Developmentalism: Market as Means Rather than Master*. Abingdon: Routledge.

Chick, V. (2013) 'Economics and the good life: Keynes and Schumacher'. *Economic Thought*, vol 2, no 2, pp 33–45.

Cypher, J. & Alfaro, J. (2016) 'Triángulo del neo-desarrollismo en Ecuador'. *Revista Problemas del Desarrollo*, vol 185, no 47, pp 163–186.

Correa, R. & Falconí, F. (2012) 'Después de "Río+20". Bienes ambientales y relaciones de poder'. *Revista de Economía Crítica*, vol 14, pp 257–276.

Currie-Alder, B., Kanbur, R., Malone, D.M. & Medhora, R. (2014) *International Development: Ideas, Experience, and Prospects*. Oxford: Oxford University Press.

Domínguez, R. (2013) 'José Luis Sampedro (1917-2013), pionero de los Estudios del Desarrollo'. *Revista Iberoamericana de Estudios del Desarrollo*, vol 2, no 1, pp 119–125.

Domínguez, R. & Caria, S. (2016) 'Ecuador en la trampa de la renta media'. *Revista Problemas del Desarrollo*, vol 187, no 47, pp 89–112.

Domínguez, R. & Caria, S. (2018) 'Raíces latinoamericanas del otro desarrollo: estilos de desarrollo y desarrollo a escala humana'. *América Latina en la Historia Económica*, vol 25, no 2, pp 175–209.

Domínguez, R., Caria, S. & León, M. (2017) 'Long live *Buen Vivir*. Praise, instrumentalization, and reproductive pathways of good living in Ecuador'. *Latin American and Caribbean Ethnic Studies*, vol 12, no 2, pp 133–154.

Emmerij, L., Jolly, R. & Weiss, T. (2005) 'Economic and social thinking at the UN in historical perspective'. *Development and Change*, vol 36, no 2, pp 211–235.

Escobar, A. (1995) *Encountering Development: The Making and Unmaking of the Third World*. Princeton, NJ: Princeton University Press.

Espinoza, J.G. (1988) 'Otro desarrollo, otra vida. ¿Fin de la civilización del egoísmo?' *Nueva Sociedad*, no 42, pp 72–80.

Falconí, F. (2013) 'Crisis civilizatoria y alternativas de la humanida'. Online. http://issuu.com/falconifander/docs/ecosocialismo__11_06_2013.

Goodman, A. (2012) 'Entrevista con Manfred Max-Neef'. *Ecología Política. Cuadernos de debate internacional*, no 44, pp 97–101.

Gudynas, E. (2014) 'El postdesarrollo como crítica y el Buen vivir como alternativa'. In Delgado Ramos, G.C. (ed.), *Buena Vida, Buen Vivir: Imaginarios alternativos para el bien común de la humanidad*. Mexico: CEIICH, UNAM, pp 61–95.

Hidalgo-Capitán, A.L. & Cubillo-Guevara, A.P. (2014) 'Seis debates abiertos sobre el sumak kawsay'. *Íconos. Revista de Ciencias Sociales*, no 48, pp 25–40.

Hidalgo-Capitán, A.L. & Cubillo-Guevara, A.P. (2018) 'Orto y ocaso del Buen Vivir en la planificación nacional del desarrollo en Ecuador (2007–2021)'. *América Latina Hoy*, no 78, pp 37–54.

Houtart, F. (2011) 'El concepto de Sumak Kawsay (Buen vivir) y su correspondencia con el bien común de la humanidad'. *Ecuador Debate*, vol 84, pp 57–75.

Jolly, R., Emmerij, L., Ghai, D. & Lapeyre, F. (2009) *UN Contributions to Development Thinking and Practice*. Bloomington, IN: Indiana University Press.

Macas, L. (2010) 'Sumak Kawsay: La vida en plenitud'. *América Latina en Movimiento*, vol 452, pp 14–16.

Max-Neef, M., Elizalde, A. & Hopenhayn, M. (1986) *Desarrollo a Escala Humana. Una opción para el futuro*. CEPAUR and Fundación Dag Hammarskjöld, Santiago. Available in English as Max-Neef, M. (1991) *Human Scale Development. Conception, Application and Further Reflections*. New York and London: The Apex Press.

Max-Neef, M. (1986 [1982]) *La economía descalza. Señales desde el Mundo Invisible*. Montevideo: Editorial Nordan. Available in English as Max-Neef, M. (1992) *From Outside Looking In: Experiences in 'Barefoot' Economics*. London: Zed Books.

Patiño, R. (2010) 'Diferencias entre el socialismo del siglo xx y el socialismo del siglo XXI. La democracia participativa y el nuevo sujeto revolucionario'. In SENPLADES (ed.), *Los nuevos retos de América latina: socialismo y Sumak Kausay*. Quito: SENPLADES, pp 133–140.

Ramírez, R. (2010a) 'La transición ecuatoriana hacía el Buen Vivir'. In León, I. (ed.), *Sumak Kausay/Buen vivir y cambios civilizatorios*. Quito: FEDAEPS, pp 125–141.

Ramírez, R. (2010b) 'Socialismo del Sumak kawsay o biosocialismo republicano'. In SENPLADES (ed.), *Los nuevos retos de América latina: socialismo y Sumak Kawsay*. Quito: SENPLADES, pp 55–76.

Sampedro, J.L. (1978 [2009]) 'De cómo dejé de ser *Homo oeconomicus*'. In Sampedro, J.L. (ed.), *Economía humanista. Algo más que cifras*. Barcelona: Debate, pp 83–95.

Sampedro, J.L. (1979) 'Economía y ecología'. In Sampedro, J.L.(ed.), *Economía humanista. Algo más que cifras*. Barcelona: Debate, pp 210–219.

Sampedro, J.L. (1980) 'Desarrollo económico'. In Martínez, R. (ed.), *Economía Planeta. Diccionario Enciclopédico*, Vol 3. Barcelona: Planeta, pp 352–367.

Sampedro, J.L. (1982a) 'La economía'. In Sampedro, J.L.(ed.), *Economía humanista. Algo más que cifras*. Barcelona: Debate, pp 239–255.

Sampedro, J.L. (1982b) 'La crisis del desarrollo y el medio ambiente'. In Sampedro, J.L. (ed.), *Economía humanista. Algo más que cifras*. Barcelona: Debate, pp 323–350.

Sampedro, J.L. (1982c) 'El desarrollo, dimensión patológica de la cultura industrial'. In Sampedro, J.L.(ed.), *Economía humanista. Algo más que cifras*. Barcelona: Debate, pp 351–361.

Sampedro, J.L. (1983) 'Triple nivel, doble estrategia y otro desarrollo'. *El Trimestre Económico*, vol 50, no 199/3, pp 1655–1675.

Seers, D. (1969) 'The meaning of development'. *IDS Communication*, 44. Publicado ese mismo año en. *International Development Review*, vol 11, no 4, pp 1–28.

SENPLADES (2009) *Plan nacional para el Buen Vivir 2009–2013. Construyendo un estado Plurinacional e Intercultural*. Versión resumida. Quito: SENPLADES.

SENPLADES (2013) *Plan Nacional para el Buen Vivir 2013–2017*. Quito: SENPLADES.

Stewart, F. (2006) 'Basic needs'. In Clark, D.A. (ed.), *The Elgar Companion to Development Studies*. Cheltenham: Edward Elgar, pp 14–18.

Tinbergen, J. (ed.) (1977) *Reestructuración del Orden Internacional. Informe al Club de Roma*. Mexico: Fondo de Cultura Económica.

Vanhulst, J. & Beling, A. (2013) 'Buen Vivir: la irrupción de América Latina en el campo gravitacional del desarrollo sostenible'. *Revista Iberoamericana de Economía Ecológica*, vol 21, pp 1–14.

Waldmüller, J.M. (2014) 'Buen Vivir, Sumak Kawsay, "good living": An introduction and overview', *Alternautas*, vol 1, pp 17–28.

4
REVISITING TRANSITION

S. Charusheela

Introduction

In his field-defining book, *Encountering Development: The Making and Unmaking of the Third World*, Arturo Escobar (1995) argued that the problem with development was that a modernist vision of the world was so deeply embedded in its discourse that nothing less than a revision of the concept-frames through which we understood the world would do. Escobar's critique drew on and joined the work of a range of scholars (Godelier 1986; Gudeman 1986; Yanagisako & Collier 1989; Ferguson 1990) who pointed out that the emergence of 'economy' as a seemingly self-evident field of activity acted as a power-knowledge complex that rendered alternate forms of knowing and being in the world unintelligible, irrational, or backward.

Subsequent scholarship has taken two paths, one *genealogical/deconstructive*, the other *re-constitutive/re-interpretative*. The genealogical (and/or deconstructive) project traces the histories and legacies of dominant development discourse in order to denaturalize it. The re-constitutive (and/or re-interpretative) project generates revised concept-frames for creating alternate ways of being in the world. It is easy to dismiss the genealogical project as failing the test of Marx's Eleventh Thesis, '[t]he philosophers have only interpreted the world, in various ways; the point is to change it' (Marx 2002). But as Kathy Ferguson (1993) reminds us, genealogy keeps re-constitutive projects honest, identifying locations where we may need further revisions of our concept frames as we seek the 'impossible "no" to a structure which one critiques, yet inhabits intimately' (Spivak 1993: 281, quotation marks in original).

This chapter will provide a postcolonial genealogical intervention into one of the major re-constitutive projects: the revised Marxist framework of 'diverse economies' (Gibson-Graham 1993, 1996, 2006; Gibson-Graham, Resnick & Wolff

2000, 2001; Gibson-Graham, Cameron & Healy, 2013). I have chosen the word 'intervention' with care – this is not a rejection of the diverse economies framework. My aim is to highlight some limiting assumptions embedded in the approach and suggest revisions to address these limits.

Rethinking Marxism

Marx's analysis of economic relations remains both central for liberatory postdevelopment projects, and a vexed location of developmentalist eurocentrism. On the one hand, as Escobar points out, we would not wish to overlook the achievements of Marx's approach (historical materialism), which include

> [...] the formulation of an anthropology of use value in lieu of the abstraction of exchange value; the displacement of the notion of absolute surplus by that of surplus value and, consequently, the replacement of the notion of progress based on the increase of surplus by that based on the appropriation of surplus value by the bourgeoisie (exploitation); the emphasis on the social character of knowledge, as opposed to the dominant epistemology, which placed truth on the side of the individual's mind; the contrast between a unilinear concept of history, in which the individual is the all-powerful actor, and a materialist one, in which social classes appear as the motor of history; a denunciation of the natural character of the market economy and a conceptualisation, instead, of the capitalist mode of production, in which the market appears as the product of history; and finally the crucial insight of commodity fetishism as the paradigmatic feature of capitalist society.
>
> *(Escobar 1995: 60–61)*

On the other hand, as postcolonial scholars (Spivak 1999; Chakrabarty 2000) have shown, classical Marxism shares substantially in the modernist and orientalist frameworks that are part of the discourse of progress. This can be seen in Marxism's concept of 'pre-capitalist' modes of production and in its analysis of the rise of Europe's capitalist hegemony.

Escobar's list of Marxism's achievements features insights that Marxism provides about capitalism and the rise of capitalist modernity. Some are insights that historicize capitalism, some are insights that challenge the self-description of progress provided by capitalist elites, some are alternate analyses of the operation of capitalism. All of these are insights we conventionally associate with a structuralist Marxist approach to history and global political economy.

This understanding of what is valuable about Marx is not unique to Escobar. Whether it is in terms of the stages of capitalist development (Jameson 1991), or the dynamics of capitalist accumulation (Harvey 1982, 1989), or the relation between economic relations or technologies of production and social organization (Virno & Hardt 1996; Hardt & Negri 2001, 2004), for most scholars, it is Marxism's systemic approach to capitalist social totality and Marxism's understanding of capitalism as a world bestriding global order that is most valuable. Unfortunately, these insights rest on at least two major elements of the conceptual code of modernity that has been so forcefully critiqued by Escobar and others: economism/economic determinism and eurocentric teleology.

As Gibson-Graham (1993, 1996) rightly identified, this understanding of what is valuable in Marxism is a form of *capitalocentrism*. It is not only modernist, it also (hence?) blocks another substantial achievement of Marxism (one not noted in Escobar's list): that of envisaging alternates to capitalism, of imagining other worlds. It is a testament to the importance of Gibson-Graham's intervention, and of the work emerging from the Association for Economic and Social Analysis (AESA) in general, that the element of Marx they decided would become the core for a re-constitution was exploitation and the possibility of creating a world free of it, rather than capitalism's singular globe-bestriding logic – a decision that reflects Marx's critical discussion of the role of philosophy and theory (Marx 2002). In the process, they developed an approach that removed the two assumptions of economic determinism/economism and eurocentric teleology identified above as core elements of Marxism's modernist legacy.[1]

In brief, having identified capitalocentrism as a blockage to imagining alternate ways of being in the world, Gibson-Graham (1996, 2004, 2006) propose the overdetermined class analysis developed by Resnick, Wolff, and members of AESA as an alternative (Resnick & Wolff 1987; Gibson-Graham, Resnick & Wolff 2000, 2001). They argue that the social world consists of multiple processes in four categories – economic, political, natural, and cultural. Thus 'economy' does not exhaust the social totality or provide the master code through which to understand all societies. Next, economic processes themselves are diverse, and include processes of production, circulation, ownership, regulation, taxation, and exchange. Class – understood not as a subject position but as a social practice – is a subset of the totality of economic processes, and describes the practices of producing, performing, appropriating, and distributing surplus. Some of these class processes are exploitative (where the surplus is appropriated by a group of people different from the producers of surplus), and some are not. Capitalism is no longer a world bestriding logic, but a narrower and more specific relationship of appropriating surplus value that takes place between capitalist and worker at the level of the capitalist enterprise. The social field is a map of different types of economic relations and activities, only some of which are capitalist – we no longer assume a singular transition from 'feudal' to 'capitalist/modern' as describing the world well, and thus a second element of the code that ordered societies as more or less developed in terms of capitalist development disappears. Further, the causal relations between these different processes are contingent, contradictory, and overdetermined – this removes the economism and the eurocentric teleological theory of history from the concept frame.

Thus, the diverse economies framework, in the process of addressing the poststructuralist critiques of classical Marxism, creates a Marxist approach in which we can envisage fields of economic activity far beyond capitalist modernity.

Because we are no longer tied to the modernist logics that lead us to capitalocentrism, we are no longer limited by the economism and eurocentrism of previous approaches. What we lose in grand theories of the global march of capitalism, we gain in terms of envisaging and cultivating alternate ways of being in the world. Finally! A concept-frame that really integrates the postcolonial critique of Marxism's modernism, and which can be used to analyze the social world without the lenses and values of eurocentric capitalist modernity.

Or so we hope.[2]

Modes of production and transition

Marxism's eurocentric and modernist legacies can be seen in two interrelated locations – its theory of history, and its theory of subjectivity as expressed in and through the concept of a mode of production. In brief, Marxism adopted the teleological ordering of history as a transition from less to more advanced/developed stages, from primitive communist to ancient to slave to feudal to capitalist, which would hopefully eventuate in the culminating transition to communism. What made Marxism's modernism distinct from other types of modernism is that Marx was under no illusion that 'advanced' meant more ethical, more democratic, more civilized. Advanced simply reflected the advancing of the *material* forces, with the concomitant shifts to social knowledge that generated. That said, Marx did value 'advanced' over 'pre-capitalist' forms, even though capitalist development did not colonize or expand into other spaces through altruism, and capitalist expansion was a bloody and violent process. This is because capitalism removed the hold of pre-capitalist modes of production and their attendant pre-capitalist social subjects. This elimination of traditional forms of social and cultural control was a necessary step, in his view, removing the hold of religion and superstition over the lives and minds of people. Thus, the spread of capitalism would pave the way for a new organization that would create the modern worker who could, with the development of worker consciousness and activism, eventually lead us to a society that would be advanced in the ethical sense as well.

Subaltern Studies scholars (Guha 1982; Guha & Spivak 1988) famously disputed this imagination of a necessary progressive role for capitalism in two ways. First, they argued that 'pre-colonial' or non-modern subjects (e.g., peasants and indigenous communities) showed themselves capable of radical protest and activism against exploitation and colonialism, even if we did not always understand their protests and dismissed them as traditionalist, irrational, or backward.[3] Second, they argued that wage labor and capitalism, when they arrived, did not actually do the progressive work of removing religiosity and superstition, and dissolving the hold of cultural understandings of role and rank, that classical Marxist teleology assigned to it. Thus, Subaltern Studies argued for a revision of Marxism that undid teleology and orientalism both in terms of the backwardness of the pre-colonial or non-modern subject, and in terms of the progressive potential of capitalist modernity. These two mistakes were built into the intellectual architecture of modes of production, they pointed out, and could not simply be set aside without substantially revising the Marxian typology.

Spivak (1999: 88), argues that the now-neglected 'Asiatic Mode of Production' (AMP) is important not in terms of whether or not it was a good description of Asia, but because it was 'the crucial theoretical fiction to set the machinery of the emancipatory transformation of Hegelianism presenting itself as a general system'. The AMP therefore allows the theorist to ignore the possibilities of agency and internal historical transformation in this pre-capitalist formation, and treat colonialism, for all its pillage and blood, as essential to start the motor of History moving in the direction of emancipation. Colonizers may not be nice agents, but they are nevertheless the true agents of History.

This problem is not resolved by jettisoning the AMP and reading pre-colonial and pre/non-capitalist social formations as iterations of the feudal mode. We see the non-capitalist world as essentially reflecting Europe's past, and imagine that these societies will/should progress along the same path of development and the rise of capitalist-modernity that had been previously followed by Europe. In disparate locations across the Third World/Global South, we now saw feudalism everywhere. But as multiple scholars have argued, it is just as erroneous (and as eurocentric) to map Europe's historical past onto the diverse social formations of pre-colonial Asia, Africa, and Latin America.[4]

Class and classification

At first glance, the diverse economies approach does not face the problems identified in the previous section. It does not seek to provide a grand narrative of the sweep of History and the transition from one mode of production to another. It makes no claim that capitalism progressively destroys other modes for good or bad, nor suggests that we can map Europe's so-called past or present on any particular historical location or era in an *a priori* fashion. In large part, this is because the diverse economies framework, having eschewed capitalocentrism, eschews all the attendant analytical problems associated with Marxism's theory of History – Marxism no longer *has* a theory of History. Marxism is useful for understanding processes of historical *change*, but that is mainly through a careful, on the ground reading of the details of particular conjunctures and specific sites.

Similarly, an initial examination of the approach leads us to conclude that the diverse economies approach avoids the problem of orientalist descriptions of subaltern subjectivity and culture. In this approach, class does not denote groups of people with particular mentalities. A given social subject is a fragmented self occupying multiple class positions that may or may not cohere to reinforce each other. Identity formation is a result of discursive and cultural process, and these processes have no *a priori* causal relation to class processes. Since a given individual may occupy multiple class positions, we no longer associate subjective agency with any one of these. The concept of class as describing large social groups exhibiting particular mental frames has disappeared. Class is a process without a subject, hence there is no specific subaltern psyche or mentality that is built into the analysis, resolving the problem of orientalism.

But on closer examination, we find the problem of modernist orientalism has not been adequately addressed. To see this, let us turn our attention to the *classification* scheme used by the diverse economies approach to organize analysis. One of the features of modernist thought is not merely its teleology, but its concept frame. The problem is not that different societies have different economies, the problem is that even as we note that, we assume the concept field 'economy' is a self-evident universal. And this is not merely a problem of how mainstream economics understands the economy, or even of disciplinarity, which we can fix by using interdisciplinary approaches, drawing on other disciplines like anthropology to create our alternate approaches to the economy. As Escobar (1995: 61) points out,

> Anthropologists have been complicit with the rationalization of modern economics, to the extent they have contributed to naturalizing the constructs of economy, politics, religion, kinship, and the like as fundamental building blocks of all societies. The existence of these domains as presocial and universal must be rejected.
>
> *(Escobar 1995: 61)*

Citing Yanagisako and Collier (1989: 41), he continues, 'we must ask what symbolic and social processes make these domains appear self-evident, and perhaps even "natural," fields of activity in any society?'

In the approach developed by Resnick and Wolf and used by the diverse economies framework (Resnick & Wolff 1987; Gibson-Graham, Resnick & Wolff 2000, 2001), the social totality is a constellation of different types of processes, which provide the overdetermined and contradictory conditions of existence for each other. To organize our social analysis and identify the diversity of economies, we begin by sorting out these social processes into four categories – economic, political, cultural, and natural. The purpose of this sorting is to first establish that 'economy' does not exhaust the social totality, and that economic and non-economic processes provide conditions of existence for each other. This move addresses the economic determinism of the base-superstructure hierarchy from classical Marxism, as no claim is made that class provides the sole explanation for social interactions or that economy explains all other elements of society.

However, when we examine the four categories into which the diverse economies approach organizes social processes – economic, political, cultural, and natural – they correspond to the organization of the social world that is critiqued by Escobar in the quote above. The problem is not simply that classical Marxism assumed that class and economics explained the entirety of the social world, the problem is that we have taken the division of social life into the spheres of economic, political, cultural, and natural as self-evident. We face the problem of trying to eschew capitalocentrism even as we organize our analysis via a categorization scheme that reflects the symbolic order of modernist imagination.

The organization of processes into such categories emerges out of the institutional organization of social life in modern Western social democracies through states, markets, firms, households, and the separation of the elements of social life into economic, political, civic, and cultural spheres. As I have shown elsewhere (Charusheela 2009), one of the ways in which ethnocentric modernism operates is by proceeding as if social analysis based on the institutions of modern Western life can be universalized. This results in an epistemic erasure of alternate ways of being in the world, replacing them with a new, modernist episteme and symbolic order.

As Colin Danby (2017) shows, the constitution of the 'economic' as a visible and measurable subset of social life is a knowledge project that anchors the post-World War II Bretton Woods order of nation-states – an order on which the development project critiqued by Escobar and others is based. Danby's work carries forward the scholarship of Ferguson (1990), Mitchell (1991), and others who show us how the problem with economics is not simply that it provides a mis-analysis of the developing world, but that it acts as a knowledge project that reorganizes social life in problematic ways. Thus, by adopting a classification scheme that is derived from the symbolic order of modernism, the diverse economies approach implicitly naturalizes the 'economic' as a self-evident subset of social life, and thus remains tied to the modernist framework critiqued by Zein-Elabdin and Charusheela (2004).

In addition to sorting/classifying processes within a social totality, the diverse economies framework categorizes class processes. As discussed above, in this framework, class denotes processes and practices of producing, performing, appropriating, and distributing surplus. The diverse economies approach recognizes six forms of the class process: primitive communist, ancient, slave, feudal, capitalist, and communist. Of these, three are non-exploitative (primitive communist, ancient, and communist), and three are exploitative (slave, feudal, and capitalist). By categorizing six different ways in which the production, performance, appropriation, and distribution of surplus happens across different sites within a social totality, we can reveal a field of (economic) activity that far exceeds the capitalist firm, thus eschewing capitalocentrism. And by identifying at least three ways in which one may recognize non-exploitative forms of producing and appropriating surplus, we vastly expand our imagination of what it means to live and work in non-exploitative ways and can create a practical politics for the here-and-now.

Though the diverse economies approach has addressed the problems of capitalocentrism and teleological eurocentrism that beset the older modes of production framework, the trace of the old typology is retained in adverbial form to describe the difference between different forms of the class process. But what does it mean to organize our analyses of class processes around these concepts once we have given up the mode of production framework? The diverse economies approach does not retain the AMP as a category by seeking to identify an 'Asiatic form' of the class process because of the well-recognized orientalist problems with that category. But as noted above, simply removing the AMP from the analytical field and replacing it with the category 'feudal' does not actually resolve the problems of orientalism and eurocentrism that the AMP reflected. Hence, the questions asked about the role of the AMP and about the use of the category feudal to describe the Third World as pre-capitalist in the modes of production debates can be raised here as well – how are we defining the distinctions between these forms of the class process?

I have argued elsewhere (Charusheela 2007, 2010) that the way the diverse economies approach identifies distinctions between the different exploitative forms of the class process continues to reflect the deeper orientalist code through which difference is mapped within the modes of production typology. Instead of rehearsing that discussion in depth here, I will simply provide a quick example: Fraad, Resnick, and Wolff's (1989) discussion of households.[5]

Fraad, Resnick, and Wolff argue that far from living in a capitalist world, we live in a world in which vast swathes of surplus production take place in households, appropriated in a feudal form. To make their case, having successfully argued that we see surplus production and appropriation at the site of the household, they turn their attention to the problem of deciding what type of exploitation this is.

They first note that the exploitation in the household is clearly not capitalist.

> Now this form of the fundamental class process is clearly not capitalist. The husband does not buy the labor power of the wife by paying her wages, no exchange of commodities occurs between them, nor does he sell on the market as commodities the use-values she produces. Since the products of her surplus labor are not sold, her surplus labor has no exchange value as it would if she were participating in a capitalist fundamental class process. The husband does not engage in the drive to maximize some 'profit' derived from her surplus labor, nor does he compete with others to do so. Therefore, if our class analysis of this household is to proceed, we must inquire as to what other, noncapitalist form of the fundamental class process best captures what is happening.
>
> *(Fraad, Resnick & Wolff 1989: 16–17)*

Having decided that it is not-capitalist, their next move is to consult the other-than-capitalist options within the classical Marxist typology. Since household exploitation does not look like slavery, and we no longer use the AMP, that leaves feudalism:

> A consideration of the various noncapitalist forms of the fundamental class process discussed in the Marxist literature readily suggests which form best fits our household. It is the feudal form, that particular kind of fundamental

> class process which takes its name from medieval Europe, although it has existed at many other times both in Europe and elsewhere across the globe. The feudal form is appropriate because it requires no intermediary role for markets, prices, profits, or wages in the relation between the producer and the appropriator of surplus labor. The producer of surplus on the medieval European manor often delivered his/her surplus labor (or its products) directly to the lord of the manor, much as the wife delivers her surplus to her husband. Ties of religion, fealty, loyalty, obligation, tradition, and force bound serf and lord much as parallel marital oaths, ideology, tradition, religion, and power bind husbands and wives in the sort of household we are analyzing here.
>
> (Fraad, Resnick & Wolff 1989: 17)

First, note that despite the vocabulary that seems to posit some positive definition, the argument is really one of difference-from-capitalism. The feudal form is appropriate because it does not require intermediary roles for *capitalist* forms (markets, prices, profits, wages). But, slavery too does not require such intermediaries, so what makes us move so quickly from these capitalist absences into feudal? Slavery, like the capitalist form, possesses a positive content, which means it cannot be used extensively everywhere. The positive content of slavery's definition is not surprising, since the logic of ownership used to define modern notions of chattel slavery fits the modernist concept frames of property and ownership and modernist conceptions of freedom as self-ownership. The feudal form, however, is a capacious category whose boundaries are defined mainly through difference, with 'culture' functioning as a code for marking a broad swath of subject-constitution that is not-capitalist/not-modernist.

> The slave form, like the earlier category slavery, seems to be clear: the laborer is completely, visibly and openly, owned and controlled by the appropriator of surplus. We also think we know what the capitalist form, previously capitalism, means: wage labor in a system in which the equality of modern institutions and markets masks the process of surplus extraction in value form, and consent emerges through the act of masking exploitation and making it invisible.
>
> But feudal or feudalism has been used as a catchall category for everything else: all cases in which there is exploitation that is neither fully 'masked' by the languages of equality and market valuation nor upheld through the exploited being completely and formally owned by the exploiter. That is, 'feudal' spans that vast terrain where we see exploitation that is not fully masked (i.e., where the exploitation is 'out in the open', as it were), and those who are exploited seem to consent to this openly recognised performance and appropriation of surplus despite not being completely and formally owned and controlled by the exploiters. 'Culture' then becomes the necessary terrain for defining the feudal form/mode – people

caught in tradition, religious belief, role, who seem to keep accepting their subordinate position despite the absence of either a direct and visible control as with slavery, or invisibility and pretense of equality as under capitalism. In short, the slavery/feudalism/capitalism typology functions as a way to avoid, or at least to contain, the problem of subjectivity.

(Charusheela 2007: 14)

Fraad, Resnick, and Wolff are, of course, aware of the problems with mapping a category derived from discussions of Europe's past onto other locations. What makes this specific mapping unique is that it posits this categorization not for some Third World location, but for discussing the relations within contemporary US households. Going further, they write:

Of course, the presence of the feudal form of the fundamental class process is not the same as the presence of the feudalism that existed in medieval Europe. The feudal form will be different depending upon the social context in which it occurs. Just as feudal class processes in seventeenth century China differ from those in Latin America in the nineteenth century, so do feudal class processes in contemporary United States households differ from those present on medieval European manors.

(Fraad, Resnick & Wolff 1989: 17)

This willingness to open up a much broader ambit for defining the feudal is welcome, but not sufficient. This is because the problem is not that Europe's past was mapped onto other locations, the problem is that the conceptual frame through which we interpret other-than-capitalist subjectivity is what allows there to be so many different types of feudalism – there are many ways in which subjects may turn out to be insufficiently modern. Thus, the way they give content to the cultural space reveals the ongoing hold of a particular imagination of non-modern subjects: 'Ties of religion, fealty, loyalty, obligation, tradition, and force bound serf and lord much as parallel marital oaths, ideology, tradition, religion, and power bind husbands and wives in the sort of household we are analyzing here' (Fraad, Resnick & Wolff 1987: 17). It is unclear what it means to posit that the psychic and emotive ties that bind spouses in US households to each other are equivalent to the relation between landord and peasant in India, for example, beyond the fact that both are about relations that fall outside the logic of the market. Going further, it is even unclear that religion, fealty, loyalty, obligation, tradition, and force are particularly unique to feudal forms, since one could just as strongly note the role of religion and the Protestant work ethic, or of concepts of loyalty to firms and co-workers, as part of the actual way in which the conditions of existence of surplus appropriation in value form takes place within capitalist firms.

The problem with the typology of class used in the diverse economies framework, then, is how it treats culture and subjectivity, with 'feudal' standing in as a code for difference-from-capitalist-modernity. As long as the typology retains this mode of defining 'feudal', the deeper issue of how we come to know and see other-than-capitalist from without the capitalocentric nexus remains unresolved. While my discussion here has focused on the feudal form within the typology of exploitative forms, one could similarly ask what distinguishes the primitive communist from the communist class process on the side of the non-exploitative forms, since these are no longer ordered in historical progression.

A postfeudal politics

Given the difficulties that retaining the classification schemes generates for moving away from the limiting hold of modernist analysis, why bother to retain classification? What is the value of the classification of social processes into economic, political, cultural, and natural, and classification of class processes into feudal, slave, capitalist, ancient, primitive communist, and communist, for the diverse economies framework? As I have discussed above, both these typologies are important for the framework. The categorization of processes allows one to see a field of social activity that exceeds the market and allows the diverse economies framework to eschew the limiting economic determinism of previous approaches. The typology of multiple ways of appropriating surplus allows us to see a diversity of surplus production and appropriation beyond capitalocentrism.

In deploying the diverse economies framework, we have proceeded as if it were the logic of the external world, the 'on-the-ground realities' of different types of social processes and different forms of surplus appropriation the scholar-activist encounters and describes, rather than the inner logic of difference generated from inside modernist approaches of capitalocentrism itself, that provides the code we use for classification. But on closer examination, we see that the diverse economies approach did not adequately address the problem of how we think of the different-from-capitalist and other-than-modern. It simply submerged the problem of how we discuss subaltern subjectivity – the subjectivity of peasants, indigenous, non-modern subjects whose lives seem to be incomprehensibly tied to land and bound by tradition and fealty and religion and superstition – into the area of classification, so that it disappeared from view.

It has been hard to see this because so far, we have been asking the 'capitalism question'. In *The Man Question*, Kathy Ferguson (1993) points out that reframing an issue can help us see the limits of a concept frame – the man question is no more about men than the woman question was ever about women. Rather, if we pose the question of difference and diversity raised under the ambit of the woman question through the lens of the man question, we can denaturalize the concept frame that the woman question conceals. Proceeding in this spirit, let us ask ourselves the 'feudalism' question.

The question of how to analyze non-capitalist social formations has been at the center of a variety of transition debates within Marxism. One such debate was the Indian Modes of Production debate, which took place from the late

1960s to the 1980s.[6] The question taken up in the debate was, on the surface, a simple one of empirical verification – how would one classify Indian agriculture? Had it become capitalist? Or was it still pre-capitalist/feudal? As the debate proceeded, it became clear that the issues of classification could not be resolved simply by observation, as there were substantial problems of how one would define capitalism and feudalism in undertaking social analysis. Going further, moving the issue of definition more narrowly to the level of the production unit (in this case the farm – note that this narrowing of the location where we define class relations is also the strategy used by the diverse economies framework as discussed above), didn't end up resolving the underlying problems of applying the typology of Marxian classification to Indian peasantry.

In this context one of the participants in the debate, Ashok Rudra, argued that, given the difficulty in applying Marxist typology to the Indian case, we should step back and ask: if we are to undertake a re-constitutive project in Marxian thought, what would we identify as valuable and core for our approach? Rudra, like the diverse economies approach, identified Marx's concept of exploitation and Marx's materialist method of social analysis as the things we should retain. But he did not merely let go of capitalocentrism – he let go of further classification of the exploitation process along lines such as capitalist and feudal altogether (Rudra 1988).

There is much that can be theoretically resolved by simply rejecting the usefulness of classifying class processes beyond sorting them into exploitative versus non-exploitative. In analytical terms, we do not face the problem of trying to fit all the forms that surplus appropriation can take into one of the available categories. In ethical terms we gain a clear anchor for social change – the focus is on moving us from exploitative to non-exploitative forms of organizing social life. The need to make ethical or other adjudications between the different ways of appropriating surplus among the exploitative forms and the problem of overvaluing one of them, even in opposition, disappears.

This is a resolution worth considering. But another one is to accept the value of categorizing different types of class processes in a way that lets us sort through what is distinct about a specific way of coordinating the production, performance, appropriation, and distribution of surplus. But this does not automatically lead us to the process-without-a-subject resolution of the diverse economies approach. Figuring out what concept map we should use to categorize class processes will depend on what reason we have for engaging in such classification.

As noted above, the taxonomy of forms of the class process was important for populating the sphere of economy beyond the narrowly capitalocentric frame, which is the primary role that the classification plays in the diverse economies approach. A second important role for undertaking such taxonomies is that it can refocus our ethical imagination on the different ways in which we could perform and sustain non-exploitative forms of producing and appropriating surplus in the here-and-now. And here, I would like to suggest that an additional reason to retain the classification of different types of class processes is that it can give us a way to think about the different types of subjectivities that different ways of coordinating surplus production, performance, appropriation, and distribution reflect. Surfacing this is not simply a realist social science project, it is a project of making the potential for radical change in 'other-than-capitalist' spaces visible.

If we bury subjectivity by hiving it off to a separate sphere of the cultural while class becomes a process without a subject, we remove one of the reasons to engage in such sorting. While exploitation is a process without a subject, the classification of exploitation is precisely about building subjectivity back into our analysis. It *matters* that the surplus is extracted and performed in this or that manner – for if it was an irrelevant distinction, why bother with the classification? Serap Kayatekin and I (Kayatekin & Charusheela 2004) have argued for redefining the 'forms' of the class process in and through the effort to make alternate subjectivities visible. Specifically, we argue that we should not leave our discussions of feudal subjectivity at the level of norms of fealty, but actually use the Marxian concepts of hegemony – normally reserved for discussions of capitalism – to understand the ways in which non-modernist symbolic orders and world views constitute a 'common sense' that generates consent to exploitation. This gives us a path to a richer analysis of subjectivity. Going further, in Charusheela (2010) I suggest that taking this hegemonic common sense seriously can also generate a very rich vocabulary and ethical imagination for radical politics that far exceeds the particular experience of non-modern subjects, and acts as a contrast and supplement to the visions of communism that derive from modernist world views.

These strategies of recasting the Marxian typology allow us to ask the postfeudal politics question in a different way. Both, how would one move from feudal exploitative relations to communist ones, and, how would one open up and recompose the subaltern subjects hidden from view under the postcapitalist question? Ajit Chaudhury (1987) asked if we could envisage a subaltern Lenin. This was not merely a search for a figure who could lead a revolutionary movement of peasants, but a theoretical proposition about the possible emergence of radical socialist/communist consciousness from subaltern movements. Chaudhury argues that what we require here is a theorization akin to Lenin's analysis of the distinction between workers' consciousness and socialist consciousness. Workers' consciousness becomes radical, rather than reformist, only once it absorbs the contradictions of bourgeois ethics and, through a dialectical transformation, integrates this 'outside' into worker consciousness so that it becomes a consciousness not just for the worker but for society more generally.

This question about the emergence of a radical subaltern consciousness, which is hidden within a postcapitalist framework, can be asked under a postfeudal politics. If we follow Chaudhury's lead, we could begin to theorize the characteristics of radical subaltern consciousness. This would entail moving beyond imagining subaltern movements primarily in terms of their efforts to address particular issues or grievances. We would need to recognize and imagine subaltern leaders who reorganize the common sense that non-modern symbolic orders may generate, who are able to absorb and transform the contradictory aspects of concept-frames such as fealty, loyalty, gratitude, reciprocity, care that provide conditions of existence for feudal forms of appropriating and distributing surplus, much as a genuine socialist consciousness emerges when workers dialectically absorb and transform bourgeois frameworks of democracy and equality to create something that is qualitatively different. We would have to imagine the possibility of radical subaltern consciousness that can give us a vision for socialism that is generalized to all society and not limited to their own specific group, rank, or class.

To get there, we need a much more robust analysis of subject-constitution in relation to non-capitalist arrangements of surplus production and appropriation. Without that, the particular *positive* value of alternate frameworks such as indigenous and decolonial approaches or *adivasi* logics as places where one looks for a subaltern Lenin, disappears from view, leaving behind mainly their negative value of not being capitalist. And what is a specifically postcolonial approach to diverse economies if not the ability to make such subaltern visions for radical change legible under and against the modernist project of development?

Notes

1 The title of this section is a tribute to AESA's journal and signals the distinctiveness of this specific project to re-constitute Marxism in response to the critiques of its determinism and teleology.
2 At this point, it is worth remembering that the actual development of the diverse economies framework did not take place in the linear manner described above, beginning with an identification of specific problems, and followed by the revision that addressed them. The critique of classical Marxism and the revision of the framework went hand in hand. Substantial portions of this work preceded Gibson-Graham's critique of capitalocentrism. Consequently, the alignment between the diverse economies framework and postcolonial critiques of modernism has been uneven, since though the diverse economies framework developed in response to poststructuralism, *specifically* postcolonial concerns about orientalism and eurocentrism (as opposed to the broader poststructural turn more generally) have not been its central drivers. (A complete listing of the work that went into this creating this framework is far beyond the scope of this chapter. A brief glimpse into the immense theoretical work that was being generated within AESA in the decade from the mid-1980s to the mid-1990s, which went into the eventual consolidation of the approach as seen in Gibson-Graham, Resnick & Wolff 2000, 2001, and Gibson-Graham 2006, can be seen in, for example, Amariglio 1984, 1987, 1988; Norton 1988; Resnick & Wolff 1987; Amariglio, Resnick & Wolff, 1988; Amariglio & Callari 1989; Gabriel 1990; Callari 1991; Ruccio 1991; Ruccio, Resnick & Wolff 1991; Diskin & Sandler 1993; Cullenberg 1994; Amariglio & Ruccio 1994; Callari, Cullenberg & Biewener 1995; Callari & Ruccio 1996, to name just a few of the numerous publications by members of AESA during that period.)
3 Subaltern Studies used the term subaltern to describe these subjects. They derived this term from Gramsci's use of it in 'On the Subaltern Question' (Gramsci 1971). The issue that concerned Gramsci was the failure of the Communist Party of Italy to address the cultural imagination and political aspirations of Southern Italian peasants facing displacement by the rise of capitalism. Emerging from villages and cultural spheres shaped by the vast field termed traditional, religious, or superstitious, Gramsci

spoke to the need for addressing the grievances and tensions of this class of Italians, who were forming the subaltern ranks of Mussolini's army, and providing a base for the National Fascist Party. I remind readers of this here, mainly because I will be returning to the question of 'hegemony' that was a crucial aspect of Gramsci's work later in this chapter. I agree substantially with Marcus Green's (2002) argument that the interpretation of Gramsci that sparked Subaltern Studies rested on a misreading of his work, but my note here is genealogical – that is, to trace how the concept got deployed in the debates about transition and postcoloniality – rather than an effort to present the correct way to interpret Gramsci.

4 In late-1920s Latin America, Mariátegui (1971) was already developing an initial framework to critically distinguish the Latin American experience from Europe. Such efforts to critically distinguish non-Western experiences from the European case can be seen in other parts of the world as well. See Mukhia (1981) for a discussion of the South Asian case, and Goody (1963) for a discussion of the use of the concept for Africa. Byres and Mukhia (1985) provide a good theoretical overview of the debate.

5 Exemplars work only when they are good and strong, rather than weak, representations of the approach being critiqued. Fraad, Resnick, and Wolff's 'For every knight in shining armor, there's a castle waiting to be cleaned' (1989) has been an important contribution to the diverse economies framework. Twice anthologized as a major exemplar and key originary text for the development of this approach (Fraad, Resnick & Wolff 1994; Cassano 2009), it has been the point of development and departure for some of the more compelling analyses of households and other-than-capitalist spaces that the diverse economies approach has produced. To my mind, despite its flaws, it remains one of the more imaginative and pathbreaking works to have emerged from the AESA project. It showed us a way out of the domestic labor debates that could break past the previous limits of capitalocentrism and functionalism that reflected Marxism's 'unhappy marriage' with feminism (Hartmann 1979). It allowed us to recognize exploitation and acknowledge women's unpaid labor without falling back into reductive and narrow conceptions of gender. It let us examine the role played by culture without representing issues of gender identity as simply superstructural or reflective of false consciousness. And, it let us see that these spaces that had been viewed as troublesome distractions from the 'real' revolution, with these not-properly-modern-capitalist subjects, were actually locations of radical transformation, places where some of the most important experimentation with communist ways of living together could be found. One could, no doubt, find various types of realist objections to the framework around this or that detail of historical accuracy in particularity of description – which would be to miss the point. As Cameron notes in her review of *Bringing it All Back Home*:

> This book is, as Spivak notes in her introduction, a beginning. (Indeed Spivak suggests ways in which the approach might be used in the Third World and transnationally, in particular to breakdown distinctions between the West and the Third World). The authors are not presenting a completed social analysis, the accuracy of which needs to be debated, they are offering us a way of doing social analysis. Theirs is an approach for taking apart not only familiar sites like the household but familiar concepts such as class. And in the hands of the authors these sites and these processes become powerful tools for social analysis. They offer us new ways of seeing and new ways of making sense of the social world. And for those concerned about the political effectiveness of an approach that decries the notion of right and wrong theories, it offers new ways of thinking about political action.
>
> *(Cameron 1996: 206)*

Thus, my critical discussion here must be read in the spirit it is offered – not as a simple realist critique of the approach, but as addressing the broader intellectual architecture of the approach, with an eye to refining it and further enabling new ways of seeing the world.

6 See Patnaik (1990); Thorner (1982a, 1982b); and Chakrabarti and Cullenberg (2003: chapters 2–5) for an overview of this debate. For a more extended discussion of the point made in this paragraph, see Charusheela (2010).

References

Amariglio, J. (1984) '"Primitive communism" and the economic development of Iroquois society'. Ph.D. dissertation, University of Massachusetts Amherst.

Amariglio, J. (1987) 'Marxism against economic science: Althusser's legacy'. *Research in Political Economy*, vol 10, pp 159–194.

Amariglio, J. (1988) 'The body, economic discourse and power: An economist's introduction to Foucault'. *History of Political Economy*, vol 20, no 4, pp 583–613.

Amariglio, J. & Callari, A. (1989) 'Marxian value theory and the problem of the subject: The role of commodity fetishism'. *Rethinking Marxism*, vol 2, no 3, pp 31–60.

Amariglio, J., Resnick, S. & Wolff, R.D. (1988) 'Class, power, and culture'. In Nelson, C. and Grossberg, L. (eds.), *Marxism and the Interpretation of Culture*. London: MacMillan, pp 487–502.

Amariglio, J. & Ruccio, D. (1994) 'Postmodernism, Marxism, and the critique of modern economic thought'. *Rethinking Marxism*, vol 7, no 3, pp 7–35.

Byres, T. & Mukhia, H. (eds.) (1985) *Feudalism and Non-European Societies*. London: Routledge.

Callari, A. (1991) 'Economic subjects and the shape of politics'. *Review of Radical Political Economics*, vol 23, nos 1–2, pp 201–207.

Callari, A., Cullenberg, S. & Biewener, C. (eds.) (1995) *Marxism in the Postmodern Age*. New York: Guilford.

Callari, A. & Ruccio, D. (1996) *Postmodern Materialism and the Future of Marxist Theory: Essays in the Althusserian Tradition*. Middletown, CT: Wesleyan University Press.

Cameron, J. (1996) 'Review of H. Fraad, S. Resnick and R. Wolff *Bringing It All Back Home: Class, Gender and Power in the Modern Household*'. *Antipode*, vol 28, no 2, pp 204–206.

Cassano, G. (ed.) (2009) *Class Struggle on the Home Front: Work, Conflict, and Exploitation in the Household*. New York: Palgrave MacMillan.

Chakrabarti, A. & Cullenberg, S. (2003) *Transition and Development in India*. New York: Routledge.

Chakrabarty, D. (2000) *Provincializing Europe: Postcolonial Thought and Historical Difference*. Princeton, NJ: Princeton University Press.

Charusheela, S. (2007) 'Transition, telos, and taxonomy'. *Rethinking Marxism*, vol 19, no 1, pp 8–17.

Charusheela, S. (2009) 'Social analysis and the capabilities approach: A limit to Martha Nussbaum's universalist ethics'. *Cambridge Journal of Economics*, vol 33, no 6, pp 1135–1156.

Charusheela, S. (2010) 'Engendering feudalism: Modes of production debates revisited'. *Rethinking Marxism*, vol 22, no 3, pp 438–445.

Chaudhury, A. (1987) 'In search of a subaltern Lenin'. In R. Guha (ed.), *Subaltern Studies No. 5: Writings on South Asian History and Society*. Delhi: Oxford University Press, pp 236–251.

Cullenberg, S. (1994) *The Falling Rate of Profit: Recasting the Marxian Debate*. London: Pluto Press.

Danby, C. (2017) *The Known Economy: Romantics, Rationalists, and the Making of a World Scale*. London: Routledge.

Diskin, J. & Sandler, B. (1993) 'Essentialism and the economy in the post-Marxist imaginary: Reopening the sutures'. *Rethinking Marxism*, vol 6, no 3, pp 28–48.

Escobar, A. (1995) *Encountering Development: The Making and Unmaking of the Third World*. Princeton, NJ: Princeton University Press.

Ferguson, J. (1990) *The Anti-Politics Machine: 'Development,' Depoliticization, and Bureaucratic Power in Lesotho*. Cambridge: Cambridge University Press.

Ferguson, K. (1993) *The Man Question: Visions of Subjectivity in Feminist Theory*. Berkeley, CA: University of California Press.

Fraad, H., Resnick, S. & Wolff, R.D. (1989) 'For every knight in shining armor, there's a castle waiting to be cleaned: A Marxist-feminist analysis of the household'. *Rethinking Marxism*, vol 2, no 4, pp 9–69.

Fraad, H., Resnick, S. & Wolff, R.D. (1994) *Bringing It All Back Home: Class, Gender and Power in the Modern Household*. London: Pluto Press.

Gabriel, S. (1990) 'Ancients: A Marxian theory of self-exploitation'. *Rethinking Marxism*, vol 3, no 1, pp 85–106.

Gibson-Graham, J.K. (1993) 'Waiting for the revolution, or how to smash capitalism while working at home in your spare time'. *Rethinking Marxism*, vol 6, no 2, pp 10–24.

Gibson-Graham, J.K. (1996) *The End of Capitalism (As We Knew It): A Feminist Critique of Political Economy*. Oxford: Blackwell Publishers.

Gibson-Graham, J.K. (2004) 'The violence of development: Two political imaginaries'. *Development*, vol 47, no 1, pp 27–34.

Gibson-Graham, J.K. (2006) *A Postcapitalist Politics*. Minneapolis: University of Minnesota Press.

Gibson-Graham, J.K., Cameron, J. & Healy, S. (2013) *Take Back the Economy: An Ethical Guide for Transforming Our Communities*. Minneapolis: University of Minnesota Press.

Gibson-Graham, J.K., Resnick, S. & Wolff, R.D. (eds.) (2000) *Class and Its Others*. Minneapolis: University of Minnesota Press.

Gibson-Graham, J.K., Resnick, S. & Wolff, R.D. (eds.) (2001) *Re/presenting Class: Essays in Postmodern Marxism*. Durham, NC: Duke University Press.

Godelier, M. (1986) *The Mental and the Material: Thought, Economy and Society*. London: Verso.

Goody, J. (1963) 'Feudalism in Africa?' *Journal of African History*, vol 4, no 1, pp 1–18.

Gramsci, A. (1971) *Selections from the Prison Notebooks*, trans. and ed. Hoare, Q. & Nowell Smith, G. New York: International Publishers.

Green, M. (2002) 'Gramsci cannot speak: Presentations and interpretations of Gramsci's concept of the subaltern'. *Rethinking Marxism*, vol 14, no 3, pp 1–24.

Gudeman, S. (1986) *Economics as Culture: Models and Metaphors of Livelihood*. London: Routledge and Kegan Paul.

Guha, R. (ed.) (1982) *Subaltern Studies No. 1: Writings on South Asian History and Society*. Delhi: Oxford University Press.

Guha, R. & Spivak, G.C. (eds.) (1988) *Selected Subaltern Studies*. Delhi: Oxford University Press.

Hardt, M. & Negri, A. (2001) *Empire*. Cambridge, MA: Harvard University Press.

Hardt, M. & Negri, A. (2004) *Multitude: War and Democracy in the Age of Empire*. New York: Penguin Press.

Hartmann, H. (1979) 'The unhappy marriage of Marxism and feminism: Towards a more progressive union'. *Capital & Class*, vol 3, no 2, pp 1–33.

Harvey, D. (1982) *The Limits to Capital*. Oxford: Basil Blackwell.

Harvey, D. (1989) *The Condition of Postmodernity: An Enquiry into the Origins of Cultural Change*. Oxford: Blackwell Publishers.

Jameson, F. (1991) *Postmodernism, or, The Cultural Logic of Late Capitalism*. Durham, NC: Duke University Press.

Kayatekin, S. & Charusheela, S. (2004) 'Recovering feudal subjectivities'. *Rethinking Marxism*, vol 16, no 4, pp 377–396.

Mariátegui, J.C. (1971) *Seven Interpretative Essays on Peruvian Reality*, trans. Basadre, J. Austin: University of Texas Press.

Marx, K. (2002) *Theses on Feurbach*. Marx/Engels Internet Archive. www.marxists.org/archive/marx/works/1845/theses/theses.htm.

Mitchell, T. (1991) *Colonizing Egypt*. Los Angeles: University of California Press.

Mukhia, H. (1981) 'Was there feudalism in Indian history?' *Journal of Peasant Studies*, vol 8, no 3, pp 273–310.

Norton, B. (1988) 'Epochs and essences: A review of Marxist long-wave and stagnation theories'. *Cambridge Journal of Economics*, vol 12, no 2, pp 203–224.

Patnaik, U. (ed.) (1990) *Agrarian Relations and Accumulation: The 'Mode of Production' Debate in India*. Published for Sameeksha Trust, Mumbai. London: Oxford University Press.

Resnick, S. & Wolff, R.D. (1987) *Knowledge and Class*. Chicago, IL: University of Chicago Press.

Ruccio, D. (1991) 'Postmodernism and economics'. *Journal of Post-Keynesian Economics*, vol 13, no 4, pp 495–510.

Ruccio, D., Resnick, S. & Wolff, R.D. (1991) 'Class beyond the nation-state'. *Capital & Class*, vol 43, pp 25–42.

Rudra, A. (1988) *Non-Eurocentric Marxism and Indian Society*. Calcutta: People's Book Society.

Spivak, G.C. (1993) *Outside in the Teaching Machine*. London: Routledge.

Spivak, G.C. (1999) *A Critique of Postcolonial Reason: Toward a History of the Vanishing Present*. Cambridge, MA: Harvard University Press.

Thorner, A. (1982a) 'Semi-feudalism or capitalism? Contemporary debate on classes and modes of production in India, Part 1'. *Economic and Political Weekly*, vol 17, no 49, pp 1961–1968.

Thorner, A. (1982b) 'Semi-feudalism or capitalism? Contemporary debate on classes and modes of production in India, Part 2'. *Economic and Political Weekly*, vol 17, no 51, pp 2061–2066.

Virno, P & Hardt, M. (1996) *Radical Thought in Italy: A Potential Politics*. Minneapolis, MN: University of Minnesota Press.

Yanagisako, S. & Collier, J. (1989) *Gender and Kinship: Toward a Unified Analysis*. Stanford, CA: Stanford University Press.

Zein-Elabdin, E. & Charusheela, S. (2004) *Postcolonialism Meets Economics*. London: Routledge.

5

PRAXIS IN WORLD OF THE THIRD CONTEXTS

Beyond third worldism and development studies

Anup Dhar and Anjan Chakrabarti

This chapter is bifocal. On the one hand, it takes us beyond development studies and makes space for 'praxis', praxis as the foreclosed of the University Discourse (Lacan, 2007 [1969–1970]) obsessed with 'studies', praxis as also the foreclosed of a development sector obsessed with 'intervention' and 'implementation'.

On the other hand, it puts to critical interrogation the extant cartography 'first world/third world' and developed/*under*developed (Spivak 1985; Berger 1994: 269). The interrogation also stems from the 'desire to assert a logic of difference and possibility against the homogenizing [and hegemonic] tendencies of globalization and the teleological generalities of political economy' (Gibson-Graham 2016: 288). The chapter makes space for a new cartography marked by the *overdetermined*[1] and dynamic boundaries between the 'circuits of global capital' and the 'world of the third', where the world of the third is marking contingent *outsided-ness* with respect to the circuits of global capital and capital's language-logic-experience-ethos; where the world of the third is also about a *third* that is both present and absent – present in terms of 'forms of life' but absent in discourse: the discourse of global capitalism and inclusive developmentalism, a discourse marked in turn by 'capitalocentrism' (Gibson-Graham 1996) and 'orientalism' (Said 1978). It is about a *third* world (not 'third world'), a world beyond what are conventionally known as first worlds and third worlds. It is about a *third* kind of experience: an experience that is neither capitalist nor *pre*-capitalist but *non*-capitalist (which in turn could be the ground for postcapitalist subject formation and 'a politics of emplacement'). 'Not a politics of identity *per se*, but a politics of the co-production of subjects and places. A politics of becoming in place' (Gibson-Graham 2016: 288).

The movement from (i) third world to (ii) the world of the third as space and (iii) the world of the third as place is a movement from (a) 'space-as-*lacking*' (where third world is seen as the pre-capitalist 'lacking Other' of a capitalist first world) to (b) space-as-marking-*difference* to (c) place – place as the 'site and spur of [possible] becoming'.[2] *Possible* becoming, because it is praxis that births the world of the third *as* place. There is, however, no guarantee that the world of the third as (non-capitalist) space (unhooked from the circuits of global capital) shall transform into the world of the third as (postcapitalist) place; the transformation is birthed through (postdevelopmental) praxis. The world of the third births the necessity of transformative praxis, postcapitalist praxis. Praxis in turn births the possibility of the world of the third as place.

The chapter also turns to the *know-how* in/of the 'world of the third'; the assumption: the world of the third is the space where some of the 'know-how' of what Lacan (2007) calls 'slave' and what we call the *adivasi* (original inhabitants or the Indigenous people) and the *dalit* reside. 'The recovery of the other selves of cultures and communities, selves not defined by the dominant global consciousness' is perhaps 'the first task of social criticism and political activism and the first responsibility of intellectual stock-taking' (Nandy 1989: 265) in postdevelopment praxis.

The nascent *idea* of development practice (*not* development studies), which at present has taken the form of an 'immersion' and 'action research'-based MPhil programme at Ambedkar University Delhi, tries to 'span the gap between the academy and activism, engaging in place-based action research involving both university and community-based researchers/activists' and inaugurate in the 'beehive' of the university (Derrida 2003) the foreclosed question of praxis and of the 'slave's know-how'. The idea of development practice – inspired by the reflection of Tagore's (2011: 137–160) *Sriniketan* in the rearview mirror and Gibson-Graham's (2016: 289) 'a politics of becoming in place' in the windscreen view – is an attempt at also 'breaking the silo' and at *integrating* (development) studies and practice. Our action research projects at the Centre for Development Practice (see www.cdp.res.in) have aimed to 'recognize and value' the distinctive economic, political, cultural, and nature-nurturing 'capabilities of localities' or 'world of the third' (Chakrabarti & Dhar 2009), and have tried to build upon the know-how and the ethics of practices within, through nourishing extant communal practices, as also constructing alternative economic, political, and cultural institutions.

Postdevelopment: beyond global-local

In the context of this chapter, the postdevelopmental perspective gestures towards three related moves. One, the 'post' of postdevelopment, gestures towards 'critique', critique of existing paradigms of development. Two, postdevelopment is about rethinking space, rethinking the 'local' as against globality-globalisation, rethinking third world. The space-designated world of the third is in that sense in tune with the postdevelopment perspective of rethinking space (Chakrabarti & Dhar 2009; Chakrabarti, Dhar & Cullenberg 2016). Three, the postdevelopmental perspective is also about thinking praxis beyond statist developmental interventions or mere intervention-implementation programmes. It is to think developmental praxis in terms of local contexts, community participation as also to learn to learn from below. This is where the action research programme in development practice becomes relevant in terms of three departures: one, immersion (as against field work) in community contexts, rural and forest societies; two, co-researching *with* community to arrive at the action research problematic; and three, co-authoring with community 'transformative social praxis', which is, in turn, informed by social justice and well-being considerations.

To make sense of postdevelopment as also to practise postdevelopment, this chapter brings to dialogue the immanent praxis of the 'located micro-political' in Gibson-Graham (2006) and the utopian near-transcendent gesture of an 'alternative *to* development' in Escobar (1995) and Nandy (1989). The former marks difference with respect to capitalocentrism (capitalocentrism is 'capitalism of thought'; critiques of capitalism are not immune to capitalism of thought) (see Spivak 1994); the latter marks difference with respect to modernism. Further, if development is the substitute signifier for capitalism, postdevelopment needs to gesture towards postcapitalist politics. Postdevelopment also gestures towards a post-orientalist perspective; hence the need to rethink *topos*, rethink cartographies, rethink third wordlism; hence the turn to the world of the third.

Five questions thus become important in postdevelopmental praxis: (a) *doing*, not just knowing (postdevelopment is not just *writing* about wrongs, but about *righting* wrongs [Spivak 2004: 523–581]), (b) doing *what*: i.e., doing *differently*, doing postdevelopmentally and not developmentally, marking economic difference, (c) doing *with* and not doing on (hence immersion, hence co-researching, co-authoring transformation as in the action research programme in development practice), (d) doing *where*, not 'third world' but the 'world of the third', and (e) doing with *who*: not the underdeveloped, but the different; not the appropriate(d), but the inappropriate(d) in subaltern subject positions; not the third worldist subject of *lack*.

The university unthought:[3] from 'field-work' to 'working-in-the-fields'

Two departures create the ground for postdevelopment praxis. One, the movement from third world as the space-of-lack to the world of the third as place of difference. Two, the movement beyond (development) 'studies'. One can turn to Rabindranath Tagore (1861–1941), poet, writer, educationist, philosopher, and founder of *Sriniketan* (the 'abode of the aesthetic') – an institution of alternative pedagogy and grassroots-level *transformative social praxis* involving the *lokavidyas* (see Basole 2015), i.e., the 'know-how of subaltern bricoleurs' – to get a sense of such a beyond to mere 'studies' as also to the classical university imagination, an imagination steeped in and limited to the teaching of the theoretical sciences. While the focus on 'studies' sharpened largely the intellectual self, Tagore inaugurated in the 'culture of the self' in *Sriniketan* the creative expression and praxis of the affective, the aesthetic, and the ethical; the praxis of being-in-the-world;[4] being-with-nature; the praxis of labouring activities in the 'average everydayness' of the ashram; the praxis of self- and social transformation. Tagore's turn to Sriniketan could thus be seen as a departure from the kind of cognitivist student subject the university mass produces; such mass production of cognitivist student subjects in turn creates a culture of *turning away* from the masses.

Thus Tagore was not only outgrowing the discursive liminalities of enlightened progressivism and state-driven top-down official developmental fantasies, but was also formulating his own theories and practice of integrated and grounded 'human development' (Sen 1984; Tagore 2011: 160). We argue in this chapter that the experience of an experiment called *Sriniketan* could also be seen as his way of re-creating, re-constructing the rural everyday and the hugely important role education and educational institutions should play in that exercise (Roy 2010: 679; Tagore 2017). *Sriniketan* would, for Tagore, 'ultimately bridge the ever-widening gap between the country and the city; a gap, that originated from the unleashing of forces of "colonial modernity" by the imperial rulers' (Roy 2010: 679). *Sriniketan* was also the site for projects for rural reconstruction, co-operative movements, agricultural banking, and new methods in agriculture, largely amongst *adivasis* and *dalits*. Tagore states in the 1925 prospectus of the 'A Viswa-Bharati Institute for Rural Reconstruction at Sriniketan'; the aim of the Institute is the *coordination of brain and hand* (Tagore 2011: 137–139). The objectives of *Sriniketan* were (somewhat postdevelopmental): (a) 'to bring back life in its completeness into the villages making then self-reliant and self-respectful, acquainted with the cultural tradition of their own country, and competent to make an efficient [and critical] use of the modern resources', (b) 'to win the friendship and affection of the villagers and cultivators by taking real interest in all that concerns their life and […] by making a lively effort to assist them in solving their most pressing problems', (c) 'to take the problems of the village and field to the classroom', (d) 'to carry the knowledge and experience gained in the classroom and experimental farm [back] to the villages', etc. The coordination between knowing and doing, thought and action, theory and practice, however, remained central in *Sriniketan*. Tagore thus was not just *studying* the village – or gathering data, or conducting surveys – he was trying to *reconstruct* village life.

Beyond *theoria*: return to phronesis-praxis

Lacan foregrounds the *theft, abduction* and *stealing* of the slave's 'know-how' (not just 'surplus labour', as suggested by Marx), through the maneuvers of the Master in Plato's dialogues, a know-how that was intimately tied to labouring practices. What we call *episteme* is, as if, premised on the *extraction* of the essence of the know-how embedded in the everyday praxis of the craftsmen, of the serfs, of women working in households. Theoretical knowledge or what Aristotle calls *theoria* in its historical function is *this* extraction, of the slave's know-how, in order to obtain its transmutation (first) into the 'Master's Discourse' and then into the 'University Discourse' (2007 [1969–1970]). This would also lead to a historical *hyper-separation* of theory and practice (this hyper-separation is of course not a feature of the slave's life-world; this is what Lacan would like to argue) – a hyper-separation Marx and Tagore (as also Heidegger 1985 [1962] and Arendt 2005) would be worried about. The abduction of the slave's or subaltern's know-how thus resulted in, one, a 'loss of concepts' (see Lear 2006) in what we have designated the world of the third. It also led, two, to a distilling of the 'know-ing' component of the register of the 'know-how' from the slave or the subaltern's world to the Master's grip. The 'know-ing' component appropriated by the Master later came to be known as the university's knowledge repository as also the *function* of the university. The 'how' component of the register of the 'know-how' (i.e., the 'how to' or the 'how of doing things') got relegated to the now-denigrated register of 'hand' (of the brain/hand binary), 'labour' (of the intellect-labour binary), and practice (of the studies/practice binary). The hand-labour-practice space also became the space of the slave/subaltern; or the space of the slave/subaltern became the space of the use of the hand, of labour and of practice. Thought was on the Master's side; or inside the secure perimeters of the university. Postdevelopmental praxis inaugurates a relationship not just with the world of the third, but the know-how that resides inside the world of the third. It thus takes us beyond mere *theoria* or mere knowing and opens space for transformative praxis. It re-integrates, on the one hand, know-how and the world of the third and, on the other, the register of the know-how and the slave/subaltern.

This chapter on postdevelopment praxis and the action research programme in development practice also remains informed by Heidegger's (1985 [1962], 1997; Long 2002) turn to the Aristotelian concept (invoked in Book IV of the *Nicomachean Ethics*) of *phronesis* (as distinct from episteme), *phronesis* as *practical reason* (as distinct from theoretical reason), *phronesis* as reasoning based on concrete practical action (as distinct from speculative reason), *phronesis* as reason based on experience (as distinct from abstract deductions) (see Dhar & Chakrabarti 2016).[5] The action research programme in development practice is an attempt at turning to the 'lost tradition' of practical philosophy and its forgotten companion concepts: *phronesis* and praxis, concepts that have been 'rendered marginal' and 'face something approaching total obliteration' in the dominant culture of modernity (see Gadamer 1980; Carr 2006: 434).

Beyond practice: beyond *poiesis*

> 'Practical' behaviour is not 'atheoretical' in the sense of sightlessness [i.e., a lack of seeing]. The way it differs from theoretical behaviour does not lie simply in the fact that in theoretical behaviour one observes, while in practical behaviour one acts [*gehandelt wird*], and that action must apply theoretical cognition if it is not to remain blind; for the fact that observation is a

kind of concern [or taking care] is just as primordial as the fact that action has its own kind of sight [seeing].

(Heidegger 1985 [1962]: 99)

If one side of the problem is *theoria* or observation without concern/care, the other side of the problem is practice or action that is blind. Practice is also normalised through repetition. One hence needs to re-conceptualise practice beyond *poiesis* and *techne*. *Poiesis* usually refers to a form of 'making' whose end is known prior to the practical means taken to achieve it; *poiesis* is guided by the form of reasoning that the Greeks called *techne* and that we would today call instrumental 'means-end' reasoning. *Poiesis* is thus a form of instrumental action that requires a prior mastery of the knowledge, methods, and skills that together constitute technical expertise. Developmental practices often take the form of 'applied science', which provide the principles, procedures, and operational methods that together constitute the most effective means for achieving some pre-determined end (see Carr 2006: 426; Chakrabarti & Dhar 2013). Development could be thought from the perspective of *poiesis*; it could also be thought from the perspective of praxis. Praxis is to progressively realise the idea of the 'good' that is constitutive of a morally worthwhile form and quality of life. The 'end' of praxis hence is not to make or produce some object or artefact. The good of praxis, however, cannot be 'made'; it can only be 'done' or realised. Praxis is thus a form of 'doing' action precisely because its 'end' – to arrive at good life – '*only* exists, and can *only* be realised, *in and through* praxis *itself*' (Carr 2006: 426).

Praxis also differs from *poiesis* in that knowledge of its end cannot be theoretically specified in advance and can only be acquired on the basis of an understanding of how, in a particular concrete situation, this knowledge is being interpreted and applied. Praxis is thus nothing other than a practical manifestation of how the idea of the good is being progressively understood, just as knowledge of the good is nothing other than an abstract way of specifying the mode of human conduct through which this idea is given practical expression. In praxis, acquiring knowledge of what the good is and knowing how to apply it in particular situations are thus not two separate processes but two mutually constitutive elements within a single dialectical process of practical reasoning (see Carr 2006: 426; also see Dunne 1993).

This chapter hence tries to replace *poiesis* in development with praxis. It also connects praxis to *phronesis*. The chapter presents development as not just a technique but as a question of praxis – where theories of development and practices of development are in a mutually constitutive relationship – as also *phronesis*. By turning to the concept of phronesis the chapter puts to question universalist theories and practices of development and makes development a particularised endeavour, an endeavour intimately and inalienably tied to what Heidegger calls the *with-which* – the with-which of the community context or what Haraway (1992) designates as a 'series of "situated knowledges," part fact and part fiction, which are "artifactual"' (Watts in Crush 2005 [1995]: 55).

We thus highlight the need to move, in contexts of development, first, from *theoria* to practice; second, from mere repetitive practice to praxis, thus bringing *theoria* and practice to dialogue; third, from *poiesis* to praxis, i.e., from repetitive making/production to reflective doing, from instrumental action to reflexive processes; fourth, relate to and engage with the particularities of the community with which the praxis of development is attempted. We also highlight the need to move, in contexts of development, from material development to human development, and from human development to community-initiated 'new social movements' – new social movements as the medium through which alternative discourses *to* (rather than *of*) development are being articulated – new social movements as ground for 'a more radical imagining of alternative futures' – new social movements as polyvalent, local, dispersed, and fragmented (Porter in Crush 2005 [1995]: 61–84; Escobar in Crush 2005 [1995]: 205–222).

Praxis also concerns the transition from what Althusser (see Dhar & Chakrabarti, 2015: 225) designated 'practical truth' (which is practiced or experienced) to the 'theory of that truth or to its concept'; as also the inundating of theory, truth, or concept in the 'dirty' immanence of practice (see Marx 2016 [1845]). Althusser credits Lacan for having shown that the problems of psychoanalytic technique cannot be resolved at the level of technique, that 'a leap' and 'recourse to theory' was needed; the problems of theory may also not get resolved at the level of theory, a 'dip' into practice and polis (see Arendt 2005) was needed. This, however, does not mean that there is, on the one hand, pure and simple technique, which would be practiced by people without any idea of theory and to whom that theory must be taught so that they can then nuance or reform their technique. The conflict is not between a pure technique without theory and pure theory. There is no pure technique. Any technique that wants to be pure technique is, in fact, according to Althusser, an 'ideology of technique', that is, a 'false theory'. Such 'ideology' or 'false theory' is most often the 'obligatory mate' of one's 'false innocence as pure technicians'. How would one, in the turning away from 'pure studies' and the turn to practice, not become pure 'technicians' of development? How would one reach the 'truth' of one's developmental practice(s)? How would one refine, temper, and re-form truth in practice? Praxis – postdevelopmental praxis – attempts to bring the 'practice of truth' and the 'truth of practice' to dialogue.

Beyond development

Development can be disaggregated into hegemonic forms of development (i.e., growth, industrialisation, progressive journey from a 'third world-ish' traditional economy to a modern capitalist economy so as to get rid of mass poverty), 'alternative forms of development' (i.e., the human development approach, growth with redistribution, means to better quality of life and well-being, etc.), and 'alternatives to development'[6] (i.e., postdevelopmentalist positions). While the first two share a somewhat unexamined commitment to modernisation and capitalism, the third problematises modernism. One can also argue for a fourth position that problematises *both* modernism and capitalism. Not just modernism and capitalism, but orientalism (i.e., the hierarchical division of the world into the [developed] West and the [*under*developed] 'rest') and capitalocentrism (i.e., the description of world and experience from the standpoint of capital and the consequent division of the world into the capitalist/developed and the *pre*-capitalist/*not-yet*-capitalist/*under*developed remainder). The fourth position problematises 'socio-economic dualism', which is the process of representing and interpellating an otherwise complex, decentered, disaggregated, and heterogeneous socio-economic reality into the logic of the two, 'p' and '~p', where the former (p) is valued and the *other* (~p) is seen as 'lacking p' and is hence devalued, where developed is valued, underdeveloped is devalued; capital is valued, *non*-capital is devalued and represented in turn as *pre*-capital; modern is valued, pre-modern is devalued. Resultantly, asserting 'a logic of *difference* and possibility against the homogenizing [and hegemonic] tendencies of globalization and the teleological generalities of political economy' (Gibson-Graham 2016: 288) nurturing 'what are not capitalist' class existences into postcapitalist futures becomes impossible.

We argue that the experience of development is not structured on the logic of the two, but, instead, on the logic of the three: (i) modernism/capitalism as 'p', (ii) the lacking Other/third world as '~p', which is, however, foregrounded, and (iii) the foreclosed Other/world of the third. If third world is the *constitutive inside*, or the 'appropriate(d) Other' of development, then world of the third is the *constitutive outside*, the 'inappropriate(d) Other'. Development's object of control and regulation is not third world, but instead world of the third. The world of the third as the harbinger of a *non*-capitalist language-logic-lived experience-ethic *outside* of and *beyond* the circuits of (global) capitalist modernity, and that puts *under erasure* capitalist ethic and language. However, in developmental logic world of the third is displaced into 'third world' – third world as *pre*-capitalist – as a lower step in the ladder of linear time. The world of the third as also the *critique of the capitalist present and future* is thus reduced to a *third wordlist past*. Building on Gibson-Graham (2006) and the work of the Community Economies collective, we in the action research programme in development practice have tried to work through the world of the third as non-capitalist space to the world of the third as postcapitalist place; Bhavya Chitranshi's chapter in this volume (Chapter 7) is a narrative of this difficult, uncertain, and incomplete 'working through' from space *to* place.

Beyond third worldism: rethinking development as reconstruction

Development has been the primary mechanism through which the third world has been imagined and has imagined itself, thus precluding other ways of seeing and doing (Escobar in Crush 2005 [1995]: 206–207). This section argues that the world of the third as space is another way of *seeing* what has hitherto been designated 'third world' and engendering the world of the third as place is another way of *doing* what has hitherto been designated as developmental practices. This section generates the angle of such seeing and the axis of such doing through a remapping of what the discourse of development has designated as third world. It remaps through the deployment of the 'entry point' of economic qua class as processes of surplus labour (Resnick & Wolff 1987) in an otherwise overdetermined reality. Through class as processes of surplus labour this section revisits the capitalist/pre-capitalist divide that has become paradigmatic for much of our description of the third world. This section critiques this description of the third world as *lacking/lagging* Other and as *pre*-capitalist or *under*developed. Through a close study of class as processes of surplus labour we arrive at a new cartography of 'circuits of global capital'-'world of the third' in a hyphenated (*not* slash) relation of mutual, dynamic and ever-shifting constitutivity. The cartography of the circuits of global capital and the world of the third is important because what was hitherto known as first world and third world is now seen to be split and splintered in many directions; or perhaps it was always already split in an infinite multiplicity of possibilities; it was we who had rendered the real infinity and the multiplicity hostage to a homogeneously pre-capitalist, underdeveloped, backward, and superstitious bloc: *the* third world. This is an attempt to not lapse into the either/or that is currently dominating us; either the third world is a homogeneous presence, somewhat eternal, pure, and pristine; or the third world is slowly getting annihilated and erased from existence – representative of unthinking modernist positions. This section shows that what was known as first world and third world could be re-written as the unresolved and unfinished dialectic between the circuits of global capital and the world of the third. The redrawing of the cartography of the third world creates conditions or ground for the *political* or, more precisely, the politics of place. The third world has hitherto been seen as our *past*; a past to be transcended. The redrawing of the cartography helps us see the world of the third as the *future*; not the whole of the world of the third; not the world of the third as a homogeneous entity; but a fragment of the world of the third (Chakrabarti, Dhar & Cullenberg 2012); a fragment that is *cocooned* in the world of the third as space, but which, however, is also *crypted* (see Abraham & Torok 1986). Cocooned designates *presence*; that which is cocooned (is) inside. Crypted points to *absence*; that which is crypted is hidden, veiled, occulted from view, from consideration. We contend that that which is cocooned yet crypted in the world of the third as *space* constitutes the postdevelopmental or postcapitalist future/politics of place. The study of economic qua class as processes of surplus labour takes us to the doorstep of that which is 'cocooned *yet* crypted'.

This section of the chapter looks at 'economic reality' in terms of a multiplicity of mutually constitutive and even contradictory subject positions/forms of life or praxis (in this case practices of labouring) – contradictory because the same subject may occupy non-exploitative and exploitative class positions – and not in terms of the paradigmatic framework 'p/~p' (developed/underdeveloped, modern/traditional, capitalist/feudal, progressive/backward, scientific/superstitious). Table 5.1 gives us a sense of the class positions one could possibly occupy with respect to performance and appropriation of surplus (Chaudhury & Chakrabarti 2000). The first and second alphabet in Table 5.1 stands for performance and appropriation of surplus respectively. For example, AA signifies performance and appropriation by the same 'undivided' self. AB signifies performance by an individual 'A' and appropriation by another non-performing individual 'B'. C signifies a collective of performers/appropriators:

In Table 5.1, the disaggregation was in terms of *exploitative* and *non-exploitative*. One can see through Table 5.1 how what the development sector calls the third world is not all exploitative, not all 'victim-hood' in need of rescue/development, not all 'evil' in need of annihilation or dystopian (with no futurity), but a space of also non-exploitative praxis. For example, it is indeed a space of AA class process – a single woman peasant [A] working on her own land and appropriating the surplus alone [A]; AC class process – number of single woman peasants [A] working on their respective lands and coming together to appropriate the surplus [C]; and CC class process – a collective of woman peasants working together [C] and appropriating the surplus together [C], as in the *Eka Nari Sanghathan* (see Chitranshi, Chapter 7, this volume).

We shall now add to the institutional configuration of performance and appropriation of surplus labour (as in Table 5.1) the dimensions of (i) output distribution – whether in commodity ('com.') or non-commodity ('non-com.') form and (ii) labour remuneration – whether in wage and non-wage to make

TABLE 5.1 Class process and modes of appropriation

Performance of surplus labour	Appropriation of surplus labour		
	Individual labour (A)	*Non-labour* (B)	*Collective labour* (C)
	AA (surplus produced by individual performer [A] appropriated by same individual performer [A] – hence non-exploitative)	**AB** (surplus produced by individual performer [A] appropriated by non-performer [B] – hence exploitative)	**AC** (surplus produced by multiple individual performers [A] appropriated by the collective of the same individuals [C] – hence non-exploitative)
	CA (surplus produced by the collective [C] is appropriated by one of the performers [A] – hence exploitative)	**CB** (surplus produced by collective [C] appropriated by non-performer [B] – hence exploitative)	**CC** (surplus appropriated by the collective [C] that produces [C] the surplus – hence non-exploitative)

sense of which class processes are hooked to the circuits of global capital and which are *outside*. The six class processes (in Table 5.1) thus get disaggregated further into 24 class sets (see Chakrabarti, Dhar & Cullenberg 2012: 138–142).

In Table 5.2, class sets 5 and 17 designate the capitalist class sets (both are exploitative; and in both labour power and output distribution are in the commodity-form). The rest (i.e., the 22 class sets from 1–4, 6–16, and 18–24) are non-capitalist class sets (by virtue of at least being non-exploitative).

Of the 22 'what are not capitalist class sets', at least 12 (i.e., class sets 2, 4, 6, 8, 10, 12, 14, 16, 18, 20, 22, and 24) are *outside* the circuits of global capital by virtue of their output distribution being in the non-commodity form.

The other ten non-capitalist class sets – even if they are non-capitalist, could be either inside (i.e., hooked to) or outside the circuits of global capital, depending on whether their produce is exchanged in the local-global market (see column 6 above) or the local market (see column 7 above). Interestingly, class sets 5 and 17, if they are not global capitalist enterprises, could also be inside (i.e., hooked to) or outside the circuits of global capital.

Thus depending on a host of mutually constitutive and contradictory contexts, the odd-numbered class sets in the above matrix can be inside or outside the circuits of global capital. *The even-numbered ones are, however, outside*. Thus, an *outside* to the circuits of global capital, marked by the even-numbered class sets and a few of the odd-numbered class sets, including (interestingly) even capitalist class sets, can be conceptualised as 'the world of the third as space'. No kind of *a priori* value can be imputed to the world of the third as space.

However, of the 12 non-capitalist class sets that are outside the circuits of global capital six (i.e., class sets 2, 4, 14, 16, 22, and 24) are non-exploitative in addition to being non-capitalist. Those six could be the ground and condition for a postcapitalist future. Also, of the 12 class sets (i.e., the odd-numbered ones) that could be hooked to the circuits of global capital, once again, six (class sets 1, 3, 11, 15, 21, and 23) are non-exploitative.

Thus class sets 2, 4, 14, 16, 22, and 24 constitute (and class sets 1, 3, 11, 15, 21, and 23 *could* also constitute) the *cocooned* fragment of the (a) non-capitalist and (b) non-exploitative sets in world of the third as space.

What is *crypted*, however, is that class sets 2, 4, 14, 16, 18, and 20 (as also class sets 1, 3, 11, 15, 21, and 23) are also the condition and ground for postcapitalist futures. It is postdevelopment praxis that takes us to an appreciation of that which is cocooned yet crypted within world of the third as space. Postdevelopmental praxis inaugurates world of the third *as* place.

To conclude, postdevelopment *and* postcapitalist praxis require a shift from conventional development studies and standard forms of developmental practices, which in turn needs to move beyond the local/global axis. This entails putting to question the extant idea of local as mere space and as a given ground of self-, social, and political transformation. For that one needs a concomitant interrogation of capitalocentrism, modernism, and orientalism. One hence needs to distinguish the concept of local from the third world 'local'; the mere invocation of the local without an

TABLE 5.2 Class sets and world of the third

No	Performance	Appropriation	Distribution	Workers' remuneration	Local-global markets[7]	Local Markets	World of the third (WOT)	Modes of appropriation
1	A	A	COM	WAGE	Possible	Possible		Non-E
2	**A**	**A**	**NON-COM**	**WAGE**	Possible	Possible	**WOT**	**Non-E**
3	A	A	COM	NON-WAGE	Possible	Possible		Non-E
4	**A**	**A**	**NON-COM**	**NON-WAGE**	Possible	Possible	**WOT**	**Non-E**
5	A	B	COM	WAGE	Possible	Possible	WOT	E
6	A	B	NON-COM	WAGE	Possible	Possible	WOT	E
7	A	B	COM	NON-WAGE	Possible	Possible	WOT	E
8	A	B	NON-COM	NON-WAGE	Possible	Possible	WOT	E
9	C	A	COM	WAGE	Possible	Possible	WOT	E
10	C	A	NON-COM	WAGE	Possible	Possible	WOT	E
11	C	A	COM	NON-WAGE	Possible	Possible	WOT	E
12	C	A	NON-COM	NON-WAGE	Possible	Possible	WOT	E
13	A	C	COM	WAGE	Possible	Possible		Non-E
14	**A**	**C**	**NON-COM**	**WAGE**	Possible	Possible	**WOT**	**Non-E**
15	A	C	COM	NON-WAGE	Possible	Possible		Non-E
16	**A**	**C**	**NON-COM**	**NON-WAGE**	Possible	Possible	**WOT**	**Non-E**
17	C	B	COM	WAGE	Possible	Possible	WOT	E
18	C	B	NON-COM	WAGE	Possible	Possible	WOT	E
19	C	B	COM	NON-WAGE	Possible	Possible	WOT	E
20	C	B	NON-COM	NON-WAGE			WOT	E

(*Continued*)

TABLE 5.2 (Cont.)

No	Performance	Appropriation	Distribution	Workers' remuneration	Local-global markets[7]	Local Markets	World of the third (WOT)	Modes of appropriation
21	C	C	COM	WAGE	Possible	Possible		Non-E
22	C	C	**NON-COM**	**WAGE**	Possible	Possible	**WOT**	**Non-E**
23	C	C	COM	NON-WAGE	Possible	Possible		Non-E
24	C	C	**NON-COM**	**NON-WAGE**	Final produce sold in local-global markets – hence class set hooked to circuits of global capital	Final produce sold in local markets – hence class set is *outside* circuits of global capital	Final produce not Sold in markets – hence class set is *outside* circuits of global capital	**Non-E**

A = individual, B= none, C = shared,
com: market commodity, non-com: non-market commodity and non-commodity
E: Exploitation; non-E: non-exploitation

interrogation of third worldism will not extricate us from local as space. The undertheorised local will emerge as the *substitute signifier* of the *unspoken/uncited* world of the third; this will keep us complicit with 'global capitalist hegemony'. Working through capitalocentrism-modernism-orientalism and local-global, we hence arrive at the circuits of global capital and world of the third as space-place via a class-focused analysis. This in turn shows how the local qua world of the third as space is replete with repositories of exploitation (non-capitalist class sets 6, 8, 10, 12, 18, 20) and requires struggle (from) within. The problem is not just that of the universalising global but also that of an under-examined local. The re-writing of the local initially as world of the third as space and then world of the third as *place* (Gibson-Graham 2016), opens the process of cultivating subjects (ourselves and others). Such subjects who inhabit non-capitalist economic spaces and non-orientalist cultural spaces could move in the direction of the politics of postcapitalist or post-orientalist place, birthing in the process the arduous work of postdevelopment praxis.

Notes

1 www.marxists.org/reference/archive/althusser/1962/overdetermination.htm.
2 'Place signifies the possibility of understanding local economies as *places* with highly specific economic identities and capacities rather than simply as *nodes* in a global capitalist system. In more broadly philosophical terms, place is that which is not fully yoked into a system of meaning, not entirely subsumed to a (global) order; it is that aspect of every site that exists as potentiality. Place is the 'event in space', operating as a 'dislocation' with respect to familiar structures and narratives. It is the unmapped and unmoored that allows for new moorings and mappings (Gibson-Graham 2016: 288).
3 Debaditya Bhattacharya (ed.) (2018) *The University Unthought: Notes for a Future*. London and New York: Routledge.
4 Sadler (in Sharr 2006: xii) shows how the thinking of the Frankfurt School on the one hand and of Heidegger's school on the other continue to define 'two forms of modern truth': 'the one discovered, through work in the metropolitan library and urban loft, by the dialectic of ideal and real, the other revealed by an encounter with an uncorrupted ideal at the rural retreat'. Tagore opted for the latter form.
5 An ontology directed by *phronesis* rather than *sophia* would not seek refuge in the realm of 'universal knowledge' or 'eternal certainty' (i.e., what cannot be otherwise) but would recognise its own inherent embeddedness in the world of praxis (i.e., what can be otherwise) and being-related to the with-which (see Long 2002: 36–37; Bowler 2008).
6 'Development, to paraphrase David Harvey (1993), and alternative development are dialectically organized oppositions within the history of modernity, to be seen less as mutually exclusive but as "oppositions that contain the other" (Harvey 1993: 15)' (see Watts in Crush 2005 [1995]: 59). Escobar has a different take on alternatives: 'to think about "alternatives to development" […] [marked by] a critical stance with respect to established scientific knowledge, an interest in local autonomy, culture and knowledge, and the defence of localized, pluralistic grassroots movements […] requires a theoretical and practical transformation in existing notions of development, modernity and the economy. This can best be achieved by building upon the practices of the social movements, especially those in the Third World. These movements are essential to the creation of alternative visions of democracy, economy and society' (Escobar in Crush 2005 [1995]: 206). Some social movements are concerned with 'resource mobilization'; some others 'emphasize struggles to constitute new identities as a means to open democratic spaces for more autonomous action' (Cohen 1985, as quoted by Escobar in Crush 2005 [1995]: 215).

7 When we refer to the local–global market with reference to a commodity, we mean the chain of local–local and global–global exchanges that make up the entire value chain of that commodity, via processes of outsourcing, subcontracting, off-shoring, body shopping, and so on. Generalising the structure, we can say that local markets and global markets are part of the same market chain as long as they connect to the circuits of global capital. Markets that connect to the circuits of global capital are, thus, a component of *local–global markets*. In contrast, there are *local markets* that do not form part of the circuits of global capital in the sense that none of the concerned enterprises there are connected to the circuits of global capital. We define such markets as *world of the third markets*.

References

Abraham, N. & Torok, M. (1986) *The Wolf Man's Magic Word: A Cryptonymy*, trans. Rand, N. Minneapolis: University of Minnesota Press

Arendt, H. (2005) *The Promise of Politics*, ed. Kohn, J. New York: Schocken Books.

Basole, A. (ed.) (2015) *Lokavidya Perspectives: A Philosophy of Political Imagination for the Knowledge Age*. New Delhi: Aakar Books.

Berger, M. (1994) 'The end of the "third world"'. *Third World Quarterly*, vol 15, no 2, pp 257–275.

Bowler, M. (2008) *Heidegger and Aristotle: Philosophy as Praxis*. New York and London: Continuum.

Carr, W. (2006) 'Philosophy, methodology and action research'. *Journal of Philosophy of Education*, vol 40, no 4, pp 421–435.

Chakrabarti, A. & Dhar, A. (2009) *Dislocation and Resettlement in Development: From Third World to World of the Third*. New York and London: Routledge.

Chakrabarti, A. & Dhar, A. (2013) 'Social funds, poverty management and subjectification: Beyond the World Bank approach'. *Cambridge Journal of Economics*, vol 37, no 5, pp 1–21.

Chakrabarti, A., Dhar, A.& Cullenberg, S. (2012) *World of the Third and Global Capitalism*. New Delhi: Worldview Press.

Chakrabarti, A., Dhar, A.& Cullenberg, S. (2016) '(Un)doing Marxism from the outside'. *Rethinking Marxism*, vol 28, no 2, pp 276–294.

Chaudhury, A. & Chakrabarti, A. (2000) 'The market economy and Marxist economists: Through the lens of a housewife'. *Rethinking Marxism*, vol 12, no 2, pp 81–103.

Crush, J. (ed.) (2005 [1995]) *Power of Development*. New York and London: Routledge.

Derrida, J. (2003) 'Women in the beehive'. In Jardine, A. & Smith, P. (eds.), *Men in Feminism*. New York and London: Routledge, pp 189–202.

Dhar, A. & Chakrabarti, A. (2015) 'The Althusser-Lacan correspondence as ground for psycho-social studies'. *Psychotherapy and Politics International*, vol 12, no 3, pp 220–233.

Dhar, A. & Chakrabarti, A. (2016) 'Marxism as ascetic: Spiritual as phronetic'. *Rethinking Marxism*, vol 29, no 1, pp 563–583.

Dunne, J. (1993) *Back to the Rough Ground: 'Phronesis' and 'Techne' in Modern Philosophy and in Aristotle*. London: University of Notre Dame Press.

Escobar, A. (1995) *Encountering Development: The Making and Unmaking of the Third World*. Princeton, NJ: Princeton University Press.

Escobar, A. (2005) 'Imagining a post-development era'. In Crush, J. (ed.), *Power of Development*. London and New York: Routledge, pp 205–222.

Gadamer, H.G. (1980) 'Practical philosophy as a model of the human sciences'. *Research in Phenomenology*, vol 9, pp 74–85.

Gibson-Graham, J.K. (1996) *The End of Capitalism (As We Knew It): A Feminist Critique of Political Economy*. Oxford: Blackwell.
Gibson-Graham, J.K. (2006) *A Postcapitalist Politics*. Minneapolis: University of Minnesota Press.
Gibson-Graham, J.K. (2016) 'Building community economies: Women and the politics of place'. In Harcourt, W. (ed.), *The Palgrave Handbook of Gender and Development*. London: Palgrave Macmillan, pp 359–368.
Haraway, D. (1992) 'Promises of monsters'. In Grossberg, L., Nelson, C., & Treichler, P. (eds.), *Cultural Studies*. London: Routledge, pp 295–337.
Harvey, D. (1993) 'From place to space and back again'. In Bird, J. et al. (eds.), *Mapping the Futures: Local Cultures, Global Change*. London: Routledge.
Heidegger, M. (1985 [1962]) *Being and Time*, trans. Macquarrie, J. & Robinson, E. Oxford: Basil Blackwell.
Heidegger, M. (1997) *Plato's Sophist*. Bloomington, IN: Indiana University Press.
Lacan, J. (2007) *The Seminar of Jacques Lacan – The Other Side of Psychoanalysis – Book XVII*, ed. and trans. Miller, J.-A., with notes by Grigg, R. New York and London: W. W. Norton & Company.
Lear, J. (2006) *Radical Hope: Ethics in the Face of Cultural Devastation*. Cambridge, MA and London: Harvard University Press.
Long, C.P. (2002) 'The ontological reappropriation of phronesis'. *Continental Philosophy Review*, vol 35, no 1, pp 35–60.
Marx, K. (2016). *Theses on Feuerbach*, trans. Smith, C. Marxists Internet Archive. Available at www.marxists.org/archive/marx/works/1845/theses/
Nandy, A. (1989) 'Shamans, savages and the wilderness: On the audibility of dissent and the future of civilisations'. *Alternatives*, vol 14, no 3, pp 263–278.
Porter, D.J. (2005) 'Scenes from childhood: The homesickness of development discourses'. In Crush, J. (ed.), *Power of Development*. London and New York: Routledge, pp 61–84.
Resnick, S. A. & Wolff, R.D. (1987) *Knowledge and Class*. Chicago: University of Chicago Press.
Roy, D. (2010) 'The poet as a polemicist and a prophet'. *Rupkatha Journal on Interdisciplinary Studies in Humanities*, vol 2, no 4, pp 677–682.
Said, E. (1978) *Orientalism*. New York: Pantheon.
Sen, A. (1984) '"Well-being, agency and freedom", The Dewey Lectures'. *Journal of Philosophy*, vol 82, no 4, pp 169–221.
Sharr, A. (2006) *Heidegger's Hut*. Foreword by Sadler, S., Prologue by Benjamin, A. Cambridge, MA: MIT Press.
Spivak, G.C. (1985) 'Three women's texts and a critique of imperialism'. *Critical Inquiry ("Race," Writing, and Difference)*, vol 12, no 1 (autumn), pp 243–261.
Spivak, G.C. (1994) 'Supplementing Marxism'. In Magnus, B. & Cullenberg, S. (eds.), *Whither Marxism? Global Crises in International Perspective*. New York: Routledge.
Spivak, G.C. (2004) 'Righting wrongs'. *The South Atlantic Quarterly*, vol 103, no 2/3, pp 523–581.
Tagore, R. (2011) *The Oxford India Tagore: Selected Writings on Education and Nationalism*, ed. Dasgupta, U. New Delhi: Oxford University Press.
Tagore, R. (2017) *The Parrot's Tale*, trans. Pal, P.B. Available at www.parabaas.com/translation/database/translations/stories/gRabindranath_parrot.html.
Watts, M. (2005) 'A new deal in emotions: Theory and practice and the crisis of development'. In Crush, J. (ed.), *Power of Development*. London and New York: Routledge, pp 43–60.

6
CRISIS AS OPPORTUNITY
Finding pluriversal paths

Ashish Kothari, Ariel Salleh, Arturo Escobar, Federico Demaria, and Alberto Acosta

There is no doubt that after decades of what has been called 'development', the world is in crisis – systemic, multiple, and asymmetrical; long in the making, it now extends across all continents. Never before did so many crucial aspects of life fail simultaneously, and people's expectations for their own and children's futures look so uncertain. Crisis manifestations are felt across all domains: environmental, economic, social, political, ethical, cultural, spiritual, and embodied. We need actions for renewal and re-politicization, where 'the political' means a collaboration among dissenting voices over the kinds of alternative worlds we want to create.[1]

A project concerned with postdevelopment should deepen and widen an agenda for research, dialogue, and action, for scholars, policymakers, and activists. It would offer a variety of worldviews and practices relating to our collective search for an ecologically wise and socially just world. This agenda would investigate the What, How, Who, for Whom, and Why of all that is transformative, as distinct from that which is not.[2] In the transition to 'a postdevelopment world', there may be companions with strategic vision, as well as others with good short-term tactical proposals. Democracy – as a process in permanent radicalization of itself – should speak to all areas of life, starting from the body and moving on to affirm its place in a living Earth Democracy.[3]

The seductive nature of development rhetoric – sometimes known as developmentality or developmentalism[4] – has been internalized across virtually all countries. Even some people who suffer the consequences of industrial growth in the Global North accept a unilinear path of progress. Many nations of the Global South have resisted attempts at environmental regulation with the charge that the North is preventing the South from reaching its own level of development. The international debate then moves on to 'monetary and technology transfers' from Global North to South, which, conveniently for the former, does not challenge basic premises of the development paradigm. These terms, 'Global North and South', are not geographic designations but have economic and geopolitical implications.[5] 'Global North' therefore may describe both historically dominant nations as well as colonized but wealthy ruling elites in the South. Similarly, for new alter-globalization alliances, 'South' can be a metaphor for exploited ethnic minorities or women in affluent countries, as much as the historically colonized or 'poorer' countries as a whole.

Decades after the notion of development spread around the world, only a handful of countries called 'underdeveloped', or 'developing', or 'Third World' – to use deprecating Cold War terms – really qualify as 'developed'. Others struggle to emulate the North's economic template, and all at enormous ecological and social cost. The problem lies not in lack of implementation, but in the conception of development as linear, unidirectional, material, and financial growth, driven by commodification and capitalist markets. Despite numerous attempts to re-signify development, it continues to be something that 'experts' manage in pursuit of economic growth, and measure by gross domestic product (GDP), a poor and misleading indicator of progress in the sense of well-being. In truth, the world at large experiences 'maldevelopment', not least in the very industrialized countries whose lifestyle was meant to serve as a beacon for the 'backward' ones.

A critical part of our problems lies in the conception of 'modernity' itself – not to suggest that everything modern is destructive or iniquitous, nor that all tradition is positive. Indeed, modern elements such as human rights and feminist principles are proving liberatory for many people. We refer to modernity as the dominant worldview emerging in Europe since the Renaissance transition from the Middle Ages to the early modern period, and consolidating towards the end of the eighteenth century. Not least among these cultural practices and institutions has been a belief in the individual as independent of the collective, and in private property, free markets, political liberalism, secularism,[6] and representative democracy. Another key feature of modernity is 'universalism' – the idea that we all live in a single, now globalized world, and, critically, the idea of science as the only reliable truth and harbinger of 'progress'.

Among the early causes of this multiple crisis is the ancient monotheistic premise that a father 'God' made the Earth for the benefit of 'His' human children. This attitude is known as anthropocentrism.[7] At least in the West, it evolved into a philosophic habit of pitting humanity against nature, and gave rise to related dualisms such as the divide between subject versus object, mind versus body, masculine versus feminine, civilized versus barbarian. These classic ideological categories legitimize devastation of the natural world, as well as the exploitation of sex-gender, racial, and civilizational differences. Feminists emphasize the 'masculinist culture of domination' carried by these artificial pairs; intellectuals in the Global South emphasize their 'coloniality'. The modern colonial capitalist patriarchal world system[8] thus marginalizes and demeans forms of knowing, such as caregiving and non-Western law, science, or economies. This is the prevailing political pattern globally, yet there have been alternative forms in Europe, as well as 'modernities' in Latin America, China, and so forth.

The global crisis is not manageable within existing institutional frameworks. It is historical and structural, demanding a deep cultural awakening and re-organization of relations both within and between societies across the world, as also between humans and the rest of so-called 'nature'. As humans, our most important lesson is to make peace with the Earth and with each other. Everywhere, people are experimenting with how to meet their needs in ways that assert the rights and dignity of Earth and its threatened inhabitants. The search is a response to ecological collapse, land grabs, oil wars, and forms of extractivism, such as agroindustry and plantations of genetically engineered species. In human terms, this theft brings loss of rural livelihoods and urban poverty. Sometimes Western 'progress' gives way or leads to diseases of affluence, alienation, and rootlessness. But people's resistance movements are now taking place across every continent. *The Environmental Justice Atlas* documents and catalogs over 2000 conflicts,[9] proving the existence of an active global environmental justice movement, even if it is not yet a united one.

There is no guarantee that 'development' will resolve traditional discrimination and violence against women, youth, children, and intersex minorities, landless and unemployed classes, races, castes, and ethnicities.[10] As globalizing capital destabilizes regional economies, turning communities into wasted lives and refugee populations, some people cope by identifying with the macho power of the political Right. This prioritizes national identity and promises to 'take the jobs back' from the migrant scapegoats. At times, an insecure working-class Left can adopt this stance too, not recognizing the culpability of banks and corporations for their predicament. A drift towards authoritarianism is taking place all over the world, from India to Brazil, to the USA and Europe. The illusion of representative democracy is kept alive by a privileged technocratic class with its neoliberal trajectory of innovation for green growth. There is a fuzzy line between the Right and the orthodox Left when it comes to productivism, modernization, and progress. Moreover, each such ideology builds on eurocentric and masculinist values, so reinforcing the status quo.

Karl Marx reminded us that when a new society is born from inside the old, it drags many defects of the old system along with it. Later, Antonio Gramsci would observe of his time that 'The crisis consists precisely in the fact that the old is dying and the new cannot be born; in this interregnum a great variety of morbid symptoms appear.'[11] What these European Left intellectuals did not anticipate was how, today, alternatives are also emerging from the political margins – from both the colonial periphery and the domestic periphery of capitalism. The Marxist analysis remains necessary but it is not sufficient; it needs to be complemented by perspectives such as feminism and ecology, as well as imaginations emanating from the Global South, including Gandhian. In a time of transition such as this, critique and action call for new narratives combined with hands-on material solutions. Doing more of the same, but better, or less of the same is not enough. The way forward is not simply to make corporations more accountable or to set up regulative bureaucracies; it is not even a matter only of recognizing full citizenship for the 'colored', 'elderly', 'disabled', 'women', or 'queer' through liberal pluralist policy. Likewise, the conservation of a few 'pristine' patches of nature at the margins of urban capitalism will have little effect on the collapse of biodiversity.

We write at a time when the great twentieth-century political models – liberal representative democracy and state socialism – have become incoherent and dysfunctional forms of governance, even if achieving welfare and rights for a few.

***

Following these critical perspectives, it is important to examine the limits of developmentalism as it shapes reformist solutions to global crises. Here we see the ghost of modernity reincarnated in infinite ways, as short-sighted crisis remedies of those in power keep the North–South status quo in place. These include, amongst other topics, market-mechanisms, geo-engineering and climate-smart agriculture, the population question, green economics, reproductive engineering, and transhumanism. An over-arching theme is the much-celebrated political gesture of 'sustainable development'. Of course, even well-intentioned people may inadvertently promote superficial or false solutions to global problems. Then again, it is not so easy to distinguish mainstream or superficial initiatives from 'radical transformative' ones, in these days when the military-industrial-media complex and greenwashing industry promotions are at their most seductive best.

Criticism of industrialization is not new. Mary Shelley (1797–1851), Karl Marx (1818–1883), and Mohandas Gandhi (1869–1948), each in their own way, expressed misgivings about it, as have many people's movements throughout the last two centuries. The earlier twentieth-century debate on sustainability was strongly influenced by the Club of Rome's *Limits to Growth* argument,[12] and official circles have expressed concern about mass-production technologies and consumption patterns since the 1972 United Nations Conference on Environment and Development in Stockholm. Regular conferences at a global level would reiterate the mismatch between 'development and environment', with the 1987 report *Our Common Future* bringing it sharply into focus. However, the UN and most nation-state analyses have never included a critique of social structural forces underlying ecological breakdown. The framing has always been on making economic growth and development 'sustainable and inclusive' through appropriate technologies, markets, and institutional policy reform. The problem is that this mantra of sustainability was swallowed up by capitalism early on, and then emptied of ecological content.

In the period from the 1980s on, neoliberal globalization advanced aggressively across the globe. The UN now shifted focus to a program of 'poverty alleviation' in developing countries, without questioning the sources of poverty in the accumulation-driven economy of the affluent Global North. In fact, it was argued that countries needed to achieve a high standard of living before they could deploy resources in protecting the environment.[13] So, economic 'growth' was redefined as a necessary step.[14] This watering down of earlier debates on limits opened the way for the ecological modernist 'green economy' concept. The new millennium has seen a plethora of such Keynesian proposals – the bio-economy, Green Revolution for Africa, Chinese and European promotion of the Circular Economy, and the 2030 Agenda for Sustainable Development.[15]

At the UN Conference for Sustainable Development in 2012, this hollow sustainability ideology was the guiding framework for multilateral discussions. For some time, the United Nations Environmental Programme (UNEP), together with the corporate sector, some even on the political Left,[16] had been talking enthusiastically about the need for a 'green new deal'. In preparation for Rio+20, UNEP published a report on the Green Economy, defining it 'as one that results in improved human well-being and social equity, while significantly reducing environmental risks and ecological scarcities'.[17] In line with the pro-growth policy of sustainable development advocates, the report conceptualized all living natural forms across the planet as 'natural capital' and 'critical economic assets', so intensifying the marketable commodification of Life-on-Earth. However, opposition from alter-globalization activists was fierce.

The official Rio+20 final declaration advocates economic growth in more than twenty of its articles. This approach is based on a supposed greening of neoclassical economic theory called 'environmental economics', a belief that growth can de-link or decouple itself from nature through dematerialization and de-pollution by what is called 'eco-efficiency'. However, empirical cradle-to-grave and social metabolism studies from ecological economics show that such production has 'dematerialized' in relative terms – using less energy and materials per unit of GDP – but it has not reduced overall or absolute amounts of materials and energy, which is what matters for sustainability. Historically, the only periods of absolute dematerialization coincide with economic recession.[18] The popular idea of 'economic efficiency' falls far short of respecting biophysical limits – in nature and natural resources, in ecosystem assimilative capacity, or in planetary boundaries.

The international model of green capitalism carried forward in the declaration *Transforming Our World: The 2030 Agenda for Sustainable Development*[19] reveals the following flaws in what have become known as the Sustainable Development Goals (SDGs)[20]:

- no analysis of how the structural roots of poverty, unsustainability, and multi-dimensional violence are historically grounded in state power, corporate monopolies, neocolonialism, and patriarchal institutions;
- inadequate focus on direct democratic governance with accountable decision-making by citizens and self-aware communities in face-to-face settings;
- continued emphasis on economic growth as the driver of development, contradicting biophysical limits, with arbitrary adoption of GDP as the indicator of progress;
- continued reliance on economic globalization as the key economic strategy, undermining people's attempts at self-reliance and autonomy;

- continued subservience to private capital, and unwillingness to democratize the market through worker–producer and community control;
- modern science and technology held up as social panaceas, ignoring their limits and impacts, and marginalizing 'other' knowledges;
- culture, ethics, and spirituality sidelined and made subservient to economic forces;
- unregulated consumerism without strategies to reverse the Global North's disproportionate contamination of the globe through waste, toxicity, and climate emissions;
- neoliberal architectures of global governance becoming increasingly reliant on technocratic managerial values by state and multi-lateral bureaucracies.

This 2015 framework of Sustainable Development Goals (SDGs), now global in its reach, is a false consensus.[21] For instance, SDG 8 calls for 'sustained economic growth', which entails several contradictions with the majority of the other SDGs. If 'development' is seen as a toxic term to be rejected,[22] then 'sustainable development' becomes an oxymoron. More specifically, the degrowth theorist Giorgios Kallis has commented: 'Sustainable development and its more recent reincarnation "green growth" depoliticise genuine political antagonisms between alternative visions for the future. They render environmental problems technical, promising win-win solutions and the impossible goal of perpetuating economic growth without harming the environment.'[23] This is what happens with reformist solutions.

We do not mean to belittle the work of people who are finding new technological solutions to reduce problems, for instance, in renewable energy, nor do we mean to diminish the many positive elements contained in the SDG framework.[24] Rather, our aim is to stress that in the absence of fundamental socio-cultural transformation, technological and managerial innovation will not lead us out of the crises.[25] As nation-states and civil society gear up for the SDGs, it is imperative to lay out criteria to help people make such a distinction.

***

In counterpoint to the blinders of conventional political reason, a range of complementary notions and practices that form radical and systemic alternatives have been put forward.[26] Some of these revive or creatively re-interpret long-standing Indigenous worldviews; others come from recent social movements; yet others revisit older philosophies and religious traditions. All of them ask: what is so badly wrong with everyday life today? Who is responsible for it? What would a better life look like? And, how do we get there? As feminists for the '*sostenibilidad de la vida*' ask: 'What is a life worth living? And, how can conditions that allow it to happen be met?'[27]

Together, these perspectives compose a 'pluriverse': a world where many worlds fit, as the Zapatistas of Chiapas put it. All people's worlds should co-exist with dignity and peace without being subjected to diminishment, exploitation, and misery. A pluriversal world overcomes patriarchal attitudes, racism, casteism, and other forms of discrimination. Here, people re-learn what it means to be a humble part of 'nature', leaving behind narrow anthropocentric notions of progress based on economic growth. While many pluriversal articulations synergize with each other, unlike the universalizing ideology of sustainable development, they cannot be reduced to an overarching policy for administration by a UN or some other global governance regime, nor by regional or state regimes. We envision a world confluence of alternatives, provoking strategies for transition, including small everyday actions, towards a great transformation.

The project of deconstructing development opens into a matrix of alternatives, from universe to pluriverse. Some visions and practices are already well-known in activist and academic circles. For instance, *buen vivir*, 'a culture of life' with various names throughout South America; *ubuntu*, emphasizing the southern African value of human mutuality; *swaraj* from India, centred on self-reliance and self-governance.[28] There are thousands of such transformative alternatives around the world. Others, less well known but equally relevant, would be *kyosei, minobimaatisiiwin, nayakrishi*, as well as critically reflective versions of major religions including Islam, Christianity, Hinduism, Buddhism, and Judaism. So, too, political visions such as eco-socialism and deep ecology share points of convergence with earlier communal ideals. While many terms have a long history, they reappear in the narrative of movements for well-being and, again, co-exist comfortably with contemporary concepts such as degrowth and ecofeminism.[29]

From North, South, East, or West, each strand in the postdevelopment rainbow symbolizes human emancipation 'within nature'.[30] It is the latter bond that distinguishes a pluriversal project from cultural relativism. As Aldo Leopold would say: 'A thing is right when it tends to preserve the integrity, stability, and beauty of the *biotic community*. It is wrong when it tends otherwise.'[31] While making peace with the Earth, another peacemaking goal is linking ancestral and contemporary knowledges together in a process that will demand horizontal and respectful dialogue. That said, there are no blueprints valid for all times and places, just as no theory is immune to questioning. Indeed, this kind of historical reflexivity is only now becoming recognized as a terrain of politics. The response to macro-power structures like capital and empire is a well-travelled landscape; what is still largely unexplored is the field of micro- or capillary power that feeds everyday violence. Honorable rhetorics of abstract justice, even spiritual paeans to Mother Earth, will not suffice to bring about the changes we want. Building a pluriversal house means digging a new foundation.

Transformative alternatives differ from mainstream or reformist solutions in a number of ways. Ideally, they will go to the roots of a problem. They will question what we have already identified as core features of the development discourse – economic growth, productivism, the rhetoric of progress, instrumental rationality, markets, universality, anthropocentrism, and sexism. These transformative alternatives will encompass an ethic that is radically different from the one underpinning the current system. Transformative alternatives reflect values grounded in a relational logic; a world where everything is connected to everything else.

There are many paths towards a bio-civilization, but we may envisage societies that encompass the following values and more:

- diversity and pluriversality
- autonomy and self-reliance
- solidarity and reciprocity
- commons and collective ethics
- oneness with and rights of nature
- interdependence
- simplicity and enoughness
- inclusiveness and dignity
- justice and equity
- non-hierarchy
- dignity of labor
- rights and responsibilities
- ecological sustainability
- non-violence and peace[32]

Political agency will belong to the marginalized, exploited, and oppressed. And transformations will integrate and mobilize multiple dimensions, though not necessarily all at once. One exemplar of that vision might be the set of confluences called Vikalp Sangam taking place in India since 2014.[33] The principles and goals advanced by this movement are the following.

- *Ecological wisdom, integrity and resilience*: where primacy is given to maintaining eco-regenerative processes that conserve ecosystems, species, functions, and cycles; respecting ecological limits from local to global; and where there is an infusion of ecological ethics into all human activities.
- *Social well-being and justice*: where fulfilment is physical, social, cultural, and spiritual; there is equity in socio-economic and political entitlements and responsibilities; non-discriminatory relations and communal harmony replace hierarchies based on faith, gender, caste, class, ethnicity, ability, and age; and where collective and individual human rights are ensured.
- *Direct and delegated democracy*: where consensus decision-making occurs at the smallest unit of settlement, in which every human has the right, capacity, and opportunity to take part; establishing democratic governance by directly accountable delegates in ways that are consensual, respectful, and supportive of the needs and rights of those currently marginalized, for example, young people or religious minorities.
- *Economic democratization*: where private property gives way to the commons, removing the distinction between owner and worker; where communities

and individuals – ideally 'prosumers' – have autonomy over local production, distribution, and markets; where localization is a key principle, with trade built on the principle of equal exchange.
- *Cultural diversity and knowledge democracy*: where a plurality of ways of living, ideas, and ideologies is respected; creativity and innovation are encouraged; and the generation, transmission and use of knowledge – traditional or modern, including science and technology – is accessible to all.

***

So where are women – 'the other half' of humanity – in all this? How do we ensure that a postdevelopment pluriverse does not dissolve coloniality while keeping women 'in their place' as the material bearers of everyday life activities? A first step in the anticipation of deep systemic change is to question how both traditional and modern practices and knowledges privilege 'masculinity' and the opportunities that go with it. Originally, the two words 'economy' and 'ecology' shared the one Greek root – *oikos*, meaning 'our home'. But soon enough, this unity was broken apart as men's self-appointed domination over nature came to include the exploitation of women's energies. Whole civilizations have been built on the sex-gendered control of women's fertility – the quintessential resource for continuance of any political regime. This turned women into 'means' not 'ends', mere chattels, so taking away their standing as full human individuals in their own right.

Ironically, the economy or productive sector, as it is known in the Global North, now destroys its very own social and ecological foundations in the reproductive sector. Women across the world, and especially in the Global South, have challenged this irrational development ethos – Latin American and Pacific feminisms; PeaceWomen; matriarchies; wages for housework; body politics; gift economies; and ecofeminism. Most of these initiatives are grounded in women's struggles for survival. They link political emancipation with environmental justice, local problems with global structures, usually arguing for sustainable subsistence against linear progress and 'catch-up development'.[34] Conversely, mainstream Western feminism tends to be anthropocentric, such that liberal and even socialist feminists may be pacified with the goal of 'equality'. In this way, their politics unwittingly band-aids existing masculinist institutions.

Official UN and government analyses have never included a thorough critique of structural forces underlying ecological breakdown. Similarly, the deep structure of ancient patriarchal values carried forward by global development remains unexamined. Known as 'the longest revolution', the liberation of women from social domination by men will be no easy matter. Even policy experts too often conflate the well-being of household or community with the well-being of the breadwinner, ignoring a domestic power hierarchy. In academia, the postmodern tendency to reduce embodied sexual identity to the construct of 'gender' is another unhelpful convention. In the same way, treating 'class, race, and gender' as abstract 'intersectional structures' can deflect attention from the raw materiality of lived experience.

Formal democratic gestures – the vote or wage equality for women – barely scratch the surface of centuries-old habits of sex-gender oppression.[35] An adherence to spiritual virtues, or strong secular principles such as diversity and solidarity, can help, but do not guarantee an end to the biophysical impacts of sex-gender violence.

Activists seeking just and sustainable alternatives need to acknowledge this unspoken level of political materiality. To varying degrees, women both in the North and the South face silencing and harassment; they lack not only resources, but often freedom of movement. They live with issues such as culturally sanctioned indignities over menstruation, clitoral excision, polygamy, dowry murder, honor killing, suttee, pinching, groping, and now digitized revenge porn. They endure enforced child bearing, domestic violence, marital rape, youth gang rape, genocidal rape as a weapon of war, stigmatization as widows and persecution as 'witches' in old age. In the twenty-first century, a combination of female foeticide, privatized violence, and militarized collateral damage on civilian populations is resulting in a falling demographic ratio of women to men globally. In Asia alone, one-and-a-half million women have lost their lives in the last decade due to such factors.

The abuse of children and cruelty to animals are further aspects of the ancient yet widespread patriarchal prerogative over 'lesser' life forms. These activities are a form of extractivism; a gratification through energies drawn from other kinds of bodies, those deemed 'closer to nature'. Following Elizabeth Dodson Gray's pioneering analysis, ecofeminist scholars have offered a deep historical critique of the global capitalist patriarchal order – its religions, economics, and science. In deconstructing the continuing potency of ancient ideological dualisms – humanity over nature, man over woman, boss over worker, white over black, they have shown different forms of social domination to be interrelated.[36] Thus, a 'politics of care' enacted by women from Global North and South converges with the mores of *buen vivir, ubuntu,* and *swaraj,* because across the hemispheres women's everyday labors teach 'another logic', not controlling and instrumental but 'relational' – like the rationality of ecological processes.[37] In its deepest articulation, these pluriversal voices contest both modernity and traditionalism by locating the material embodiment of class, race, sex-gender, and species inside an eco-centric frame. There can be no pluriverse until the historical underpinnings of masculine entitlement are part of the political conversation.

***

Readers will rightly question the confidence that we, and numerous other critical scholars and activists, invest in the idea of 'community'. True, it is a contested term, one that can readily hide oppressions based on sex-gender, age, class, caste, ethnicity, race, or ability. We recognize, too, that 'localized' governance or economies are often xenophobic – a parochialism seen currently in the nationalist opposition to refugees in many parts of the world. Beset by intolerance on the Right, and a defensive 'identity politics' on the Left, our compendium of alternatives reaches for integrative and inclusive practices. Hopefully, life-affirming elements can be discovered even in some of the world's patriarchal religions, and we hope to cultivate that potential.

The ideal of communality envisaged here carries the paradigmatic sense of today's movements towards 'commoning' or *la comunalidad*. As in the case of the initiatives networked by Vikalp Sangam, these collectives are based on autonomous decision-making via face-to-face relations and economic exchange directed at meeting basic needs through self-reliance.[38] Our understanding of community is a critical one: 'in process' and always questioning the modern capitalist patriarchal hegemony of the 'individual' as kernel of society. We hope this book inspires counter-movements to that globally colonizing pressure, just as we are inspired, in turn, by cultural groups across the world that still enjoy a collective existence.[39] In this context, Mexican sociologist Raquel Gutiérrez Aguilar proposes a concept of *entramados comunitarios* or communitarian entanglements.

> [T]he multiplicity of human worlds that populate and engender the world under diverse norms of respect, collaboration, dignity, love, and reciprocity, that are not completely subjected to the logic of capital accumulation even if often under attack and overwhelmed by it [...] such community entanglements [...] are found under diverse formats and designs. [...] They include the diverse and immensely varied collective human configurations, some long-standing, others younger, that confer meaning and 'furnish' what in classical political philosophy is known as 'socio-natural space'.
>
> (Gutiérrez Aguilar 2013: 33)

Many radical worldviews and practices make the pluriverse visible. In speaking about them, we enhance their existence and viability. In fact, the very proliferation of assertions coming from these 'other' worlds makes alternatives possible. Conversely, it is in this sense that mainstream or reformist development solutions can be proven false. In responding to the ecological crisis, 'experts' in the Global North take the categories of One World responsible for devastation of the planet as the very point of departure for their alleged solutions! However, their commitment to *la dolce vita* cannot enlighten us on the fundamental task of making the pluriverse sustainable. To repeat: the notion of the pluriverse questions the very concept of universality that is central to eurocentric modernity. With their phrase 'A world where many worlds fit', the Zapatistas give us the most succinct and apt definition of the pluriverse.

Whereas the West managed to sell its own idea of One World – known only by modern science and ruled by its own cosmovision – the alter-globalization movements propose pluriversality as a shared project based on the multiplicity of 'ways of worlding'. Under conditions of asymmetric power, Indigenous peoples have had to alienate their own common-sense experience of the world and learn how to live with the eurocentric masculinist dualism between humans and non-humans, which led to the treatment of Indigenous Peoples as non-human and 'natural resources'. They resist this separation when they mobilize on behalf of mountains, lakes, or rivers, arguing that these are sentient beings with 'rights', not mere objects or resources. Complementarily, many people in the industrialized world are demanding rights for the rest of nature to be expressed in law and policy. In so doing they are taking a step toward incorporating something that Indigenous peoples have always integrated into their worldview, but they are doing so in the formal ways that they are familiar with.[40] There is a long way to go for the multiplicity of worlds to become fully complementary with each other, but movements for justice and ecology are finding increasing common ground. So, too, women's political struggles converge upon this same point.

In both the Global North and South, it is most often ordinary care-giving mothers and grandmothers who join this entanglement – defending and reconstituting communal ways of being and place-based forms of autonomy. In doing so, they, like the Indigenous Peoples described earlier, draw on non-patriarchal ways of doing, being, and knowing.[41] They invite participation, collaboration, respect, and mutual acceptance and horizontality; they honour sacredness in the cyclic renewal of life. Their tacitly matriarchal cultures resist ontologies, founded on domination, hierarchy, control, power, the negation of others, violence, and war. From the worldwide movement of Peace Women to African anti-extractivist networks, women are defending nature and humanity with the clear message that there can be no decolonization without de-patriarchalization.

Such initiatives resonate powerfully with the postdevelopment concepts profiled in our book.[42] For the pluriverse is not just a fashionable concept, it is a *practice*. Societal imaginaries based on human rights and the rights of nature are impossible to arrive at through top-down intervention. Initiatives such as the Transition Movement or Ecovillages can contain a mix of reformist and broader systemic changes. Emancipatory projects will rely on solidarity across continents and they can work hand-in-hand with resistance movements. This is exemplified by the Yasuní–ITT initiative in Ecuador, which urges: 'leave the oil in the soil, the coal in the hole, and the tar sands in the land'.[43] To live according to the insights of multiple partially connected, if radically different, worlds may mean holding traditional and modern certainties and universals at bay in our personal and collective lives. We are striving to provide some concept-tools and practices for honoring a pluriverse, fostering a bio-civilization that is eco-centric, diverse, and multidimensional, and one that is able to find a balance between individual and communal needs. This living, pre-figurative politics is based on the principle of creating right now the foundations of the worlds we want to see come to fruition in the future; it implies a contiguity of means and ends.

How do we get from here to there? We are, after all, talking about profound shifts in the spheres of economy, politics, society, culture, and lived sexuality! Transitioning implies accepting an ensemble of measures and changes in different domains of life and at different geographic scales. Transitions can be messy and not fully radical, but can be considered 'alternative' if they at least hold a potential for living change. Given the diversity of imaginative visions across the globe, the question of how to build synergies among them remains open. There will be setbacks; strategies will fade along the way and others will emerge. Differences, tensions, even contradictions, will exist, but these can become a basis for constructive exchange. The ways towards the pluriverse are multiple, open, and in continuous evolution.

Notes

1 This chapter is based on the introduction to the recently edited volume by Kothari, A., Salleh, A., Escobar, A., Demaria, F. & Acosta, A. (2019) *The Post-Development Dictionary*. Delhi: Authors Upfront and Tulika. Where the chapter mentions 'our book' or 'compendium', it is this publication that is being referred to.
2 For initial thoughts on the *Post-Development Dictionary* agenda, see Demaria & Kothari (2017). For an early attempt to articulate different alternatives to development, see Kothari, Demaria & Acosta (2015) and Beling, Vanhulst, Demaria, Rabid, Carballo & Pelenc (2018). The latter discusses discursive synergies for a 'great transformation' towards sustainability among human development, degrowth and *buen vivir* advocates.
3 Shiva: www.navdanya.org/earth-democracy.
4 Nandy (2003: 164–175); Mies (1986); Deb (2009); Shrivastava & Kothari (2012).
5 Salleh (2006).
6 Used here in the sense of an anti- or non-spiritual and religious orientation, not in the sense of an orientation that equally respects all faiths and non-faith belief systems.
7 Or, as Dobson (1995) argues, 'human instrumentalism', since we may all inevitably be a bit human-centered in a neutral way. However, the analysis of ideological dualism, as such, is owed to ecofeminist thinker Elizabeth Dodson Gray (1979).
8 Grosfoguel & Mielants (2006).
9 The Environmental Justice Atlas (EJ Atlas) collects the stories of struggling communities and is the largest worldwide inventory of such conflicts. It aims to make these mobilizations more visible, highlight claims and testimonies, and make a case for true corporate and state accountability for injustices inflicted through their activities (Martinez-Alier, Temper, Del Bene & Scheidel 2016; Scheidel, Temper, Demaria & Martínez-Alier 2018): https://ejatlas.org/.
10 Navas, Mingorria & Aguilar (2018).
11 Gramsci (1971 [1930]: 275–276).
12 Meadows, Meadows, Randers & Behrens (1972).
13 See, for instance, a presentation by former Indian Prime Minister Manmohan Singh (1992), and a critique of this in Shrivastava & Kothari (2012: 121–122).
14 Gómez-Baggethun & Naredo (2015).
15 Salleh (2016).
16 For example, the New Economics Foundation, London, and Rosa Luxemburg Stiftung, Berlin.
17 UNEP (2011); Salleh (2012).
18 Ecological economists have provided significant empirical evidence with their sociometabolic analyses, which measure the energy and material flows of the economy. For an example, see Krausmann, Gingrich, Eisenmenger, Erb, Haberl & Fischer-Kowalski (2009) and Jorgenson & Clark (2012). For a discussion of method, see Gerber & Scheidel (2018).
19 SDSN (2013); UNEP (2011); UN Secretary General Panel (2012); United Nations (2013); United Nations (2015).
20 Adapted from Kothari (2013).
21 This phenomenon was anticipated in pioneering work by Shiva (1989) and Hornborg (2009).

22 Dearden (2014).
23 Kallis (2015).
24 For a critical but appreciative view of the potential of the SDG framework, see Club de Madrid (2017), *A New Paradigm for Sustainable Development?* Summary of the deliberations of the Club de Madrid Working Group on Environmental Sustainability and Shared Societies. www.clubmadrid.org/en/publicacion/a_new_paradigm_for_sustainable_development.
25 See also www.lowtechmagazine.com/about.html.
26 For earlier contributions: Salleh (2017 [1997]); Kothari, Demaria & Acosta (2015); Escobar (2015); Beling, Vanhulst, Demaria, Rabid, Carballo & Pelenc (2018).
27 The phrase is Spanish for 'sustainability of life': Pérez Orozco (2014).
28 Gudynas (2011); Metz (2011); Kothari (2014).
29 Demaria, Schneider, Sekulova & Martinez-Alier (2013); D'Alisa, Demaria & Kallis (2014); Bennholdt-Thomsen & Mies (1999); Salleh (2017 [1997]).
30 Salleh (2017/1997); Sousa Santos (2009).
31 Leopold (1994: 224).
32 For an extensive and intensive process of visioning the elements and values of radical alternatives, see the Vikalp Sangam (Alternatives Confluences) process in India, ongoing since 2014: http://kalpavriksh.org/our-work/alternatives/vikalp-sangam/ and the vision note emerging from this at www.vikalpsangam.org/about/the-search-for-alternatives-key-aspects-and-principles/.
33 Adapted from the Vikalp Sangam vision note, at www.vikalpsangam.org/about/the-search-for-alternatives-key-aspects-and-principles/.
34 Bennholdt-Thomsen & Mies (1999).
35 Wages for women in developed economies stand at approximately seventy per cent of the male wage for equivalent work. Men in developed economies spend less than twenty minutes a day with their children. In modern India, only fifteen percent of women are in the paid workforce.
36 Dodson-Gray (1979), Merchant (1980), Waring (1987).
37 Salleh (2017 [1997], 2011, 2012).
38 For a detailed narrative on the legitimacy of using 'community' and its various derivatives, one acknowledging the contestations, see Escobar (2010, 2014).
39 See www.congresocomunalidad2015.org/ for details of the First International Congress on Comunalidad, 2015, convened at Puebla, Mexico, where these issues were discussed at length.
40 See, for instance, Kauffman & Sheehan (2018); and https://therightsofnature.org.
41 This ethic should not be read through the lens of liberal ideology; that is, as women's 'essential nature'. It is a learned outcome of the experience of care-giving labors, historically assigned to women across most cultures.
42 Acosta & Brand (2017).
43 Acosta (2014).

References and further reading

Acosta, A. (2014) 'Iniciativa Yasuní-ITT: La difícil construcción de la utopía'. *Rebelión*. www.rebelion.org/noticia.php?id=180285.

Acosta, A. & Brand, U. (2017) *Salidas del laberinto capitalista. decrecimiento y postextractivismo*. Barcelona: Icaria.

Beling, A., Vanhulst, J., Demaria, F., Rabid, V., Carballo, A. & Pelenc, J. (2018) 'Discursive synergies for a "great transformation" towards sustainability: Pragmatic contributions to a necessary dialogue between human development, degrowth, and buen vivir'. *Ecological Economics*, vol 144, pp 304–313.

Bennholdt-Thomsen, V. & Mies, M. (1999) *The Subsistence Perspective*. London: Zed Books.

D'Alisa, G., Demaria, F. & Kallis, G. (2014) *Degrowth: A Vocabulary for a New Era*. London: Routledge.

Dearden, N. (2014) 'Is development becoming a toxic term?' *Guardian*, 22 January 2014. www.theguardian.com/global-development-professionals-network/2015/jan/22/development-toxic-term?CMP=share_btn_tw.

Deb, D. (2009) *Beyond Developmentality*. Delhi: Daanish Books.

Demaria, F. & Kothari, A. (2017) 'The post-development dictionary agenda: Paths to the pluriverse'. *Third World Quarterly*, vol 38, no 12, pp 2588–2599.

Demaria, F., Schneider, F., Sekulova, F. & Martinez-Alier, J. (2013) 'What is degrowth? From an activist slogan to a social movement'. *Environmental Values*, vol 22, no 2, pp 191–215.

Dobson, A. (1995) *Green Political Thought*. London: Routledge.

Dodson-Gray, E. (1979) *Green Paradise Lost*. Wellesley, MA: Roundtable Press.

Escobar, A. (1995) *Encountering Development*. Princeton, NJ: Princeton University Press.

Escobar, A. (2010) 'Latin America at a crossroads: Alternative modernizations, postliberalism, or postdevelopment?' *Cultural Studies*, vol 24, no 1, pp 1–65.

Escobar, A. (2011) 'Sustainability: Design for the pluriverse'. *Development*, vol 54, no 2, pp 137–140.

Escobar, A. (2014) *Sentipensar con la tierra: Nuevas lecturas sobre sobre desarrollo, territorio y diferencia*. Medellín: Universidad Autonoma Latinoamericana (UNAULA).

Escobar, A. (2015) 'Degrowth, post-development, and transitions: A preliminary conversation'. *Sustainability Science*, vol 10, no 3, pp 451–462.

Escobar, A. (2018) *Designs for the Pluriverse: Radical Interdependence, Autonomy, and the Making of Worlds*. Durham, NC: Duke University Press.

EZLN, Ejército Zapatista de Liberación Nacional. (1997) 'Fourth declaration of the Lacandon jungle'. www.struggle.ws/mexico/ezln/jung4.html.

Gandhi, M. (1997/1909) 'Hind Swaraj'. In Parel, A. (ed.), *M. K. Gandhi: Hind Swaraj and Other Writings*. Cambridge: Cambridge University Press.

Gerber, J.-F. & Scheidel, A. (2018) 'In search of substantive economics: Comparing today's two major socio-metabolic approaches to the economy - MEFA and MuSIASEM'. *Ecological Economics*, vol 144, pp 186–194

Gómez-Baggethun, E. & Naredo, J.M. (2015) 'In search of lost time: The rise and fall of limits to growth in international sustainability policy'. *Sustainability Science*, vol 10, no 3, pp 385–395.

Gramsci, A. (1971/1930) *Selections from the Prison Notebooks*. New York: International Publishers.

Grosfoguel, R. & Mielants, E. (2006) 'The long-durée entanglement between islamophobia and racism in the modern/colonial capitalist/patriarchal world-system: An introduction'. *Human Architecture: Journal of the Sociology of Self-Knowledge*, vol 5, no 1. http://scholarworks.umb.edu/humanarchitecture/vol5/iss1/2.

Gudynas, E. (2011) 'Buen vivir: Today's tomorrow'. *Development*, vol 54, no 4, pp 441–447.

Gupte, M. (2017) 'Envisioning India without gender and patriarchy: Why not?' In Kothari, A. & Joy, K.J. (eds.), *Alternative Futures: India Unshackled*. New Delhi: Authors Upfront.

Gutiérrez Aguilar, R. (2013) 'Pistas reflexivas para orientarnos en una turbulenta época de peligro'. In Gutiérrez, R., Sierra, N., Davalos, P., Olivera, O., Mongragon, H.,

Almendra, V., Zibechi, R., Rozental, E., & Mamani, P. (eds.), *Palabras para tejernos, resistir y transformar en la época que estamos viviendo*. Oaxaca: Pez en el árbol.

Hornborg, A. (2009) 'Zero-sum world'. *International Journal of Comparative Sociology*, vol 50, no 3/4, pp 237–262.

Jorgenson, A. & Clark, B. (2012) 'Are the economy and the environment decoupling? A comparative international study: 1960–2005'. *American Journal of Sociology*, vol 118, no 1, pp 1–44.

Kallis, G. (2015) 'The degrowth alternative'. Great Transition Initiative. www.greattransition.org/publication/the-degrowth-alternative.

Kauffman, C. & Sheehan, L. (2018). 'The rights of nature: Guiding our responsibilities through standards'. In Turner, S., Shelton, D., Razaqque, J., Mcintyre, O., & May, J. (eds.), *Environmental Rights: The Development of Standards*. Cambridge: Cambridge University Press.

Kothari, A. (2013) 'Missed opportunity? Comments on two global reports for the post-2015 goals process'. Pune, Kalpavriksh and ICCA Consortium. www.un-ngls.org/IMG/pdf/Kalpavriksh_and_ICCA_Consortium_-_Post-2015_reports_critique_-_Ashish_Kothari_July_2013.pdf.

Kothari, A. (2014) 'Radical ecological democracy: A way for India and beyond'. *Development*, vol 57, pp 36–45

Kothari, A. (2016) 'Why do we wait so restlessly for the workday to end and for the weekend to come?'. *Scroll*, 17 June. https://scroll.in/article/809940/.

Kothari, A., Demaria, F. & Acosta, A. (2015) 'Buen vivir, degrowth and ecological Swaraj: Alternatives to development and the green economy'. *Development*, vol 57, no 3, pp 362–375.

Krausmann, F., Gingrich, S., Eisenmenger, N., ErbK.H.E., Haberl, H. & Fischer-Kowalski, M. (2009) 'Growth in global materials use, GDP and population during the 20th century'. *Ecological Economics*, vol 68, pp 2696–2705.

Latouche, S. (2009) *Farewell to Growth*. London: Polity.

Leopold, A. (1994) *A Sand County Almanac and Sketches Here and There*. New York: Oxford University Press.

Martinez-Alier, J., Temper, L., Del Bene, D. & Scheidel, A. (2016) 'Is there a global environmental justice movement?'. *Journal of Peasant Studies*, vol 43, pp 731–755.

Marx, K. & Engels, F. (1959/1872) *The Manifesto of the Communist Party*. Moscow: Foreign Languages Publishing House.

Meadows, D., Meadows, D., Randers, J. & Behrens, W. (1972) *The Limits to Growth*. New York: Universe Books.

Merchant, C. (1980) *The Death of Nature: Women and the Scientific Revolution*. New York: Harper.

Metz, T. (2011) 'Ubuntu as a moral theory and human rights in south Africa'. *African Human Rights Law Journal*, vol 11, no 2, pp 532–559.

Mies, M. (1986) *Patriarchy and Accumulation on a World Scale*. London: Zed Books.

Nandy, A. (2003) *The Romance of the State and the Fate of Dissent in the Tropics*. New Delhi: Oxford University Press.

Navas, G., Mingorria, S. & Aguilar, B. (2018) 'Violence in environmental conflicts: The need for a multidimensional approach'. *Sustainability Science*, vol 13, no 3, pp 649–660.

Pérez Orozco, A. (2014) *Subversión feminista de la economía: Aportes para un debate sobre el conflicto capital-vida*. Madrid: Traficantes de Sueños.

Rahnema, M. & Bawtree, V. (1997) *The Post-Development Reader*. London: Zed Books.

Rist, G. (2003) *The History of Development: From Western Origins to Global Faith*. London: Zed Books.

Sachs, W. (ed.) (2010/1992) *The Development Dictionary: A Guide to Knowledge as Power*. London: Zed Books.

Salleh, A. (2006) 'We in the North are the biggest problem for the South: A conversation with Hilkka Pietila'. *Capitalism Nature Socialism*, vol 17, no 1, pp 44–61.

Salleh, A. (2011) 'Climate strategy: Making the choice between ecological modernisation or "living well"'. *Journal of Australian Political Economy*, vol 66, pp 124–149.

Salleh, A. (2012) 'Green economy or green utopia? Rio+20 and the reproductive labor class'. *Journal of World Systems Research*, vol 18, no 2, pp 141–145.

Salleh, A. (2016) 'Climate, water, and livelihood skills: a post-development reading of the SDGs'. *Globalizations*, vol 13, no 6, pp 952–959.

Salleh, A. (2017/1997) *Ecofeminism as Politics: Nature, Marx, and the Postmodern*. London: Zed Books.

Scheidel, A., Temper, L., Demaria, F. & Martínez-Alier, J. (2018) 'Ecological distribution conflicts as forces for sustainability: an overview and conceptual framework'. *Sustainability Science*, vol 13, no 3, pp 585–598.

SDSN, Sustainable Development Solutions Network (2013) *An Action Agenda for Sustainable Development*. Report for the UN Secretary General, Sustainable Development Solutions Network, United Nations. http://unsdsn.org/wp-content/uploads/2013/06/140505-An-Action-Agenda-for-Sustainable-Development.pdf.

Shelley, M. (2009/1818) *Frankenstein*. London: Penguin.

Shiva, V. (1989) *Staying Alive: Women, Ecology and Development*. London: Zed Books.

Shrivastava, A. & Kothari, A. (2012) *Churning the Earth: The Making of Global India*. Delhi: Viking/Penguin.

Singh, M. (1992) 'Environment and the new economic policies'. Foundation Day Lecture, Society for Promotion of Wastelands Development, Delhi, 17 June.

Sousa Santos, B. de (2009) 'A non-occidentalist West? Learned ignorance and ecology of knowledge'. *Theory, Culture and Society*, vol 26, nos. 7–8, pp 103–125.

UNEP (2011) *Towards a Green Economy: Pathways to Sustainable Development and Poverty Eradication: A Synthesis for Policy Makers*. Nairobi: United Nations Environment Programme. www.unep.org/greeneconomy.

United Nations (2013) *A New Global Partnership: Eradicate Poverty and Transform Economies Through Sustainable Development*. The Report of the High-Level Panel of Eminent Persons on the Post-2015 Development Agenda. New York: United Nations.

United Nations (2015) *Transforming Our World: The 2030 Agenda for Sustainable Development*. New York: United Nations. https://sustainabledevelopment.un.org/post2015/transformingourworld/publication.

United Nations Secretary-General's High-level Panel on Global Sustainability (2012) *Resilient People, Resilient Planet: A Future Worth Choosing*. New York: United Nations.

Waring, M. (1987) *Counting for Nothing*. Sydney: Allen & Unwin.

Ziai, A. (2015) 'Post-development: Pre-mature burials and haunting ghosts'. *Development and Change*, vol 46, no 4, pp 833–854.

PART II
Siting postdevelopment practice

Where is postdevelopment being put into practice? Where and how is this work being done? The second, and larger, part of the volume presents a wide range of contemporary approaches drawing from postdevelopment and critical theory, diverse economies and science and technology studies, decolonial scholarship and pluriversality, feminisms and art work, all in order to inform these practices of postdevelopment. The chapters are oriented by and closely follow experiences, stories, political projects, art works, policy and development projects, communities and indigenous experiences, all the while building upon theoretical debates and discussions showing the diverse ways in which postdevelopment is already practiced.

7
BEYOND DEVELOPMENT

Postcapitalist and feminist praxis in *adivasi* contexts

Bhavya Chitranshi

A postdevelopmental dream in practice

Amidst the perils of an ongoing developmental dream, '*sabka sath, sabka vikas*' (collective efforts, inclusive development) that has been haunting the Indian political scenario for quite some time, another dream or a dream of a subaltern Other (who remains excluded from the inclusive model of development) was envisioned in 2016 in the far-away *Kondh adivasi* (tribal)-dominated village named Emaliguda in the Rayagada district of Odisha.[1] It was a dream co-created (not individually dreamt) by the *Eka Nari Sanghathan* (ENS), a collective of *adivasi* single women farmers as a hope to live, labour and love in harmony. Arnalu Miniaka (member, ENS, 2016), sharing the dream shyly, said,

> we [the single women in the *Sanghathan*] wish to live on a land surrounded by the forest and a river where we would labour together to produce and share the food, look after each other, sing and dance in harmony and where we shall be free of all our pain and misery.

Contrary to the national developmental dream, which as usual made false promises to 'enhance the profitability in agriculture, by ensuring a 50% profit over the cost of production' for 49% of the total workforce engaged in agriculture (NSSO 2011–2012; as cited in Kumar 2017), the subaltern dream of 35 single women in Emaliguda village was driven by a desire to collectively work towards making agriculture a liveable condition rather than a profitable economic system. In the mainstream developmental discourse and practice in India, agriculture is considered an income-generating livelihood activity that can be made profitable with the help of capitalist interventions and modern techniques of farming. Perceived as an economic procedure alone, its cultural, environmental and socio-political aspects are overlooked with a singular focus on enhanced production and global market linkages that can ensure profitability. Thus, agriculture in developmental imagination remains merely a form of livelihood that is necessary to feed the nation(s); detached from its cultural, social, political context and diverse life forms, it becomes a 'commodity' understood in terms of exchange value generating surplus for the global market.

Can this kind of developmental thinking make sense out of the subaltern imagination that claims that 'the land is (her) womb and the crop is like (her) growing child' (Mami Pedenti, member, ENS)? Can this relationship to nature and agriculture be understood by the developmental processes subordinated to the logic of profit and income enhancement? The answer, perhaps, is a simple 'no'. For the women farmers in Rayagada, agriculture is intimately tied to their life; it is not only a primary source of livelihood, rather the *adivasi* existence, their food, culture, festivals, their relationship to nature, forms of labouring and living life in general depend upon this significant process of agriculture. Agriculture is considered a *form of life* dependent upon an ethical relationship with more-than-human entities and ecosystems that together make it more than an economic process. De la Cadena (2015) in the South American indigenous context argues for a rethinking of reality and modernist notions to be able to understand the indigenous-environment relationship that she refers to as 'earth beings'. In the same light, this work argues for an alternative understanding of agriculture that remains embedded in the larger *adivasi* culture, history and context.

Thus, unlike *sabka sath, sabka vikas*, an electoral strategy premised upon promises of inclusive development through capitalist growth, the postdevelopmental attempt in the *Sanghathan* has been towards building a collective life through engaging in collective farming. In so-called modern and developing times, when farmers are being encouraged to produce and appropriate on an individual basis, keeping self-interest in mind, when they are being lured into cash crop production serving as input for big industries and in times of increasing reliance on capitalist markets for inorganic and chemical farming emphasising the use of marketed fertilizers, pesticides and hybrid/high-yielding seeds, this attempt at collective cultivation is an experiment exploring alternative ways of farming involving indigenous seed varieties and ecologically sensitive methods and techniques. In its efforts towards a 'transformed' practice of agriculture that goes beyond capitalist and developmentalist approaches, the *Sanghathan* engages in farming processes that build upon logic of nurturance, sharing, co-labouring and co-dependence along more-than-human life forms. Thus, collective farming in Emaliguda is an initiative towards cultivating a common life of well-being not just with other women in the *Sanghathan* but also along what Roelvink and Gibson-Graham (2009) call 'earth others'.

My engagement with Emaliguda village and the single women in the *Kondh* community began in 2013 as part of the MPhil Development Practice programme (cdp.res.in/) housed at the Centre for Development Practice, Ambedkar University, Delhi (AUD). As an MPhil action researcher, I was immersed in Emaliguda village for a period of one year. I lived with a separated single woman, Arnalu Miniaka

(Aiya), who mothered me like her own daughter. She had no family and I was far away from mine; our loneliness brought us together. As Aiya slowly introduced me to her life full of suffering and pain, she also taught me her language and how to live and relate in the village setting. I would spend most of my time labouring with her and other women in the fields and inside-outside the household. As we worked together, bathed in the same stream of river and slept in close proximity in the dead of night, my relationship with other single women in Emaliguda also strengthened over time. We often engaged in the affective exchange of our memories and life stories and instances of the lived experience of singleness surfaced and connected us. Finding resonance in each other's stories and drawing strength from each other's experiences, women in Emaliguda, for the first time, according to Barkini Pedenti (member, ENS), 'began making time for themselves'. They delved deeper into their lives and articulated and analysed their condition of singleness as they came together every night after a long tiring day of hard work and toil. Eventually, the collective creation of a new 'time-space' in the gendered lives marked by singleness led to the forging of the *Eka Nari Sanghathan*, a single women's collective, in 2013.

Singleness in our work has been understood: (a) as a condition of loneliness and alone-ness, including economic, political and cultural othering and exclusion, perpetual states of financial and emotional insecurity, life devoid largely of relationships and care, a huge work burden residing entirely on a woman's shoulders, and the everyday life of a woman subjected to varied forms of socio-political discriminations and violence; and, (b) as also a condition that has enabled women to lead at least a negotiated gendered existence in comparison to women under strict control of the hetero-patriarchal institution of marriage. In other words, singleness is as much about negotiating, and coping with, as also resisting patriarchal structures, as it is about everyday pain and suffering.

This process of conceptualising singleness enabled the *Sanghathan* members and me to disaggregate the *adivasi* gendered reality. When singleness is read as both a site of oppression and resistance and affirmation, it shows that all of the socio-cultural reality in the *Kondh* society is not patriarchal in nature. Moreover, this understanding of singleness was tied to a discursive shift we made from singlehood (as a particular social identity resulting from the absence of a husband, such as the identity of a widowed, separated, abandoned, deserted, divorced, never-married woman), to singleness (as a condition; as an experience of living and feeling singleness in the absence or even in the presence of a husband – more as a 'contingent emergent subject position'). The meaning of singleness thus extended itself to also involve women who are married and have husbands yet face conditions that are similar to those faced by women who do not have or live without a male sexual partner (see Chitranshi 2016; Chitranshi & Dhar 2016).

The meaning of singleness in our work has been evolving with the meaning of the *Sanghathan* and vice-versa. Keeping these two central ideas as contingent-emergent, the work in Rayagada has been exploring several directions and inter-connections. As a result of singleness due to familial/social othering, the *Sanghathan* was forged as a space of companionship and sense of security for women who have been either abandoned by their families or are treated as burdens and liabilities. In the words of Debi Pedenti (member, ENS, 2016),

> attending to each other's pain, providing each other emotional and financial support and looking after one another in times of difficulty, despair and illness, we also laugh, sing and work together creating moments of joy and happiness every time we meet.

Thus, along with sheltering women's varied experiences, the *Sanghathan* has been emerging as a support group hosting and re-creating relationalities.

Moreover, reimagined beyond repressive structures of family, the *Sanghathan* has also been evolving as a space for transformative thinking and practice. Caught in the clutches of capitalist development, the lives of *adivasi* single women farmers are also marked by economic exploitation, primitive accumulation, foreclosure of their subjective being, third-worldisation (Chakrabarti & Dhar 2009) and victimisation. The *Sanghathan*, through its critique of development, has been grappling with critical questions around gender, sexuality, modernity, capitalism, rights-based and/or representative forms of politics (discussed later).

In the process, the imagination of a postcapitalist (Gibson-Graham 2006) and feminist practice of agriculture was born *in* the *Sanghathan*; or perhaps I should say it was born *with* the *Sanghathan*. This alternative practice has been a movement beyond the illusory woman-centric[2] and orientalist-capitalocentric[3] frameworks of development (Gibson-Graham 1996; Gibson-Graham & Ruccio 2001; Chakrabarti & Dhar 2009) marking an ontological and epistemological shift. Rethought beyond dominant frameworks of development, this postcapitalist-feminist engagement takes us to postdevelopmental imagination and practice (Escobar 2005).

This chapter tries to engage with the relationship between the *Sanghathan* as an *adivasi* single women's group and the *Sanghathan* enacting postcapitalist (St. Martin, Roelvink & Gibson-Graham 2015) being/becoming-in-common in the 'world of the third' (Chakrabarti, Dhar & Cullenberg 2016) context.[4] In doing so, I ask, does postdevelopment practice with the *adivasi* life-world enable us to understand how gender work and economic transformation overdetermine each other? Can the *Sanghathan*, although embedded in the hegemony of developmental context, resist the capitalist and hetero-patriarchal order through cultivating alternative commons, variegated practices and diverse realities?

Hitherto, certain feminist works focussed upon socio-political concerns have offered us a way towards resisting hetero-patriarchal systems, raising feminist consciousness and building solidarities. Similarly, postcapitalist politics through diverse economic transformations have taken us to cultivating commons and ethical economic relationalities. The work of the *Sanghathan* aims to combine the two. What does it mean to 'conceptualize economic difference through the prism of gender as a social construction (rather than through the lens of capitalist reproduction)', building not only upon women's unpaid labour processes within the family (as argued by Gibson-Graham, Erdem & Özselçuk 2013b: 280) and in the larger community context but also upon the condition of singleness and gendered roles and relationships? How do gendered realities and relationalities transform through transforming economic processes?

In its postcapitalist-feminist praxis, the *Sanghathan* simultaneously attempts to build ethical interpersonal relationalities between women (by acknowledging the differences among them and moving beyond regressive frameworks of a woman-man binary) and work through ethical economic ties that shape collective subjectivities. Can non-economic affective exchanges and shared economic subjectivities combine to work towards a common future? Can processes of common becomings be accompanied by processes of 'becoming-woman'? Becoming-woman, for Deleuze and Guattari, is not to imitate or imbibe womanliness but to defy dominant molar forms and relations in order to conceive 'molecular woman' and a 'molecular political movement' (Deleuze & Guattari 2005: 276). It is through (remaining in) practice that one searches for epistemological and philosophical reflections.

Towards a postcapitalist-feminist practice

In June 2016, Aiya and Mami Pedenti, members of the ENS, joined me for a visit to Basudha. Basudha, a 2.3-acre demonstration farmland founded by Dr. Debal Deb and Mr. Debdulal Bhattacharjee, is in the deep forests of Bissumcuttack, Odisha. Over 1200 folk rice varieties and 30 other crops are grown and preserved on this farm every year, as a model of ecological agriculture combining 'traditional' and 'scientific' ways of multiple cropping. The forest, agriculture and humans come to co-exist in Basudha.[5] As we spent the whole day understanding the work in Basudha, Mami and Aiya were surprised to see how traditional methods of farming that over the years had been lost to modern techniques and chemical farming could still be useful and productive. Moreover, this farm had all the variety produce that once used to be part of their diet before transgenic Bt cotton and other cash crops were brought in to the area.

Mami and Aiya gathered a few rooted stems and leaves, a handful of seeds and plenty of memories from Basudha. They returned quite fascinated, though almost in disbelief. How was agriculture without chemical fertiliser and pesticides possible in today's time? Why were some people preserving what the *adivasi* communities were leaving behind as a sign of backwardness? They were quiet on the way back. I could sense that their morning excitement of seeing their past alive had by evening turned into a mournful nostalgia. A sad realisation of all they have lost over time had set in. When we reached Emaliguda, Aiya asked me hesitatingly if it was possible for us to build our own Basudha. I smiled; I had no immediate answer for her. But her hope had made me hopeful.

So far, the single women in Emaliguda had collectivised themselves around the issue of singleness and had been engaging in various collective endeavours like claiming pensions and financial assistance to build houses from the state, opening bank accounts and organising/mobilising women in different villages (see Chitranshi

2018). However, Aiya's dream of building our own Basudha initially seemed impossible to many. The women in the *Sanghathan* had laughed at her suggestion; however, not dismissively. I could sense the dream had somewhere touched each one of us. Perhaps the laughter symbolised co-existence of an initiated hope and its limits.

I was apprehensive of how 35 women from the *Sanghathan* would do agriculture together. Was it possible for so many women to work together? That the *Sanghathan* may fall apart in the process was my biggest fear. But over time the enthusiasm for collective farming in the *Sanghathan* built in intensity. The desire for a new beginning had come to life; it was breathing. The *Sanghathan* was looking forward to building something new, a new that was ingrained in the old; a future was being imagined through a recovery of the 'past'.

With this inspiration filling me up, I decided to discuss the Mondragon Corporation model with the *Sanghathan* members.[6] The intention behind this discussion was not to simply narrate an account of a successful cooperative but to also plant a seed of hope that could make us think about collective and ethical practices that we could engender. Women in the *Sanghathan* could relate to the idea of working together and collectively appropriating the surplus. For them, this was not something new.

Collective labouring and community participation on different occasions is a part of *adivasi* life in Rayagada. Sharing labour, helping each other and voluntary involvement in labouring activities is part of cultural life among the *Kondh*. Women work in each other's fields, co-perform household chores, look after each other's children, share the produce whenever need be and undertake roles and responsibilities on behalf of each other. Most of these exchanges and collective work remain outside monetary accounting. Over time these community value systems are slowly fading away. However, there are still many instances of collaborative processes of labouring, appropriation and exchange that are in place. In other words, alongside several capitalist class processes, *adivasi* lifeworlds are also organised around an assemblage of noncapitalist class processes, non-monetary and non-market exchanges and non-commodity production.

Some of these range from single women farmers engaging in what Resnick and Wolff (1987) call 'independent' or 'self-appropriative' class processes: individual performance of surplus labour with individual appropriation of surplus generated from a common piece of land; local market trading and local credit systems; non-monetary exchanges like barter, labour exchange and sharing, cooperative exchange, gift economy; shared household labour, social reproductive work and care work undertaken mainly by women.

With collective farming in the *Sanghathan*, three significant postcapitalist (Gibson-Graham, Cameron & Healy 2013a; St. Martin, Roelvink & Gibson-Graham 2015) possibilities and shifts could be explored through: (1) engagement in ecologically sensitive ways of farming ensuring ethical relationship between human and other-than-human forms, as opposed to chemical farming methods and techniques that rely on a capitalist market and lead to environmental degradation, including impacts on human body and health; (2) understanding and exploring collective forms of labouring, appropriation and distribution in order to re-create new processes and practices. In other words, through collective farming we could generate learnings from already existing non-exploitative and noncapitalist class processes and could work towards strengthening postcapitalist practices; (3) reorienting from individualised/self-interested subjectivities in capitalism (that are slowly overtaking *adivasi* life) towards cultivation of common and ethical subject positions through collective action, creation, exchange and sharing. In other words, through an exploration and enactment of diverse economies and cultivation of collective processes and ethics, a postdevelopmental affirmation beyond mere opposition was possible.

Development organisations have overtime mobilised 'poor-third-world-women' into micro-credit-based self-help groups (SHGs) to work on developmental issues such as livelihood, health, education etc. These agendas claiming to 'empower' women and developing rural spaces through them continue to leave behind issues of women's subjective being and their nodal experiences. It comes as no surprise that in spite of a large number of single women in the *Kondh* society, singleness as an issue has always remained absent in the developmental work in Rayagada over the years. Regardless, these women are exposed to income-generating opportunities, cash crop cultivation, use of marketed seeds and chemicals and as a token are trained in lessons on patriarchy and gender that have little or no connection to their socio-cultural context.[7]

In the process, *adivasi* reality is rendered backward, pre-capitalist and underdeveloped; *adivasi* women are perceived as helpless victims in need of external guidance and support. Tearing them away from their culture, history and knowledge, developmental interventions assert to pull *adivasi* women out of their misery of economic poverty through connecting them to circuits of global capital. Thus, all other-than-capitalist or noncapitalist class processes in the *adivasi* context are marked as the lacking Other – the pre-capital of modern European industrial capitalism. What are 'not capitalist' spaces are represented as what are 'not yet capitalist' spaces; as third world-ish, and in need of integration into the logic-language-ethos of the developed first world; as signposts of economic backwardness. The noncapitalist class processes are thus left with only two possible futures – mutation into capitalist class processes or outright annihilation (through state-sponsored primitive accumulation).

As a result of conceiving the economy as a binary between capitalist and pre-capitalist forces rather than as a heterogeneous radical space marked by overdetermination and contradiction of capitalist and noncapitalist constellations of surplus (Resnick & Wolff 1987), there is a foreclosing of diverse economic processes and noncapitalist modes of being, operational in what Chakrabarti, Dhar & Cullenberg (2012, 2016) have called the 'world of the third'. In turn, development discourse, as it foregrounds the woman farmer as a lacking/lagging subject of capitalism, i.e., as a pre-capitalist (as a not-yet-capitalist) subject, simultaneously forecloses resisting subject positions and possible futures that could emanate from a noncapitalist outside the expanding circuits of global capital and affirmative/alternative politics.

Opposed to this kind of developmental thinking and practice, our work in Rayagada attempts to learn from the *adivasi* life-world and women's subjective experiences in order to cultivate transformative practices. The women from the *Sanghathan* in Emaliguda have been working as my co-action-researchers exploring and understanding the experiences of women in different contexts, the condition of singleness, their everyday lived reality and the nature of gender(ed) relationships. About 130 women from other villages have come together to be part of the *Sanghathan* and despite contextual and experiential differences, women have been engaging with each other on several issues and instances. Issues related to different forms of gender discrimination, sexual division of labour, devaluation and invisibilisation of women's unpaid and paid work, women's health, alcoholism leading to abuse, marital/sexual violence, masculinity, body and sexuality have been surfacing and women have been sensitively engaging, reflecting and acting towards co-creating mechanisms of negotiation, resistance and affirmation that can take us to non-violent ways of doing transformative gender work.

These engagements drawing upon the *adivasi* context at large, however, do not romanticise the *adivasi* history and culture; they also do not render women's experience as sacrosanct. Nevertheless, the attempt has been to arrive at collaborative thinking and practices that along with theoretical insights place value in what *adivasi* knowledge and way of life has to offer. The work relies heavily on *adivasi* culture, the spiritual and ethical value systems, different forms of knowledge and practices. It regards *adivasi* women as 'capable' subjects creating possibilities for a collective (transformed) future rather than training them in Western perspectives on gender or motivating them to become equal to men or more like men through inculcating masculine characteristics. The *adivasi* context thus plays a crucial role in historically situating the understanding of gender (Lugones 2016; Icaza & Vázquez 2016) and economy and towards redrawing ethical and transformed relationalities.

The inherent antagonisms, conflicts, discriminations and marginalisations that are part of *adivasi* culture and life are often encountered, acknowledged and negotiated within the process of our efforts at collectivising and building socio-political and economic ties. These are efforts geared towards reorienting processes of subject-power-desire that can take us to contingent-emergent 'ethical becomings' rather than seeking ultimate reconciliation of inevitable antagonisms. Moreover, this work revisits the familiar idiom of 'representation' and 'leadership' that are accorded consistent value in developmental and mainstream feminist interventions. We resist the formation of 'woman leaders' as the very idea of 'leadership' (privileging and placing power in the hands of a few) comes across as patriarchal. The *Sanghathan* thus has no elected/selected 'leaders'. All the members of the collective form the core of decision making and facilitation among themselves. Different roles and responsibilities are fulfilled by taking turns that are decided through consensus.

Collective farming for us was a next step towards re-imagining the ethic of the social by cultivating 'what are not capitalist' class existences in the world-of-the-third context; the world of the third for us harboured a possibility. As we explored ways in which we could engage in collective and ethical processes of labouring, production, appropriation and distribution in agriculture, we realised it was important to take things in our own hands rather than depend upon external aid, development organisations and agencies. As we prepared ourselves for the agriculture season (2017–2018), we decided to engage in a collective endeavour of producing pickle with mangoes gathered from the forest. Every year, women prepare this pickle individually for family consumption; this time the women got together, distributed the work amongst each other, took responsibility at each step and enjoyed the whole process. This initiative was not simply to create a business venture but to come together as labouring-creating subjects and experience the joy of it. The pickle was kept for self-consumption and the rest was sold to generate surplus that could be collectively appropriated and used for the agriculture process. It was also to generate surplus for women in the *Sanghathan* who are old and unable to sustain themselves. This was our first attempt at a postcapitalist practice in the *Sanghathan*, which we plan to continue each year.

Alongside, we leased a three-acre plot of land using our savings, surplus from the sale of mango pickle and a little contribution from some of my friends. By this time, my friend Ashutosh had also joined us in Rayagada and, given his interest in alternative agricultural practices, we felt more confident about this initiative. Ashutosh was easily accepted in the *Sanghathan* given his polite and accommodating nature. As he laboured with the women, a relationship began to develop between him and the *Sanghathan* members. In the meantime, we invited Mr. Dulaldeb from Basudha to survey the land and conduct workshops with us that helped us understand the problems of chemical farming and ways in which we could engage in ecologically sensitive methods. Dulalda also offered the *Sanghathan* indigenous seed varieties from Basudha for the first year on the trust that with our production next year we shall return him double the amount of seeds. This is one of the ways in which Basudha engages in ethical exchange of seeds, knowledge and agricultural practice with the farmers in the area.

As women listened, they questioned. For them, using chemical fertilisers and pesticides was a given now. It was hard for them to believe agriculture was possible without chemical inputs from the market. Even though the women were convinced about planting indigenous seeds, to do agriculture without the use of chemical inputs was a huge risk. They were aware that the excessive use of chemical fertilisers, pesticides and herbicides for agriculture in general and cotton production in particular had been responsible for environmental degradation and adverse effects on body and health over time, but they were also sure that in the present times there was no way out of it. Chemical fertilisers and pesticides seemed necessary now given the soil had lost its fertility and health over the years.

Finally, Ashutosh and I had to enter into a negotiation where women from the *Sanghathan* decided to use chemical fertilisers and pesticides in regulated amounts during the early stage of plant growth. Slowly, as we progressed, the women agreed to substitute chemical inputs with natural substances (like cow dung manure and *neem* residue) and their openness towards trying alternatives increased. The blind belief in marketed inputs was slowly shaken, as we shifted to more natural and organic inputs, methods and techniques. In the first year, in order to experiment, we sowed both indigenous seed varieties and high-yielding seed varieties. With the indigenous seed varieties offering a good yield on the same area of land, some faith in the traditional methods of farming got restored. Post the harvest, looking at the production and the health of the seed, women were convinced that the indigenous seed variety did not require chemical inputs. Ashutosh and I were happy to witness women from the *Sanghathan* discussing benefits of ecologically sensitive farming with other neighbouring farmers. They insisted if the other farmers were interested in cultivating these seed varieties they could share the seeds with them but on the condition that they would not engage in chemical farming.

With respect to collective labouring, beginning from the work of preparing the land, cutting and building the boundary, treating and sowing the seeds, transplanting the crop, regulating water in the field, harvesting of paddy, thrashing and separating paddy from hay, straw and husk, packaging of the harvest, loading, unloading, distributing paddy to the members, drying paddy, preserving seeds for the next year, milling it into rice, storing of rice for sale and handling the finances throughout, all the work was done collectively. The work was mostly distributed among the members according to age, with younger women taking up more laborious tasks and older women engaging in less strenuous tasks. However, each and every one, irrespective of their age (varying from 35 to 80 years), participated and contributed to the labouring process, except Daima Pedenti (member, ENS), who unfortunately had met with an accident a few days before sowing of seeds and hence could not participate in the process.

There were many hurdles and challenges that we faced in the process. The unpredictability and delay in monsoon led to lack of irrigation in the initial days followed by delay in ploughing and sowing. The bridge that connected Emaliguda and Pujariguda (the village where the land we were cultivating is) got washed away in the flash flood that hit us just before the sowing process began. As a result, the women had to walk for about eight or ten kilometres to reach the field. They also performed all the heavy work that men usually do in the agricultural lands. Except ploughing, which was done with the use of a tractor, all other 'masculine' jobs, from breaking and building the boundary of the land, spraying organic pesticides, carrying loads of harvested paddy over their heads and thrashing the entire produce, were done by women. Women also stayed up till late at night in the fields in order to regulate the amount of water on the land.

There were also times when the *Sanghathan* members broke into heated arguments and disagreements with regards to sharing labouring activities[8]. As some women were occupied with the cultivation of family lands, the responsibility of looking after the land and the crop fell on the shoulders of a few. However, soon such crisis situations would be brought to notice in the weekly meetings and solutions would be arrived at. For example, given the former problem, it was finally decided that all the women would pair up to pay regular visits rather than just a few. In spite of these momentary disagreements and conflict, the collective spirit of the *Sanghathan* kept us going and we managed to work through all kinds of constraints, ranging from financial to physical, psychological and environmental.

The women walked long distances to reach the land, lifted heavy weights, performed back-breaking work all day, stood without shade whether it rained down or the sun scorched above and still they sang in harmony as they worked, laughed their hearts out during the small *pika* (local rolled tobacco) break, ate together under the mangrove and walked back home in joy after completing the work day after day. Their bond strengthened as they laboured, walked, sang, smoked and ate together. Their happiness was beyond measure on the days all of them would come and finish day-long work in just a couple of hours. They would often say, 'when we work together, the work feels so easy. It becomes difficult both physically and psychologically when we have no one to share it with'.

The first day when all the 34 women gathered for sowing of seeds, it was a sight to see. I was told that 'one earns the right to eat only when one sows the seed'. The story behind the food that easily reaches my plate every day was as if unfolding before me. I wondered if I had the right to eat the food I had never produced. As I struggled to find my ground in the wet muddy fields with half my legs submerged and back continuously bent, I sowed the seeds with the women and my body felt the pain that goes into producing the food we eat. The ease with which women performed the work and finished it was surprising to me. I was half their age, and I was less than half as capable of what they could do. Throughout this agricultural cycle, I engaged in each and every labouring activity to make my body aware of the efforts that go behind cultivating food. At the same time, I was also becoming aware of my body and its limits as it had never known labouring in this manner before.

As we finished harvesting, it was time for distribution. Not only the performance of labour, even appropriation of produce was a collective process. Everyone, including Daima (who could not participate this year given health reasons), was allotted the same share of produce as was distributed to those who had laboured through the process. In the enactment of a postcapitalist practice, the *Sanghathan* witnessed a shared collectivity. The appropriation took place on a shared/communitic basis rather than women's individual ability to perform labour. Apart from distribution for self-consumption, the rice was sold to generate surplus for the *Sanghathan*. A part of this surplus has been used for the production process this year (2018–2019) and the rest will be collectively appropriated to cater to social needs of the

Sanghathan members in the future. The remuneration, hence, has been in the form of appropriation of the produce and the common surplus rather than individual wages to women. With respect to exchange, the rice was sold locally in the village and to urban consumers who were put in direct contact with the *Sanghathan* members. Most of the urban consumers who have been part of the process and have continued to support this work have been willing to pay much more than the set price for the rice.

To celebrate this collective journey, the women from the *Sanghathan* organised a *bhoji* (feast) on 2 January 2018. Next to the river under the mangrove we (including people from outside who have been supporting the work and are our loyal customers) met, cooked amazing food, sang, danced, played and ate together the rice we had cultivated. This year (2018–2019) the process of collective farming has begun in full swing again with the use of preserved indigenous seeds from last year. No high-yielding seed varieties have been planted and no chemical inputs have been used. However, this year also represents an experiment in our method of farming. At what distance the seeds should be sown and whether it will be line sowing or random sowing is the debate this year. Both random sowing as part of the traditional method and line sowing as part of the scientific method have been done this year to explore which method works best for us. Moreover, many farmers in the nearby villages have taken the indigenous seeds and agreed to experiment on small portions of their land; seeds have been distributed on the same logic of non-monetary seed exchange. Keeping these experiments, questions, explorations and experiences alive, we hope to continue to learn, labour, live and love for times to come. Like Gibson-Graham, we too 'are excited to be living in these terrible times' (Gibson-Graham 2016: 307).

Acknowledgements

This action research work in the rural villages of Odisha remains indebted to many people and contributions that have before us and with us made this possible. Firstly, it draws heavily from the works of Anjan Chakrabarti-Anup Dhar, J.K. Gibson-Graham, the Community Economies Collective and Dr. Debal Deb. Although not quoted here enough, it is along these ideas and practices that our work develops. Secondly, without Ashutosh and Dulalda this work would never have been the same. Their expertise in agriculture, continuous engagement and patience have converted an imagination into a transformed reality.

Notes

1 *Sabka Sath, Sabka Vikas*, inclusive development along with unity, is a national plan used in the form of a slogan by the current prime minister of India, Narendra Modi. This slogan supposedly aims to focus on the growth and progress of the country (mostly based upon capitalist development) alongside ensuring participation of all groups and interests.

2 When development institutions and international aid agencies began to take account of gender, as they did under feminist pressure in the 1970s, their understanding of the concept was minimal. In the usual policy model, there were two categories of people, the men here and the women there, and the reform needed was to add the women into the development programme. But the dichotomy of men versus women was a radically simplified idea of gender, and the simplification had important consequences. It homogenized each of the two categories, ignoring the vast variations within them. 'Gender' in policy language usually meant women (Connell in Harcourt 2016: xii).
3 'In a capitalocentric field, capitalism is the norm and noncapitalist economic relations or entities are understood with respect to capitalism, as either the same as, complements to, opposites of or contained within capitalism' (Gibson-Graham 2016: 291).
4 Through marking *difference* with the capital-logic, remaining outside the expanding and marauding circuits of global capital, the world of the third as the harbinger of a noncapitalist language-logic-experience-ethic outside of and beyond the circuits of (global) capitalist modernity puts under erasure capitalist ethic and language.
5 http://cintdis.org/basudha/.
6 Mondragon Corporation is the embodiment of the cooperative movement that began in 1956. The values that mark this model are cooperation, participation, social responsibility and innovation. The corporation's mission combines the core goals of a business organisation competing on international markets with the use of democratic methods in its business organisation, the creation of jobs, the human and professional development of its workers and a pledge to development with its social environment.
7 Maria Lugones discusses the concept of 'coloniality of gender' as a modern system that was violently imposed on the non-Western Other through the process of colonisation in order to overshadow diverse social forms and experiences and control territories, capital, subjectivities and lives (Lugones 2016). This coloniality continues to exist in the orientalist framework of development that leaves behind the socio-historical context of the woman thereby drawing her into homogeneous and universalised understandings of gender.
8 Cameron (2015) discusses two community-supported agriculture initiatives in Australia in order to highlight how communities are not pre-existing entities but are rather constructed in the process of negotiations, struggles and uncertainities that unfold as concerns of survival, production, consumption, appropriation, distribution and market relations etc. are encountered.

References

Cameron, J. (2015) 'Enterprise innovation and economic diversity in community-supported agriculture'. In Roelvink, G., St. Martin, K. & Gibson-Graham, J.K. (eds.), *Making Other Worlds Possible: Performing Diverse Economies*. Minneapolis and London: University of Minnesota Press, pp 53–71.

Chakrabarti, A. & Dhar, A. (2009) *Dislocation and Resettlement in Development: From Third World to World of the Third*. New York and London: Routledge.

Chakrabarti, A., Dhar, A. & Cullenberg, S. (2012) *World of the Third and Global Capitalism*. New Delhi: Worldview Press.

Chakrabarti, A., Dhar, A. & Cullenberg, S. (2016) '(Un)doing Marxism from the outside'. *Rethinking Marxism*, vol 28, no 2, pp 276–294.

Chitranshi, B. (2016) 'Singleness and the Sanghathan'. *CUSP: Journal of Studies in Culture, Subjectivity, Psyche*, vol 1, no 2, pp 75–100.

Chitranshi, B. (2018) 'The story retold: Singleness and the Sanghathan'. www.pradan.net/wp-content/uploads/2017/02/Newsreach-January-February2018-.pdf, pp 2–14.

Chitranshi, B. & Dhar, A. (2016) 'The living dead'. In Cuéllar, D.P. & Junior, N.L. (eds.), *From Death Drive to State Repression: Marxism, Psychoanalysis and the Structural Violence of Capitalism (De la pulsión de muerte a la represión de Estado: Marxismo y psicoanálisis ante la violencia estructural del capitalism)*. Mexico: Porrúa, pp 59–77.

Connell, R. (2016) 'Foreword'. In Harcourt, W. (ed.), *The Palgrave Handbook of Gender and Development: Critical Engagements in Feminist Theory and Practice*. London: Palgrave Macmillan, pp xii–xvii.

de la Cadena, M. (2015) *Earth Beings: Ecologies of Practice across Andean Worlds*. Durham, NC: Duke University Press.

Deleuze, G. & Guattari, F. (2005) *A Thousand Plateaus: Capitalism and Schizophrenia*, ed. and trans. Massumi, B. Minneapolis and London: University of Minnesota Press.

Escobar, A. (2005) 'Imagining a post-development era'. In Crush, J. (ed.), *Power of Development*. London and New York: Routledge.

Gibson-Graham, J.K. (1996) *The End of Capitalism (As We Knew It): A Feminist Critique of Political Economy*. Oxford: Blackwell.

Gibson-Graham, J.K. (2006) *A Postcapitalist Politics*. London: University of Minnesota Press.

Gibson-Graham, J.K. (2016) 'Building community economies: Women and the politics of place'. In Harcourt, W. (ed.), *The Palgrave Handbook of Gender and Development: Critical Engagements in Feminist Theory and Practice*. London: Palgrave Macmillan, pp 287–311.

Gibson-Graham, J.K., Cameron, J. & Healy, S. (2013a) *Take Back the Economy: An Ethical Guide for Transforming Our Communities*. Minneapolis and London: University of Minnesota Press.

Gibson-Graham, J.K., Erdem, E. & Özselçuk, C. (2013b) 'Thinking with Marx for a feminist postcapitalist politics'. In Jaeggi, R. & Loick, D. (eds.), *Marx' Kritik der Gesellschaft*. Berlin: Akademie Verlag, pp 275–284.

Gibson-Graham, J.K. & Ruccio, D. (2001) 'After development: Re-imagining economy and class'. *From the Margins*, vol 1, no 2, pp 155–180.

Icaza, R. & Vázquez, R. (2016) 'The coloniality of gender as a radical critique of developmentalism'. In Harcourt, W. (ed.), *The Palgrave Handbook of Gender and Development: Critical Engagements in Feminist Theory and Practice*. London: Palgrave Macmillan, pp 62–73.

Kumar, M. (2017) '3 years of PM Modi: "*Sabka Sath, Sabka Vikas*" remains just a slogan'. www.thecitizen.in/index.php/en/newsdetail/index/2/10713/3-years-of-pm-modi-sabka-saath-sabka-vikas-remains-just-a-slogan.

Lugones, M. (2016) 'The coloniality of gender'. In Harcourt, W. (ed.), *The Palgrave Handbook of Gender and Development: Critical Engagements in Feminist Theory and Practice*. London: Palgrave Macmillan, pp 13–33.

St. Martin, K., Roelvink, G. & Gibson-Graham, J.K. (2015) 'An economic politics for our times'. In Roelvink, G., St. Martin, K. & Gibson-Graham, J.K. (eds.), *Making Other Worlds Possible: Performing Diverse Economies*. Minneapolis and London: University of Minnesota Press, pp 1–25.

Momsen, J.H. (2004) *Gender and Development*. London and New York: Routledge.

Resnick, S.A. & Wolff, R.D. (1987) *Knowledge and Class: A Marxist Critique of Political Economy*. Chicago: University of Chicago Press.

Roelvink, G. & Gibson-Graham, J.K. (2009) 'A postcapitalist politics of dwelling: Ecological humanities and community economies in conversation'. *Australian Humanities Review*, vol 46, pp 145–158.

8
POSTDEVELOPMENT ALTERNATIVES IN THE NORTH

Daniel Bendix, Franziska Müller, and Aram Ziai

The discourse of 'development' is based on the dualism of 'developed' and 'underdeveloped' societies and the technique of focusing on aspects of the latter, which do not correspond to the norms of the former. In this perspective, 'development' consists of universalizing the Western models of the economy, politics, and knowledge. Postdevelopment questions this approach and looks for alternatives to these models of liberal capitalism, the nation-state and representative democracy, and science – often in social movements and communities in the South that revive other worldviews and practices (see Sachs 2010 and Ziai 2015 for the debate).

However, designating these models as 'Western' neglects that they have become hegemonic in the West only through conflictive historical processes – and that they remain contested. As researchers and postdevelopment activists located in the North, we therefore would like to shift our gaze towards the alternatives to 'development' that can be found here, instead of pointing to examples of vernacular societies in the South, from which we can learn, but which can hardly serve as models for social change in the North. In the allegedly 'developed' societies, the war against subsistence and privatization of the commons for the most part took place quite a while ago, but pockets of resistance can nonetheless be found, and especially in times of crisis still provide a vivid repertoire for autonomy and self-organization, as the examples of Greece and Argentina in the aftermath of socio-economic crisis show.

It is in this light that postdevelopment in the North has to address the North's imperial mode of living in its attempt at social change (Bendix 2017). As our aim is to consider alternatives to the hegemonic and imperial models, we focus on three elementary aspects that form part and parcel of any livelihood: food systems, housing, and energy supply. One example for the first aspect is 'Solidarische Landwirtschaft' ('agriculture of solidarity'), i.e., groups engaged in community-supported agriculture, which establish close links between consumers, producers, and the soil in agriculture. Alternative practices regarding housing can be found in the 'Mietshäusersyndikat', an association for collective housing that withdraws living space from the real estate market. The third practice is situated in the field of energy, thus touching on a crucial issue in times of climate change and global ecological destruction. Situated within the broader degrowth movement, the initiative 'Ende Gelände' aims at leaving coal in the ground, the objective being to stop climate change and end the imperial way of producing and living.

These examples are scrutinized as potential postdevelopment alternatives in the North according to four criteria: first of all, we explore whether we can identify economic practices that follow a non-capitalist logic (Escobar 1995: 58–61; Gibson-Graham 2006 [1996]: xiii). Second, we examine whether we find so-called 'new commons', spaces where people appropriate decision-making from elites and experts in order to regain control over their own lives (Esteva 1992: 20f). Third, we ask to what extent we can observe an interest in local culture and knowledge and a critique of Western science as the only form of knowledge (Escobar 1995: 215). Finally, we address in what way practices break with a colonial system of exploitation (continued by the ideology of 'development' after World War II) (Rahnema 1997: ix).

The North in the postdevelopment debate

Postdevelopment authors have been accused of reactionary romanticism by uncritically celebrating the 'traditional' as well as local resistance and by disregarding those in the so-called developing world who desire 'development' in the form of capitalist, eurocentric socio-economic change (Corbridge 1998; Kiely 1999). They have also been accused of romanticism nurtured by armchair scholarship with no connection to people's day-to-day struggles (McGregor 2009: 1693). This chapter follows the more optimistic work of postdevelopment that empirically explores people's livelihood practices and on this basis suggests that 'alternatives to development' are indeed a concrete possibility (Gibson-Graham 2005; McGregor 2009). It thus focuses on the perspectives of particular struggles in Germany, which are connected to concrete practices, to enquire to what extent they reject dominant notions of 'development'.

The idea that 'development' is something that happens in the South because the North is already 'developed' (Chari & Corbridge 2008: 1) implies that the South has to change, and that the North provides the models to be followed. However, with the nascent realization of the limits to capitalist growth by Northern scientific and political elites comes the partial recognition of the postdevelopment perspective that 'the priority should not be Third World development, [...] but First World "de-development"' (Bennett 2012: 983). This idea has also been put forward under the banner of 'Undeveloping the North' (Ziai forthcoming), but has scarcely been touched upon. The few works of postdevelopment that mention 'over(-)development' do not tackle the question in depth, but merely point out the necessity to delve into this issue (Power 2006: 36–37; Bennett 2012).

This chapter attempts to contribute to postdevelopment in the North by exploring how actors/initiatives criticize 'development' in the North and how it may enhance the postdevelopment agenda.

While postdevelopment work criticizes development studies and the practice of development for 'notions of difference, between here and there, now and then, us and them, developed and developing' (White 2002: 413), it at times reifies this colonial separation of the world by inverting the stereotypes, by dividing 'the world [...] into an evil West and a noble South' (Kiely 1999: 38). This not only disregards the diversity of interests and struggles in the South, but also ignores those undertaking postdevelopment initiatives in the North. Ideas and practices of 'development' are not restricted to the Global South, and the North can thus be explored with a similar perspective (Cowen & Shenton 1995). To overcome this stereotypical division, it is important to stress that struggles against capitalist expropriation, racism, and colonialism, and for global solidarity have taken place also in the North (Federici 2004; Linebaugh & Rediker 2008). This study builds on these insights by exploring activities in Germany as contributing to postdevelopment in the North. Even though the case for turning the gaze towards activities in the North has been made (Habermann & Ziai 2007; Habermann 2012), this has to date not included a systematic examination of potential postdevelopment ideas in the North. This chapter aims to provide a small step in this direction.

Food and agriculture: Solawi[1]

Community-supported agriculture (CSA) was first developed by US small-scale farmers in the 1980s on New England farms. It can be read as a furious response to the nation-wide farming crisis following radical liberalization policies by the Reagan government (Henderson & van En 1999; Lyson 2004). Since the late 1990s CSAs can also be found in Europe. In Germany, several food crises such as mad cow disease raised questions of food safety and underlined the need to transform industrial agriculture production (Feindt, Gottschick, Mölders, Müller, Sodtke & Weiland 2008). CSAs – in German terms called 'Solidarische Landwirtschaft', which translates to 'solidary agriculture' – spread widely in the 2000s. Today we can find nearly 200 CSA projects across Germany, with each one being able to supply between 100 and 500 members with food.[2]

CSA as a concept is based on the idea that sustainable agriculture should hold a balance between supply (by producers) and demand (by consumers). CSA is based on direct relationships between producers and consumers that are stabilized through mutual trust, economic burden-sharing, and monetary and labour commitments. On the farmer's side regaining independence from market pressures and agricultural subsidies is the main asset for engaging in CSAs. The income security offers a way to escape the growth imperative and embark on food production based on sufficiency. Seasonal and climate risks are carried by the group as a whole.[3] Participation instruments such as open (and often consensual) decision-making are used to decide collectively on agricultural issues, such as cultivation methods, choice of crop varieties, use of fertilizers, organic certification labels, or farm wages. During bidding rounds between farmers and members it is declared how much the members would be willing and able to pay for a weekly vegetable delivery. A subsidized solidary price paid by well-off members ensures that other members can participate despite a lower income.

Members' activities within a CSA address, as Flora and Bregendahl (2012) argue, a broad range of nutritional, social, economic, and political dimensions: nutritional demands for safe, healthy, and fresh food are met, as is the desire for more intense nature-society relations as well as the interest to develop economic alternatives to the EU's and the WTO's 'global agriculture paradigm' (Coleman, Grant & Josling 2004), by shortening and localizing the production chain. Also, political and economic dimensions are met concerning questions of food security, food sovereignty, or agricultural monopolies (Macias 2008).

While the postdevelopment debate and the CSA concept seem to be quite natural partners, connections between both concepts have seldom been highlighted in the still scarce literature on CSA. We will discuss this with respect to postdevelopment's four central claims. CSA provides an alternative farming model that promotes rural livelihoods and mutual exchange between producers and consumers. This also includes a commitment towards agrobiodiversity, for instance, the cultivation of rare vegetable or animal species. CSA therefore bears the *potential to thwart processes of commodification*, which are one of the backbones of a capitalist production system. In line with David Harvey's (1990) works on the commodification of nature, Nost (2014) investigates how the value relations between food, growers, and consumers develop in the case of CSA. While CSA does not entirely put an end to value creation, the direct relationship between members and food – mostly accentuated through holistic practices such as volunteering on farms, mutual exchange of vegetables and traditional recipes – reduces alienation in capitalist relations. As there is no individual price for each vegetable, and as the food prices may vary, alternative forms of non-material valorization – i.e., the ritual of exchange, the celebration of common soil, the feeling of belonging and kinship in relation to the land – may come to the forefront, whereas commodification processes lose in relevance. CSA members can therefore be considered as 'holistic microeconomic agents' (Bloemmen, Bobulescu, Tuyen Le & Vitari 2015: 113) acting in a *convivial manner*, rather than as *homines oeconomici*.

CSA promotes *rural livelihoods and sometimes even creates new commons*, which have come under pressure following the rise of industrialized agriculture and the 'global agriculture paradigm' resulting in numerous farm closures and succession problems[4] since the 1980s in both the USA and Western Europe. While farm lifestyles should not be romanticized in terms of caring for the elderly, women's roles, or debt, CSA provides a viable option for safeguarding and transforming rural livelihoods as an alternative to modern contract farming. CSA cultivation practices such as voluntary work or celebration of the harvest may therefore alter the relationship to the land, resulting in a sense of connectedness to food and land (MacMillan, Alexandra, Winham & Wharton 2012; Hvitsand 2016). While this does not normally alter the property regime itself, the collective cultivation and harvesting practices, but also the participatory and often consensual decision-making on land use contribute to an understanding of the CSA land as new commons. Furthermore, several CSAs have re-introduced commons or non-commercial agriculture, such as Munich's 'Kartoffelkombinat', the European Longo Maï communes, or the 'Karl*ahof' on the outskirts of Berlin.

Regarding the *preservation of local knowledge*, CSAs do not give a clear picture. The US examples often refer to well-established farming practices including industrial agriculture, but statutes of the German Solawis promote the preservation of small-scale agriculture, as this is an iconic – and increasingly endangered – form of farming especially in the German southwest, Austria, and Switzerland. This supports local agricultural knowledge, such as cultivation of traditional landraces or the exchange of organic seeds. Also, the structure of CSA and the focus on sufficiency as such is at odds with the established business recommendations of agricultural consultancy, which would – as an expression of the growth imperative – opt for contract farming and making the most of EU agricultural subsidies.

Having started as local agricultural alternatives, many CSAs now regard themselves as political projects in connection to transnational agricultural movements. Still, *explicit references to colonial exploitation systems* are rare. In the German context, the umbrella organization, the 'Netzwerk Solidarische Landwirtschaft', expresses this through a commitment towards internationalism and transnational solidarity.[5] This is articulated politically as a critique of the EU agricultural policy structure at the annual demonstrations titled 'Wir haben es satt!' (We've had enough but also: We're full) that promote radical agricultural change and food sovereignty. Many German CSAs participate in transnational movements such as La Via Campesina, Slow Food, or transition town initiatives. In this light CSA activities also raise consciousness about colonial and postcolonial production chains in agriculture and about fair agricultural work.

Overall, we can conclude that CSAs are able provide viable societal alternatives, in line with postdevelopment aspirations. Still one needs to consider that the CSA concept promotes alternative livelihoods mainly to a quite specific political subject: the urban, well-educated middle class (Hinirchs & Kremer 2002; Brehm & Eisenhauer 2008), and often fails to reach out to economically disadvantaged consumers and communities of color (Slocum 2006; Macias 2008; Andreatta, Rhyne & Dery 2008). In theory, CSA bears the potential to not only preserve traditional rural livelihoods, but also to 'hybridize' them by overcoming centre-periphery dynamics on the urban-rural continuum, and by building connections to soil reaching across heritage, gender, or nationality, thereby feeding into the 'emancipatory postdevelopment' narrative. To facilitate access to projects of solidarity economy for a more pluralist collective, we argue that 'intersectional' strategies such as community outreach and representation of a more mixed crowd of members are needed.

Alternative housing: the case of the 'Mietshäuser Syndikat'

Even though housing is a key good for capitalist production and reproduction and a prime terrain of social conflict, it has to date not been central to the postdevelopment debate. Looking at the case of Brazil's Rio de Janeiro, Hamdi, Hilf, and Schmidt have characterized hegemonic urban development policy as 'eurocentric, depoliticising and authoritarian' and '(re)produced through global and local power structures' (2012: 36). The appropriation of housing space by the *sem-teto* ('without roof') movement in the centre of Rio de Janeiro constitutes an alternative to hegemonic development practice for those parts of the population that are excluded from formal housing markets and political participation.

For Europe, Cattaneo (2017) has explored squatting in Spain as a practice that ruptures dominant notions of development. Looking at migrant waste-pickers in Barcelona, he points to the 'interconnectedness of degrowth in urban metabolism, squatting and open border policy, to sustain an economically efficient, ecologically effective and socially just strategy for degrowth' (Cattaneo 2017: 257). According to Cattaneo, squatting abandoned warehouses puts back

> into use properties that would otherwise be left to decay (with future material costs for managing the abandoned wreck) or be subject to real estate speculation, transformed into other uses through a demolition and further reconstruction, which is an extremely resource-intensive activity.
> *(Cattaneo 2017: 267)*

This seems to fit well with the idea that the castaways of the development project make use of its ruins and shipwrecks, which is how some postdevelopment writers have characterized the creative survival strategies of the marginalized (Sachs 1992; Latouche 1993).

In the 1970s, West German cities saw the emergence of a significant squatting movement, described as 'a self-confident urban counterculture with its own infrastructure of newspapers, self-managed collectives and housing cooperatives, feminist groups, and so on, which was prepared to intervene in local and broader politics' (Mayer 1993). Squats were thus mainly used for residential and social purposes but had wider repercussions for housing policy. Inhabitants and supporters of the movement protected squats against eviction by the police as well as against attacks by neo-Nazis. After the end of the Soviet Union and the annexation of East Germany and in the context of a political vacuum, East Berlin and other cities in East Germany became a hub for the squatter movement as many buildings were vacated (Holm & Kuhn 2016). In the 1990s many squats became legalized housing projects. According to the website

'Berlin Occupied', between 1970 and 2015, '641 occupations of houses, trailer parks and public squares and sites' in Berlin alone took place, of which 200 have been legalized.[6] A few illegal squats still exist today in Germany, and occupations continue to be attempted again and again – albeit unsuccessfully in most cases.

Under pressure and to prevent eviction, a number of former squats have linked themselves to the non-commercial initiative 'Mietshäuser Syndikat'[7] (tenement union) to collectively buy the properties they had been occupying illegally (Holm & Kuhn 2016). The syndicate was founded in the early 1990s in the context of the squatting scene in Hamburg and today encompasses over 130 projects that involve more than 2,500 resident members and 600 non-resident members all over Germany (Buchholz 2016: 205).[8] The syndicate describes its principles as follows:

> Common to all is the collective desire for a house in which it is possible to live a self-determined life, without the Damocles sword of eviction or the wrecker's ball; with affordable living space that is not latently threatened by the sale of the house or the conversion of apartments into upscale condominiums, offices, etc.[9]

The properties are owned collectively through a particular model that allows for autonomous decision-making on internal matters in the case of each project, but prevents houses being privatized and thus effectively withdraws them from the market indefinitely (Schipper 2017: 9–10). The Mietshäuser Syndikat has set up re-sale formulas (or vetoes, also by non-resident members) that limit or eliminate the re-sale option of property (Buchholz 2016: 201). This is assured through a 'dualistic membership structure' that 'implies that resident members autonomously decide all matters that contribute to their quality of life', but that '[i]n case of an intended re-sale of the property, however, the resident community relies on the agreement of the (non-resident) syndicate, which holds a veto option' (Buchholz 2016: 202).

In the context of the sale of public housing stock and the commodification of space, it provides an alternative housing solution that enacts a change to property relations by explicitly rejecting the exchange value of property. By withdrawing private property from the market, the Mietshäuser Syndikat 'makes sure that political ideals (i.e., affordable housing) are secured in the long-run' (203). When the mortgage is paid back, usually profit sets in. This is not the case in the syndicate and while rents may be rising elsewhere, they remain fairly stable and low in the syndicate. Moreover, through the principle of a solidarity transfer 'existing house projects pay into a common pot, the Solidarity Fund, from which new house projects are supported during and beyond the start-up phase'.[10] Active across Germany, Mietshäuser Syndikat constitutes a unique organizational model to combine projects' alternative or radical character and their economic sustainability.

In addition to the grassroots democratic structure and the solidarity principle between the different projects and non-resident members of the syndicate, it also provides the opportunity to live communally and in solidarity in times in which the property market favors single households, couples, and nuclear families – while classism, racism, and sexism make it hard for marginalized spectra of the population to gain access to the rental housing market (I.L.A.-Kollektiv forthcoming). What is more, equipment and space can be used communally by a larger number of people, and marginalized identities can find secure housing and living. Many of the syndicate's projects practice solidarity economies internally and thus secure and improve the livelihoods of its members. The structure of the Mietshäuser Syndikat thus offers the possibility to counter neoliberal individualization in society beyond the mere issue of housing. Mietshäuser Syndikat's alternative modes of organizing communal living economically, politically, and culturally can be seen as ways of practicing postdevelopment. At the same time the initiative does not operate outside of capitalist and bourgeois structures in terms of acquiring property and its legal status – all the while keeping alive the vision of organizing society radically different. In the conceptualization of a diverse economy by Gibson-Graham (2006 [1996]: xiii), the Mietshäuser Syndikat can be identified as engaging in market transactions to transfer privately owned assets into communal ownership, allowing for non-market transactions within the project and contributing to an economy of solidarity.

Housing projects such as those assembled in the Mietshäuser Syndikat also address the extractive dimension of urban development in Germany. The creation and preservation of housing involves immense destruction of nature and use of natural resources. Here, the point is not only the actual sealing of soil, but also the demand for energy and sand for construction. The increase in individual use of living space in the past years in Germany (Behnisch, Kretschmer & Meinel 2018) thus also exacerbates the exploitation of the ecology and societies in the Global South. And the de-individualization apparent in Mietshäuser Syndikat counters this tendency.

The main structural limitation for collective housing in terms of society-wide institutionalization is the lacking capability to purchase reliable objects at an affordable price. It thus continues to be a small-scale development without wider structural repercussions for housing in Germany. What is more, it is not entirely immune to exclusionary tendencies, because participation is often (not formally, but effectively) reserved to people with considerable social and cultural capital – access depends on social relations, knowing the right people. It thus needs to be seen how far it can provide viable alternatives for different spectra of society beyond white, German academic leftist circles. In this context, it may be a promising sign that the contemporary refugee movement has changed the perspectives on vacant property and conditions of use in European countries to a certain degree. Especially in Germany, squatters' practices have changed: 'Instead of accommodating themselves or claiming social centres, more recent squatting activism [at times also led by refugees themselves] has focused on the accommodation of refugees' (Buchholz 2016: 99). Here, Mietshäuser Syndikat projects as well as other housing projects regularly make use of their experience with solidarity structures to offer so-called solidarity rooms for often illegalized migrants (personal experience).

Alternative energy: the case of 'Ende Gelände'

In Germany, climate change has since long been accepted as a real phenomenon and a serious global problem. While it is often regarded as a merely ecological problem that can be solved through new technology and a transition to renewable energy by the Green Party and other politicians, more critical voices such as the climate justice movement or the degrowth movement point to its political, social, and cultural dimensions. Those who profit(ed) most from the burning of fossil fuels also tend to have the means (or geographical locations) to protect themselves from the consequences. Hurricane Katrina's destruction of New Orleans in 2005 was a case in point: the wealthy, predominantly white population was able to get away in their cars, while the mainly black, poor segments of society bore the brunt of the disaster (Elliott & Pais 2006). Ecological racism and classism at the national level are mirrored on a global scale. Poorer, formerly colonized countries are already facing the effects of climate change, even though they have historically contributed little to carbon emissions.

In 2015 at the United Nations Framework Convention on Climate Change in Paris, the international community of states agreed to limit the global temperature increase to well below 2°C. This will require a transition to zero emissions sometime between 2030 and 2050. While Germany has significantly increased the share of renewable energy, the provision of electricity through the burning of coal has not decreased. Germany is home to twelve gigantic opencast lignite pits, burns more lignite than any other country, and one-fifth of overall German carbon emissions can be attributed to lignite-fired power plants (Kemfert 2017). According to Greenpeace (2016), to achieve the goals of the Paris declaration, Germany would have to stop the power supply via lignite and hard coal at the latest in 2025. Energy companies envisage to continue with lignite mining, and while the mining of stone coal is phased out, the German stone coal-fired power plants will continue to burn imported coal from South Africa, Colombia, Russia, and other countries where mining causes serious social and ecological harm.

There has been a controversial debate in Germany on whether and how quick to depart from coal, but the focus of the government, major unions, and the corporate sector continues to be energy efficiency and not a reduction of energy production and consumption. However, recently the emergence of the climate justice movement as well as the degrowth movement in Germany and particularly the campaign 'Ende Gelände' have managed to garner more public and political attention for a socially and ecologically just energy transition (Sander 2017: 26). The climate justice movement 'is a descendant of the environmental justice movement [...] originated in the global south [...], and aims to focus less on technical change and more on basic social structures' (Müller 2016). In its more radical form, degrowth means a 'redistributive downscaling of production and consumption in industrialised countries as a means to achieve environmental sustainability, social justice and well-being' and 'implies an equitable redistribution of wealth [...] across the Global North and South' (Demaria, Schneider, Sekulova & Martínez-Alier 2013: 209). The climate justice and degrowth movement in Germany have a close relationship as they both want to abandon the fossil fuel-based energy system and the capitalist logic it is based on.

The Ende Gelände campaign is characterized by 'a clear rejection of all varieties of green capitalism (green market economy)' and 'through its focus on the tactics of civil disobedience (often mass civil disobedience) and deliberate rule-breaking, in contrast to the more legalistic tactics of traditional environmental organisations' (Müller 2016). A related example of climate activism in Germany is direct action in opencast coal mines. For example, in 2015, the Climate Camp together with participants of the Degrowth Summer School managed to enter the lignite mining area in the Rhineland and disrupt mining activities. This has been done in other opencast pits as well, reaching a high point in November 2017 with more than 1,000 activists occupying the opencast mine Hambach.[11]

The participants of Ende Gelände can be categorized as mainly belonging to what Eversberg and Schmelzer (2016a) with reference to the degrowth movement call the 'libertarian practical left', rooted in an activist alternative social milieu. This current opts for taking 'part in direct actions or lives in alternative projects', where 'openness to spirituality and rejecting the romanticization of nature, [...] and a critique of industrial society [...] go hand in hand' (Eversberg & Schmelzer 2016b). Just as postdevelopment has been described as an anarchist critique of development (Wald 2015), this

> current stands for an anarchist-inspired critique of growth and capitalism that [...] stress[es] aspects of social justice, but also focuses on experiences of *alienation* caused by the perpetual pressure to expand, thereby seeking the leverage point for transformative action in one's own practice.
>
> *(Eversberg & Schmelzer 2016b)*

In comparison to the two postdevelopment practices discussed above, Ende Gelände does not attempt to build niches and alternative practices of energy production and consumption, but to stop the destruction of the regions in which lignite mining is undertaken as well as the negative effects for the South in terms of climate change (global warming, more frequent and more intensive droughts and floods). This could well be seen as a Northern variant of resistance against projects carried out in the name of 'development'. Although the compensations are usually better and there hardly is any othering of displaced persons as backward peoples standing in the way of progress, the parallels to infrastructure projects in the South are clear. Ende Gelände itself does not achieve sustainable livelihoods, but its approach can be regarded as a necessary precondition for the preservation of livelihoods in the Global South while pointing to the need for a just energy transition (Swilling & Annecke 2012). It is an antagonistic practice that focuses on, to use Spehr's (1996: 209) words, 'undeveloping the North'. As part of the climate justice movement, it not only aims at leaving fossil fuels in the ground and shifting to 'appropriate energy-efficiency and safe, clean and community-led renewable energy', but also demands a reduction of consumption, especially by the Global North. Ende Gelände's slogan 'Leave it in the ground' highlights an internationalist awareness as it is evidently a reference to the Yasuní-ITT Initiative, which was linked to the inclusion of *buen vivir* in the Ecuadorian constitution and sought to not exploit the oil reserves in a large area of Ecuador's eastern Amazon.

Concluding reflections

We now return to our four questions derived from postdevelopment theory: do the examples provide economic practices based on an alternative logic, can we find claims for a 'new commons', is Western science challenged by other local knowledges, and is there a break with colonial legacies? Regarding the question whether we can identify economic practices that function according to a non-capitalist logic, community-supported agriculture in Germany is in most cases based on individual ownership of land and on the logic of exchange. However, the relation between producer and consumer is not anonymous but rather characterized by cooperation. The prices are negotiated within this relationship, based on a dialogue on needs and available means. The maximization of production and profits seems largely absent, although it has not been eliminated through structural transformation. Yet CSA includes elements of postdevelopment economic practices. The tenement trust, while also functioning within a capitalist framework, clearly challenges the foundational idea of private ownership of living space. In contrast, collective ownership, the principle of solidarity and removing housing from a market system – a system in which some cannot afford housing while others own houses they do not live in and are able to extract rent from those without property – are the hallmarks of this alternative. The tenement trust thus easily qualifies as a postdevelopment alternative in this respect. In contrast, the anti-coal movement does not engage in economic practices of production, consumption, and exchange at all. It is therefore difficult to portray it as an economic alternative. Still, it not only resists projects of 'development' in the North but explicitly transgresses the property rights of energy corporations by occupying the opencast mines.

This leads us to our second point: the activists against coal mining claim a voice in the decision-making over the production of energy, rejecting the exclusive rights of corporations and politicians in that matter. They can thus be seen as appropriating new commons in line with the ideas of postdevelopment. According to them, the decision to leave the coal in the ground or to exacerbate global warming is a public one, or at least one in which all affected parties should have a say (including people in the Global South and future generations). This constitution of a new commons and the act of taking back control over livelihoods is also present in the other two examples where food production and housing are also being reclaimed from industrial agriculture and a housing market. Instead of being able to exert influence in these areas only on an individual basis through purchasing power, decisions on what to plant and how to live are taken collectively in CSA and the tenement trust.

The third point concerning local culture and scientific knowledge is the most challenging for postdevelopment in the North. In most radical alternatives claims concerning cultural difference are absent and critiques of science are nowhere to be seen. On the contrary, scientific knowledge is sometimes evoked as a resource, e.g., to prove that a transition towards renewable energies is feasible with the next years. References to other, spiritual knowledge systems have not been found in the examples. In this respect, alternatives in the North seem to differ from the original postdevelopment agenda. What we do find, however, are elements of a different relation to nature in two of the examples. CSA participants mention that the involvement in agricultural production and the cycles of organic growth changed the way they perceive the 'fruits of the earth'. And while the rejection of coal mining is entirely compatible with a strong belief in the necessity of technological progress in the field to wind, solar, and geothermal energy plants, at least a portion of the Ende Gelände activists is sympathetic to ideas of *buen vivir* and the rights of nature, as the taking over of the Yasuni slogan ('Leave it in the ground') suggests. Traces of an alternative nature-society relation could be discerned here, but not in the tenement trust. (Of course, if one sees alternative values concerning economic practices and political decision-making also as a form of cultural difference, the results will look different.)

As for the last point, the break with a colonial legacy of global exploitation, results differ between the three examples. The tenement trust seems to be little entangled in (and thus concerned with) relations of neocolonialism, at least not consciously. At first glance, the same might hold true for CSA, but the reorientation towards local networks of agricultural production and consumption is at odds with the colonial division of labor in which the South produces and exports fruit and vegetables to consumers in the North. Thus an increasing focus on local agriculture in the North could be seen as a complimentary element to struggles for food sovereignty in the South. Ende Gelände's anti-coal activism, finally, is explicitly concerned with the 'imperial mode of living' (Brand & Wissen 2017) of the global middle class (which is increasingly located also in the South, see Sachs 2010) and thereby with questions of climate justice between North and South and the legacy of two centuries of industrialization in Europe and North America – in part made possible by colonialism.

Our analysis yields the following: if we apply the criteria for postdevelopment derived from the literature to the examples of alternatives in the North, they are only partially met. The focus on cultural difference and alternative knowledge can be found only in traces of a different relation to nature in some examples, and addressing neocolonialism is no standard element either. However, all three examples seem to be inspired by a widespread sense of discontent of the participants with specific aspects of the existing economic system (regarding healthily and locally produced food, affordable housing, and sustainable energy production) and all aspire to create a 'new commons' in which they regain control over some part of their lives. Therefore we can conclude that also in the North the crisis of the economic and social system (some still say 'of development') leads to new movements looking for creative ways to deal with and overcome these predicaments collectively, trying to increase their autonomy. In this sense, we can also call them postdevelopment alternatives.

Notes

1 The following analysis relates to existing CSA research, but most significantly to Franziska's own experience as a co-founder and member of a CSA in Darmstadt, Germany from 2011 to 2014. If not stated otherwise she refers to the German context.
2 www.solidarische-landwirtschaft.org/solawis-finden/liste-der-solawis-initiativen/.
3 This holds true for German CSAs and has been notified in the statutes of the umbrella organization.
4 The intergenerational transfer of farms from the owner family to their children or grandchildren.
5 www.solidarische-landwirtschaft.org/fileadmin/media/solidarische-landwirtschaft.org/pdf/Mitglied-werden/Netzwerk-Solidarische-Landwirtschaft_Statuten.pdf.
6 www.berlin-besetzt.de/#!.
7 www.syndikat.org/en/.
8 www.syndikat.org/de/projekte/.
9 www.syndikat.org/en/.
10 www.syndikat.org/en/solidarity_transfer/.
11 At the time of writing, in September 2018, hundreds of activists are defying the police in their attempt to evict the treehouse dwellers in Hambach forest for deforestation and the enlargement of a mine by energy corporation RWE.

References

Andreatta, S., Rhyne, M. & Dery, N. (2008) 'Lessons learned from advocating CSAs for low-income and food insecure households'. *Southern Rural Sociology*, vol 23, no 1, pp 116–148.

Behnisch, M., Kretschmer, O. & Meinel, G. (2018) *Flächeninanspruchnahme in Deutschland: Auf dem Wege zu einem besseren Verständnis der Siedlungs- und Verkehrsflächenentwicklung*. Wiesbaden: Springer VS.

Bendix, D. (2017) 'Reflecting the post-development gaze: The degrowth debate in Germany'. *Third World Quarterly*, vol 38, no 12, pp 2617–2633.

Bennett, C. (2012) 'Supporting the posts in development discourse: Under-development, over-development, post-development'. *Sociology Compass*, vol 6, no 12, pp 974–986.

Bloemmen, M., Bobulescu, R., Tuyen Le, N. & Vitari, C. (2015) 'Microeconomic degrowth: The case of community supported agriculture'. *Ecological Economics*, vol 112, pp 110–115.

Brand, U. & Wissen, M. (2017) 'Crisis and continuity of capitalist society-nature relationships: the imperial mode of living and the limits to environmental governance'. *Review of International Political Economy*, vol 20, no 4, pp 687–711.

Brehm, J.M. & Eisenhauer, B.W. (2008) 'Motivations for participating in community-supported agriculture and their relationship with community attachment and social capital'. *Southern Rural Sociology*, vol 23, no 1, pp 94–115.

Buchholz, T. (2016) *Struggling for Recognition and Affordable Housing in Amsterdam and Hamburg: Resignation, Resistance, Relocation*. PhD thesis, University of Groningen. www.academia.edu/26789728/Struggling_for_recognition_and_affordable_housing_in_Amsterdam_and_Hamburg_resignation_resistance_relocation.

Cattaneo, C. (2017) 'Natural resource scarcity, degrowth scenarios and national borders: The role of migrant squats'. In Mudu, P. & Chattopadhyay, S. (eds.), *Migration, Squatting and Radical Autonomy. Resistance and Destabilization of Racist Regulatory Policies and b/Ordering Mechanisms*, pp 257–271. London: Routledge.

Chari, S. & Corbridge, S. (eds.) (2008) *The Development Reader*. London: Routledge.

Coleman, W, Grant, W. & Josling, T. (2004) *Agriculture in the New Global Economy*. Cheltenham: Edward Elgar Publishing.

Corbridge, S. (1998) '"Beneath the pavement only soil": The poverty of post-development'. *The Journal of Development Studies*, vol 34, no 6, pp 138–148.

Cowen, M. & Shenton, R. (1995) 'The invention of development'. In Crush, J. (ed.), *The Power of Development*, pp 27–43. London: Routledge.

Demaria, F., Schneider, F., Sekulova, F. & Martínez-Alier, J. (2013) 'What is degrowth? From an activist slogan to a social movement'. *Environmental Values*, vol 22, no 2, pp 191–215.

Elliott, J.R. & Pais, J. (2006) 'Race, class, and Hurricane Katrina: Social differences in human responses to disaster'. *Social Science Research*, vol 35, no 2, pp 295–321.

Escobar, A. (1995) *Encountering Development. The Making and Unmaking of the Third World*. Princeton, NJ: Princeton University Press.

Esteva, G. (1992) 'Development'. In Sachs, W. (ed.), *The Development Dictionary. A Guide to Knowledge as Power*, pp 6–25. London: Zed Books.

Eversberg, D. & Schmelzer, M. (2016a) 'Über die Selbstproblematisierung zur Kapitalismuskritik. Vier Thesen zur entstehenden Degrowth-Bewegung'. *Forschungsjournal Soziale Bewegungen*, vol 29, no 1, pp 9–17.

Eversberg, D. & Schmelzer, M. (2016b) 'Critical self-reflection as a path to anti-capitalism: The degrowth-movement'. *Degrowth Blog* (blog). 23 February 2016. www.degrowth.info/en/2016/02/critical-self-reflection-as-a-path-to-anti-capitalism-the-degrowth-movement/.

Federici, S. (2004) *Caliban and the Witch: Women, the Body and Primitive Accumulation*. New York: Autonomedia.

Feindt, P.H., Gottschick, M., Mölders, T., Müller, F., Sodtke, R. & Weiland, S. (2008) *Nachhaltige Agrarpolitik als reflexive Politik*. Berlin: Edition Sigma.

Flora, C.B. & Bregendahl, C. (2012) 'Collaborative community-supported agriculture: Balancing community capitals for producers and consumers'. *International Journal of Society of Agriculture & Food*, vol 19, no 3, pp 329–346.

Gibson-Graham, J.K. (2006 [1996]) *The End of Capitalism (As We Knew It). A Feminist Critique of Political Economy*. 2nd ed. Minneapolis: University of Minnesota Press.

Gibson-Graham, J.K. (2005) 'Surplus possibilities: Postdevelopment and community economies'. *Singapore Journal of Tropical Geography*, vol 26, no 1, pp 4–26.

Greenpeace (2016) 'Was bedeutet das Pariser Abkommen für den Klimaschutz in Deutschland?' www.greenpeace.de/files/publications/160222_klimaschutz_paris_studie_02_2016_fin_neu.pdf.

Habermann, F. & Ziai, A. (2007) 'Development, internationalism and social movements. A view from the North'. In Ziai, A. (ed.), *Exploring Post-development. Theory and Practice, Problems and Perspectives*, pp 212–227. London: Routledge.

Habermann, F. (2012) 'Von Postdevelopment, Postwachstum und Peer-Ecommony: Alternative Lebensweisen als 'Abwicklung des Nordens''. *Journal für Entwicklungspolitik*, vol 28, no 4, pp 69–87.
Hamdi, A., Hilf, S. & Schmidt, K. (2012) 'Alternativen in der Stadt: Der Kampf der Sem-Tetos in Rio de Janeiro'. *Journal Für Entwicklungspolitik*, vol 28, no 4, pp 30–47.
Harvey, D. (1990) 'Between space and time: Reflections on the geographical imagination'. *Annals of the Association of American Geographers*, vol 80, no 3, pp 418–434.
Henderson, E. & van En, R. (1999) *Sharing the Harvest: A Citizen's Guide to Community Supported Agriculture*. White River Junction, VT: Chelsea Green Publishing Company.
Hinirchs, C.C. & Kremer, K. (2002) 'Social inclusion in a Midwest local food system project'. *Journal of Poverty*, vol 6, no 1, pp 65–90.
Holm, A. & Kuhn, A. (2016) 'Squatting and gentrification in East Germany since 1989'. In Anders, F. & Sedlmaier, A. (eds.), *Public Goods versus Economic Interests: Global Perspectives on the History of Squatting*, pp 278–304. London: Routledge.
Hvitsand, C. (2016) 'Community supported agriculture (CSA) as a transformational act - distinct values and multiple motivations among farmers and consumers'. *Agroecology and Sustainable Food Systems*, vol 40, no 4, pp 333–351.
I.L.A.-Kollektiv (forthcoming) *Die Solidarische Lebensweise. Aufbruch in das gute Leben für alle*. München: Oekom.
Kemfert, C. (2017) *Das Fossile Imperium schlägt zurück. Warum wir die Energiewende jetzt verteidigen müssen*. Hamburg: Murmann.
Kiely, R. (1999) 'The last refuge of the noble savage? A critical assessment of post-development theory'. *European Journal of Development Research*, vol 11, no 1, pp 30–55.
Latouche, S. (1993) *In the Wake of the Affluent Society. An Exploration of Post-Development*. London: Zed Books.
Linebaugh, P. & Rediker, M. (2008) *Die vielköpfige Hydra: Die verborgene Geschichte des revolutionären Atlantiks*. Berlin: Assoziation A.
Lyson, T.A. (2004) *Civic Agriculture: Reconnecting Farm, Food, and Community*. Lebanon: University of New England Press.
Macias, T. (2008) 'Working toward a just, equitable, and local food system: The social impact of community-based agriculture'. *Social Science Quarterly*, vol 89, no 5, pp 1086–1101.
MacMillan, U., Alexandra, L., Winham, D.M. & Wharton, C.M. (2012) 'Community supported agriculture membership in Arizona. An exploratory study of food and sustainability behaviours'. *Appetite*, vol 59, no 2, pp 431–436.
Mayer, M. (1993) 'The career of urban social movements in West Germany'. In Risher, R. & Kling, J.M. (eds.), *Mobilizing the Community: Local Politics in the Era of the Global City*, pp 149–170. London: Sage.
McGregor, A. (2009) 'New possibilities? Shifts in post-development theory and practice'. *Geography Compass*, vol 3, no 5, pp 1688–1702.
Müller, T. (2016) 'Climate justice. Global resistance to fossil-fuelled capitalism'. www.degrowth.info/en/dim/degrowth-in-movements/climate-justice/.
Nost, E. (2014) 'Scaling up local foods. Commodity practice in community-supported agriculture'. *Journal of Rural Studies*, vol 34, pp 152–160.
Power, M. (2006) 'Anti-racism, deconstruction and "overdevelopment"'. *Progress in Development Studies*, vol 6, no 1, pp 25–39.
Rahnema, M. (1997) 'Introduction'. In Rahneema, M. & Bawtree, V. (eds.), *The Post-development Reader*, pp ix–xix. London: Zed Books.
Sachs, W. (1992) *The Development Dictionary. A Guide to Knowledge as Power*. London: Zed Books.

Sachs, W. (2010) 'Preface to the new edition'. In Sachs, W. (ed.), *The Development Dictionary. A Guide to Knowledge as Power*, pp vi–xiv. London: Zed Books.

Sander, H. (2017) 'Ende Gelände: Anti-Kohle-Proteste in Deutschland'. *Forschungsjournal Soziale Bewegungen*, vol 30, no 1, pp 26–36.

Schipper, S. (2017) *Wohnraum dem Markt entziehen? Wohnungspolitik und städtische soziale Bewegungen in Frankfurt und Tel Aviv*. Wiesbaden: Springer VS.

Slocum, R. (2006) 'Anti-racist practice and the work of community food organizations'. *Antipode*, vol 38, no 2, pp 327–349.

Spehr, C. (1996) *Die Ökofalle. Nachhaltigkeit und Krise*. Wien: Promedia.

Swilling, M. & Annecke, E. (2012) *Just Transitions: Explorations of Sustainability in an Unfair World*. New York: United Nations University Press.

Wald, N. (2015) 'Anarchist participatory development: A possible new framework?' *Development and Change*, vol 46 no 4, pp 618–643.

White, S. (2002) 'Thinking race, thinking development'. *Third World Quarterly*, vol 23, no 3, pp 407–419.

Ziai, A. (2015) 'Post-development: Premature burials and haunting ghosts'. *Development and Change*, vol 46, no 4, pp 833–854.

Ziai, A. (forthcoming) 'Undeveloping the North'. In Kothari, A., Salleh, A., Escobar, A., Demaria, F. & Acosta, A. (eds.), *Pluriverse. A Post-development Dictionary*. Delhi: Authors Up Front.

9

WHO WANTS A 'DEVELOPMENT' THAT DOESN'T RECOGNISE ALTERNATIVES?

Working with and against postdevelopment in Jagatsinghpur, India

Sandeep Pattnaik and Samantha Balaton-Chrimes

Introduction

In the district of Jagatsinghpur, in the eastern Indian state of Odisha, a community of betel-farmers, fisherfolk and livestock herders spent more than a decade in a protracted struggle against South Korean steel giant POSCO to retain their coastal farming, grazing lands, waterbodies and other environmental resources that are shared in common and used for livelihoods. In 2017, POSCO finally withdrew, and the community has enjoyed a temporary reprieve from forced land acquisition threats, though rumours are rife that other companies are interested in the land. The communities believe that their struggle is not over.

In this chapter, we examine the anti-POSCO People's Movement (*POSCO Pratirodh Sangram Samiti*, PPSS) as an example of postdevelopment in practice. The movement's anti-corporate stance, its defence of its members' common and private land and resources, its resistance to a forcible transition to wage labour and exclusion from land-based sustainable livelihoods, its concern for the environment and its insistence on members' rights to determine their own futures all align with key tenets of postdevelopment. Because the movement has developed as inherently oppositional, and is situated within a highly polarised political economy of development in Odisha, it is easy and indeed tempting to understand the movement as almost quintessentially postdevelopment. However, upon closer inspection, there are a number of axes on which the movement's stance is more aligned with some quite traditional (pre-neoliberal) ideas around development, including the importance of access to markets for petty commodities, and a strong belief in the state as both the inevitable and appropriate site of self-governance and an agent of development (in this case through the provision of infrastructure for petty commodity production and trade). We offer this actually existing practice, then, as an example of how an exceptionally resilient community has resisted unwanted development, while also engaging in and negotiating not only postdevelopment principles, but also development ones, generating its own vision of the future and the good life that rejects globalised and heavily industrialised capitalism, but seeks engagement with and benefit from local small-scale industrialised capitalist trade and the state. In general, villagers have not displaced development as the set of discourses and practices through which living conditions are understood (Escobar 2012: xii–xiii), but rather they imagine a development alternative (not an alternative to development). As Corbridge (1998: 139) notes, opting out of development is not the only option.

In this chapter we draw on publicly available documents and qualitative research with PPSS leaders. We draw on research we have conducted independently and together since Sandeep began working with the movement in 2009, and Samantha began researching the POSCO case in 2011. This includes knowledge Sandeep has gleaned as a solidarity activist working on displacement and the rights of scheduled tribes and castes, and documenting the movement's work (Pattnaik 2011) and knowledge Samantha has gained researching the movement's efforts to oust POSCO (Balaton-Chrimes 2016; Balaton-Chrimes & Haines 2016). In addition, we also draw on recent interviews (five with PPSS members, two with PPSS leaders) conducted by Sandeep in April 2018, a time in which the movement was regrouping after POSCO's withdrawal a little over a year earlier, strategising about possible future threats of land acquisition, and reflecting on how to reconfigure its goals in light of POSCO's exit.

We are exploring here the movement's ideas of what it is to live well, their formulation of the good life. At this point, a few methodological caveats are in order. In speaking of 'the movement's' view of the good life, we are not suggesting this is a singular vision. The villagers who are members of the movement include different people with different skills and livelihoods, and different property rights, and these differences (among others) generate variation in people's desires. We consider this normal and attend to the variation in our analysis. We also wish to be clear that, when we deal with recent interview material, this picture of villagers' aspirations is a snapshot of a particular point in time, albeit situated against the lengthy backdrop of opposition to globalised and industrialised capitalist expansion. We are not suggesting this snapshot captures a fixed set of desires, nor that it covers everything members of the movement might want now or in the future. We labour this point in order to ward against a common criticism made of postdevelopment, namely that it romanticises and essentialises social movements (Ziai 2017: 2547–2548). We wish to do neither, but rather to keep open a space for internal diversity and changes over time in how these communities conceptualise what it is to live well. Finally, our research has been conducted only with members of the movement, and so does not take into account the desires of villagers who were pro-POSCO because they expected (unrealistically high levels of) compensation and benefits from the project (Balaton-Chrimes 2016: 21). These pro-POSCO villagers have formed the United Action Committee, consisting of around 1000 members, demanding a compensation package for loss of betel vines, prawn gheries and cultivable land at the proposed project site. We exclude these people from our research not to invalidate their development aspirations, but because of the focus of this edited volume on postdevelopment in practice.

We focus here on PPSS in order to contribute to the growing postdevelopment literature that is rich in empirical detail, and therefore much greater nuance than the early work on postdevelopment (Escobar 2012: xv–xvi). We are not suggesting our analysis of PPSS can be generalised to all people's movements, or even all anti-displacement or anti-corporate people's movements in India. Rather, this snapshot is intended to be generative of insights about the interplay between development and postdevelopment principles and aspirations (Hage 2016). It is, in de Sousa Santos' (2014: ix, 44) terms, 'rearguard theory', anchored in an empirical account of the movement that seeks to know *with*, understand, facilitate and share, rather than acting as a theoretical vanguard that claims to know *about*, explain and guide.

In what follows, we outline the history of the movement in the context of Odisha, where a very traditional modernist development project is being vigorously pursued by the state government. We go on to explore two areas in which there is tension between development and postdevelopment sensibilities: the role of the state in self-governance, and a commitment to state-supported small-scale light industrial capitalist production and trade. We conclude by arguing that if we are committed to building a pluriverse, then we need to attend to aspirations that entail tensions between postdevelopment and more traditional development principles.

Oppositional development politics

The political economy of Odisha is one that heavily privileges a modernist imaginary of development as occurring through economic growth, fuelled by industrialisation (especially private sector) and hostile to alternative understandings of development or ways of life. Until the 1980s, Odisha's economy was predominantly agricultural, with some light manufacturing (Adduci 2012). Where there were industrial developments, such as the state-owned Rourkela steel plant, NALCO Aluminium or the Hirakud dam, these were designed to meet the needs of the state for energy or broader India for the expansion of its industrial base, but they did little to contribute to the state's economic growth (Adduci 2012). Beginning as early as the 1980s and accelerating under the Biju Janata Dal (BJD) government with Naveen Patnaik as chief minister since 1997, the state government has sought to reorient the economy towards industrialisation.[1] The state government sees industrialisation, particularly through mining of the state's abundant mineral resources (Department of Steel & Mines 2015) and value-adding processes (such as steel manufacturing) as the key to generating employment (Adduci 2012: 78). In order to exploit these natural resources, the state has sought to out-compete other states to attract private, including foreign, capital and concentrated its efforts in the iron ore and steel sectors.[2] A progressively established policy framework seeks to facilitate this investment through committing to deregulation, with a focus on the mineral sector, and orienting the government's role to the establishment of infrastructure through public–private partnerships (via the Odisha Industrial Policy 2001, Industries Facilitation Act 2004 and Industrial Policy 2007, Policy for Special Economic Zone 2015), providing special security for industrial projects through the Odisha Industrial Security Forces Act (2012) and the establishment of the country's first Single Window Clearance mechanism (following the Odisha Industries (Facilitation) Act 2004) to speed up clearances and approvals (Odisha State Government 2018). The government has been particularly proactive in providing support for land acquisition through the Industrial Infrastructure Development Corporation (IDCO) of Odisha, which is a state nodal agency for land acquisition. The IDCO has already reserved at least 59,000 acres under a land bank project for industrial infrastructure, partly in response to POSCO's withdrawal over difficulties in land acquisition (*Times of India* 2017).

The shift in state economic policy towards industrialisation and liberalisation has led to high economic growth rates, an estimated 7.14% for 2017–2018, surpassing the national growth rate of 6.5% (*New Indian Express* 2018). Poverty has also decreased significantly in the state, from 57.2% in 2004–2005 (60.8% in rural areas and 37.6% in urban areas) to 32.59% in 2011–2012 (35.69% in rural areas and 17.29% in urban areas). Nevertheless, Odisha remains one of the poorest states in India (where national poverty rates had dropped to 21.92% in 2011–2012 (Planning Commission 2014: 28–29) and poverty is particularly concentrated among the state's large population of vulnerable populations, where poverty rates are at 63.52% for scheduled tribes and 41.39% for scheduled castes in 2011–2012 (Planning and Coordination Department 2014: 271).

Conventional critics of the state's development model have not departed from a modernist imaginary of development, but rather focus on problems with its implementation. Some have argued that increases in mining and industry have not had the anticipated effect of also increasing production and employment in downstream sectors such as manufacturing (Adduci 2012: 86–88). Others argue that the failure of mining-led industrialisation to bring benefit to all the people of Odisha is, in part, the result of the government's failure to adequately regulate the industry to ensure that private investments adhere to the rule of law and make adequate assessments of the costs and benefits of private (or public) industrial projects (Maringanti, Mathew & Naidu 2013: 71). Some on the Indian left attribute this 'growth without inclusion' to the parallel neglect of agriculture (Mishra 2010; Panda 2008). The agricultural sector provides more employment than the industrial sector, yet the state government has allowed the sector to stagnate through lack of investment, as well as slow but steady dispossession of agricultural land and other forms of common property, such as forests and water resources, that traditional agriculturalists use in farming (Mishra 2011).

Both the state's development model and the most common criticisms of it subscribe to what Ziai (2013: 126–127) identifies as the core assumptions of development that postdevelopmentalists are concerned about: the existential assumption that there is such a thing as development, the normative assumption that development is a good thing, the practical assumption that development can be achieved and the methodological assumption that units (states) can be compared according to their development.[3] Furthermore, both the state's model and its main critics also share in three additional assumptions Ziai identifies as associated with the *classical* paradigm of development: that the goal is to be industrialised like the countries of North America and Europe; that this is to be achieved through economic growth, industrialisation and modernisation; and that such interventions can be readily legitimated by basing them on expert knowledge.[4]

Though academic criticism of this development model in Odisha has largely shared in these assumptions and sought to better implement programs of industrialisation and growth, a number of anti-corporate and anti-displacement people's movements have mounted more fundamental challenges to this model. These movements have questioned the extreme social, economic and environmental costs that ordinary people face when displaced for large-scale industrial projects. They typically seek to stop major industrial projects, but sometimes seek to negotiate better terms for benefit sharing, usually in cases where there is no realistic hope of retaining their land (Dash & Samal 2008). By rejecting industrialisation and global capitalism as development mechanisms, these people's movements share postdevelopment concerns. Between 2005, when the state government signed a Memorandum of Understanding with POSCO, and 2017 when the company pulled out, PPSS was one of the most resilient and successful of these movements.

The proposed POSCO project was a US$12 billion investment – the biggest foreign direct investment India has ever seen – that would have included construction of an integrated steel plant, mine and associated infrastructure. It had unprecedented levels of support from the state government of Odisha, as well as the Union government of India, and the South Korean Government, and the MoU offered particularly generous terms for POSCO with respect to access to land and minerals, taxes and support for clearing regulatory hurdles (Balaton-Chrimes 2016: 14–15). The most controversy was around the proposed plant site of 4004 acres, covering eight villages in the three *gram panchayats* of Dhinkia, Gobindapur and Gadakujanga, and a total population of 22,000 people (Asher 2009: 11; IHRC & ESCR-net 2013: 12; MZPSG 2010: 6; Pingle, Pandey & Suresh 2010: 52). A total of 718 families would have been displaced (Balaton-Chrimes 2016: 14). The compensation package offered by POSCO was inadequate to protect against impoverishment, there was inadequate consultation around the project and its impacts and there were high levels of government-sponsored violence, intimidation and harassment against PPSS members (Balaton-Chrimes 2016; IHRC & ESCR-net 2013). Supporters helped the movement with legal and regulatory appeals, national and transnational campaigning and a complaint to the OECD National Contact Point (Balaton-Chrimes 2016), but the most decisive factor in making the project untenable for POSCO was the resistance of the people's movement.

Formed within weeks of the signing of the POSCO MoU, PPSS claims to represent 80% of the people in the areas affected by the proposed POSCO steel plant in Jagatsinghpur, with Dhinkia Panchayat the movement's consistent stronghold (Ceresna 2011: 20). The movements' objective was to prevent the POSCO project from going ahead; to retain their ancestral lands and livelihoods; and to protect the local environment. Its strategy to achieve these objectives has been two-fold: non-violent direct action and a policy of non-engagement with the company or government on anything other than protection of their land and environmental rights. The movement is structured through village committees, an inter-village general council of 1000–1500 members of approximately 20,000 people potentially displaced (it changes over time), an executive committee consisting of 51 members, 40% of whom are women (who strategically take the lead in rallies, demonstrations and confrontations with the police), and a smaller core leadership group of approximately ten people responsible for urgent decisions, led by the movement's chairman, Abhay Sahoo, who is a member of the Communist Party of India (CPI) (Pattnaik 2011: 54; Interview with Prasant Paikray, spokesperson PPSS, Bhubaneshwar, December 2012; Interview with Abhay Sahoo, leader PPSS, Jagatsinghpur, December 2013). Members of PPSS make small financial contributions to the movement to sustain its activities, and participate in non-violent direct-action protests. Day to day, members of the movement provide mutual support, for example, through resolving conflict to avoid having to deal with the police, or through working on collective projects such as unblocking waterways, or preparing for cyclones (Pattnaik 2011: 58; Interview with Prasant Paikray, spokesperson PPSS, Bhubaneshwar, December 2012).

PPSS thus functions both as a resistance movement and a self-help movement that filled the gap left by a state they saw as promoting POSCO's interests over that of its citizens. PPSS liaises with more formal organisations, such as civil society organisations, legal activists or journalists, academics, anti-displacement movements, political parties and national and international solidarity committees to take advantage of their technical expertise and networks. Other organisations can make their own decisions regarding their strategies and tactics, which, by engaging the law and other more formal channels, are complementary to non-violent direct action and non-engagement with the government on matters other than protection of land and environmental rights. However, PPSS operates on the principle of solidarity, constituted by a strict policy of non-interference from outside organisations in PPSS's internal matters (Interview with Prasant Paikray, spokesperson PPSS, Bhubaneshwar, December 2012). Though POSCO has quit the project, the issue of land already acquired and transferred to POSCO still remains. Odisha's industry minister has told the state assembly the land will be kept in a land bank and plans are being made to fence the land. Since POSCO's withdrawal, PPSS has called on the government to return the land, and has mobilised people to repossess their farm lands and reconstruct their vineyards for the cultivation of betel leaves.

As an 'anti'-movement, PPSS's goals have been defined primarily in oppositional terms – what they are against, rather than what they are for. The initial formation of the movement was facilitated by Ghandian activists who had a presence in the area as part of a humanitarian effort after the 1999 super cyclone, and who shared the early information about the project and its impacts with the villagers. Their non-violent approach, even in the face of attacks from pro-POSCO villagers, attracted many new members to the movement. They organised mass *dharanas* (sit-ins) outside government offices, and had roving *satyagrahis* (proponents of non-violence) raising awareness throughout the villages (Pattnaik 2011: 55). A few months later, opposition political parties, particularly CPI, began touring the area and also became involved in the movement (Pattnaik 2011: 56), quickly forming a leadership group. The movement therefore has its ideological origins both in Ghandian notions of *swaraj* (self-rule) and in leftist opposition to (particularly global) capitalism.[5] However, neither of these ideological orientations has firmly shaped the aspirations of the villagers, who instead hold a less ideologically developed commitment simply to a source of livelihood that is both adequate and sustainable over the long term, and which is often (but not always) deemed by villagers to include guaranteed access to communal resources.

Development and postdevelopment

PPSS's emphasis on political self-governance (particularly through the activities of the *gram sabhas* (Village Councils)), economic self-determination and ecological preservation in many ways aligns neatly with a postdevelopment sensibility. The movement does not trust that the state's modernist development will deliver on its promise of improved quality of life (Sachs 2010: xii). It is critical of disvaluing of non-industrial and non-economised ways of life, and of the violence and domination that takes place in the name of the expansion of capitalism and a Westernised way of life (Ziai 2015: 840–842; 2017: 2457–2458). More specifically, the movement objects to the enclosure of the commons, the associated transformation of farmers or fisherfolk into (surplus) wage labourers, and the risks this poses to their very survival, and adopts civil disobedience as a strategy to combat these risks (Shiva 2005). However, looking more closely, villagers' aspirations – as opposed to their rejections – reveal a more complex engagement with some of the core tenets of postdevelopment scholarship.

The state and self-governance

The postdevelopment literature, in its earliest iterations, held a stance of suspicion toward the state. Esteva and Prakash's (2014: 13) idealised postmodern grassroots movements, for example, were 'independent from and antagonistic to the state and its formal and corporative structures'. More recent scholarship both within and critical of postdevelopment has rightly corrected this hostile stance to ask more nuanced questions about the role of the state in what this volume is calling postdevelopment in practice. Following Corbridge's call for field research that reveals the everyday experiences of state (and market) (Corbridge 2010: 87; see also Corbridge, Williams, Srivastava & Véron 2005), we agree that attention to actually existing practices of state-citizen relations is more useful for understanding and advancing the aspirations of people in the South. In the case of India, Vandana Shiva (2005: 35) characterises the state as having an ambivalent role in a 'zone of contest in conflicts between enclosures and reclamation of the commons'. While the state can sometimes be 'inverted', more committed to foreign investment than its citizens' wellbeing (Shiva 2005: 77–78), it is also the case that some postdevelopment arguments are problematic insofar as they call for a weakening of states that can expose communities to the vagaries and violence of global capitalism (McGregor 2009: 1696). PPSS's struggle is situated within precisely this predicament; the actually existing state *is* more committed to foreign capital than citizen welfare, but if not the state, then who will protect the villagers from that very same capital?

PPSS has been continuously and keenly alive to the dilemma this poses. One of the movement's most central and consistent strategies has thus been to advocate for proper implementation of citizen rights to self-governance outlined in Indian legislation via the *panchayati raj* (rule by village councils) system. The 73rd amendment of the Indian Constitution recognises the *panchayats* as self-governing units at the district and sub-district levels, and as the main locus of democratic decentralisation.[6] In 2006, a further important piece of legislation, the Scheduled Tribes and Other Traditional Forest Dwellers (Recognition of Forest Rights) Act, commonly known simply as the Forest Rights Act (FRA), came into force. This Act proposes to set right the historical injustices done to those living in and around forests. In order to protect their existing livelihoods and way of life, people in the villages affected by the proposed POSCO project applied – without success – for recognition of their status as Other Traditional Forest Dwellers (Balaton-Chrimes 2016: 17). This is a category afforded special land rights under FRA, namely (in Sections 2 and 3a) the 'right to hold and live in the forest land under the individual or common occupation for habitation or for self cultivation for livelihood'. In short, Indian law provides for considerable decision-making autonomy for PPSS members, and one of the movement's primary objectives is to activate these laws.

Since the signing of the POSCO MoU in 2005, *gram sabha* resolutions rejecting the POSCO project were passed in all three *gram panchayats*, though these have been ignored by the state government (Balaton-Chrimes 2016: 18). These resolutions demonstrate how the movement has utilised a robust collective decision making process and a strong sense of camaraderie among themselves to combat the state's efforts to avoid its responsibilities and forcibly displace them, of which they are keenly aware.

This strategy reflects the movement's commitment to strengthen existing mechanisms of self-governance. We deliberately use the term self-governance here, rather than self-determination, because the implication is not that the movement's members seek some form of independence from the state, either in the sense of separatism or in the sense of a lack of dependence.[7] On the contrary, the movement sees the state as having responsibilities to respect and fulfil the aspirations of villagers. This does not necessarily mean the claim is not a radical one, however – it is quite radical insofar as it calls on the state for resources and investment, but in a way that is *entirely deferent* to local decision-making processes. The relationship the movement is trying to establish, then, is one of mutual interdependence between people and the state. The effort is to move from the current state hostility towards a situation in which the state is theirs.

The state, small-scale industrialised capitalism and wage labour

Perhaps even more so than the state, the postdevelopment literature has a very hostile attitude toward markets. Ziai (2017: 2458) identifies one of the core tenets of postdevelopment as conceptualising development as an economic rationality centred around accumulation, and possessing a capitalist logic of privileging activities earning money through the market. Esteva (2010: 17) claims that 'disengaging form the economic logic of the market or the plan has become the very condition for survival'. Shiva (2010: 238) is also critical of market-centred economies, compared to earth-centred economies, which she holds are infinitely better at 'providing better human sustenance for all'. Yet, PPSS and its members depend on national- and state-level markets in petty commodities for their survival, and intend to continue to do so.

The district of Jagatsinghpur hosts a highly productive and relatively (by rural Indian standards) lucrative agricultural economy. The majority of villagers cultivate a range of crops including betel,[8] paddy, cashew and other tree species, as well as collecting minor forest products such as bamboo and fuel (Pingle, Pandey & Suresh 2010: 19), while some engage in fishing, operate shrimp farms (pisciculture) or practice animal husbandry (IHRC & ESCR-net 2013: 12–13). Of these livelihood activities, betel cultivation and trading is the most lucrative, earning an average annual profit of about Rs 200,000 (US$ 3374) in 2010 for the owner (IHRC & ESCR-net 2013: 12), and providing additional employment for landless labourers (Asher 2009: 12). In addition to the income stream provided by cultivation of betel, shrimp or cashews, families in the affected villages in Jagatsinghpur also supplement their livelihood in significant ways by accessing common resources, including rice, fish and forest products that are gathered locally and used for household consumption (MZPSG 2010: 37–38). Furthermore, these livelihoods engage all members of the family in productive work (MZPSG 2010: 35). In a context of deteriorating agricultural production and associated impoverishment and marginalisation of rural populations in Odisha, this successful agricultural way of life is significant (cf. Mishra 2011).

As such, PPSS members are very committed to retaining these livelihood sources. The vision articulated in our interviews with PPSS members, and in PPSS communications with supporters (sent out via email regularly), is one of a light industrial form of capitalism that supports small-scale petty commodity production and trade. The emphasis is on livelihoods that are both sustainable, in terms of protecting natural resources for the long-term future, and dignified, in terms of enabling people some autonomy, financial security and a reasonable standard of living. To support these aspirations, villagers want the state to provide infrastructure, such as roads and small-scale processing factories for commodities like cashews. In this sense, they want to benefit from modern technologies, not to return any kind of idealised pre-technological era, as postdevelopmentalists can sometimes demand (see also Nanda 1999). However, they see technology as playing a complementary role in the preservation of livelihood and natural resources. Far from constituting Rahnema's vernacular society, in which 'abundance is perceived as a state of nature' (2010: 187), villagers are, in fact, worried about the security of their natural resources, and actively seek to protect them, but in order that they might be exploited over the long-term, in a sustainable way. The effort here is, then, to push the state to become a sustainably developmental state.

In addition to this commitment to small-scale petty commodity production and trade, supported by the state, there is some ambivalence around wage labour among PPSS members that also complicates the postdevelopment paradigm. Though there is some willingness among men to become proletarianised or semi-proletarianised by accepting wage labouring positions in nearby heavy industry, this is generally only understood as acceptable as a supplement to secure land rights and ongoing production of betel and so on. PPSS members do not want to sacrifice their own land and resources, but are willing to benefit from the employment opportunities offered by heavy industrialisation in other areas. Women are much less enthusiastic about a move to wage labouring, understandably given the very few employment opportunities for women in heavy industry. Equally, many people who either were landless to begin with, or have become landless through forcible land acquisition, are *dalit* or low-caste people. They find themselves in a particularly precarious position, living barely hand-to-mouth on wages earned labouring on other people's land, and are therefore willing to take wage labour positions in factories, but ultimately still desire land or land restitution as their first priority.

One of the reasons for the ambivalence around wage labour and the staunch commitment to land-based livelihoods is the villagers' witnessing of the experience of a nearby village with heavy industrialisation – the Indian Oil refinery. PPSS members have seen the plight of 5000 displaced villagers of Trilochanpur (part of Dhinkia Panchayat but not in the proposed POSCO area) who gave their land to Indian Oil Corporation Ltd. in the 1990s, but did not get ongoing employment in the factory built there. In 2017, affected villagers – neighbours of PPSS members – organised under the banner of *Jamihara Krushak Ekta Manch* (Solidarity platform of families who lost land to Indian Oil) and launched an indefinite hunger strike demanding permanent jobs, and more adequate compensation and rehabilitation for their earlier displacement. This case, and many others like it in the state, have demonstrated that the promise of a position in the proletariat is often a false one, and that displaced people are far more likely to be surplus to labour demands, and to fall into a vicious cycle of impoverishment and social dysfunction. Individual villagers' interest in becoming wage labourers is, then, contingent upon their degree of optimism regarding opportunity, and their assessment of their other livelihood options, particularly for women (who have few wage opportunities) and the landless (who are more in need of income than those with land).

Concluding reflections

One of the long-standing critiques of postdevelopment scholarship is that is has an inconsistent theory of power (Lehmann 1997: 573; Ziai 2004: 1047). On the one hand, postdevelopmentalists (especially the early ones) paint a picture of a developmental power so ubiquitous it is inescapable, and yet on the other they glorify autonomous and untainted people's movements that have somehow escaped development's reach to imagine and pursue alternative life projects. Our research with PPSS shows that neither extreme is the case. In practice, the power of the conventional development imaginary is significant and has shaped the aspirations of members of the people's movement, but not so much that they have come to resemble only *homo oeconomici* desiring nothing but a Western way of life. Desires for improvement are a negotiation on a messy terrain of power's effects.

The case of the anti-POSCO people's movement is inspiring in many ways. Their resilience in the face of more than a decade of violence and hostility from government and the private sector in order to protect a dignified and sustainable way of life is remarkable. However, the movement does not align neatly with all that the postdevelopment literature proposes as core to postdevelopment. It is our contention that this does not simply mean the movement has been co-opted by the development machine, but that the pluriversality the movement aims at is more subtle in nature and practice. We don't want to imply some kind of pure and autochthonous emergence of untainted ideas and desires, but nor do we wish to imply false consciousness. What this research shows instead is a thick social, economic and political fabric in which a plurality of desires exists in conversation with each other.

Notes

1 Naveen Pattnaik is son of Biju Pattnaik, the founding father of the state of Odisha. Pattnaik and his party, BJD, were in an alliance with the Bharatiya Janata Party (BJP) from 1998 until 2009, after which time BJD was able to gain a majority in the Legislative Assembly alone. BJD's platform is one of neoliberal economic policy and industrialisation. The party's success is often attributed to the lack of a strong opposition, as neither BJP nor Congress are strong at state level. BJD is not, however, popular in tribal areas or areas where there are peoples' movements.
2 Eighty per cent of mining leases in the state since liberalisation have been for private companies (Adduci 2012: 79).
3 Ziai is referring to states as in nation-states, though the same principle applies when considering comparison of states within India.

4 This is particularly so in the case of POSCO, where its use of technology was one of the major justifications for seeking foreign rather than domestic investment.
5 CPI and other opposition parties also had clear electoral interests in joining and leading these movements.
6 An additional piece of important legislation for decentralised democratic decision-making is The Panchayat (Extension to Scheduled Areas) (PESA) Act 1996, which extended Part IX of the Constitution, constituting the *panchayat* system, to scheduled areas. The Fifth Schedule deals with administration of scheduled areas where tribal communities are in a majority. The PESA Act aims to empower the *panchayati raj* institutions in the scheduled areas for economic development and social justice. Under this Act, a *gram sabha* has the power to safeguard and preserve the traditions and customs of the people of the area, their cultural identity, community resources and customary dispute resolution processes. However, Jagatsinghpur was not a scheduled area so this legislation is less directly relevant to PPSS, but important in empowering other anti-corporate and anti-displacement people's movements in the state.
7 In addition, the term 'self-determination' has connotations of state secession in India that are not relevant here.
8 *Paan* is a mix of betel leaves and other ingredients that is consumed widely in Asia.

References

Adduci, M. (2012) 'Neoliberalism and class reproduction in India: The political economy of privatisation of the mineral sector in the Indian state of Orissa'. *Forum for Social Economics*, vol 41, no 1, pp 68–96.
Asher, M. (2009) *Striking While the Iron Is Hot: A Case Study of the Pohang Steel Company's (POSCO) Proposed Project in Orissa*. Pune: National Centre for Advocacy Studies.
Balaton-Chrimes, S. (2016) *POSCO's Odisha Project: OECD National Contact Point complaints and a Decade of Resistance*. Melbourne: The Non-Judicial Grievance Mechanisms Project.
Balaton-Chrimes, S. & Haines, F. (2016) 'Redress and corporate human rights harms: An analysis of new governance and the POSCO Odisha project'. *Globalizations*, vol 14, no 4, pp 596–610.
Ceresna, L. (2011) *A Manual on Corporate Accountability in India*. Bangalore: Cividep India.
Corbridge, S. (1998) 'Beneath the pavement only soil: The poverty of post-development'. *The Journal of Development Studies*, vol 34, no 6, pp 138–148.
Corbridge, S. (2010) 'Beyond developmentalism: The turn to cultural anthropology'. *New Political Economy*, vol 6, no 1, pp 81–88.
Corbridge, S., Williams, G., Srivastava, M. & Véron, R. (2005) *Seeing the State: Governance and Governmentality in India*. Cambridge: Cambridge University Press.
Dash, K.C. & Samal, K.C. (2008) 'New mega projects in Orissa: Protests by potential displaced persons'. *Social Change*, vol 38, no 4, pp 627–644.
Department of Steel & Mines (2015) Orissa website, 'Mineral based industries'. www.orissaminerals.gov.in/website/MineralProc.aspx?GL=mines&PL=2.
de Sousa Santos, B. (2014) *Epistemologies of the South. Justice against Epistemicide*. Boulder, CO and London: Paradigm Publishers.
Escobar, A. (2012). *Encountering Development: The Making and Unmaking of the Third World*. Princeton, NJ: Princeton University Press.
Esteva, G. (2010). 'Development'. In Sachs, W. (ed.), *The Development Dictionary*. London and New York: Zed Books, pp 22–44.
Esteva, G. & Prakash, M. (2014) *Grassroots Post-modernism: Remaking the Soil of Cultures*. London: Zed Books.

Hage, G. (2016) 'Towards an ethics of the theoretical encounter'. *Anthropological Theory*, vol 16, no 2–3, pp 221–226.
International Human Rights Clinic & ESCR-Net (2013) *The Price of Steel: Human Rights and Forced Evictions in the POSCO-India Project*. New York: NYU School of Law.
Lehmann, D. (1997) 'An opportunity lost: Escobar's deconstruction of development'. *The Journal of Development Studies*, vol 33, no 4, pp 568–578.
Maringanti, A., Mathew, B. & Naidu, S.C. (2013) 'Contemporary fault lines in applied economic research'. *Economic & Political Weekly*, vol XLVIII, no 3, pp 71–77.
McGregor, A. (2009) 'New possibilities? Shifts in post-development theory and practice'. *Geography Compass*, vol 3, no 5, pp 1688–1702.
Mining Zone Peoples' Solidarity Group (2010) *Iron and Steal: The POSCO-India Story*. USAMining Zone Peoples' Solidarity Group.
Mishra, B. (2010) 'Agriculture, industry and mining in Orissa in the post-liberalisation era: An inter-district and inter-state panel analysis'. *Economic and Political Weekly*, vol XLV, no 20, pp 49–68.
Mishra, D.K. (2011) 'Behind dispossession: State, land grabbing and agrarian change in rural Orissa'. *International Conference on Global Land Grabbing*, Institute of Development Studies, University of Sussex.
Nanda, M. (1999) 'Who needs post-development? Discourses of difference, green revolution and agrarian populism in India'. *Journal of Developing Societies*, vol 15, pp 5–31.
New Indian Express (2018) 'Odisha's economy estimated to grow at 7.14% 2017–18'. 22 March 22.
Odisha State Government (2018) 'Single window clearance'. Invest Odisha website. https://investodisha.gov.in/eodb/single-window.
Panda, M. (2008) *Economic Development in Orissa: Growth Without Inclusion?* Mumbai: Indira Gandhi Institute of Development Research.
Pattnaik, S.K. (2011) 'Case study 3: Story from India'. In National Centre for Advocacy Studies (ed.), *Organising and Mobilising in People Centred Advocacy in South Asia*. Pune: National Centre for Advocacy Studies.
Pingle, U., Pandey, D. & Suresh, V. (2010) *Majority Report of the Committee Constituted to Investigate into the Proposal Submitted by POSCO India Pvt. Limited for Establishment of an Integrated Steel Plant and Captive Port in Jagatsinghpur District, Orissa*. New Delhi: Ministry of Environment and Forests.
Planning and Coordination Department (Government of Odisha) (2014) *Odisha Economic Survey 2013–2014*. Bhubaneshwar: Planning and Coordination Department, Government of Odisha.
Planning Commission (Government of India) (2014) *Annual Report 2013–2014*. New Delhi: Planning Commission, Government of India.
Rahnema, M. (2010) 'Poverty'. In Sachs, W. (ed.), *The Development Dictionary*. London and New York: Zed Books, pp 195–215.
Sachs, W. (ed.) (2010) *The Development Dictionary*. London and New York: Zed Books.
Shiva, V. (2005) *Earth Democracy: Justice, Sustainability and Peace*. Cambridge, MA: South End Press.
Shiva, V. (2010) 'Resources'. In Sachs, W. (ed.), *The Development Dictionary*. London and New York: Zed Books, pp 249–263.
Times of India (2017) 'Odisha government sets aside 59,000 acres as land bank for industrial use'. 31 December. https://timesofindia.indiatimes.com/city/bhubaneswar/odisha-government-sets-aside-59000-acre-as-land-bank-for-industrial-use/articleshow/62313808.cms.

Ziai, A. (2004) 'The ambivalence of post-development: Between reactionary populism and radical democracy'. *Third World Quarterly*, vol 25, no 6, pp 1045–1060.

Ziai, A. (2013) 'The discourse of "development" and why the concept should be abandoned'. *Development in Practice*, vol 23, no 1, pp 123–136.

Ziai, A. (2015) 'Post-development: Premature burials and haunting ghosts'. *Development and Change*, vol 46, pp 833–854.

Ziai, A. (2017) 'Post-development 25 years after the development dictionary'. *Third World Quarterly*, vol 38, no 12, pp 2547–2558.

10
ECONOMIC HYBRIDITY IN REMOTE INDIGENOUS AUSTRALIA AS DEVELOPMENT ALTERITY

Katherine Curchin

Introduction

This chapter considers the potential contribution of economic hybridity to postdevelopment in practice. It does this by focusing on Jon Altman's application of a hybrid economy lens to the search for alternatives to development in Australia. Many regions in the centre and north of the Australian continent are distant from labour markets, centres of economic and political power and the lived experience of the non-Indigenous people who govern them from afar. Just over 70,000 Indigenous people – roughly 10% of the Indigenous population of Australia – live on land held under exclusive Indigenous title in these 'remote' regions (Altman & Markham 2015: 135). Unlike the individualistic culture brought to Australia by colonisers from Britain, Indigenous cultures emphasise 'a set of relationships that bind particular persons inter-generationally to specific places via carefully delineated bodies of cosmological knowledge' (Altman & Hinkson 2010: 189). Today Indigenous people inhabit intercultural social worlds formed from 'a mix of customary and western (global) social norms and values' (Altman 2009a: 7).

Through regular fieldwork over almost four decades, Altman has documented the resilience and adaptability of the Kuninjku people's customary economic practices on their ancestral land. He has highlighted their agency in pursuing a valued lifeway shaped by ongoing commitments to kin, country and ceremony. His work seeks to make visible and to legitimate what orthodox development discredits and ignores. Underpinning his work is a rejection of the central tenets of the hegemonic development paradigm: that humanity progresses down a single path; that the West provides a model other parts of the world should emulate; that noncapitalist economic relations are backward; and that local knowledges and practices are inferior (de Sousa Santos 2004; Sachs 2017). He contests the hegemonic assumption that 'the future for Indigenous Australians lies in modernity, urbanization, a full embrace of the market and ultimately, assimilation' (Altman 2001: 9–10). Altman criticises the settler state's development agenda for Indigenous Australians for its hubris, inequity, ecological unsustainability and failure to appreciate difference. His work can be read as a celebration of a form of postdevelopment pursued in remote regions of Australia since the 1970s.

The concept of economic hybridity has been key to the way Altman understands existing institutions and envisions alternatives to the dominant development paradigm. Altman's central contribution to development debates has been 'expanding and diversifying what counts as economic activity in remote Australia' (Muecke & Dibley 2016: 149). If we understand economic activity as 'laboring activity to provide goods and services to satisfy human needs' (Wright 2010: 36), we realise the conventional exclusion of nonmonetised activity is arbitrary and distorting. In 2001, Altman proposed a provocative 'conceptual framework for understanding the nature of the economy' in remote regions of Australia (Altman 2001: 10). He made the case that actually existing regional economies are comprised of market, state and customary sectors (Altman 2001). Non-monetised customary production should not be understood as merely cultural, but as making an important contribution to people's livelihoods, he argued. Conventional economics, blinkered by its preoccupation with the market and state, fails to see the customary economic production of remote regions. Viewing regional economies through the three-sector lens, rather than a conventional two-sector lens, has important implications for evaluating policy options (Altman 2001). In particular, the ways that the different sectors articulate are important for thinking about alternative, ecologically sustainable futures. Economic hybridity offers a vantage point from which to critique both the hegemonic discourse of capitalist expansion and the punitive behavioural policy seeking to shift Indigenous norms. Policy proposals that appear common sense from a neoliberal vantage point are reframed as unproductive, costly and risky.

This chapter describes how economic hybridity figures in Altman's work and explains how it connects with his empirical research as an economic anthropologist. I then examine a range of critiques of the hybrid economy framework from empirical and ideological perspectives. Finally, I draw tentative lessons from the Australian experience that may be relevant to postdevelopment thinkers in other parts of the globe.

Economic hybridity in Indigenous Australia

Altman's theorising of alternatives to orthodox development can be traced back to the ethnographic fieldwork he – a Balanda (non-Indigenous) man, initially trained in economics – conducted among the Kuninjku in central Arnhem Land in Australia's Northern Territory in 1979–1980. There he documented the marked revival of the Indigenous subsistence economy as the Kuninjku chose to move from the township of Maningrida to tiny satellite communities (outstations) on their clan lands (Altman 1987). His study of economic life on the outstation at Mumeka left him convinced that the demise of the Indigenous customary economy was not inevitable.

The reoccupation by the Kuninjku of their ancestral lands was part of a larger 'rural exodus' (Altman 1987: xiii) in the 1970s and 1980s initiated by Aboriginal groups and facilitated by the government policy that it termed 'self-determination'. The voluntary revival of the customary economy after years, often decades, of dependence on the colonisers contradicted powerful assumptions about the flimsiness of non-capitalist economic formations once in contact with capitalism. In 1979, the people of Mumeka were not living a pre-contact existence, but they were resisting the adoption of Western economic rationality. They furthered their own purposes (which were shaped by a kin-based worldview) by engaging with the market when it suited them, for example, using cash from sales of artefacts to buy weapons for hunting, and then distributing the kill according to customary obligations. Outstation residents' production of artefacts for sale and engagement in subsistence hunting and gathering resulted in a higher standard of living for them than those who remained in the town (Altman 1987: 11). Here were Aboriginal people, in the late 1970s, creating, in the cracks of capitalism, flexible economic arrangements; this was postdevelopment in practice. Living beyond the institution of waged labour, the Kuninjku cobbled together their livelihoods from various available sources, none of which would be sufficient on their own. Rather than hapless victims of modernity, Altman interpreted them as 'exploiters of the capitalist system' (Altman 1987: 9). So much for universal capitalist domination.

In his doctoral work at Mumeka, Altman was concerned to highlight Indigenous agency in maintaining and creatively adapting economic institutions. The concern with the capacity of Indigenous people to control 'the intensity of their interaction with the wider Australian economy' has been an enduring theme in his work (Curchin 2015: 417). Adopting the language of economic hybridity has helped Altman think more systematically about the kind of economic institutions the Kuninjku and other Aboriginal groups in similar circumstances had created. This has entailed paying attention to the way the present-day customary sector *articulates* with the state and market sectors. Importantly, the task has not been to categorise economic activities or products – sorting them into boxes marked customary, state or market – or to measure the relative size of each, so much as to make visible the interdependencies between the customary, state and market.

In the articulation of customary, market and state sectors Indigenous peoples have discovered sources of income compatible with continuing 'distinctively Indigenous forms of personhood and sociality' (Curchin 2016: 69). The hybrid economies of northern Australia nurture a series of niche industries that draw on distinctive Aboriginal advantages. These include art, craft and artefact production for international markets, cultural tourism, wild harvesting of bushfoods and environmental management services informed by traditional ecological knowledge. Such industries 'enable people to reside on or close to their ancestral land and to maintain a valued connection with a sentient landscape' while using local resources in sustainable ways (Curchin 2016: 69). Drawing on cultural inheritance to produce goods for export beyond the region comes with the threat of repressive demands for authenticity (Wolfe 1999; Altman & Fogarty 2010). However, experience has shown that savvy Indigenous art centres can mitigate this problem by educating the tastes of art buyers, thereby enabling artists the freedom to paint how and what they wish.

These intercultural industries – which are often not commercially viable without state subsidisation due to their distance from markets or their small scale – may better suit the values and aspirations of (some) local people than the economic opportunities presented by, for example, capital-intensive extractive industries (Curchin 2016: 70). The livelihood solutions they offer are likely to fly under the radar of conventional development thinking, which prioritises commercial profitability over social or ecological sustainability.

Altman has emphasised the importance of not just thinking creatively about potential income sources, but in carefully evaluating livelihood options according to local aspirations (Curchin 2013: 23). Conventional employment opportunities in capital-intensive industries, such as mining, should not be rejected out of hand but considered in relation to valued livelihoods. For example, through a stint in mining a person may save enough money to buy a boat enabling them to earn a living fishing (Altman 2009b). The hybrid economy paradigm does not seek to arbitrarily foreclose such opportunities.

I have argued that the concept of 'partial commodification' is key to understanding how hybrid economies function (Curchin 2016). Appreciating the appeal of partial commodification means acknowledging that exchanging goods for money does not necessarily turn them into 'mere commodities, mere instruments of profit and use' (Curchin 2016: 71). According to the liberal political philosopher Elizabeth Anderson 'what confers commodity status on a good is not that people pay for it, but that exclusively market norms govern its production, exchange and enjoyment' (Anderson 1993: 156). By insisting on the right to retain their own non-market norms, Aboriginal Australians have engaged with markets 'while resisting the full commoditisation of their labour, their cultural inheritance or the local environment' (Curchin 2016: 70).

Engagement with the market does not always mean total submission to the logic of capitalism. Many Indigenous art centres choose to balance business imperatives with social and cultural purposes such as maximising participation, making them less commercially profitable (and more reliant on government funding) than they might otherwise be (Curchin 2015: 422). An analogous phenomenon can be seen in the fishing industry in the Torres Strait (off the northern tip of Queensland). Annick Thomassin (2016) observes that the livelihoods of Masig fishers involve an 'interplay between [...] commercial and customary fisheries' (Thomassin 2016: 101). Though Masig fishers catch seafood for the market, they decline to organise their labour for optimal commercial profit. Instead, their preferred fishing arrangements reflect the continuing importance of the 'customary marine tenure regime' and the cultural imperative to 'take only what you need' (Thomassin 2016: 103). By refusing to internalise the ethos of the market they place less stress on the marine resources they depend on. Rather than viewing customary production as a remnant of the past, which will inevitably give way to the superior technology of modernity, Altman views it as an enduring component of alternative livelihoods. Economic hybridity is here to stay, rather than a transitory arrangement on the road to industrial capitalism (Curchin 2015: 421).

An important strategy for resisting the pressure towards full commoditisation is state subsidisation. It is clear that an innovative government programme called the Community Development Employment Projects scheme (CDEP) was practically important in growing hybrid regional economies. CDEP, which operated from 1977, provided funds for small-scale Aboriginal-controlled organisations to employ Aboriginal workers – the majority of whom would otherwise have been unemployed – on local projects decided upon by local people. Organisations received ongoing government funding rather than one-off grants. The form of employment made possible by CDEP was compatible with the maintenance of ceremony and customary production because of its flexibility. Work shaped by rhythms of the land and the sea doesn't fit well with rigid nine-to-five employment. CDEP attended the birth of various niche industries and thereby expanded Indigenous livelihood options. Altman describes the scheme as 'replete with postcolonial possibility' (Altman 2019: 17). After the official retreat from self-determination as government policy, CDEP fell out of favour. It came to be viewed as an obstacle to the full assimilation of Aboriginal people into the norms of a modern labour market (Altman & Hinkson 2010) and was replaced by active labour market programmes aimed at transitioning Aboriginal people to the mainstream workforce. Its opponents were correct, I believe, in their view that CDEP was insulating Aboriginal participants to some extent from the norms of the capitalist economy.

The state has played an important role in facilitating the development of community-based rangering as a livelihood option. Initially part of a grassroots movement driven by the Indigenous belief that 'the land needs its people' (Altman 2010: 261), Indigenous ranger groups have become formalised as the state came to recognise the positive externalities of Indigenous customary production. They now receive government support to undertake important environmental management work, such as bushfire management and invasive species control, on the vast Indigenous estate. Preventing massive late dry season bushfires by adapting customary burning practices has become a scientifically verified form of carbon abatement that provides a highly significant, sustainable income stream from private companies for Indigenous ranger groups in Arnhem Land (Cooke 2012). Just as the intersection of market and customary sector has its tensions, the interface of the state and customary sectors can be fraught. There is contestation over which norms – customary or state – will prevail in determining objectives, priorities and work practices (Kerins 2012; Fache 2017). Ranger groups are subject to bureaucratic forms of accountability and their funding is vulnerable to changes in government budgetary priorities. The interaction of the customary with the state in Indigenous rangering programmes also poses the threat of essentialism, potentially constraining Aboriginal peoples' space to interpret their own identities (de Rijke, Martin & Trigger 2016: 50).

Whereas in other tri-sector conceptualisations of economy, the non-market, non-state component is labelled civil society (see Wright 2010), the notion of civil society rarely features in Altman's work. The reason for this is likely to be that the Western concept of civil society is a poor fit for Indigenous relational ontologies. Civil society is a sector comprised of associations voluntarily entered into by adult citizens. In a kin-oriented society the most politically significant relationships are those one is born into, rather than those freely chosen in adulthood.

Hybrid economies are dynamic, living economies. Altman insists that fluidity is ever present. Peck observes that the livelihood strategies afforded by the hybrid economy of the Pilbara region are 'precarious' – they have enabled Aboriginal communities to 'survive, although hardly thrive' (Peck 2013: 256). Different sectors within regional economies grow and contract over the years in accordance with changes to the external environment. Though place-based, they are globally connected. For example, as the financial crisis of 2007–2008 depressed art sales prices internationally, the revenue of Aboriginal art centres fell substantially. Regulatory decisions of the state also impact the viability of livelihood options. For example, tighter gun regulations can make it harder to access the particular types of firearm needed to hunt certain species (Altman 2009c). Ecosystem health also has an impact on available livelihoods.

Pursuing diverse sources of income (both monetised and non-monetised) and willingness to shift between occupations can be interpreted as a sensible way of managing risk (Altman 2005; Altman & Hinkson 2010). Altman and Hinkson (2010) highlight the irony that the neoliberal state perceives Aboriginal alterity as a source of risk which must be managed or even eradicated. By contrast the risks of advanced capitalism are often underplayed; industrial capitalism concentrates wealth and power in ways that are socially unsustainable while depleting non-renewable resources, decreasing biodiversity and putting the climate at risk.

The hybrid economy framework foregrounds Aboriginal strengths of skill, knowledge, responsibility, identity, land ownership and kinship. This contrasts with the dominant discourse of deficit suffusing Indigenous policy in Australia – deficits of income, employment, literacy, education. Government policy fixates on the 'gap' between Indigenous and non-Indigenous socio-economic indicators such as income and educational attainment. Altman questions whether closing the 'gap' is the most appropriate objective, suggesting that it imposes Western priorities on people with a different worldview (Altman 2010: 262).

Critiques

Some scholars have criticised as over-optimistic the idea that economic hybridity offers Indigenous Australians an alternative development pathway. For example, there is scepticism about the extent to which subsistence hunting and gathering contributes to Indigenous diets in the twenty-first century. Some anthropologists have suggested hunting and gathering is significant in specific tropical regions where game is more plentiful, but far less important in more arid areas (de Rijke, Martin & Trigger 2016), but this is contested by studies of Martu hunters in the Western Desert (Scelza, Bird & Bliege Bird 2014). Nicolas Peterson has called the hybrid economy approach a 'Rolls-Royce' solution to surplus labour – an economic option available only to a small proportion of remote-living Aboriginal people, which inevitably leaves intact the larger surplus labour problem in remote Australia (2016: 61). The Kuninjku are lucky not to be separated from the means of subsistence, but not all Indigenous groups have the option of self-provisioning on their own land. Peterson also queries whether the growing demand from Aboriginal people in remote communities for expensive consumer goods, such as smartphones, is undermining the sustainability of a low-cash lifestyle (Peterson 2016: 60). Others have emphasised the contemporary challenges to maintenance and inter-generation transmission of customary knowledge and practice, including 'material and cultural attractions of the wider Australian society as well as the realities of socioeconomic inequality, structural discrimination, interpersonal violence, and related social crises' (de Rijke, Martin & Trigger 2016: 45). John, an older Kuninjku man, said 'If you stay here in Maningrida you don't learn anything about your country and how to gather food from it. You only think about chicken and Balanda food' (in Altman 2018: 187). Similarly, his contemporary Samuel observed, 'We are the last generation to eat bush tucker but the children today are not used to eating bush food' (in Altman 2018: 186).

Alternatives to development involving subsistence hunting are controversial in a policy era where the received wisdom is that the only solutions to the problem of Indigenous surplus labour are industrialisation of Australia's tropical north and Indigenous migration to urban centres. From a conventional economic framework, the decision by Aboriginal people to remain living on their ancestral land in places with no functioning labour market is seen as irrational. Programmes that support the aspiration to live on ancestral lands garner hostility from opponents who perceive them as consigning Aboriginal communities to be living 'museums'. This 'museum' critique misses the mark because it conveys the idea that outstation residents are shaping themselves to the colonisers' nostalgic desire for unchanging tradition, while the picture Altman paints is of dynamic peoples exploiting new economic opportunities. He recognises the interculturality of the contemporary Kuninjku economy. The model is not anti-technology; rather, state-of-the-art technology is incorporated when it serves a valued purpose. For example, Indigenous rangers use equipment such as helicopters and incendiaries for fire management and sophisticated remote sensing and digital technology for recording and monitoring carbon emission offsets and biodiversity benefits of environmental work (Altman 2012: 16).

The modest livelihoods offered by hybrid economies contrast with an aspirational discourse of 'prosperity' championed by some Indigenous thought-leaders

(Curchin 2015; Empowered Communities Alliance 2015). These influential policy entrepreneurs are convinced that the only viable solution for Indigenous poverty is for Indigenous people to accommodate themselves to the imperatives of capitalism. For example, Richard Ah Mat argues that he and his fellow Indigenous leaders in Cape York in Queensland need to make wealth accumulation 'respectable amongst our people' (Ah Mat 2003: 10). Greater autonomy and greater dignity require, in their view, Indigenous economic independence from the state, which in turn entails full integration of Indigenous peoples into the capitalist economy. Key steps towards this goal include integration of Aboriginal people into the mining workforce of remote regions, support for the development of Indigenous-owned business enterprises and greater relocation from homelands to urban centres for education and employment. Inculcation of the practice of household saving rather than distributing income among kin are part of this project. The objective of reducing Indigenous dependence on the state has government backing. In support of greater private sector employment, social policy has sought 'to reshape those Aboriginal values, beliefs, social relations and practices that remain distinct from mainstream norms' by, for example, making government income support contingent on certain behaviours (Altman 2010: 277).

It seems the question of how much pressure should be placed on Indigenous peoples to assimilate to the individualistic norms of settler Australians is a central point of contention (Curchin 2013). Noel Pearson, a nationally prominent Aboriginal leader and social reformer, sees value in the continuation of hunting and gathering, yet opposes Altman's larger philosophy on development (Curchin 2015: 420). 'You cannot live a traditional lifestyle underwritten by passive welfare', he claims, because 'in the long run passive welfare is socially and culturally corrosive' (Pearson 2005). In his view, any strategy predicated on alternatives to waged employment – or, in his terminology, 'real jobs' – amounts to a plan for 'passive welfare dependency' (Pearson 2000: 13). Though the hybrid economy model promises meaningful activity rather than idleness, for Pearson at least this is not enough to overcome the deep stigma of income support.

Altman has explicitly sought to propose alternatives to development which are 'realistic'. More utopian thinkers might criticise the hybrid economy approach for a lack of ambition. The economic form exemplified by the Kuninjku economy poses no real challenge to capitalism as a system. It does not promise genuine postcolonial justice, but merely the possibility of survival as a society organised around kinship and reciprocity in the crevices of the liberal capitalist state. Indigenous people remain encapsulated by the more powerful settler society and vulnerable to domination (Altman 2012: 18). Yet in the current political climate, defending the right of Indigenous peoples to remain on their lands and continue their customary economic activities is radical: 'The existence and resilience of a customary sector is anathema to dominant neoliberal ways of thinking and the goal to bring all human action within the realm of the market' (Altman 2010: 272).

Economic hybridity elsewhere

Altman's argument is not that Aboriginal economies are uniquely hybrid. Rather, his project has been to document the particular shape economic hybridity takes in a particular part of Australia. While numerous geographic, demographic and cultural features make remote Indigenous Australia highly distinctive – the rich biodiversity and very low population density, as well as Aboriginal peoples' relational ontology and deep spiritual attachment to land and sea – there is much here that could be learnt from.

The notion of economic hybridity is an important intervention into the discursive contestation over the legitimacy of non-market economic forms. It has obvious relevance to people in other countries struggling to preserve local norms and values rather than succumb to the homogenising impact of hegemonic development. Economic hybridity reclaims the concept of 'productivity' from neoliberalism, interpreting productivity as not about profitability, but about meaningful activity to provision a society.

Economic hybridity holds particular promise for those thinking about the problem of surplus labour. Increasing automation is predicted to render the labour of huge numbers of skilled workers surplus to capitalist economies, creating development problems within affluent nations (Frey & Osborne 2017). The hybrid economies of northern Australia demonstrate that people can create livelihoods beyond the institution of waged labour that fit their priorities, especially if they creatively bundle complementary productive activities. The concept of economic hybridity might help people resist paternalistic policy aimed at disciplining people to accept a lifestyle based upon waged employment alone. It insists on the diversity of motivations for productive labour beyond cash remuneration.

By unhiding the actually existing hybrid economies of remote Australia, Altman rebuts the message that there is no alternative to capitalist development (see also Gibson-Graham 2005). As Altman has documented through his long relationship with Kuninjku, postdevelopment is not a recent phenomenon. This points to the possibility of excavating histories of postdevelopment from other places.

Economic hybridity helpfully clarifies that it is market fundamentalism rather than markets per se which pose such a threat to diversity. Partial commodification is a generative concept, often enabling people to find valued livelihoods without forfeiting their autonomy to an unacceptable extent. I would urge more attention to the nature of the interaction between market and non-market sectors of local economies: the compromises and trade-offs which are made, as well as the synergies which are possible, as the relative sway of different sectors changes over time (Curchin 2016). This is very similar to Wright's project of studying the way actually existing economies are comprised of varying degrees of capitalism, statism and socialism (Wright 2010).

The intersection of market and non-market spheres creates potential for conflict, necessitating assessments of instances of partial commodification to determine whether market norms are crowding out non-market norms in undesirable ways (Curchin 2016). State funding (for example, of Indigenous art centres, so that they are only partially reliant on art sales to cover operating costs) can be a useful way of buffering producers from market forces, thereby enabling them to resist full commodification of their knowledge and talents. Livelihood options are broadened enormously when governments are willing to underwrite community-controlled organisations which coordinate productive activity in pursuit of local goals. But this depends upon the capacity of the state to see and to value difference. The coercive state can also aid neoliberalism's creative destruction of customary practice and Indigenous identity (Altman & Hinkson 2010).

The ups and downs of actually existing hybrid economies may have something to teach us about the potential challenges and vulnerabilities of postdevelopment, too. It is worth reflecting on the political opposition Indigenous attempts to remain beyond the confines of waged labour have inspired. In the Australian context, influential commentators continue to view government-subsidised employment and non-monetised forms of productive activity as inherently less dignified and less psychologically fulfilling than waged employment, even in regions where there is no demand for labour (Pearson 2000, 2001). This contrasts with Kuninjku assessments of the relevance of conventional employment to their lives. In Joshua Jununwangga's words, 'I am far too busy for a full-time Balanada job' (cited in Altman 2019).

Strong norms of sharing among kin and tolerance for a lower material living standard than the Australian norm have enabled Indigenous peoples to survive in the interstices of capitalism. According to John (quoted above): 'Being able to get to your country and being able to live here [the township of Maningrida] too, that's the good life. Sometimes going bush, sometimes living here; the main thing is to have enough food. When you have enough food to eat, that's good' (cited in Altman 2018: 163).

It remains to be seen whether the younger generations' dreams of prosperity, fuelled by international mass media and entertainment, will undermine their resistance to displacement from their land. Consumerism is a powerful ally to capitalist expansion. The growing dependency among Indigenous people on consumer goods, especially expensive digital communications technology, is threatening the viability of economic institutions that generate only modest incomes. This strikes me as the Achilles' heel of attempts to live beyond neoliberalism.

Conclusion

Altman has sought to stretch the discipline of economics: to make visible economic plurality, and thereby do justice to Aboriginal productivity obscured by more conventional approaches to economics. A 'will to improve' (Li 2007) ultimately underpins this project – not the desire to reshape the subjectivity of Aboriginal people, but the desire to improve the government policies that thwart or support Aboriginal peoples' capacity to pursue their chosen life projects.

Altman has at times despaired at the inability or unwillingness of governments to respond to social scientific evidence and is alive to the danger of governments and public commentators misusing anthropological concepts (Altman 2010). Yet his research and writing on alternatives to development have been predicated on the conviction that deliberate choices made by the state can hinder or facilitate Aboriginal groups in pursuing their aspirations, and that well-founded social-scientific expertise can support these deliberate choices. Indeed, why else despair when governments make decisions flagrantly counter to the weight of evidence on what will promote social and ecological sustainability? This faith, albeit fragile, in the possibility of improving policy through better evidence seems to me worth preserving.

Despite Altman's commitment to postdevelopment, he does not denounce the term 'development'. Instead he employs it strategically, framing policy options that facilitate the revival of subsistence hunting as 'development alternatives' (Altman 2001). Altman makes this choice as an activist-scholar intent on influencing government policy (Altman 2009c). Much of Altman's output has been written with a policy audience, rather than an academic audience, in mind. The positive valence that 'development' has for his audience of policymakers helps legitimate a radical idea: the use of state resources to enable Kuninjku to make a living on country. Altman's reason for writing in terms of 'development alternatives' is not to reform and rehabilitate 'development' in response to postdevelopment critique. It is clear that Altman's commitment is not to 'development', but the Kuninjku struggle to choose lifeways they value.

The hybrid economy framework speaks to many of the concerns animating postdevelopment theory. If postdevelopment is taken to include the struggle to fashion diverse lifeways based on relational ontology rather than exploitation of the Earth (Demaria & Kothari 2017), it might be argued that in the remote regions of Australia a form of postdevelopment is already underway. Altman's anthropological commitment to grounded research brings into focus the agency of Indigenous people adapting and co-opting the possibilities available to them regardless of official attempts to control their lives or theorists' attempts to foretell their economic destinies. This general spirit of inquiry, and the concept of economic hybridity, might be creatively appropriated by people in other settings envisioning economic futures. The Indigenous Australian experience may offer some inspiration for other people who wish to benefit from some market engagement without being confined within capitalism.

References

Ah Mat, R. (2003) 'The moral case for Indigenous capitalism'. Paper presented at AIATSIS Native Title Conference: Native title on the Ground. Alice Springs, NT. 3–5 June.

Altman, J.C. (1987) *Hunter-Gatherers Today: An Aboriginal Economy in North Australia.* Canberra: Australian Institute of Aboriginal Studies.

Altman, J.C. (2001) 'Sustainable development options on Aboriginal land: The hybrid economy in the twenty-first century'. *Centre for Aboriginal Economic Policy Research*

Discussion Paper No. 226. Canberra: Centre for Aboriginal Economic Policy Research, Australian National University.

Altman, J.C. (2005) 'Economic futures on Aboriginal land in remote and very remote Australia: Hybrid economies and joint ventures'. In Austin-Broos, D. & MacDonald, G. (eds.), *Culture, Economy and Governance in Aboriginal Australia*. Sydney: University of Sydney Press, pp 121–133.

Altman, J.C. (2009a) 'Contestations over development'. In Altman, J.C. & Martin, D. (eds.), *Power, Culture, Economy: Indigenous Australians and Mining*. Canberra: Australian National University Press, pp 1–15.

Altman, J.C. (2009b) 'Indigenous communities, miners and the state in Australia'. In Altman, J.C. & Martin, D. (eds.), *Power, Culture, Economy: Indigenous Australians and Mining*. Canberra: Australian National University Press, pp 17–49.

Altman, J.C. (2009c) 'The hybrid economy and anthropological engagements with policy discourse: A brief reflection'. *Australian Journal of Anthropology*, vol 20, pp 318–329.

Altman, J.C. (2010) 'What future for remote Indigenous Australia? Economic hybridity and the neoliberal turn'. In Altman, J.C. & Hinkson, M. (eds.), *Culture Crisis: Anthropology and Politics in Aboriginal Australia*. Sydney: UNSW Press, pp 259–280.

Altman, J.C. (2012) 'People on Country as alternate development'. In Altman, J.C. & Kerins, S. (eds.), *People on Country: Vital Landscapes, Indigenous Futures*. Sydney: Federation Press, pp 1–22.

Altman, J.C. (2018) '"The main thing is to have enough food": Kuninjku precarity and neoliberal reason'. In Gregory, C.A. & Altman, J.C. (eds.), *The Quest for the Good Life in Precarious Times: Ethnographic Perspectives on the Domestic Moral Economy*. Canberra: Australian National University Press, pp 163–196.

Altman, J.C. (2019) 'Of pizza ovens in Arnhem Land: The state quest to realign Aboriginal labor in remotest Australia'. In Stead, V. & Altman, J. (eds.), *Labour Lines and Colonial Power: Indigenous and Pacific Islander Experiences of Labour Mobility in Australia*. Canberra: Australian National University Press (in press).

Altman, J.C. & Fogarty, B. (2010) 'Indigenous Australians as "no gaps" subjects: Education and development in remote Australia'. In Snyder, I. & Niewenhuysen, J. (eds.), *Closing the Gap in Education? Improving Outcomes in Southern World Societies*. Melbourne: Monash University Publishing, pp 109–128.

Altman, J.C. & Hinkson, M. (2010) 'Very risky business: The quest to normalise remote-living Aboriginal people'. In Marston, G., Moss, J. & Quiggin, J. (eds.), *Risk, Responsibility and the Welfare State*. Melbourne: Melbourne University Press, pp 185–211.

Altman, J.C. & Markham, F. (2015) 'Burgeoning Indigenous land ownership: Diverse values and strategic potentialities'. In Brennan, S., Davis, M., Edgeworth, B. & Terrill, L. (eds.), *Native Title from Mabo to Akiba: A Vehicle for Change and Empowerment?* Sydney: Federation Press, pp 126–142.

Anderson, E. (1993) *Value in Ethics and Economics*. Cambridge, MA: Harvard University Press.

Cooke, P. (2012) 'A long walk home to Warddewardde'. In Altman, J.C. & Kerins, S. (eds.), *People on Country: Vital Landscapes, Indigenous Futures*. Sydney: Federation Press, pp 146–161.

Curchin, K. (2013) 'Interrogating the hybrid economy approach to Indigenous development'. *Australian Journal of Social Issues*, vol 48, no 1, pp 15–34.

Curchin, K. (2015) 'Two visions of Indigenous economic development and cultural survival: The "real economy" and the "hybrid economy"'. *Australian Journal of Political Science*, vol 50, no 3, pp 412–426.

Curchin, K. (2016) 'If the market is the problem, is the hybrid economy the solution?' In Sanders, W. (ed.), *Engaging Indigenous Economies*. Canberra: Australian National University Press, pp 65–77.

Demaria, F. & Kothari, A. (2017) 'The *Post-development Dictionary* agenda: Paths to the pluriverse'. *Third World Quarterly*, vol 38, no 12, pp 2588–2599.

de Rijke, K., Martin, R. & Trigger, D. (2016) 'Cultural domains and the theory of customary environmentalism in Indigenous Australia'. In Sanders, W. (ed.), *Engaging Indigenous Economies*. Canberra: Australian National University Press, pp 43–53.

de Sousa Santos, B. (2004) 'The World Social Forum: Toward a counter-hegemonic globalization (part I)'. In Sen, J., Anand, A., Escobar, A. & Waterman, P. (eds.), *World Social Forum: Challenging Empires*. New Delhi: Viveka Foundation, pp 235–245.

Empowered Communities Alliance (2015) *Empowered Communities: Empowered Peoples, Design Report*. Sydney: Wunan Foundation.

Fache, E. (2017) 'Mediation between Indigenous and non-Indigenous knowledge systems: Another analysis of "two-way" conservation in northern Australia'. In Dussart, F. & Poirier, S. (eds.), *Entangled Territorialities: Negotiating Indigenous Lands in Australia and Canada*. Toronto: University of Toronto Press, pp 91–116.

Frey, C.B. & Osborne, M.A. (2017) 'The future of employment: How susceptible are jobs to computerisation?' *Technological Forecasting and Social Change*, vol 114, pp 254–280.

Gibson-Graham, J.K. (2005) 'Surplus possibilities: Postdevelopment and community economies'. *Singapore Journal of Tropical Geography*, vol 26, no 1, pp 4–26.

Kerins, S. (2012) 'Caring for Country to working on Country'. In Altman, J.C. & Kerins, S. (eds.), *People on Country: Vital Landscapes, Indigenous Futures*. Sydney: Federation Press, pp 26–44.

Li, T.M. (2007) *The Will to Improve: Governmentality, Development and the Practice of Politics*. Durham, NC: Duke University Press.

Muecke, S. & Dibley, B. (2016) 'Five theses for reinstituting economics: Anthropological lessons from Broome'. In Sanders, W. (ed.), *Engaging Indigenous Economies*. Canberra: Australian National University Press, pp 143–152.

Pearson, N. (2000) *Our Right to Take Responsibility*. Cairns: Noel Pearson and Associates.

Pearson, N. (2001) 'Rebuilding Indigenous communities'. In Botsman, P. & Latham, M. (eds.), *The Enabling State*. Annandale: Pluto Press, pp 132–147.

Pearson, N. (2005) 'Peoples, nations and peace'. Inaugural Mabo Oration, Brisbane, 3 June. www.adcq.qld.gov.au/resources/a-and-tsi/mabo-oration/2005-inaugural-mabo-oration-noel-pearson/mabo-oration-noel-pearson.

Peck, J. (2013) 'Polanyi in the Pilbara'. *Australian Geographer*, vol 44, no 3, pp 243–264.

Peterson, N. (2016) 'What is the policy significance of the hybrid economy?' In Sanders, W. (ed.), *Engaging Indigenous Economies*. Canberra: Australian National University Press, pp 55–64.

Sachs, W. (2017) 'The Sustainable Development Goals and *laudato si*: Varieties of post-development?' *Third World Quarterly*, vol 38, no 12, pp 2573–2587.

Scelza, B.A., Bird, D. & Bliege Bird, R. (2014) 'Bush tucker, shop tucker: Production, consumption, and diet at an Aboriginal outstation'. *Ecology of Food and Nutrition*, vol 53, no 1, pp 98–117.

Thomassin, A. (2016) 'Hybrid economies as life projects? An example from the Torres Strait'. In Sanders, W. (ed.), *Engaging Indigenous Economies*. Canberra: Australian National University Press, pp 95–110.

Wright, E.O. (2010) *Envisioning Real Utopias*. London: Verso.

11
PLURINATIONALITY AS A STRATEGY

Transforming local state institutions toward *buen vivir*

Miriam Lang

In which ways does the challenge to move out of the development paradigm involve the state? How can we envision institutional arrangements, structures and relations in a postdevelopment society? Even if we imagine a postdevelopment society without a state in its current forms – the shapes political power has taken in the context of modern/colonial capitalist societies (Brand & Görg 2018) – some sort of institutional transition will have to occur. In order to contribute a few elements to this rather incipient quest (Walsh 2009; Kippler 2010; Escobar 2015; Schavelzon 2015), this chapter analyzes recent experiences from Ecuador, where Rafael Correa's progressive government (2007–2017) constitutionalized *buen vivir* as a postdevelopment paradigm, but quickly turned towards extractivist neodevelopmentalism. After years of neoliberalism, the state was recovered as the only legitimate, central actor of social transformation. However, while this was the predominant narrative at the national level, other kinds of relations were furthered by local, territorialized processes.

In the following, I will shortly depict how, as long as *buen vivir* was just fed into existing state apparatuses as a new public policy horizon, apparently neutral institutional mechanisms, procedures and regulations deployed their own momentum and reverted transformative impulses away from postdevelopment. But I will also analyze how at the local level, different logics of doing government could be introduced into existing institutional settings, opening spaces for the practice of *buen vivir* by transforming the mechanics of the modern/colonial state itself.

Buen vivir does not outline a single path for political practice. As a paradigm rooted in orality, it rather wraps up a set of principles around which the organization of collective life has evolved in practice in many diverse Indigenous societies of the American continent – often in tension with the values introduced by colonial/modern intrusion and power; many of these societies have no word for 'development' in their languages.[1] It is those principles which, in their ultimate consequence, are incompatible with the idea of a linear, unlimited 'bettering' of living conditions, and thus with the promise of development as capitalism framed it since World War II in close association to economic growth.

Instead of unlimited material accumulation, *buen vivir* proposes equilibrium, balance and harmony as the highest values of coexistence. Instead of being pursued as a goal, accumulation of material wealth or individual power is considered a threat to the community, and its possibilities are systematically deactivated by mechanisms of redistribution, reciprocity and rotation of duties. At the same time, communitarian life is not fixed in tradition, but evolves according to the needs of all, in situated historical processes actively shaped by collective deliberation. Instead of competition, *buen vivir* proposes collaboration. Instead of the capitalist *homo oeconomicus*, always rationally interested in getting the best for just himself, it proposes an ontology of being collectively, in community, in awareness of our deep interdependences with other human and non-human beings. Instead of dividing life into different realms of the social, the political and the economical, it conceives life as a whole. Instead of defining nature as a set of resources external to human life and prone to exploitation, it defines human life as a part of all forms of life as a whole.

The sensational introduction of *buen vivir* into Ecuador's 2008 Constitution boosted its visibility, caused it to circulate around the world and also to enter the academic sphere. It inspired numerous struggles and promised, in the eyes of many, an answer to a multi-dimensional, even civilizational crisis. To those who had identified 'development' as a potent machine of ongoing and intensifying primary accumulation and dispossession in the Global South, it formulated a common reference point for social transformation. Thus, the introduction of *buen vivir* into the Constitution was celebrated as a step of historical dimensions (Chuji 2014).

The ambiguity of the constitutionalization of *buen vivir*

But at the same time, as several authors have pointed out (Gudynas & Acosta 2011; Caria & Domínguez 2016), the concept underwent several processes of deep resignification. One dimension of resignification was its very inclusion into the format of a 'political constitution of the state', which has a specific function in the modern/colonial/patriarchal/capitalist state. A constitution is elaborated according to a set of rules, protocols and procedures, within a pre-established structure, which operate as a powerful filter of possible outcomes, featuring some while making others invisible. They are part of a finely woven network of exclusion along lines of ethnicity, gender and class, which are constitutive to this kind of state.[2] Moreover, an elected constituent assembly always reflects the political correlation of forces of a specific historical moment. In Ecuador in 2007/2008, while this correlation of forces, after a decade of strong Indigenous mobilizations, made it possible to constitutionalize *buen vivir*, it did not allow the ruling out of 'development', a concept so deeply inscribed in the subjectivities of the Global South – naturalized as the ideal to strive for and at the same time legitimizing state action and the state itself – that it has become practically unquestionable. As a result, development paradoxically coexists with *buen vivir* in the 2008 Ecuadorian Constitution, where it still holds a central place and perpetuates the doxa of modernization and progress (Manosalvas 2014).

But the introduction into the Constitution was only a first step in the reformatting of *buen vivir* via the specific momentum of modern state bureaucracy; once enshrined as a guiding principle for future public policies, *buen vivir* was subjected to the efficiency and management logics of the neoliberal state. It was translated into the language and structures of development plans – soon to be called 'National Plans for *Buen Vivir*' – with their sets of objectives, indicators and goals. It became governed by a management framework bound to show quick results in order to ensure re-election. Thus, *buen vivir* was recodified in the short-term logic of electoral democracy and fitted into the metric mindset characteristic of the era of development, which tends to represent complex realities in simple, comparable numbers (Engle Merry 2011; Moreno, Speich & Fuhr 2015; Lang 2017). As a result, and in spite of a certain eco-socialist rhetoric issued by some Ecuadorian Government officials (Ramírez 2010), *buen vivir* often ended being used simply as synonymous with modern, capitalist development, making it possible for public infrastructure like highways or dams to be promoted as 'works for *buen vivir*'.[3]

Buen vivir as a territorial postdevelopment practice

Nevertheless, this sometimes grotesque resignification of *buen vivir* by the central state under Rafael Correa's national government (2007–2017) only describes one layer of Ecuadorian social practice inspired by *buen vivir*. On a territorial level, especially in rural Ecuador and mostly in the shade of the blasting propaganda instrumented by the national government, a series of socio-political processes organized along the principles of *buen vivir* were taking place, adapting to ever-changing external conditions and often in a tense relationship with the central state. They are symbolically rooted in the long history of Indigenous resistance and communal organizational practices; however, some of them have gained force only in the last few years.

In the context of massive uprisings of the Indigenous population in the 1990s, which disrupted the colonial/modern ways of doing politics in Ecuador, in 1996, the *Confederación de Nacionalidades Indígenas de Ecuador* (CONAIE), the biggest national umbrella organization of Indigenous peoples, founded the *Movimiento de Unidad Plurinacional Pachakutik* in 1996 as its 'political arm'. This political movement opened the possibility to take part in elections, thus taking political control of some territories in order to end the white-mestizo dominion characterized by abuse, corruption and racism. Partisan electoral participation was never considered the only strategy in the move toward territorial autonomy in Ecuador's Indigenous movement. It has been a contentious issue since the 1980s (Andrade 2003: 118; Ospina 2006; Becker 2015). However, in 2000, through the second election it took part in, *Pachakutik* won thirty local governments. As Ortiz Crespo (2008) points out, those local governments were far from homogeneous; some of them only prolonged the clientelist practices of Ecuadorian colonial/patriarchal political culture, using public works as a means of political control, and others just modernized public office in some ways. But a third group not only made a bet on the multi-dimensional transformation of their territories envisioning *buen vivir*, but also built a network of political education and exchange in order to foster their collective learning and critical self-assessment, the *Coordinadora de Gobiernos Locales Alternativos*.

The two counties this chapter focuses on stand in this wider tradition: Nabón, located at the periphery of the southern province of Azuay and home to 18,000 people, and Cayambe, situated only 60 km from the capital Quito, in the central Pichincha province, with 86,000 inhabitants, including the city of Cayambe with around 40,000. Nabón has had all-female *Pachakutik* mayors since 2000, Amelia Erráez (2000–2009) and Magali Quezada (2009–2018); Cayambe, in contrast, while it also draws on a historically outstanding, strong organizational process of the Kayambi Indigenous peoples,[4] only managed to break the political rule of its mestizo-hacienda elites in 2014, when Guillermo Churuchumbi, a *kichwa-kayambi* activist of the CONAIE, became elected mayor. In this sense, both local processes have roots which reach back long before the 2008 Constitution, although they both made a strategic use of the new leeway the Carta Magna gave them. This chapter builds on a series of field visits to both Cayambe and Nabón in 2016 and 2017, where in-depth interviews were conducted with local government officials as well as representatives of social and communitarian organizations, additional to observant participation in assemblies, public hearings, local markets and organic agricultural production.

In both cases, transformative processes have been complex and multi-dimensional, including elements of depatriarchalization, decolonization, redefinition of societal relations with nature, deepening of democracy, redirecting production from capital accumulation towards the sustainability of the material conditions for the reproduction of life and towards self-reliance, mainly through agroecology and a relative decoupling from the world market and its macroeconomic imperatives (Lang & M'Barek 2018). In this text, it is not my intention to give an exhaustive account of all their dimensions – but rather to read them from the perspective of institutional arrangements which would let postdevelopment practices prosper.

It is important to note that during the period I examine, both local governments, Cayambe and Nabón, coexisted with the central government led by Rafael Correa, which strongly aimed at the modernization, centralization and standardization of all kinds of policies, in accordance with the political dynamics of a neoextractivist, neodevelopmental state, with a strong redistributive center located in the executive power (Meschkat 2015). Thus, their official documents, e.g., land-use plans or 'local development plans', had to be elaborated following the procedures issued by the central planning institution *Secretaría Nacional de Planificación y Desarrollo* (SENPLADES), which necessarily would lead them to replicate the above-mentioned conceptual ambiguities regarding development and *buen vivir*.

However, they managed to introduce important moments of contestation, for example, when the 2014 land-use plan of Nabón states:

> The dominant thesis of development has entered into a deep crisis in the Latin American political environment, not only because of the colonialist perspective from which it was built, but also because of the results it has generated in the world [...] [T]his plan proposes a moratorium on the word development, in order to incorporate the concept of *Buen Vivir* into the debate.
>
> (PYDLOS 2014: 15)

Cayambe's local government for its part was renamed as the 'Intercultural and Plurinational Autonomous Decentralized Government of the Municipality of Cayambe – *Sumak Kawsaypak* – together for *Buen Vivir*' when Guillermo Churuchumbi took office in 2014 (GADIP Cayambe 2015).

Expanding communitarian logics, transforming political relations through plurinationality

The principles of interculturality and plurinationality had been central claims of the Indigenous movement since the 1990s – especially the introduction of a 'plurinational state'. They are complementary perspectives; while plurinationality would be an acknowledgement of the social reality of countries like Ecuador and Bolivia, where Indigenous peoples claim the status of nations on the grounds of sharing a common territory, a common history and language, as well as forms of social organization, interculturality rather describes the relations and articulations that have to be built on these grounds, as a transformational project with a political, social and ethical dimension (Walsh 2009; Cholango 2012; Schavelzon 2015). In 2008, alongside *buen vivir*, both were included in the Constitution as fundamental characteristics of the Ecuadorian state. Nevertheless, the Correa administration moved in the opposite direction. Although interculturality and plurinationality would rhetorically figure in the canons of political correctness in all kinds of official documents, concrete policies, for example, regarding education or health, tended to respond to the Western 'universal' patterns of standardization, modernization, meritocracy and quality, which are characteristic of neoliberal governance. Existing structures of collective self-management that had emerged during the neoliberal period, often in absence of the state, sometimes with support from foreign development agencies, were systematically replaced by centralized, uniform public policies. Examples are communitarian health networks which were dismantled regardless of their efficacy, instead of receiving support from the state in order to improve their services, as well as the decentralized bilingual education system that had been co-administrated by Indigenous organizations and the corresponding Ministry (Lang 2017). Following the same logic, in 2013 a new law on political territorial organization was issued, the *Código Orgánico de Organización Territorial, Autonomía y Descentralización*

(COOTAD), which withdrew competences around health and education from local governments and re-centered them at the national scale.

In their own territories, the municipalities of Nabón and Cayambe chose the opposite path; they not only gave recognition to the logics of Indigenous communitarian democracy where it existed in their territories, but placed those logics at the core of political transformation. 'Plurinationality will be the tool for the transformation of the use of political power and the participation of peoples and nationalities within the transformation of the territory', declares the municipality of Cayambe in its 2015 'development plan' (GADIP Cayambe 2015).

'At the beginning, we learned from the indigenous zone how to organize, and applied this to the mestizo zone', says Mayor Quezada from Nabón.[5] In Cayambe, communitarian practices were even extended into the urban quarters of the city. This operated a significant transformation of the forms of political participation at this level of the state. Both in Cayambe and Nabón, assembly-based forms of decision making became the main instrument for deepening democracy, widening the available spaces for deliberation and strengthening communitarian self-reliance. When, in January 2015, the municipality of Cayambe faced the unpleasant disjunctive of either privatizing its drinking water grid or increasing the water tariffs in the city – a problem that had become critical because former mayors had simply found it too unpopular to address – Churuchumbi chose to call a general citizen's assembly for the first time in the history of the city; the people should receive all available information, deliberate and then make the decision themselves. The result was a legitimate, democratically decided adaptation of the urban water rates, which, as came out, until this day had been significantly lower for the city than for the rural and Indigenous zones of the county.[6]

Magali Quezada from Nabón underlines the maturity of decisions taken in assemblies:

> People know that before a decision is taken over an issue, this issue has to be well debated, the arguments have to be well presented, because they will be responsible for the decision they make. When it is a collective decision, all signs indicate that it will work out.

Communitarian logics also help to dismantle clientelist practices that have been inscribed in political culture for centuries during colonial and then postcolonial rule. For example, the habit of giving people money in order to attend certain rallies or to carry them there in buses. As Quezada points out:

> You cannot manipulate. People go to the assemblies by themselves and they like to go, there is no need to pay them or bring them in order to make them assist. […] The people are empowered; this is about their responsibility with their territory.

In the Andean region, public works are often presented as if they were a personal gift of the current ruler and are used as a tool for political control, instead of being implemented as a right of the community. Another move against the grain of this persisting colonial, paternalistic and patriarchal political culture consists in that both counties have extended the *mingas*, unpaid communitarian work normally performed collectively on weekends in rural Indigenous communities, to the mestizo zones of their territory – and even to urban neighborhoods in the case of Cayambe. When public works are to be carried out people participate with their unpaid labor power, while the municipality provides the materials, machines and technical advice if necessary. This was not only a convenient strategy of coping with severe budgetary cuts introduced after the 2013 territorial administration reform; it also establishes the principle of reciprocity in the relationship between the local government and the people, one of the core principles of *buen vivir*.

'Public works have been used to disperse and divide people', says Guillermo Churuchumbi, 'while they should be an instrument to organize them'. In Churuchumbi's vision of *buen gobierno* (good government), the state does *not* do everything *for* the people, who end up in an ongoing passive expectation. He expects people to organize and get involved. To illustrate this, he recalls the ecological recovery of a riverbank in urban Cayambe:

> The municipality is facilitating the process. We went to the neighborhoods to talk. First they told us the municipality should build a park, but we said, okay, we can build something, but what will the responsibility of the neighbors be, how is this going to be taken care of? We organized the *minga*, with the participation of the neighbors. [...] People helped collect the rubbish, we did a first, second, and third *minga* together. Now it is almost a permanent practice. Every month or every second, they come together without the municipality and do it, as a neighborhood organization, as a practice of environmental awareness.[7]

This kind of collective activity generates community, moments of conviviality, and lays the grounds for other improvements in urban life, for example, the construction of communitarian security policies. In those municipalities working for *buen vivir*, communities as a collective social and political actor are an important counterpart, which enacts a public realm beyond the state, complicating the usual picture of private/market versus public/state.

Communities have their own jurisdiction for the government of the commons (Ostrom 1990; Bollier & Helfrich 2012; Caffentzis & Federici 2013) – granted by Article 171 of the 2008 Constitution, which establishes judicial pluralism. However, the Correa administration constantly sought to limit the competences of Indigenous justice or to subordinate it to ordinary justice, while media often calumniate it as a variant of lynch justice. In practice, Indigenous justice is mainly about another principle of *buen vivir*: reestablishing the necessary balances for the well-being of the community as a whole – contrasting with ordinary justice and its focus on punishment and guilt. The municipalities of Cayambe and Nabón recognize this as an important dimension of *buen vivir*; in recent years, the judge of Nabón stood out for officially handing over cases to the Indigenous *cabildos* for resolution and pointed to a precedent of jurisprudence declaring himself incompetent to resolve conflicts originating in the realm of the Indigenous communes of the county – which brought him a lawsuit of the Correa government before he was removed from Nabón.

For Churuchumbi, communitarian jurisdiction is at the heart of plurinationality, and it is useful for far more than conflict resolution. In Cayambe, even the practices of state bureaucracy institutions like the land registry have become plurinational to some extent. By law, buildings like community education centers can only be built on land with a land title issued by the state – while the usufruct of collectively owned communal land had only been recorded in a commune book, often in handwriting. This usually prevented communities from realizing their plans for collective edifications on their own land. With the new municipality, the land registry began to issue official collective land titles for these purposes. The only condition is that there is a proper written record from a community assembly stating a collective need, and declaring that the land in question is of collective, communitarian property.

The care of commons: generating well-being collectively

Instead of public-private partnerships, Churuchumbi's municipality has established public-communitarian partnerships, for instance, a sewage system that connects different neighboring municipalities. Relations of shared responsibility between the local state and communities mainly evolve around the care for certain commons such as water management or the protection of the *páramo* highlands.[8] Communitarian water management systems have worked for centuries in Ecuador, caring for irrigation channels that carry water from the glaciers to the fields over hundreds of kilometers. In Cayambe, some *páramos* are officially state property, belonging to the Ministry of Environment. Some years ago, people from nearby communities were sending their livestock up the mountains, which would destroy the water reserves in the state-owned land. However, the communities have become aware that they have the ancestral possession and have generated the exercise of authority over those territories. They have assumed care for the *páramos*: 'When a fire breaks out like in 2016, it is the people who go up and put it out, and there the mayor went to support his people in the task of caring for the páramos', says Churuchumbi.

> There are even sanctions for offenders. […] The people have generated a process of collective empowerment beyond the law. The municipality only gives support. We want to give tax exonerations to those communities who really care for the páramos, who nurture the water sources. The water is not only for themselves, it is for all. This is where the principles of reciprocity and solidarity come in again.

Critics might argue that in these examples, the state is sneaking out of its responsibilities and shifting them onto the people, following the neoliberal recipe of privatization. But here the tasks in question are not left to households, which usually burdens individual women. They are not privatized, but commoned. Commoning the responsibility for the sustainability of life can be an act of emancipation and is certainly one of self-reliance, as it allows people to experience their ability of collectively generating well-being. The state, in this case the municipality, seeks to enable communities for this purpose, it provides them with certain conditions or infrastructure, but it does not interfere or supplant in a top-down way like a classical welfare state. As Raquel Gutiérrez puts it, the state governs 'as little as possible' (Gutiérrez Aguilar 2017: 96).

One of its most important tasks is to protect these processes of self-reliance against the appropriation interests of big capital – and this points directly to one of the main challenges for those local governments; in Nabón, the highest *páramo* around the Cerro del Mozo, at a height of more than 3000m, from where a series of communities draw both their drinking and irrigation water, has been concessioned to a gold mining firm. The mine would not only channel off most of the water for its operations, but also contaminate it with highly toxic substances. While the central state has given all environmental permissions and omitted a previous consultation of the affected people, the municipality is still pursuing by all judicial means to stop the destruction of one of the most important assets of their territory. Without water, all the efforts invested during the last 25 years in recovering soil fertility, in organic production and food sovereignty would be reverted – in the name of 'development'.

Participatory budgeting is another important instrument both municipalities use to empower people and make them co-responsible. Since the early 2000s, Nabón has implemented a method of participatory budgeting that bridges the situated needs and priorities of its people with the formal requirements of the central state and the law. Once informed about the available public funds, each community and then each parish or commune decides its spending priorities in assemblies, which are compiled by municipal employees and socialized in a sequence of general assemblies during the year. Each citizen knows exactly how much money is coming to his or her community for what purpose and can take an active part in processes of accountability. The overall municipal budget is not only assigned following a proportional rule based on the population or extension of the different territories, but also according to socio-political and ecological criteria like soil degradation, number of single mothers etc. These proceedings were also built in a participatory way, holding assemblies throughout the county. In recent years, under Mayor Magali Quezada, an additional criterion of solidarity was introduced into participatory budgeting. It allows communities or parishes to lend parts of their yearly assigned budget to one another following rules of reciprocity. In times of scarce budgeting, this has made bigger investments possible where necessary. Today, the inhabitants of Nabón are rather well informed in regard to budgetary assignments; they know exactly where there are budget remainders, and discuss their best use with the mayor or within their community.

This new institutionality, by stretching national regulations in order to deepen local democracy, has deeply affected the influence of political parties on the local process; elected members of the municipal council, instead of being 'authorities' who take decisions *on behalf of* the people, today can only ratify decisions that were already taken *by* the people at the basis level and help implement them. This way, the *concejo* decisions are generally taken by consensus. Electoral processes meet specific conditions in Nabón:

> Many candidates come here and expose their proposals not on the basis of a participatory process, but from their own point of view. And people say: no, not like that. We have already decided what to do and now they come and want to impose this on us.

Nevertheless, electoral cycles always pose a threat to these long-term transformative processes, not only because they imply the possible loss of political control. They also impose their own, short-term temporalities, and the individualistic and personalistic logics of political campaigning regularly disrupt the logic of communities as collective actors, reintroducing the vision of public office as a well-paid personal privilege instead of a simple service or duty to the community.

Poverty, well-being and standardized institutional development narratives

The municipality of Nabón also undertook an initiative to subvert the institutional statistical narratives by which the developmental state usually depicts governmental progress, which are generally taken as unquestionable truths. At the end of the twentieth century, Nabón county was listed as one of the poorest counties in the country. More than 90% of the population was considered poor according to 'unsatisfied basic needs', and 76.4% even lived in extreme poverty according to the census of 2001 (INEC 2001, cited in Brassel, Herrera & Laforge 2008: 8). In 2010, the next census only showed a slight drop in poverty, from 92.9% to 87.8% according to unsatisfied basic needs indicators, which would attest a rather meager result after ten years of local government oriented toward *buen vivir* (SIISE-INEC 2010).

On one side, the municipality contested these numbers on their same grounds, stating that 97% of houses today have access to drinking water (Quezada 2017), and sewage infrastructure coverage has improved from 13.7% in 2001 (SIISE-INEC 2001) to 20.4% ten years later (SIISE-INEC 2010), covering all houses that belong to village structures in the county. Also, income is again mainly generated by the agricultural and artisanal production of the people of Nabón (Quezada 2017). Already in 2008, female heads of household earned 270% more than a decade before, while the average income had risen by around 180% (Unda & Jácome 2009: 39).

But additionally, it contested the very narrative of development and poverty indicators like 'unsatisfied basic needs' by carrying out a *subjective well-being survey* with the University of Cuenca. This survey, applied in 2012 encompassing 15% of Nabón's households by initiative of a consortium of local governments in Azuay, inscribes itself in the current that seeks to innovate quantitative measurement of well-being in the line of Bhutan's Gross Happiness Index (Ura, Alkire, Zangmo & Wangdi 2012). It put forward questions central for well-being, e.g., asking if people were satisfied with their freedom of choice and their capacity to control their own lives – on average more than 70% of the people responded 'very satisfied'. Furthermore, the survey asked them about their satisfaction with their occupation, their family life, their financial situation, their leisure time, their environmental surroundings, their housing, their spiritual life and food security etc. As a result of this survey, 75.8% of the local population of Nabón expressed high satisfaction with their overall lives (Morocho 2013) – in stark contrast to almost 90% having been declared as having 'unsatisfied basic needs' two years earlier. This calls standardized, quantitative poverty indicators like income poverty or basic needs into question, regarding their ability to give a comprehensive, contextualized picture of well-being or quality of life (for an extensive discussion see Lang 2017).

Opening up state institutions for postdevelopment

The Ecuadorian experience shows how until present times, the coloniality of power has been inscribed into a multiplicity of state apparatuses and institutional arrangements. Far from being neutral mechanisms, they are geared towards economic growth and continuous modernization as drivers of development and capitalist accumulation. Interestingly, it is the turn towards plurinationality, the opening up towards an*other* understanding of authority, government and public service rooted in the radical difference of Indigenous/communitarian ontologies (Escobar 2012; Blaser 2014) that managed to break those dynamics in Nabón and Cayambe. It is by introducing these radically different logics or political ontologies into the ramifications of the local state, by reframing concrete procedures, but also by subverting temporalities, assumed bases of knowledge, and undermining the hierarchy of spatial scales, that *buen vivir* is allowed to flourish. In Nabón, one factor which undeniably helped this to happen was the feminization of politics, the de-patriarchalisation of socio-political relations (Lang & M'Barek 2018).

Nabón and Cayambe show how the recognition and incorporation of cultural/epistemological/ontological diversity becomes a *central tool for the transformation of the present*, instead of being only an action to protect or conserve a *heritage from the past*. There simply seems to be no *buen vivir* without plurinationality. These two experiences point at postdevelopment institutional arrangements which, instead of seeking overall control, govern as little as possible, seeking not to interfere into existing, diverse communitarian self-rule processes, while they invest their power in protecting the commons against the appropriation interests of big capital, and still enforce regulations around equality, justice and deliberative democracy *within* communities where this is necessary. In a geopolitical context where extractivism is intensifying and accelerating throughout Latin America, shielding these achievements against its onslaught is certainly a major challenge, which requires strategic alliances at a global scale.

Notes

1 In order to stress the diversity of these societies and the multiplicity of practices around *buen vivir*, I will use the Spanish term *buen vivir* in this chapter, as a cipher expressed in the colonial lingua franca of the continent, instead of the kichwa expression *Sumak Kawsay*, which has been constitutionalized in Ecuador's 2008 Carta Magna.
2 Patricia Chávez (2012) has shown in detail how these apparently innocuous mechanisms of exclusion have worked in the case of Indigenous Members of Parliament who entered the legislative power under Evo Morales in Bolivia.
3 'Works for *buen vivir*' was a recurrent phrase in President Correa's speeches when inspecting building sites or inaugurating public works. For instance, on 8 September 2015, he inspected a dam project in Cañar province and promised 'more works for *buen vivir*' (www.elciudadano.gob.ec/presidente-constata-avance-de-proyecto-de-control-de-inundaciones-canar-naranjal/). Similarly, a tweet from the then-ruling party Alianza Pais from 27 May 2015 states: 'The Citizen Revolution delivers four works for Buen Vivir in Sucumbíos' (https://twitter.com/35PAIS/status/603674579207196672).
4 In the 1940s, in the context of the liberal revolution and the raise of the socialist and communist parties of Ecuador, the first Indigenous peasant unions that organized strikes of hacienda workers, as well as illegal bilingual Indigenous schools that admitted girls and boys all alike, were founded in Cayambe by historical figures like Dolores Cacuango and Tránsito Amaguaña.
5 All citations of Magali Quezada are taken from an interview held in Quito on 23 March 2017.
6 https://vlex.ec/vid/canton-cayambe-reglamenta-administracion-581627490.
7 All citations of Guillermo Churuchumbi are taken from an interview held in Quito on 23 March 2017.
8 The *páramo* is the ecosystem of the regions above the continuous forest line in the Andes, yet below the permanent snowline. Its vegetation is composed mainly of giant rosette plants, shrubs and grasses, which act like giant sponges, leading to its most important ecological function: the storage of water.

References

Andrade, S. (2003) 'Gobiernos locales indígenas en el Ecuador'. *Revista Andina*, no 37, pp 115–136. www.revistaandinacbc.com/wp-content/uploads/2016/ra37/ra-37-2003-05.pdf.
Becker, M. (2015) *¡Pachakutik! Movimientos indígenas, proyectos políticos y disputas electorales en el Ecuador*. Quito: FLACSO and Abya Yala.
Blaser, M. (2014) 'Ontology and Indigeneity: On the political ontology of heterogeneous assemblages'. *Cultural Geographies*, vol 21, no 1, pp 49–58.
Bollier, D. & Helfrich, S. (2012) *The Wealth of the Commons*. Amherst: Levelers Press.
Brand, U. & Görg, C. (2018) *Zur Aktualität der Staatsform. Die materialistische Staatstheorie von Joachim Hirsch*. Baden-Baden: Nomos.

Brassel, F., Herrera, S. & Laforge, M. (eds.) (2008) *¿Reforma agraria en Ecuador? Viejos temas, nuevos argumentos*. Quito: SIPAE.

Caffentzis, G. & Federici, S. (2014) 'Commons against and beyond Capitalism'. *Community Development Journal*, vol 49, suppl. 1, pp 83–i91.

Caria, S. & Domínguez, R. (2016) 'Ecuador's *buen vivir*. A new ideology for development'. *Latin American Perspectives*, vol 43, no 1, pp 18–33. http://journals.sagepub.com/doi/abs/10.1177/0094582X15611126?journalCode=lapa.

Chávez, P. (2012) '¿De la colorida minoría a una mayoría gris? Presencia indígena en el legislativo'. La Paz: Friedrich Ebert Stiftung and Editorial gente común.

Cholango, H. (2012) 'Movimiento Indígena del Ecuador, su Participación en la Asamblea Constituyente de Montecristi, y la Lucha por el Estado Plurinacional'. Bachelor thesis. Quito: Universidad Politécnica Salesiana.

Chuji, M. (2014) 'Sumak kawsay versus desarrollo'. In Hidalgo-Capitán, A.L. & Guillén García, A.D. (eds.), *Sumak kawsay yuyay: Antología del pensamiento indigenista ecuatoriano sobre sumak kawsay*, pp 221–236. Huelva and Cuenca: CIM-UH/FIUCUHU/PYDLOS.

Engle Merry, S. (2011) 'Measuring the world: Indicators, human rights, and global governance'. *Current Anthropology*, vol 52, Supplement 3, pp 83–95.

Escobar, A. (2012) 'Cultura y diferencia. La ontología política del Campo Cultura y Desarrollo'. *Wale'Keru: Revista de Investigación en Cultura Y Desarrollo*, no 2. https://dugi-doc.udg.edu/bitstream/handle/10256/7724/WALEKERU-Num2-p7-16.pdf?sequence=1.

Escobar, A. (2015) 'Decrecimiento, post-desarrollo y transiciones: Una conversación preliminar'. *Interdisciplina*, vol 3, no 7, pp 217–244.

GADIP Cayambe (2015) 'Actualización del plan de desarrollo y ordenamiento territorial del Cantón Cayambe 2015–2025'. Cayambe: GADIP.

Gudynas, E. & Acosta, A. (2011) 'El buen vivir más allá del desarrollo'. *Qué hacer*, no 181, pp 70–81.

Gutiérrez Aguilar, R. (2017) 'Horizontes comunitario-populares. Producción de lo común más allá de las políticas estado-céntricas'. Madrid: Traficantes de sueños.

Kippler, C. (2010) 'Exploring post-development: Politics, the state and emancipation. The question of alternatives'. *POLIS Journal*, vol 3, pp 1–38. www.polis.leeds.ac.uk/assets/files/students/student-journal/ug-summer-10/caroline-kippler-summer-10.pdf.

Lang, M. (2017) 'Erradicar la pobreza o empobrecer las alternativas?'. Quito: Abya Yala and Universidad Andina Simón Bolívar.

Lang, M. & M'Barek, M. (2018) 'Nabón county: Building *buen vivir* from the bottom up'. In Lang, M., König, C.-D. & Regelmann, A.-C. (eds.), *Alternatives in a World of Crisis*, pp 90–133. Global Working Group Beyond Development. Brussels and Quito: Rosa Luxemburg Stiftung and Universidad Andina Simón Bolívar.

Manosalvas, M. (2014) 'Buen vivir o sumak kawsay: En busca de nuevos referenciales'. *Íconos: Revista de ciencias sociales*, no 49, pp 101–121.

Meschkat, K. (2015) 'Los gobiernos progresistas y las consecuencias políticas del neoextractivismo'. In Lang, M., Cevallos, B., & López, C. (eds.), *¿Cómo transformar? Instituciones y cambio social en América Latina y Europa*, pp 77–92. Quito: Abya Yala and Fundación Rosa Luxemburg.

Moreno, C., Speich, D. & Fuhr, L. (2015) *Carbon Metrics: Global Abstractions and Ecological Epistemicide*. Berlin: Heinrich Böll Stiftung.

Morocho, P. (2013) 'Encuesta de bienestar subjetivo. Proyecto piloto Nabón y Pucará 2012-2013. Cuenca, Nabón y Pucará'. Cuenca, Nabón and Pucará: PYDLOS, Gobierno Autónomo Descentralizado de Nabón, Gobierno Autónomo Descentralizado de Pucará.

Ortiz Crespo, S. (2008) 'Gobiernos locales indígenas en el Ecuador'. Ottawa FOCAL, Canadian Foundation for the Americas. www.focal.ca/pdf/indigenous_Ortiz%20Crespo_gobiernos%20locales%20indigenas%20Ecuador_April%202008.pdf.

Ospina, P. (ed.) (2006) *En las fisuras del poder. Movimiento indígena, cambio social y gobiernos locales*. Quito: Instituto de Estudios Ecuatorianos.

Ostrom, E. (1990) *Governing the Commons*. Cambridge: Cambridge University Press.

PYDLOS (2014) 'Plan de ordenamiento territorial del Cantón Nabón: Diagnóstico y diagnóstico integrado'. Nabón and Cuenca: PYDLOS and Gobierno Autónomo Descentralizado de Nabón.

Quezada, M. (2017) 'Participación Ciudadana, Modelo de Gestión, Presupuesto Participativo'. Talk at the seminar *Gobiernos locales alternativos y construcción del Sumak Kawsay*, 23 March. Quito: Universidad Andina Simón Bolívar.

Ramírez, R. (2010) 'Socialismo del sumak kawsay o biosocialismo republicano'. In Secretaría Nacional de Planificación y Desarrollo SENPLADES (ed.), *Los nuevos retos de América Latina: Socialismo y Sumak Kawsay*, pp 55–76, Quito: SENPLADES.

Schavelzon, S. (2015) *Plurinacionalidad y vivir bien/buen vivir: Dos conceptos leídos desde Bolivia y Ecuador post-constituyentes*. Quito: Abya Yala.

SIISE-INEC (2001) 'Censo de población y vivienda'. Quito: Sistema de Indicadores Sociales del Ecuador – Instituto Nacional de Estadísticas y Censos. www.siise.gob.ec/siiseweb/siiseweb.html?sistema=1#.

SIISE-INEC (2010) 'Censo de población y vivienda'. Quito: Sistema de Indicadores Sociales del Ecuador – Instituto Nacional de Estadísticas y Censos. www.siise.gob.ec/siiseweb/siiseweb.html?sistema=1#www.siise.gob.ec/siiseweb/siiseweb.html?sistema=1#.

Unda, R. & Jácome, R. (2009) 'Del clientelismo político a la participación ciudadana. Experiencia del presupuesto participativo en el cantón Nabón'. Nabón: Municipio de Nabón and PDDL cooperación.

Ura, K., Alkire, S., Zangmo, T. & Wangdi, K. (2012) *A Short Guide to Gross National Happiness Index*. Thimphu: The Centre for Bhutan Studies.

Walsh, C. (2009) 'Interculturalidad, Estado, sociedad. Luchas (de)coloniales de nuestra época'. Quito: Universidad Andina Simón Bolívar and Abya Yala.

12
SURVIVING WELL TOGETHER

Postdevelopment, maternity care, and the politics of ontological pluralism

Katharine McKinnon, Stephen Healy, and Kelly Dombroski

Introduction

Postdevelopment began in the domain of academic critique, a critique sometimes so scathing that it was read as a wholesale rejection of development. In our reading, however, those critiques expressed a disappointment and betrayal felt by those who saw that the development industry (multilateral or bilateral aid, INGOs, and charitable organizations) had been founded on some worthwhile altruistic intention. The intention and the promise of a more equitable world, a global sharing of knowledge and resources, and greater shared well-being were, and remain, worthwhile goals. But from the beginning the industry was mired in the ethnocentrism and arrogance of the 'First World', colonial legacies of dispossession and destruction, and the emergence of institutions that would form the bedrock of contemporary global capitalism. In the late 1980s and 1990s, postdevelopment scholars provided a minority voice against the development machine, but never rejected the idea that greater global equity was a worthwhile enterprise (McKinnon 2007; McKinnon 2012). Following these critiques, the next question is how can a global community work towards these goals without reinscribing, and re-performing imperialism? There is not, and never will be, a simple answer to that question. In this chapter we explore some examples of how a critical development scholarship now is moving past a position of critique, into the practice of engaged scholarship as postdevelopment.

Our approach to postdevelopment emerges through our collaborations with the Community Economies Collective (CEC). The CEC is a global network of scholars, activists, and practitioners elaborating diverse economies theory to explore how aspects of a diverse economy might contribute to community well-being. At the heart of this enterprise is a rearticulation of what it is we are aiming for in our community engagements and our scholarship. The goal is summed up for us in the phrase 'surviving well together', taken from Gibson-Graham, Cameron, and

Healy's book *Take Back the Economy* (2013). The idea of 'surviving well' requires us to think not only about what is required for an individual, household, or community to meet their needs, but also what is required in order to thrive, to lead a worthwhile and satisfying life, and to enjoy well-being beyond mere survival. The addition of the term 'together' is crucial. It signals that there is no surviving well without human beings working together for our shared survival, across families, communities, and the globe. In addition, our togetherness is an interspecies phenomenon – our survival as a species is dependent upon the survival and well-being of our planetary companions. Surviving well together requires a constant reprisal of ethical negotiations with our human and non-human others, across boundaries of majority and minority worlds, cultures, species, and consciousness.

As a goal, 'surviving well together' packs a lot into just three words. This chapter explores some of the implications of those three words for our efforts in an engaged postdevelopment scholarship. We reflect on three interrelated research projects from which we can discern a handful of core strategies. These strategies we see as central to our own efforts towards the practice of engaged postdevelopment research, aimed at creating an understanding of how to survive well together. Together they articulate a practice of feminist postdevelopment research that continues to take shape. In what follows, we consider three research projects to illustrate three core strategies in our approach to postdevelopment practice. The first core strategy is to appreciate the importance of co-producing knowledge and an openness to the presence of multiple ontologies. Here, we focus on a project conducted in the Pacific by Katharine McKinnon amongst a team of collaborators (see Carnegie et al. 2012; Carnegie et al. 2013; McKinnon et al. 2016) to create community-based indicators for gender equity. Following Kelly Dombroski's work in China on maternity and birthing, the second core strategy is to recognize how multiple ontologies are embodied, and that attending to this 'body multiple' (see Mol 2002, 2008) is crucial for health and for the end goal of surviving well together the context of maternal care. Finally, our discussion shifts to a collaborative project in its formative stages, which brings our interest in surviving well together into the realm of maternity care provision in Laos PDR. In reflection based on preliminary research we grapple with how to practice recognition of multiple ontologies and the body multiple in a context where politics, both formal state politics and the structural politics of aid provision, presents few openings of an alternative discourse of health or the body (see also Dombroski et al. 2016; Dombroski et al. 2018).

Defining postdevelopment

For us, the term 'postdevelopment' describes a broad set of critical commentaries and approaches. It is a field of debate characterized by an engagement with poststructural and postcolonial thought coupled with a critical reflection on the logics and practice of international aid and development work. Postdevelopment scholars draw on the poststructural interest in language and representation to explore the operations of the discourses of development: how it came into being, and how it shapes the problematization of poverty, and the actions taken to address those problems; it is thinking critically about what development discourses *do* that most concerns us and other postdevelopment scholars. To paraphrase Yvonne Underhill-Sem, we are interested in the ways that development discourse shapes us and how are we shaped by it (Underhill-Sem 2002). The purpose of seeing what the discourse does is not merely critique, but to open up a view into what *might be*. Following in the footsteps of Gibson-Graham (2005), we are interested in 'looking for difference', investigating what alternative views might be fostered, what new possibilities might be opened up as a result of seeing things differently (Gibson-Graham 2005).

The possibility for action comes with the recognition that our representations of development, our language around what the 'problem' is, have performative power. The performativity of discourse draws together both our understandings of what development is, why it is needed, and what it does, and the actual practice to doing development. As Muniesa (2014) has noted, discourse (our representations of and entangled actions upon the world) 'provoke' certain realities into being. In other words, what we believe a thing to be shapes what we think we can do about it, and how we seek to do it.

Postdevelopment *practice* has the difficult task of continuing to attend to the power of development discourse and complex politics of development practice, its colonial history and neocolonial tendencies, its compromised ideology and its failures, while seeking to still do something. Founded in poststructuralism, a postdevelopment practice cannot, however, claim the firm moral ground that most development branding enjoys. As Phil Ireland and Katharine McKinnon put it in 2013, what postdevelopment scholars must do is to find ways to 'move ahead uneasily – without confidence that any particular approach is the "right" one, and with the knowledge that any development work is always already embedded in politics' (Ireland & McKinnon 2013).

Uncertainty and uneasiness do not sit well with most development institutions. The development industry is now dominated by a marketplace approach, where monies made available for development work are subject to a competitive tender process (usually by international NGOs). Bids are assessed on a value-for-money basis. Overlaying this market approach to aid is a rich and many-layered bureaucratic system that remains deeply paternalistic, with extensive reporting requirements, strict time constraints, and a system that prioritizes accountability to donors over accountability to community. There is then a constancy, a set of unconscious commitments, that persist through development's many iterations over the past half-century. Within aid culture an open and uncertain approach is anathema because the goals remain the same. Despite the ample demonstration that social and economic change seldom progresses predictably or smoothly, the aid industry seems to still require reportable outcomes, predictable pathways, models for change, reliable blueprints.

We are interested in how development practice can work with inescapable politics and uncertainty, and what role there is for the postdevelopment scholar in enabling this. Boaventura de Sousa Santos suggests the key is to move away from what he calls 'the Great Singularity' exemplified in five monocultures he identifies: of knowledge, linear time, classification, universality, and capitalism. The idea is to move instead towards a 'sociology of absences' that gives credit to 'the diversity and multiplicity of social practices in opposition to the exclusive credibility of hegemonic practices' (de Sousa Santos 2004: 239, 240) that creates the conditions for what he terms 'cognitive justice' (de Sousa Santos 2015). Cognitive justice commits us to ontological plurality, to re-valuing other ways of knowing and being in the world. In the following section we describe a project in which cognitive justice was indeed one of the central goals of the work.

Multiple ontologies of equity

In an earlier project, Katharine McKinnon, with others, received support from the AusAID Australian Development Research Awards to conduct research on development and gender equity in the context of the Solomon Islands and Fiji (McKinnon et al. 2016). The context for this scholarly intervention was that regional leaders had signed onto an International Gender Equality Declaration, which had implications for how development was to be practiced in both of these former ex-colonial countries. This commitment to gender equity occurred precisely at a moment when the development establishment was moving from treating gender equality as a social concern to it being the pursuit of a smart economics – based on a growing global recognition that women were frequently lead actors in the informal economy and that their latent capacities as rational-actors should be harnessed in the development process (Bergeron & Healy 2013). In the context of the World Bank's 'Smart Economics', gender equity becomes a rational benefit to the whole society but also becomes one-dimensional in its meaning – equality means that women, like men, must be integrated into the market economy, ideally its formal sector. In this narrative the solution was already clear – development meant the further integration of women into the market economy. But what if this weren't the only answer? What if it were possible that in these societies gender equity was allowed to be something other than what liberal feminism and the development apparatus presumed it to mean? Drawing on previous diverse economies research, a series of workshops were held with community members in Fiji and the Solomon Islands. These were facilitated by local NGO co-researchers and engaged community members in a process of detailing all of the work done by both genders and across the lifecycle that contributed to community well-being.

What this rich description made clear was that while wage work and participation in the market economy played a role in community livelihood, it was not the only, or even the most significant, contributor to collective well-being. Conversations with community members worked to find a language for what was already there, but was absent in the visions of economic development and gender equality available in 'development-speak'. As a sociology of absence, the research allowed a new articulation of shared concern and experience, in turn enabling a different imagining of what gender equality might mean. One of the outcomes from these conversational exercises were other ways of indicating and valuing gender equity – a set of metrics that sought to place the discursive power of indicators in the hands of community by ensuring that they reflected both the concerns and aspirations of community members (see Carnegie et al. 2013; McKinnon et al. 2016). The suite of indicators sought, for example, to reflect how both non-capitalist and non-market activities like home gardens were valuable because they in turn were the basis for a system of redistribution that deepened social connections. Building a language for gender equality on the basis of community conversations also meant that conventional meanings of gender equity were challenged; rather than equal participation in the market economy, gender equity came to mean revaluing contributions of both women and men (across age groups) to shared well-being in a more-than-capitalist economy.

As scholars of development, we are interested in how our intellectual work and our engagements via action research can move beyond the monocultures that contain the development project and create spaces where cognitive justice becomes a possibility.[1] For Gibson-Graham (2005), beginning with rich description of these diverse and multiple practices is one way to think of a postdevelopment practice that is not just an inexorable move towards industrialization or capitalism. These practices might be economic, as in Gibson-Graham's work (Gibson-Graham 2014, 2016; Gibson-Graham et al. 2017; Gibson et al. 2018), or health-related, as in Dombroski's work (Dombroski 2015, 2016b). Efforts to move beyond the singularity to which de Sousa Santos alerts us forces an encounter with other ontologies and ways of being in the world that pose immediate and material challenges to the assumptions of much of development practice. If we are serious about moving beyond monocultures of knowledge and practice, we must pay attention to these ontologies, and indeed cosmologies, in any intervention towards surviving well together.

The body multiple in postdevelopment practices of engaged care

The recognition of multiple ontologies is a starting point for a practice of postdevelopment scholarship, but added to this is the recognition that we live and work in bodies that are also constructed differently in those multiple worlds. This awareness of the 'the body multiple' is a major contribution of Kelly Dombroski's work to our shared project of exploring how a practice of feminist postdevelopment research might look.

Dombroski's work in rural Qinghai, China, focuses on early child care and breastfeeding practices (Dombroski forthcoming). This region has faced decreasing breastfeeding rates and duration since the introduction of artificial formula in the 1970s (Guo et al. 2013). Because of the many benefits of breastfeeding for infant nutrition, health, and immunity, as well as effective mother and child bonding, the World Health Organization (WHO) has spearheaded efforts to increase breastfeeding rates globally (World Health Organization 2012). One example is the baby-friendly hospital initiative (World Health Organization 1981). Signatories are expected to, among other things, prohibit the marketing of artificial formula in hospital, promote rooming in and skin to skin contact for newborns and mothers, and initiate breastfeeding within two hours of birth unless medical conditions prevent this. These recommendations are understood by many as a return to simpler practices of birthing and breastfeeding and a limiting of the influence of industrialization, medicalization, and indeed 'modernization' within maternity care.

The WHO recommendations (1981, 2012) represent the human maternal body as globally homogeneous: a mammal fully capable of immediate breastfeeding. They also represent the failing hospital and unethical formula marketing as the cause of reduced breastfeeding, promoting the baby-friendly hospital accreditation as an alternative to the baby-unfriendly spaces where babies are separated from their mothers and subjected to artificial formula before breastfeeding has even been initiated. The view from the ground, however, is much more complex.

Dombroski's fieldwork in the city of Xining, China, found that for women birthing in a baby-friendly hospital a number of different understandings of the maternal and infant body were present, which produced patterns of formula use quite different from those in other parts of the world (Dombroski forthcoming). A postdevelopment approach to intervening in infant health here requires an enunciation of the complex practices of infant feeding already present.

Firstly, women in Xining were subject to two quite different understandings of how the body operates. These two physiologies of the body are ontologically distinct, with contradictory realities of what the body is actually composed of. The first of these is associated with the tradition of Chinese medicine, formalized in the People's Republic of China as Traditional Chinese Medicine (TCM), the state-funded and more highly theorized version of Chinese traditional medicine or *zhongyi* 'central/Chinese medicine' (Zhang 2007; Lei 2014). The second physiology of the body is that associated with the biomedical practice of medicine, sometimes known as 'modern medicine' or 'scientific medicine', historically known in China as *xiyi*, 'Western medicine' (Zhang 2007). In the former, breastfeeding is a practice that is intimately tied up with the functions of the *chong* and *ren* meridians, where the *ren* is linked to the uterus, menstruation, and other forms of uterine bleeding, the production of breastmilk, the lungs, and the emotion of grief and the activity of worry. In turn, the *chong* is linked to the liver, the breasts, and the emotion of anger (among other things). The flows of *qi* and blood through these linked organs mean that breastmilk is understood as being produced by sufficient flows of *qi* and blood to the area of the breasts, a flow that is disrupted if *qi* is depleted through downward flows of blood and *qi* as experienced in birthing a baby and placenta (Hsiung 1995; Men & Guo 2010). Therefore, in traditional understandings of the body, breastfeeding is understood as an activity best delayed until the flows of blood have stabilized and the mother has had a chance to replenish herself through blood and *qi*-nourishing foods. It is also important that she is enabled to remain calm through the care and attention of others. All of this is understood as good for both baby and mother.

At the same time, the mother in Xining who is birthing in a hospital is also subject to biomedical knowledge that posits the maternal body as primarily mammalian, and considers the vulnerability of the baby over that of the mother. In the biomedical understanding, breastfeeding physiology is one of supply and demand; the demand created through sucking produces the milk and simultaneously contracts the uterus and prevents excessive bleeding (Day & Australian Breastfeeding Association 2004). From a biomedical perspective delays in breastfeeding informed by TCM are understood as a superstitious withholding, although in Xining health practitioners displayed mixed attitudes. Most understood and related to the reasons for delay articulated by mothers and grandmothers, but were also concerned that the baby could become hypoglycaemic and be unable to feed if they did not intervene in a timely manner. Health professionals interviewed by Dombroski insisted that 'unless something was wrong' all women breastfed in the delivery ward before being transferred to the maternity ward. However, in twenty-five interviews only *one* woman had breastfed in the delivery ward – meaning that the criteria for something being wrong was being applied very liberally, that almost every woman's *qi* was depleted enough to prevent immediate breastfeeding. And yet, in this embodied intersection between *xiyi* and *zhongyi*, the vulnerable baby was left without immediate nutrition. The concern then arose that the baby would become too weak to stimulate supply. This provided an opening for a non-breastmilk intervention – often sugar water (a treatment for hypoglycaemia) and also artificial formula.

In Xining the practices around immediate breastfeeding, and introduction of non-breastmilk alternatives, signal the presence of two different ontologies of the body interacting in one space. Both are present in the baby-friendly hospital, but also, both are present in the one space of the maternal body. For Xining mothers and babies there is no monoculture of knowledge and the body, the situation is far more complex. This is what Annemarie Mol would call 'the body multiple' (Mol 2002).

As scholars concerned with action research, the question then arises: what kind of intervention for baby and maternal health would a postdevelopment practice make here? In the years that followed, Dombroski has been able to explore this more explicitly through community-engaged scholarly work. She was invited to do a number of training events for breastfeeding counsellors, and to review the material being translated by the Australian Breastfeeding Association for Chinese-speaking women in Australia. Her work provided a series of dialogues and scenarios breastfeeding counsellors, midwives, doctors, and other health practitioners could use in intervening in the moments after birth, when breastfeeding might be initiated (Dombroski 2016a). Presented in conferences, video materials, and training sessions with health professionals, these dialogues enabled birth to be framed as a draining and depleting act (as understood in TCM), and provided a way to broach breastfeeding in a way that acknowledged and addressed depletion. For example:

MIDWIFE: *You might be feeling a bit exhausted and depleted now after all that work. What we will do is have a little rest with baby resting on your chest, but then get some hot, nourishing food into you. Then we will give breastfeeding a go in an hour or so when you have had a chance to recover.*

In this scenario, the midwife can work with family members to provide TCM-appropriate food for the mother in order to address the concern for her depletion and need for nourishment before attempting to breastfeed. Making sure that depletion, nourishment, and recovery are mentioned is key to this intervention, recognizing the ontological reality of the birthing mother, treating it through providing appropriate foods, and provoking an affective response that reduces anxiety and worry and may lead to earlier breastfeeding and reduced use of manufactured formula. It may not be necessary for the health practitioner to necessarily accept the multiple ontological realities present in the birth room as 'actual' realities, but the recognition that a mother may experience an ontologically different reality is enough here to make an effective intervention for the health and well-being of the baby and mother.

The learning we take from Dombroski's work in Xining, and with Chinese mothers in Australia, is that engaged scholarship can make space for cognitive multiplicity: seeking interventions that honour multiplicity and do not attempt to reduce one reality to a 'perspective' that must be somehow subsumed or coalesced into a singularity. We cannot only avoid the great singularity that de Sousa Santos decries in development practice, we can create the conditions for postdevelopment as cognitive justice. In this case cognitive justice is neither expecting, nor wanting an outcome where we arrive at a shared, or correct, understanding of body, childbirth, or mothering. Instead, we look for ways to accept and work with divergent understandings of the same phenomena. In turn, care is transformed into a process of 'staying with the trouble', as Donna Haraway (2016) puts it. This process that can be carried out in relation to the body of the birthing mother for us also works at a larger scale – we can 'stay with the trouble' as part of a further effort to reimagine a postdevelopment practice.

In this next section we speculate on how the ontological and cosmological pluralism at the heart of a move beyond de Sousa Santos' singularity might be applied to rethink approaches to improving maternal health at the national scale. In the sections that follow we draw on initial findings from a project focused on maternity care delivery in Laos.

Practicing a feminist postdevelopment scholarship: maternity care in Laos

Childbirth for Lao women has become considerably safer over the last two decades but maternal mortality rate in the Lao People's Democratic Republic remains among the highest in the Western Pacific Region (World Health Organization 2018). The official health department policy to prevent mothers from dying is that all women should be receiving antenatal care that would pick up on danger signs for conditions like placenta praevia or malnutrition, and that all women should be giving birth at a clinic or hospital in the care of a trained midwife and/or obstetrician. This policy is supported by the WHO and the international funding aid agencies that subsidize the Laos health care system. In our preliminary research in the province of Luang Prabang we could see that neither clinics nor the hospitals are necessarily safe, nor able to accommodate all the women who might need them. This suggests that getting more women into clinics is not necessarily the solution.

There are many reasons why hospitals and clinics are unable to provide adequate care. From our discussions with Laos Department of Health staff, obstetricians, and midwives in the province we understood that the number of trained midwives and obstetricians remains far fewer than are needed to service the population, and the health system remains badly underfunded. Given the lack of facilities and equipment, lack of trained midwives and obstetricians (and even lack of access to relevant health research for teachers and students), it is clear that if all women did come into hospitals and clinics to give birth, this would not solve the problem. In addition, many women do not want, or are not permitted, to come to hospital. Only one study to date has explored why rural women choose not to go to hospital, and this study shows that women have very good reasons for that decision. Sychareun and colleagues (2012) found that women felt clinics were uncomfortable, not allowing freedom of movement or providing space for family members to support women. Women also felt afraid, experienced bullying and mistreatment, and were unable to communicate with health staff due to language barriers. For some women, their husbands would not give them permission to go to the clinics. A final reason was that women felt spiritually vulnerable in hospital, being unable to receive the traditional spiritual or medicinal treatments that they need for a safe and healthy birth.

The Ministry of Health officials we spoke with were particularly focused on the problem of this last point – women are 'afraid of ghosts/spirits' and therefore won't accept lifesaving treatment. The mislabelling of cultural beliefs and spiritual practice as superstition is not confined to bureaucrats. Phoxay et al. (2001) write that 'health-seeking behaviour was determined by superstitious will, which would be detrimental to mothers' (17). The solution they proposed (2001) consists of better education for mothers, which would give them up-to-date knowledge of modern medicine and cut across the knowledge transmitted by village elders on how to care for pregnancy. The danger of this recommendation is that it dismisses the value of the traditional knowledge of elders and de-legitimizes cultural practices as a whole, when not all such practices may be harmful as claimed. When scholars, doctors, and health officials dismiss the spiritual beliefs of a minority group, they are in effect dismissing the complex cosmology that forms the foundation of that culture.

A postdevelopment take on this case would be to place Indigenous knowledge and medical practice alongside that of the hospitals and clinics. This would mean recognizing that there are multiple ontologies at work in these contexts and refusing to assume that Western or even biomedical practice is always correct. Indeed, recognizing what we might learn from other ways of protecting health and well-being. It would require accepting that the knowledge and experience of, for example, Hmong women is as legitimate and as important as the knowledge and experience of the clinicians and health department policymakers. And a postdevelopment practice might take that recognition further, to work for solutions to the challenges of safe childbirth in rural Laos based on the confluence of knowledge and practice that is already available. The challenge in this case is that both the international NGOs who support the health services and the hospitals and provincial health department officials are bound by the policies endorsed by the central authorities in Vientiane. There is no room to visibly stray from the aims and intentions of that policy, even in order to respond to the particular needs of the population in different parts of the country.

It is here that we encounter the limits of the kind of postdevelopment practice for which we are equipped, forced to confront again the spectre of the political that remains at the core of the development industry. As with community development interventions of the past (and especially those McKinnon studied in northern Thailand; McKinnon 2012), the possibilities for effective/affective engagement of small players (that is, three university researchers) is extremely limited. As with the processes that unfolded in neighboring Thailand, room for dissenting voices, for community advocacy, and for a politics of multiplicity can only come into development as the political situation at the national level begins to change. Until then the options for postdevelopment practice remain limited to the quiet work of researching and practicing in solidarity with communities, and (perhaps) exercising a gentle subterfuge of the kind development professionals in northern Thailand practiced under the headline of participatory development (McKinnon 2012).

Conclusion

We began this chapter with an elaboration of engaged postdevelopment scholarship. A starting point for us is the profound sense of *unease* postdevelopment generates, calling into question what we already know is wrong or what needs to happen, or how a solution might be found. This sense of unease resonates with Donna Haraway's call to 'stay with the trouble' and is a starting point for seeking the kind of cognitive justice called for by de Sousa Santos. Unease does not excuse us from acting, for not acting is also acting. But it does open the floor to new possibilities, including what happens when we engage in a sociology of absence, when we revalue precisely what development jettisons in the name of progress.

We discussed work to create community-based indicators of gender equity, which shows that it is possible to make space for diverse place-based knowledges and aspirations for equity, and to construct interventions that achieve cognitive justice through the appreciation of multiple ontologies. Through Dombroski's work with breastfeeding as understood and practiced across Chinese and Western medicine, we showed that it is possible to make space for multiple ontologies not only in relation to discursive interventions, but also in relation to the body. In the context of maternity and early childhood care, Dombroski's postdevelopment intervention makes space for parallel, co-existing realities within the same room and within the same body. The challenge moving forward, as demonstrated by our preliminary research in Laos, is in how to formulate a feminist postdevelopment practice based on multiple ontologies and the body multiple knowing that there is little room in the structure of the development industry for the uneasiness these multiplicities introduce. Especially in the realm of health care, where biomedical knowledge and strict adherence to guidelines for clinical practice have implications around life and death, it is not so easy to trouble knowledge hierarchies. This is especially so in institutional contexts that are either overtly or subtly wedded to the unstated, unconscious, bureaucratic machinations that underwrite the development establishment.

For us, a commitment to staying with the trouble does not mean giving up on 'doing something', but it means committing to a path that transforms development and even postdevelopment as we know it. For us 'staying with the trouble' means an approach to learning and acting together in the world where we too are implicated, it means identifying our collective stakes in surviving well together. In the end what does it mean to give up on the idea of progress, and to reimagine development? For us it is to begin with a continuous affirmation that our survival as a species is dependent upon the survival and well-being of all our planetary companions, and to require the constant reprisal of ethical negotiations with our human and non-human others, across boundaries of majority and minority worlds, cultures, species, and consciousness.

Note

1 Cameron and Gibson's (2005) description of action research in a poststructural vein departs from other understandings of action research. Rather than imagining action as one where formerly marginalized subjects participate, research is recast as an open-ended, affecting, and collaborative context that may generate new desires, identifications, or forms of collective action.

References

Bergeron, S. & Healy, S. (2013) 'Beyond the business case: A community economies approach to gender, development and social economy'. In Utting, P. (ed.), *Potential and Limits of Social Solidarity Economy*. Geneva, Switzerland: UNRISD.

Cameron, J. & Gibson, K. (2005) 'Participatory action research in a poststructuralist vein'. *Geoforum*, vol 36, pp 315–331.

Carnegie, M., Rowland, C. & Crawford, J. (2013) 'Rivers and coconuts: conceptualising and measuring gender equality in semi-subsistent communities in Melanesia'. *Gender Matters*, vol 2.

Carnegie, M., Rowland, C., Gibson, K. McKinnon, K., Crawford, C., Slatter, C. (2012) *Gender and Economy in Melanesian Communities: A Manual of Indicators and Tools to Track*

Change. Sydney: University of Western Sydney, Macquarie University and International Women's Development Agency.

Day, J. & Australian Breastfeeding Association (2004) *Breastfeeding … Naturally*. East Malvern, VIC: Australian Breastfeeding Association.

de Sousa Santos, B. (2004) 'The WSF: Toward a counter-hegemonic globalization'. In Sen, J., Anand, A., Escobar, A., Waterman, P. (eds.), *World Social Forum: Challenging Empires*. New Delhi: The Viveka Foundation, pp 235–245.

de Sousa Santos, B. (2015) *Epistemologies of the South: Justice against Epistemicide*. London and New York: Routledge.

Dombroski, K. (2015) 'Multiplying possibilities: a postdevelopment approach to hygiene and sanitation in northwest China'. *Asia Pacific Viewpoint*, vol 56, pp 321–334.

Dombroski, K. (2016a) 'Breastfeeding as cultural practice: comparing Australian, Chinese and New Zealand breastfeeding practices and beliefs'. *Australian Breastfeeding Association 2016 Health Professionals Seminar Series, Breastfeeding: Making Connections*. Adelaide, Perth, Sydney.

Dombroski, K. (2016b) 'Seeing diversity, multiplying possibility: My journey from postfeminism to postdevelopment with JK Gibson-Graham'. In Harcourt, W. (ed.), *The Palgrave Handbook of Gender and Development*. Basingstoke: Palgrave Macmillan, pp 312–328.

Dombroski, K. (forthcoming) *Guarding Life*. Minneapolis: University of Minnesota Press.

Dombroski, K., Healy, S. & McKinnon, K. (2018) 'Care-full community economies'. In Harcourt, W. & Bauhardt, C. (eds.), *Feminist Political Ecology and Economies of Care*. London: Routledge, n.p.

Dombroski, K., McKinnon, K. & Healy, S. (2016) 'Beyond the birth wars: diverse assemblages of care'. *New Zealand Geographer*, vol 72, pp 230–239.

Haraway, D.J. (2016) *Staying with the Trouble. Making Kin in the Chthulucene*. Durham, NC: Duke University Press.

Gibson, K., Astuti, R., Carnegie, M., Chalernphon, A., Dombroski, K., Haryani, A.R., Hill, A., Kehi, B., Law, L., Lyne, L., McGregor, A., McKinnon, K., McWilliam, A., Miller, F., Ngin, C., Occeña-Gutierrez, D., Palmer, L., Placino, P., Rampengan, M., Lei Lei Than, M., Wianti, N.I., Wright, S. (2018) 'Community economies in Monsoon Asia: keywords and key reflections'. *Asia Pacific Viewpoint*, vol 59, pp 3–16.

Gibson-Graham, J., Cameron, J., Dombroski, K., Healy, S., Miller, E. (2017) 'Cultivating community economies: Tools for building a liveable world'. In Alperovitz, G. & Speth, J. (eds.), *The Next System Project*. Available at: http://thenextsystem.org/cultivating-community-economies/.

Gibson-Graham, J.K. (2005) 'Surplus possibilities: postdevelopment and community economies'. *Singapore Journal of Tropical Geography*, vol 26, pp 4–26.

Gibson-Graham, J.K. (2014) 'Rethinking the economy with thick description and weak theory'. *Current Anthropology*, vol 55, pp 147–153.

Gibson-Graham, J.K. (2016) 'Building community economies: Women and the politics of place'. In Harcourt, W. (ed.), *The Palgrave Handbook of Gender and Development*. Basingstoke: Palgrave Macmillan, pp 287–311.

Gibson-Graham, J.K., Cameron, J. & Healy, S. (2013) *Take Back the Economy: An Ethical Guide for Transforming Our Communities*. Minneapolis: University of Minnesota Press.

Guo, S., Fu, X., Scherpbier, R.W., Wang, Y., Zhou, H., Wang, X., Hipgrave, D.B. (2013) 'Breastfeeding rates in central and Western China in 2010: implications for child and population health'. *Bulletin of the World Health Organization* 91, pp 322–331.

Hsiung, P.-C. (1995) 'To nurse the young: breastfeeding and infant feeding in late imperial China'. *Journal of Family History*, vol 20, pp 217–239.

Ireland, P. & McKinnon, K. (2013) 'Strategic localism for an uncertain world: A postdevelopment approach to climate change adaptation'. *Geoforum*, vol 47, pp 158–166.

Lei, S.H.-l. (2014) *Neither Donkey nor Horse: Medicine in the Struggle over China's Modernity*. Chicago and London: University of Chicago Press.

McKinnon, K. (2007) 'Post-development, professionalism and the politics of participation'. *Annals of the Association of American Geographers*, vol 97, pp 772–785.

McKinnon, K. (2012) *Development Professionals in Northern Thailand: Hope, Politics and Practice*. Singapore, Honolulu: Singapore University Press, University of Hawaii and NIAS.

McKinnon, K., Carnegie, M., Gibson, K., Rowland, C. (2016) 'Gender equality and economic empowerment in the Solomon Islands and Fiji: a place-based approach'. *Gender, Place & Culture*, vol 23, pp 1376–1391.

Men, J. & Guo, L. (2010) *An Introduction to Traditional Chinese Medicine*. Boca Raton, FL, London and New York: CRC Press.

Mol, A. (2002) *The Body Multiple: Ontology in Medical Practice*. Durham, NC and London: Duke University Press.

Mol, A. (2008) *The Logic of Care: Health and the Problem of Patient Choice*. London and New York: Routledge.

Muniesa, F. (2014) *The Provoked Economy: Economic Reality and the Performative Turn*. London and New York: Routledge.

Phoxay, C., Okumura, J., Nakamura, Y., Wakai, S. (2001) 'Influence of women's knowledge on maternal health care utilization in Southern Laos'. *Asia-Pacific Journal of Public Health*, vol 13, pp 13–19.

Sychareun, V., Hansana, V., Somphet, V., Xayavong, S., Phengsavanh, A., Popenoe, R. (2012) 'Reasons rural Laotians choose home deliveries over delivery at health facilities: a qualitative study'. *BMC Pregnancy and Childbirth*, vol 12, pp 1-10.

Underhill-Sem, Y. (2002) 'Embodying post-development: bodies in places, places in bodies'. *Development*, vol 45, pp 54–73.

World Health Organization (1981) *International Code of Marketing of Breast-milk Substitutes*. www.who.int/nutrition/publications/code_english.pdf.

World Health Organization (2012) *Exclusive Breastfeeding*. www.who.int/nutrition/topics/exclusive_breastfeeding/en/.

World Health Organization (2018) *Maternal Health*. WHO Representative Office, Laos People's Democratic Republic. www.wpro.who.int/laos/topics/maternal_health/en/.

Zhang, Y. (2007) *Transforming Emotions with Chinese Medicine: An Ethnographic Account from Contemporary China*. Albany, NY: State University of New York Press.

13

STATE-FUNDED SERVICES DELIVERY AS COSMOPOLITICAL WORK

Opportunities for postdevelopment in practice in northern Australia?

Michaela Spencer

Introduction

This chapter grows from a research project being carried out under contract for the Northern Territory Government, a territory government in the north of Australia, and developed in collaboration with Indigenous researchers and Elders in several remote Aboriginal communities. The purpose of this research was to develop means for government to evaluate their practices of engaging with Aboriginal people when implementing government policies and programs in remote areas, and to develop processes for continuous learning and improvement by government staff, particularly around housing and community development programs.

From the very early days of the project, tensions arose around the requirement to separate questions of government engagement, coordination and communication, from questions of local decision-making and policy formation. While this separation was familiar for our government funders, many Elders and community members recognised engagement and decision-making as synonymous, and proposed that the best way forward is for government practices to recognise and work with the presence of two differing traditions of knowledge, governance and law as a condition for good engagement and coordination.

The facilitation of this work in practice, on the one hand accommodating the state's initially narrow terms of reference, and on the other acknowledging the contesting terms in which Indigenous participants defined their engagement, became part of our task as 'Ground Up'[1] researchers, employed at the Northern Institute, Charles Darwin University.[2] We were a small team of two researchers, one researcher/project manager and two senior advisors working to support and facilitate the collaborative development of the research project. I had the dual role of working as researcher and project manager, and at the time I was very caught up in the day-to-day activities of the project. However, now looking back there seems to be a considerable opportunity to learn from the tensions emerging in the project work, and to develop sensitivites around how such tensions these might be nurtured as opportunites for postdevelopment, rather than denied through the reassertion of the settler-colonial state and its dominant relations of knowledge production and governance practices.

There are many ways of presenting this apparent tension within a scholarly rendering of the project. My account that follows takes a largely ethnographic approach, telling stories of the project and means we employed in trying to work generatively within a government-funded program involving the collaboration of Indigenous Elders and researchers, as well as university-based researchers and government staff. In the process of undertaking this project moments arose where myself and the other CDU researchers felt in need of a productive way of seeing and understanding some of the ruptures and tensions that we were grappling with. Recognizing state-funded service delivery as cosmopolitical work offered a way to generatively understand experiences of connection and rupture within our current research project while offering a sensitising concept able to support future work of a simillar kind.

The term cosmopolitics is an elision of two words: 'cosmopolitan' and 'politics'. It was coined by the philosopher Kant at the end of the eighteenth century in Germany. But at the turn of the twentieth century two rather different meanings came to be attached to the term as two books with the title cosmopolitics were published. *Cosmopolitics I* is a book of essays about epistemic practices of science by the Belgian philosopher Isabelle Stengers (2010). The second book, edited by Cheah and Robbins (1998), is a set of collected essays by political scientists who specialise in studying international relations and who sought to extend the notion of cosmopolitics beyond a concern with relations between nation-states.

Here I join with a number of theorists in the Stengarian tradition (Blaser 2016; de la Cadena 2010; Latour 2004), taking cosmopolitics to refer to the politics of working differing worlds, or, more precisely, working differing politico-epistemic practices together and separately in going on together (Verran 2013, 2018). Paying close attention to the intersection of quite different sets of epistemo-political practices being enacted and proposed by those involved provides a way to get a handle on this project without making prior assumptions about what counts as knowledge or appropriate practices of governance. To gloss this difference very early on, there is an established norm within the tradition of settler-colonial governmentality that assumes that knowledge production is something that can happen at the periphery, while politics is something that happens in the centre, notably in parliaments. However, for Yolŋu Aboriginal Australians, this same configuration does not hold, but rather places and knowers emerge together in the ongoing work of maintaining Indigenous people-places (Verran 2002: 749). It is a tension in the epistemo-politcal practices of these differing means for constituting governed people-places that emerged within our research work, and needed to be carefully negotiated.

However, rather than racing ahead, let's first go back to the beginning and to the early days of this research project, where the activities to be undertaken were still in flux, and a rather significant difference in the understanding and aspirations between participants began to emerge.

In Galiwin'ku

I'm sitting with a small group of Indigenous researchers and advisors on the back veranda of the Yolŋu research organisation, Yalu' Marŋgithinyaraw,[3] in Galiwin'ku, East Arnhem Land. Today, like most days, this veranda it is a very busy place. This is where the director, Rosemary Gundjarraŋbuy, spends most of her time and where much of the business of the organisation is coordinated. A constant stream of Yolŋu staff and balanda[4] visitors move through, attending to various pieces of work from early in the morning till late afternoon when the office shuts. Yalu' is a go-to place for government staff and service providers, as well as university researchers like myself. The veranda has mats for those happy to sit on the floor, as well as chairs for those not so inclined, and is a breezy place where it is possible to sit quietly and talk, while still being able to see some of the things going on: people walking back and forth to the shops, cars heading up and back to the council office, kids heading to and from school, sometimes funeral processions and much other busy daily activity.

This team of researchers and advisors includes Stephen Dhamarrandji, a Yolŋu co-researcher on our project, as well as Djankirrawuy, Nyikamula and G.W.[5], three senior men who had agreed to advise on the conduct of the research project. We pulled out a small table and several chairs and sat down together to talk. These men are all very busy people, and it had taken no small amount of effort for Stephen to bring them together to discuss an upcoming research and evaluation project to be carried out in Galiwin'ku. But they all have significant experience working with government, and carry significant cultural authority. We are there to talk about the new evaluation research project that the government has proposed, and which – with their approval – might begin to take place in Galiwin'ku. I was the university researcher who would visit and work in this community, and there were also other researchers who would work with other teams of Indigenous researchers and Elder advisors in other communities. My commitment as a 'Ground Up' researcher was to work with local researchers and advisors to design the project as it would be carried out here, and this discussion with Elders was a first step towards finding out if they saw any value in the work, and seeking their guidance around the development of the research. On the one hand, the proposed project was already attractive to these Elders and the organisation as a source of income, but at the same time they were wary of research projects that do not involve significant engagement with their own methods for doing knowledge work, and were keen to avoid such projects where possible.

Stephen introduced the project and these senior men turned to each other and, speaking in Yolŋu matha, began to discuss amongst themselves appropriate ways forward. This discussion lasted some time, with some pauses, and a few exchanges back and forth in English checking aspects of the brief or clarifying things that were unclear. When these negotiations seemed to reach a natural end-point the conversation shifted back to English and G.W. explained to me some of what had been discussed and some of their interests and concerns. The first two points were ones I may have expected. He made it clear that this work was not for those sitting at the table, but for the young people who need role models of good leadership and engagement, and to learn how to work well with government. Then, also, that if it was a voice from 'the community' that the government wanted to hear coming through in the research, then there were particular appropriate ways to constitute such an entity. 'The community' wasn't a place that pre-existed the research, but a quite specific people-place that would need to be constituted through the way that the research was being carried out.

It was the third issue that made me slightly uneasy. Not because of what was being said, but because of how it seemed to conflict with other discussions I had already had with government staff in Darwin. This final point came couched in metaphor. G.W. said that the issue that they could see was that so many times before when Yolŋu have become involved in work like this, their stories and information had travelled to Darwin or Canberra, but then had *no* noticeable impact or effect on the ground in Galiwin'ku. The input offered by Yolŋu contributors becomes added as an ingredient to many other ingredients in a big dish, and gradually all the flavour offered by Yolŋu gets leached out of the food. What G.W. wanted to make clear was that there were also *other ways of cooking*; that is, of doing policy and governance work. For example, some recipes that don't have other ingredients, like the preparation of yams or the cycad nut that needs the poison to be leeched out before cooking and eating. These foods have only one ingredient, but must nonetheless be carefully prepared with their cooking resulting in a meal that can be shared by appropriate groups in different ways.

This story was told with laughter and joking, also made a significant metaphysical point. This was about the character of governance and the presence of differing practices of governance present within the Australian state. Government processes and law frequently seek many different inputs of information; they often take these inputs as equivalences that can be combined in a general milieu of market-based or parliamentary decision-making practice. Yolŋu governance and law, on the other hand, works on an assumption that there is just one kind of 'stuff' that must be worked with so as to produce distributed and amenable outcomes. This retains a situated character and does not require governance decision-making to travel to the centre to be agential, but needs to continue being practised in the right ways in-place.

In Darwin

A few weeks previously, I had been sitting in a meeting with government staff discussing their hopes and understandings for the research project. This meeting did not take place on a breezy veranda, but in an air-conditioned seminar room at the Northern Institute at Charles Darwin University. We had met to clarify general brief of the project, including a commitment to developing methods and processes with local Indigenous collaborators in each of the project sites, as well as how we would go about delivering these outcomes. In relation to their engagement and coordination activities, the Northern Territory Government (NTG) members in the room were primarily interested in getting a sense of 'how well government is doing.' Over the last few years they had invested a considerable amount of energy into supporting government staff to practice good engagement when working in remote Aboriginal communities, including through providing cultural awareness training, developing sophisticated mechanisms for consultation and seeking to engage with appropriate Indigenous groups (not just local government bureaucrats) when conducting government business. However, recognizing that this is an ongoing task requiring regular feedback if improvements are to be made, they were interested in the best ways of receiving such feedback and supporting iterative learning by staff and teams.

This evaluation work was to be associated with a new NTG strategy called the Remote Engagement and Coordination Strategy (RECS). Developing ways to assess whether people were enacting 'best practice' methods of engagement and coordination in accordance with the RECS strategy was important both for the ongoing improvement of government practice and the transparency of the strategy. Recognizing that there is a persistent blind spot around government evaluation of Indigenous policies, programs and expenditure, this project was an example of the government stepping up to accept feedback and potential criticism. Taking care of good engagement and coordination practices also meant taking care of how they would be evaluated, and getting good feedback or assessment on government performance. The state wanted to know how well 'they' were doing, as a question quite separate from modes of governance and decision-making that government staff might bring with them when doing business in Galiwin'ku, and as separate too from the policies that informed that government.

Research as state-funded service delivery

Working under contract to the NTG, our role as a small team of 'Ground Up' researchers on the Remote Engagement Coordination – Indigenous Evaluation Research (REC-IER) project[6] was to deliver research services and services products to our funding agency. The character of these products was underdetermined at the start of the research. Part of the agreement within our brief was that these research services products would not be developed within the university alone, but the process of design would involve collaboration with appropriate Indigenous knowledge authorities, as well as government staff in Darwin and in the communities where the project was being carried out. This was to be a three-way research design and development process.

Included in the research contract was provision for employment of Indigenous researchers or consultants working in their home communities, and payment for both Elder supervision and training for young mentorees paid to accompany more experienced researchers, learning through watching the project work. This was in recognition of the professional status of local researches, and to recognise that local Indigenous knowledge and expertise is valuable and deserves remuneration when contributing to the conduct of government work. As a brand, or a package, the 'Ground Up' research team had the capacity to initiate and support these engagements and the opportunity for research to be carried out in Aboriginal languages where this is desired or appropriate.

These requirements accompany a move to a more design-oriented approach[7] to research in northern Australia generally, and Indigenous contexts in particular, where the role of university researchers is not to provide expert knowledge informing policy development, but rather to develop policy design and evaluation practices through contingent on-ground negotiations where policy norms, as particular politico-epistemic practices and devices, are produced through practices of on-ground negotiation as research practice. In many ways, the freedom offered by such collaborative design approaches seemed very appealing to a well-meaning researcher such as myself.

Verran and Christie (2011) have noted that there has been a shift in the last few decades around governance in northern Australia. They suggest that:

> [...] cross-cultural knowledge practices associated with community level governance of multicultural liberal democracy, expressing 'welfare liberalism,' are being replaced by those associated with evidence-based policy formulated for governance by commissions.
>
> *(2011: 27)*

Associated with this, they suggest that

> [...] a profound change [has occurred] in the nature and location of expertise, which entails many more possibilities for Aboriginal knowledge authorities to be identified as holders of salient expertise, as well as more opportunities to challenge the ruling ontology embedded in a discourse of governmental expertise.
>
> *(2011: 27)*

However, at the same time, there has also been considerable work within the Australian academy detailing the structure failure of shifts towards neoliberal governance to account for alternative practices of knowledge and governance, and to adequately respond to Indigenous interests and voices (Altman 2007; Klein 2016; Strakosch 2015). In line with these critiques, the realization of this collaborative and potentially emancipatory potential was difficult to achieve, and the potential of the project to work postdevelopmentally often evaded our grasp. In the next few sections, I tell more stories drawn from the project, attending to moments where this difficulty appeared, and then reflecting on processes for engaging these moments differently.

An engagement scorecard: doing the state but not doing Indigenous people-places

A pressing concern for government staff involved in the project was how assessments of government engagement carried out on the ground might reliably travel back to relevant agencies and department heads in government. They wanted to learn about satisfaction associated with government staff activities as they visited the council school, clinic and employment agency and went about their business facilitating meetings, delivering services and administering funding; the idea of a scorecard was proposed by government staff as a means to receive this feedback.

We agreed to try this approach, as did researchers in Galiwin'ku. In line with the rest of the project, development of the scorecard involved carrying out interviews with senior community members, asking what good government engagement meant for them. These responses were then discussed and negotiated amongst the local research team, and translated into a series of questions that were printed in the scorecard both in English and in language. Each question could be answered by offering a score from 1 to 10, and/or by writing a comment. In Galiwin'ku the scorecard showed a picture of the research team on the front cover[8] and inside included questions such as the following.

- *Dula gapman mala marrtji ga nhäma wäŋa-wataŋuny wo ŋalapalmirriny mala*/Did government go first to the Traditional Owners and Leaders?
- *Nhä nhakuŋuny guyaŋanhawuy balayiny ŋunhi dhäwulil ŋunhi nhä nhe ŋäma walalaŋhuŋ gapmanguŋ*/Did you have enough time to think about what government was saying before making any decisions?
- *Dula yutany yolŋuny marrtji ga nhäma nhä malanynha dhäwu gapmandhu mala ga lakaram wo gurrupan?*/Were young people invited to the meeting, and given a chance to watch and learn from their Elders?

This all seemed to be going well until the Yolŋu researchers, Stephen and some of his colleagues realised that they were the people supposed to administer the scorecard in meetings as part of the evaluation research work, that the Yolŋu researchers would be the people to hand the scorecard around in meetings, and then collect it up and send it back to either the university or the government. It was at this point that this otherwise hopeful technology started to stall, becoming forgotten or accidentally left at home at times when it was supposed to be in use. Meetings with government would come and go without the scorecard being handed around to the other Yolŋu in the room until Stephen suggested that the scorecard is a good tool, but perhaps 'the government people should hand it out themselves' (Dhamarrandji, private communication).

The benefit of the scorecard for government staff seeking to know 'how well we are doing' was that it produced information that was able to travel well so as to let government assess their own practice while keeping the business of government going. Feedback could move quite easily from a meeting room in a community to offices in the NTG in Darwin or other centres, and as such these scorecards did a reasonable job of 'doing the state'. However, they were less good at 'doing an Indigenous people-place', failing to maintain particular and specialist lines of authority and leadership by which Yolŋu maintain complex relations of kinship, clan membership and land ownership. Quietly refusing to implicate themselves in this form of assessment, the Yolŋu researchers voted with their feet and found a way to avoid putting themselves in a position where they would be the ones reporting so definitively to government on their performance, and where they would be the ones sitting with their close relatives, their kin, in meeting rooms filling out scorecards saying something about government people.

Videos and elder testimony: doing an Indigenous people-place but not doing the state

At some point, as the scorecard struggled to gain traction as a useful tool, Stephen started recording video footage on an iPad that he took along to meetings where government staff and Yolŋu were working together. More than other forms of written documentation, the use of video appeared more intuitive, and a different means for evaluating government engagement and coordination activities in Galiwin'ku. However, these snippets of video footage do not speak on their own, and so as to offer interpretation and authorisation to the footage, and convert it from a digital file to a piece of feedback to government, his initial inclination was to again convene a small group of Elders who could speak to the video, and provide a small package of video and community message which could be passed onto government staff, providing an opportunity to maintain appropriate relations of Elder authority *and* to tell alternative stories around what was happening in these situations where government, as well as other business, was being done.

Sitting back on the veranda at Yalu' after a local council meeting, Stephen spoke with two elder Yolŋu – Gundjarraŋbuy the research director, and Daŋataŋa her nephew through kinship relations. He told them about several issues that had come up in the meeting and showed them small snippets of video footage he had taken. One of the key issues emerging in this meeting concerned a decision that needed to be made about the expenditure of funds available for development works in the community. Suggestions had been made about a BMX track or a swimming pool for the kids, and the Yolŋu council members were asked by the council administration which of these they would prefer.

Hearing this story, Gundjarraŋbuy and Daŋataŋa discussed some of the events of the meeting, and picked on this particular moment as a missed opportunity for good engagement between government staff and Yolŋu council members. With Stephen again using the iPad to record footage, they spoke to the camera providing a message for government regarding this contention. In the recorded testimony, they sidestepped the question of how the money should *actually* be spent. Good engagement did not start here. Rather, good engagement concerned thinking through ways to ask the question that are supportive of Yolŋu and balanda being able to work together, finding pathways to support young people and the development of Galiwin'ku.

'How can we think about this together? How can we come together to make decisions about how this money might be spent?' Gundjarraŋbuy starts. He then quickly qualifies this by saying, 'I'm just throwing some ideas around.'

Developing a short video testimony together, they then go on to point to the moment in the local council meeting, and propose that here the question should not have been posed as 'what facility do you want?' but rather 'how can we invest this money so as to produce jobs and sustainable learning pathways for Yolŋu in Galiwin'ku?' Learning employment skills in-place, developing facilities that make sense for the builders, as well as the users, made sense in relation to how Yolŋu Elders want to support and grow young people. Daŋataŋa ends the clip by saying, 'for real, this is how they (young Yolŋu) will learn, and this is how they will follow the right pathway.'

The story presented here can be read as proposing an ontologically different order of governance than that which would have been maintained in the circulation of the scorecard data. The scorecard data would have informed government staff what they had been doing badly or well, and so potentially helped them to modify their behaviour as a practice of improving government engagement. The implication of this story was that in the practice of good engagement government staff should have reconfigured their policy and decision-making practices, recognizing these decisions around funding as participating in the emergence of a community in which young Yolŋu learners and employees will have a chance of taking part.

As information, as a new kind of story about how to do good engagement, this was new for the government staff involved in the project. But at the same time, it proposed a shift that many staff felt exceeded their capacity to actualise. As government employees, they had clearly defined roles and responsibilities within an arrangement for doing governance that did not see worlds, futures and pasts emerging all apiece. So how to begin to take on the task of doing governance in this way, as part of the practice of doing good engagement, was, if not unthinkable, certainly quite difficult to practically action without at least some further guidance.

Designing feedback packages: doing cosmopolitical diplomacy

We were fortunate, throughout the duration of this project, to be able to adopt a collaborative and experimental attitude when developing research work and potential evaluation processes and techniques. With our evaluation techniques still a work in progress, we began to further explore the notion of the using iPads to collect video footage as the basis for evaluation and feedback to government. Yolŋu researchers in Galiwin'ku continued to find this visual technology was more suited to their methods than note-taking, and government staff involved in the project were enthusiastic about gathering footage direct from meetings and other engagement activities. However, the question of how to provide interpretation of, and reporting through, these video clips remained open.

It was toward the end of the project that the notion of evaluation packages emerged. These were small bundles of feedback that included a snippet of video footage, plus a feedback report (see Box 13.1 below). This report was to come in three parts: (1) a straight summary of what appeared in the footage; (2) an interpretation by an Indigenous Elder or researcher; and (3) an interpretation by a CDU researcher. The most significant difference between these packages and previous community-based video reports was the addition of this third component – the 'CDU researcher interpretation'.

BOX 13.1 SAMPLE FEEDBACK REPORT, EXCERPTED FROM REC-IER FINAL REPORT (SPENCER, CHRISTIE, MACDONALD, CAMPBELL & VERRAN 2017: 22)

Issue 1: Budget decisions

Summary from Yalu' research team:

There was a presentation by a man from the regional council. He talked about money, saying that there was a budget available for Galiwin'ku shire. The council members were asked if they wanted a BMX track for the kids, and were told other funds available if Danny Daŋataŋa (Local Authority [LA] Chairman) or the community wanted a park or recreational area, cyclone centre, swimming pool […]

Comments from Yalu' research team:

This was good, but what we were seeing is that they were talking about an issue for the community, not an issue that was for individual choice. There should have been a way to involve the community instead of the LA committee getting the story and keeping it there. It could be that in between LA and the community there is a gap that needs to be filled.

> Comments from CDU research team:
>
> For Yolŋu, the relevant constituency to discuss or be involved in decision-making is not always the same. While the LA members are supposed to represent the community, sometimes it is difficult when their opinion is prioritised over discussions with other relevant people. There may be room for further consideration of appropriate mechanisms for decision-making and communication into and out of council meetings and governance processes.

Where the video footage and Elder reports had not succeeded in initiating postdevelopment work, these packages appear more promising. The packages have been identified by both Yolŋu researchers and government staff as a good way of providing feedback, and have been identified as the basis of a second phase of this project, beginning in late 2018, which will further pursue the methods of video reporting and multi-author interpretations of video footage providing feedback to government, and evaluating their engagement activities in remote communities.

So why might this method have come to be endorsed by various project participants, when others were serially refused – first by Yolŋu researchers and then by government staff? This report does not simply reproduce the ontological commitments of a particular mode of Northern Territory state governance providing feeding back to government staff on their engagement practices. It actively perforates an assumption that engagement is only about certain forms of individual behaviour. At the same time, it provides suggestion as to alternate actionable practice, able to be taken on by the figure of the 'government worker' configured as an agential and responsible within the working governance imaginaries of the state, supporting them to operate in an alternate mode – in the service of a community and various participants which emerge all apiece, supporting them to cook a dish made from only one ingredient, but which nonetheless serves all.

The addition of the CDU researcher interpretation offered the opportunity for cosmopolitical diplomacy. The scorecard had failed because it could neither accommodate the possibility of telling different stories, or the possibility of alternate modes for doing research work. While the video testimonies of Yolŋu Elders *had* offered difference, new kinds of stories and new kinds of research work, they did not offer any support for government staff seeking to realise these insights. While maintaining the integrity of the message being presented by Yolŋu Elders and researchers, the CDU interpretation needed to also translate these stories into a mode able to be actively mobilised by government staff working actively and responsively to improve their practice. This involved rendering these stories as tangible in there here-and-now, as sensitizing concepts that could be re-realised slightly differently in different situations, but which nonetheless provide a guiding image or design that can be actualised in practice by government staff.

In this sense, while we had initially conceived of the design work of this research as residing exclusively within the project, by the end the scope of this design work had widened considerably. It now included government staff, who in the course of their daily practice could and should find ways to manage the interface and co-existence of differing ways of doing good engagement. That is, they could and should be involved in cosmopolitical work, contributing to the emergence of governed polities not only produced according to existing commitments and working imaginaries of the state.

Maintaining the possibility for postdevelopment within the performance of state-funded research as services delivery

A thread running through the stories I have assembled here is the question of whether postdevelopment is possible within forms of state-funded research as service delivery. The promise of collaborative research work would seem to herald this possibility; within the initial stages of this project, the practice of postdevelopment seemed very difficult to achieve. Myself and other members of the 'Ground Up' research team struggled to find ways within our project work to question and evade the business of simply maintaining the settler-colonial state. Throughout, the Yolŋu Elders and researchers involved in the project were very clear about what counted as good government engagement for them, and the mode of practice within which they were accustomed to producing governed people-places. They were also very clear in their refusal of particular aspects of the project that contradicted these commitments. However, how to productively maintain this refusal and our commitments to government was an ongoing challenge and tension within the project.

The first two stories of the scorecard and the video testimonies were episodes pointing to failures in maintaining these dual relationships, and failures to achieve postdevelopement-in-practice. In these episodes, the presence of my work and the 'Ground Up' team at CDU was not actively felt within the project. It was in beginning to develop techniques and tools for communication that enabled government to be engaged and supported whilst also maintaining the message of Yolŋu Elders and researchers that the practice of postdevelopment began to emerge.

Reflecting on this now, for myself and our broader group of university-based 'Ground Up' researchers, finding means to nurture a cosmopolitical sensitivity within policy evaluation and governance practice seemed a necessary step. Finding ways to explicitly develop practices connecting and separating differing modes of governance practice, involved being able to uphold government funding arrangements that prioritise the epistemic authority of the university, whilst also remaining true to our responsibilities as participants in collective knowledge work being nurtured and produced by local researchers and other involved participants in Galiwink'ku.

Being explicit about this connecting and separating work, my suggestion, foreshadowed at the start of this text, is that an attention to research services delivery as cosmopolitical work offers a repertoire for sensitizing researchers, to the performance of cosmopolitics in the everyday practice of collaborative research and service delivery, and that it is attending to the cosmopolitical embedded within emerging institutional practices that provides openings for postdevelopment within complex arrangements of state-funded research work. The production of the evaluation scorecard entailed the development of a one-world device. Differing ontological commitments present in the doing of a governed place would have been rendered invisible and unable to be commented on in any evaluation of government engagement practices assessed through this means. A cosmopolitical sensitivity alert to such affordances embedded in research objects and practices might assist with collaborative research interested in the potential of research services delivery as postdevelopment-in-practice.

Notes

1 'Ground Up' is an approach to research and service delivery that involves working collaboratively on the ground, taking seriously the knowledge and governance of both Aboriginal and non-Aboriginal people in research work. For more information, see http://groundup.cdu.edu.au.
2 Charles Darwin University has campuses located in Darwin and Alice Springs, and is the only university in the Northern Territory.
3 Yalu' Marŋithinyaraw is a Yolŋu research organisation that has been running for over twenty years. Its name means 'nest for knowledge'. For more information, see http://yalu.cdu.edu.au.
4 Balanda is derived from the Macassan word 'Hollander' and in Yolŋu communities refers to white or non-Indigenous people.
5 Initials are used to denote this advisor as he has since passed away, and out of respect it is not appropriate to list his full name.
6 For more information, visit the project website, http://recier.cdu.edu.au.
7 There is potentially a resonance here between a 'co-design' as a research and service delivery method increasingly valued by the Northern Territory Government, and recent work around the 'ontology of design' as discussed by Arturo Escobar (2012). Although, it seems that it is precisely the difficulty for state-based practices to recognise ontological difference in collaborative design practice that seems at issue here.
8 For the full version, see http://recier.cdu.edu.au/resources/galiwinku-resources/.

References

Altman, J. (2007) *Neo-paternalism and the destruction of CDEP*. Canberra: Australian National University, Centre for Aboriginal Economic Policy Research.
Blaser, M. (2016) 'Is another cosmopolitics possible?' *Cultural Anthropology*, vol 31, no 4, pp 545–570.
Cheah, P. & Robbins, B. (eds.) (1998) *Cosmopolitics: Thinking and Feeling Beyond the Nation, Vol 14*. Minneapolis: University of Minnesota Press.
de la Cadena, M. (2010) 'Indigenous cosmopolitics in the Andes: Conceptual reflections beyond "politics"'. *Cultural Anthropology*, vol 25, no 2, pp 334–370.
Escobar, A. (2012) 'Notes on the ontology of design'. Chapel Hill, NC: University of North Carolina. http://sawyerseminar.ucdavis.edu/files/2012/12/ESCOBAR_Notes-on-the-Ontology-of-Design-Parts-I-II-_-III.pdf.

Klein, E. (2016) 'Neoliberal subjectivities and the behavioural focus on income management'. *Australian Journal of Social Issues*, vol 51, no 4, pp 503–523.

Latour, B. (2004) 'Whose cosmos, which cosmopolitics? Comments on the peace terms of Ulrich Beck'. *Common Knowledge*, vol 10, no 3, pp 450–462.

Spencer, M., Christie, M., Macdonald, J., Campbell, M. & Verran, H. (2017) *Remote engagement coordination – Indigenous evaluation research: Final report*. Darwin: Charles Darwin University.

Stengers, I. (2010) *Cosmopolitics I*, trans. Bononno, R. Minneapolis: University of Minnesota Press.

Strakosch, E. (2015) *Neoliberal Indigenous Policy: Settler Colonialism and the 'Post-Welfare' State*. London: Palgrave Macmillan.

Verran, H. (2018) 'The politics of working cosmologies together while keeping them separate'. In de la Cadena, M., & Blaser, M. (eds.) *A World of Many Worlds*. Durham, NC: Duke University Press.

Verran, H. (2013) 'Engagements between disparate knowledge traditions: Toward doing difference generatively and in good faith'. In Green, L. (ed.), *Contested Ecologies: Dialogues in the South on Nature and Knowledge*. Cape Town: HSRC Press.

Verran, H. & Christie, M. (2011) 'Doing difference together towards a dialogue with aboriginal knowledge authorities through an Australian comparative empirical philosophical inquiry'. *Culture and Dialogue*, vol 1, no 2, pp 21–36.

Verran, H. (2002) 'A postcolonial moment in science studies: Alternative firing regimes of environmental scientists and aboriginal landowners'. *Social Studies of Science*, vol 32, nos 5–6, pp 729–762.

14

MYTHS OF DEVELOPMENT

Democratic dividends and gendered subsidies of land and social reproduction in Uganda

Lyn Ossome

Introduction

Throughout Uganda's history, notions of development have pervaded statist logic from colonialism to the current National Resistance Movement (NRM) government, as the source of popular legitimisation and political stabilisation, a logic that has been worked through the accommodation of various economic classes. The successive settlements (of the food and land questions) have, however, been elite pacts that did not fundamentally alter the agrarian structure, with its gendered, ethnic, regional components. Neither did legal and policy reforms fundamentally affect the class structure as the top-down approaches have restricted substantive power to a small elite of ruling classes at the expense of the majority. This suggests not only that development in Uganda has been a process engineered from above (articulated to the mode of rule), but also that an understanding of the means through which the largely rural, peasant populace has survived ought to be understood in relation to struggles from below, which have challenged and exposed the limits of consecutive states' development rhetoric.

Indeed, a number of scholars of Uganda have critiqued the notion of development, viewing it as a ruse for colonial control and postcolonial statecraft and stabilisation. This, for instance, is a significant point that Muhereza (2018) makes in his study of sedentarisation and pastoralism in northern Uganda, arguing that interventions by various governments seeking the eradication of pastoralism, the sedentarisation of pastoralists and adaptation to settled crop farming and commercial livestock ranching in the area has been fraught with contradictions. The overwhelming focus on crops by successive regimes has failed to both secure access to food and to end Karamojong vulnerability to poverty. The state, Muhereza argues, has been the primary beneficiary of the reordering of Karamojong society, either economically, in terms of resources extracted, or politically, in terms of political control over

Karamoja, or both, and paved the way for 'unbridled state exploitation of Karamoja's resources' (2018: ii).

Similarly, Mamdani (1988), in his examination of the nature of economic reforms that followed the first substantive reorganisation of Uganda's economy following the expulsion of Asians in 1972 by President Idi Amin, argues that the Amin regime was the only post-independence power in contemporary Uganda that dared to implement institutional reforms that broke with the mould of the colonial period, and, as such, whose claim to being anti-imperialist was taken seriously by the population at large. Yet the practical significance of the Africanisation programme for development instituted by Amin remained limited to the educated middle class and did not succeed in liberating labour in Uganda. Its real purpose, Mamdani argues, was

> to liberate, or rather to create, Ugandan capital [that was] by and large speculative, not productive. It could not lay the basis of growth. In the absence of economic development, then, the only way the ideology of the land of opportunity could be sustained was by a periodic repeat of the 1972 expulsion.
>
> *(1988: 1161)*

Mamdani's (1988) argument is that the regime's political stability became attached to a myth of prosperity that depended on the regime's ability to generate populist pro-regime sentiment and effect some form of redistribution roughly organised from above. This attempted repetition took two forms: on the one hand, every regime has re-appropriated the properties that were confiscated from the expelled Asian owners and redistributed them to its narrow circle of supporters at the summit; on the other hand, every regime has organised an expulsion of opponents and an appropriation of their properties – usually land and cattle and household effects, as in 1979 (of Muslims) in Bushenyi, 1980 in West Nile or 1982–1983 in Bushenyi and Mbarara and Rakai – for distribution to a broader circle of supporters at the base (Mamdani 1988).

Another body of scholarship critical of development aspirations in Uganda has examined it from below, in relation to the peasantry, highlighting the agrarian literature, which suggests that when viewing them as marginal to the economic project, states have tended to 'withdraw' from the peasantry – neither collecting taxes nor drawing any other form of economic surplus from them (Jones 2009). These peasantries have as a result been both 'freed' from and impoverished by the state through historical processes of dispossession from above and from below (the latter through processes of social differentiation). This scholarship blames agricultural stagnation in Uganda on the state's exploitation of peasants (Mamdani 1987), and while the predominant scholarship (Bates 1981; Hyden 1983; Mamdani 1987, 1996; Mafeje 2003; Jones 2009) has cast doubt on the possibility of a peasant path to development given the undemocratic nature of the state, their studies have tended to homogenise the peasantry and, in this regard, both failed to account for its differentiation (apart from class) on the basis especially of gender.

It is to this latter set of debates, which attempt to account for the *subjects* of rule and seek to understand the colonial and post-independence regimes from below, that this chapter makes a contribution. I draw rationale here from the significant insight developed by feminist scholars J.K. Gibson-Graham (2006), who argue for the need to 'move beyond the economism of theorizing class solely in terms of relations of production', and rather think of class formation as 'a complex process involving political, cultural, ideological and other forces: in effect, the constitution of social groups as an 'effect of struggle' at the workplace, community, local or national state' (2006: 50). Gibson-Graham (2006) argue that capitalism, because of its association with structural and systemic images of social totality, tends to take up the available social space, incorporating noneconomic dimensions of social life such as culture and politics, as well as noncapitalist economic realms like household production, as colonised spaces.

As such, Gibson-Graham are concerned to explicitly divorce class from structural and hegemonic conceptions of capitalist society because of the ways in which such conceptions discourage a politics of local and continual class transformation, and make it difficult to imagine or enact social diversity in the dimension of class. Insisting on the presence of class processes beyond industrial or capitalist economy, Gibson-Graham argue that industrialisation may be seen as equivalent to the proliferation of class processes and class positions that occur whenever surplus labour is produced, appropriated and distributed. In this regard, they view the household as a major site of class processes, incorporating 'feudal' class processes in which one partner produces surplus labour in the form of use values to be appropriated by the other (Gibson-Graham 2006).

The household is thus constituted as a major site of production in its own right, in which class processes are enacted (household as a zone of class conflict). The elements of such household transition include the fact that it is not governed by hegemonic structures and rules of patriarchy and capital, but, rather, is represented as a social site in which a wide variety of class, gender, sexual and other processes intersect. The meaning of this formulation for broader systemic changes is that opportunities for individual and collective struggles over exploitation are an ever-present experience with significant though not unidirectional transformative effects (Gibson-Graham 2006). Taking seriously the politics of recognition and difference, Gibson-Graham 'mobilize the possibility of emphasising economic difference and of supplanting the discourse of capitalist hegemony with one that properly acknowledges the plurality and heterogeneity of economic forms' (Leyshon n.d.: 4).

We might, furthermore, draw from Luxemburg's (1951) insights that non-capitalist forms of production are essential for capitalism even if the latter is waged in a continuous struggle to undermine the former. Non-capitalist social formations of household and family labour, specifically articulated to peasant modes of production, include unpaid labour that directly benefits the market, as well as unpaid and invisible domestic productive and reproductive labour. The latter supports the reproduction of the working classes and the reserve army of labour, thus assuming the costs of supporting a labour pool. The incursion of capital and consumer goods in rural areas and the dispossession that accompanies commodification forces rural populations to purchase from the market what they used to produce for themselves. The accompanying shrinking of the non-capitalist strata means that some rural households cannot keep up with the socially determined level of consumption, thus lowering the living standards of all workers (Naidu & Ossome 2016). Capitalism, however, does not benefit from the complete destruction of non-capitalist economies, as this would lead to a 'standstill of accumulation' (Luxemburg 1951).

As such, in contrast to explanations which have attributed political stabilisation in Uganda to attempts at development, my argument in this chapter is that the distance between the state and its rural component illustrates a paradoxical relationship of accommodation and disarticulation, within which the politics of the state ought to be understood. The core thrust of the chapter seeks to show, through a historical and materialist reading of the colonial and postcolonial states, how dispossession resulting from failed economic policies led to the reorganisation of gender norms and gender relations around land and landed resources, and subsequently reproduced women as exploited/exploitable subjects of capital, on the one hand, and as agentic postdevelopment actors, on the other. It is this articulation between social reproduction and (women's/peasant) struggles from below which I also view as providing a gendered subsidy to the state. Amidst state repression, the gendered agencies and practices of survival emanating from below – which in J.K. Gibson-Graham's theoretical framing ought to be viewed as class processes – emerge as a challenge to the state's claim of development as the basis of political stabilisation in Uganda. Women appear to be appropriating this liminal space between the household non-capitalist realm and the capitalist realm of the market and state through embodied practices of postdevelopment in the form of protest and resistance, explored later in this chapter.

Rulership and regime changes from the colonial period to the present

The state-society relations of incorporation and disarticulation in Uganda ought to be understood within a longer history of the relationships that African peoples established between food systems, social balance and political power, which long predates colonial modernity (Schoenbrun 1998; Hanson 2003). Among the Baganda, Hanson (2003) has shown in her extensive documentation of the eighteenth- and early-nineteenth-century Buganda kingdom that incessant competition among chiefs for followers and for the prestige that consolidated a chief's hold over followers characterised Ganda politics.[1] Networks of tribute and reciprocal obligation were central to these relationships. The precolonial wars of expansion brought large numbers of captive people into Buganda and, significantly, marked a change in the social status of Ganda women – 'a drastic reduction in their status as a result of the presence of nonfree people' (2003: 82). Captive people brought into the kingdom as a result of wars of expansion allowed both the *kabaka* (king) and other powerful men to create units of productive labour unhooked from networks of reciprocal obligation.

The creation of *mailo*[2] land in 1900 through an agreement between British colonial authorities and Buganda narrowed the locations of power in Ganda society, and undermined reciprocal obligations. In the years immediately following the consolidation of power by elite Protestant chiefs through the allocation of *mailo*, Ganda social institutions underwent subtle but profound transformations, among the most significant of which was the need for workers to substitute men who had left Buganda in order to avoid labour and taxes. Competition to attract followers was intense as wage labour for the colonial government and trade also removed men from rural life. Each *mailo* purchaser needed to populate his land with followers, so the accelerating process of land sale also increased the need for followers.[3] Immigrants and independent Ganda women (those unencumbered by familial obligations) became a key substituting (re)source in this regard. The doubling of labour demands, along with the new possibilities created by cash payment for cotton, caused a profound shift in the pattern of Ganda households: women began to control land independently (Hanson 2003: 178).

Women may have chosen to become the tenant of a chief/landowner over being the wife of a tenant as a result of household tensions created by the new work of planting, weeding, harvesting and carrying cotton, and also because of their newfound ability to control land independently. Women grew cotton from 1910; cotton cultivation was women's work because it was agricultural and therefore in women's sphere. This fundamental transition in the assignment of domestic labour, Hanson (2003) argues, suggests a struggle between Ganda men and women that might well have motivated women to choose to control land on their own account when the option became available.

A more significant point which Hanson (2003) does not explore is the fact that the incorporation of women into the market economy drew on their existing resources as producers and reproducers, yet, even as in their more independent positions, did not modify the structural labour exploitation and, in fact, seemed to have been predicated on the ability to exploit the resources of women. People who controlled land had many good reasons to include independent women among their followers. Giving land to women who wanted it increased the income of the land allocator; at this time, landlords/chiefs received one-tenth (and sometimes more) of a tenant's cotton crop (Wrigley 1959: 53). Amidst their exploitation in the colonial period, women did retain some agency around land access and a measure of control over crop incomes.

After independence, Milton Obote's first regime embarked on constitutional reforms that made the presidency more powerful and established him as both the head of state and chief executive, at the same time that his political base of support was diminishing and the economy was beginning to show serious signs of decline. The response from Obote's government was to reorganise the state in order for it to play a more active role in the economy, and centralisation of the economy became the new method for restructuring the basis of regime legitimacy (Khadiagala 1995). This move would provide state elites with the patronage they needed to maintain political validation from their clients (Khadiagala 1995). The economic plan adopted by the regime involved two strategies for development. The first one was to establish new state corporations (parastatals) and expand and reorganise the old ones created by the colonial state (Khadiagala 1995). Through these corporations the regime would try to win public support by using the economy as a political instrument. Through government-owned companies, state jobs and resources were doled out to supporters of the regime, thereby reinforcing the patron-client patterns of power and giving institutional support to rent-seeking behaviour. These patterns led to waste and inefficiency and subsequently to a decline in the state's capacity to deal with social and economic problems (Khadiagala 1995).

The second strategy came by way of the Second Five-Year Plan (1966/1967 to 1970/1971), in which a socialist programme was introduced, thus indicating a shift toward greater centralisation of state power. Through this five-year plan, the regime announced a 'move to the Left', a policy that was accompanied by ambitious nationalisation measures (Jørgensen 1981: 232). The details of these presidential initiatives, mostly promulgated in the *Common Man's Charter*, have been critically examined elsewhere.[4] Obote's professed motive for the move to the Left was to improve the condition of the masses by using state power to break the back of the economic elites (especially the landed gentry) in Uganda. The state would nationalise privately held enterprises and then redistribute wealth to the dispossessed – an attempt to address colonial-based social inequalities. Obote's basic claim was that this would help his war against poverty, ignorance and disease. However, a closer look at the plan shows that it was in fact a populist attempt at window dressing, the objective of which was to strengthen executive power and conflate his Uganda People's Congress (UPC) party/regime with the teleological functions of the state.

Students of Obote's so-called 'move to the Left' have made several insightful observations regarding the contradictions inherent in the strategy and, thus, its weaknesses. Kabwegyere (1995), for example, points out that the *Common Man's Charter* was anti-pluralistic; instead of giving power to the masses, it was yet another strategy for Obote to consolidate state power through centralisation. Mamdani (1976) has described the fallacy of the 'move to the Left' thus:

> […] the expansion of the state sector was identified as the building of socialism and the period of its own formation as that of transition to socialism. But in this petty bourgeois conception socialism was stripped of the class struggle, of its political content, and was set forth as an economic ideology in its static conception.
>
> *(1976: 273)*

When Obote declared socialism as the official ideology and nationalisation of individual property as the political agenda, it was no longer possible to separate the state from the regime. Moreover, one of the key instruments of state coercion, the military, was now at the heart of the state, not to protect the citizens but to force them into compliance. It did not take long for the military to assert itself as the ruling 'party'. In January 1971, General Idi Amin overthrew Obote's government by coup d'état. Amin adopted an economic nationalist philosophy and declared an 'Economic War' during 1971–1972, the policies of which were aimed at returning all means and sectors of production to Ugandan citizens. This policy gave Amin a political boost from Ugandan populists, who took over assets that had been 'abandoned' by the Asians, which included 5,655 firms, factories, ranches and agricultural estates as well as homes, cars and household goods.[5] The regime's repressive character, however, surfaced the minute it faced popular demands. The Land Reform Decree of June 1975 brought all land under the control of the state. Both 'absolute ownership of the land' and 'the power of the customary tenant to stand in the way of development' were abolished, converting all land to 99-year leasehold (Mamdani 1984: 50). Where the landlord system existed, as in Buganda, the tenant became a sub-lessee and the landlord a lessee of the state. The Land Commission was empowered to terminate any lease on 'undeveloped' land and grant it to a potential 'developer'. Such a lease-holder was 'free to evict any tenant occupying any part of the lease-hold granted to enable him to develop the land' (Mamdani 1984: 50).

Obote's second term, from 1980–1985 (Obote II), was faced with the task of restoring the rule of law, democratic legitimacy, accountability and economic productivity. Success in these three areas would at least restore the instrumentalist prerequisite of legitimacy, namely state effectiveness. Yet the UPC was too weak internally to perform the functions of mass mobilisation, interest aggregation and provision of viable policy alternatives. Under these circumstances state-society relations were so constrained as to block the emergence of a governance realm. Values of trust, reciprocity, accountability and authority were all linked to party loyalty or to personal relations with the president and other high-ranking party/government political elites. Limitations on political space precluded the expected activities of opposition parties, civil society and particularly the media. The peasantry once again exited the formal economy, resorting instead to smuggling, trading in local foodstuff or simply subsistence agriculture (Mamdani 1984).

The current National Resistance Movement (NRM) regime rose to power on the back of a coup in 1986 led by Yoweri Museveni. To scholars like Tripp, the Uganda case shows how the excesses of authoritarianism, patronage and the violence of the regimes of Amin and Obote ultimately led to state collapse and institutional decay, arguing that it was political liberalisation, even in its limited form under Museveni, that initially offered a respite from a downward spiral at least until 1995 (Tripp 2010). Alluding to the failure of past regimes' development project and suggesting that Uganda's democratisation had been influenced by economic factors, Tripp argues that the pressures for reform came from within the elite and military at a time when the country's economy was on an uptick rather than in a downturn. Economic growth served to further legitimise the status quo, thus galvanising the political opposition, which wanted a more equitable division of the country's political power and economic resources. While economic crisis may have resulted in popular pressures for political reform in the early 1990s, by 2010 economic prosperity created its own impetus for change in Uganda, where economic growth *had become a source of legitimacy for the NRM's monopoly of power* (Tripp 2010: 34–35, emphasis added). The NRM's appeal to populist legitimacy has, among other realms, been expressed in its land law reforms, in an apparent appeal to its largely peasant base.

As this account suggests, throughout Uganda's history, from colonialism to the current NRM government, a significant source of popular legitimisation and stabilisation has proceeded through the accommodation of various economic classes. The successive settlements (of the food and land questions) have, however, been elite pacts that did not fundamentally alter the agrarian structure and its gendered, ethnic, regional components. Neither did they fundamentally affect the class structure. What, then, does this mean? First, the attempts at economic reform under Obote were at best developmentalist. Neither Obote's attempts towards socialism nor Amin's populist redistributive ambitions significantly transformed the agrarian structure. Obote's 'move to the Left' was received with considerable cynicism by a large section of the population, especially those who had been squeezed out of commercial enterprises and the ordinary workers and peasants who were struggling to cope with the ever-increasing economic difficulties (Mamdani 1976: 285). Examining the NRM period (1986–present) that has renewed and continued these historical cycles of dispossession, I argue in the section below that struggles waged by peasants and the rural populace, and in particular their gendered component, appear as critique of the state and failure of its development project, and provide a counterweight to state repression to the extent that they assert radical processes of democracy from below.

Peasant struggles and postdevelopment in practice

At its infancy during the guerrilla struggle (1981–1985), the National Resistance Army/Movement (NRA/M) sought to build

> a state power with a difference in its liberated zones [and] to marshal the support of the peasantry against the Obote II regime. This form of power had to highlight the question of rights of the peasantry in the institutions it created.
>
> *(Mamdani 1996)*

The NRA/M abolished the (administrative) position of the chief and in its place created a system of Resistance Councils (RCs) and committees, which had legislative and judicial powers. The NRA/M's innovation in the arena of rights was to affirm the right of peasant communities to organise as communities and to hold state officials accountable as communities.[6] The nature of the reforms through the RCs were fundamentally agrarian, and defined the strength of the NRA/M's peasant base in the period 1981–1985. Yet hierarchies on the basis of gender remained intact in the new NRM state. Its attempts at broad-base politics had effected significant political gains which nonetheless did not guarantee the social power of the peasantry's physical majorities – women.

The argument could be made then that the recognition of women as political subjects was attached to their peasant status rather than their gender identity. In order for both identities to be salient, the NRA needed to have identified and sought to resolve a contradiction internal to the economic structure of the peasantry: that the prism of subsistence economies and the gendered labour regimes therein, which are highly predicated upon the free, exploitative and self-exploitative labour performed by rural women on a daily basis, present the peasantry as a contradictory social force in the course of agrarian transformation (Naidu & Ossome 2016: 70). In other words, the resolution of the agrarian question of gendered labour. Instead as Mamdani (1996) tells us, the NRA's attempt to build effective coalitions against established authority 'was marked by contradictory tendencies: political emancipation alongside social conservatism. As communities were reproduced, so were the internal hierarchies within these communities' (1996: 209).

The reforms had not been permanent – their partial and unstable character owing mainly to the fact that they had not been reinforced by a corresponding reform in the central state. In 1995, Resistance Councils (RCs) were renamed Local Councils (LCs) by constitutional amendment. They could make and enforce local bylaws, settle civil cases and customary land disputes and embark on local self-help projects, and were seen as an engine for rural development (Tripp 2010). LCs as the main vehicles for popular participation enhanced the political monopoly of the NRM and, in fact, became a key mechanism linking the NRM to the grassroots. The NRM's broad-based recovery and transformation was conceived in broader political terms, with concerted efforts to strengthen the political infrastructure through RCs. The aim of involving women in the RCs, though obvious in terms of democratisation, was not a benign inclusion. Women,

> who form the backbone of agriculture, were included in decision making in all political and economic structures [and] there is an unprecedented number of women in the National Resistance Council (NRC) […] [i]nvesting in women's involvement and mobilization has enormous political and economic capital that the NRM is deliberately cultivating.
>
> (Mugyenyi 1991: 73–74)

It is as critique of these structures of governance that emergent peasant struggles ought to be understood. In other words, these struggles render apparent the fact that a cornerstone innovation upon which the NRM regime staked its development plan failed to minimise dispossession of the populace. Furthermore, that women are playing an instrumental role in these struggles suggest a link between agrarian distress and gender as a basis of exploitation – what I term a gendered subsidy. Failure of the NRM regime to fully incorporate women into its LC structures suggest that women have been able to retain some agency, which materialises in resistance to land dispossession and illustrates their thrust as a form of postdevelopment in practice.

At the same time as the state was incorporating women and the peasantry into its mode of governance, it also embarked on neoliberal restructuring of agriculture from the late 1980s, which was aimed at enhancing the registration and formalisation of land, facilitating its titling and transfer, improving smallholders' integration in agricultural commodity chains and consolidating agribusiness. State-led development projects promoted the standardisation and simplification of rural spaces, facilitating their decryption and subsequent control (Martiniello 2015: 657). Mamdani (2012) argues, for instance, that the 1998 Land Act's aim of recognising customary land tenure must be seen as the latest phase in the modern state's endeavour to colonise society. While just seventeen percent of land in Uganda is held under freehold (Martiniello 2015), the state is expanding its efforts to consolidate its fiscal basis, enhancing territorial control over reluctant northern populations and actively promoting the formation of a class of politically connected businessmen (Mamdani 2012). The imposition of a new definition of property formidably biased in favour of landowners, which was aimed at eradicating use rights not juridically defined, generated exclusive and individualised access to land and undermined other communal/cooperative/collective forms of land tenure (Martiniello 2015).

The culmination of these structural changes and elite-driven development has been the various forms of resistances from below, in which women have played a decisive role. To illustrate this point, I focus here on one landmark case of social protest that took place in Amuru District in northern Uganda on 18 April 2012, during which between 80 and 100 women stripped naked in a protest to block their eviction from land they claim is rightfully theirs. They did this in front of representatives of the Local District Board and surveyors of the sugar company Madhvani Group, the firm that was seeking land in the area for sugarcane growing. The Amuru Sugar Works project owned by the Madhvani Group sought 40,000 ha of land for a new commercial sugarcane estate, and was faced with a landmark protest staged by the local community (Martiniello 2015).

Two recent scholarly articles have examined this protest in detail. Ebila and Tripp (2017) take a culturalist feminist perspective and explore the symbolic meanings behind the public displays of the female naked body in the face of repressive authority in contemporary protest movements. They show how 'the body symbolism of motherhood was successfully used as a resource for collective struggle to protect land rights' (Ebila & Tripp 2017: 1), and argue that it revealed the ways in which people draw on the repertoire of protest tactics available to them [...] [t]he symbolic association of women with the land made their revolt all the more powerful. The reproductive connotation of motherhood became the basis and justification for political action rather than a [traditional] symbol of passivity as is often regarded in Western societies.

(Ebila & Tripp 2017: 18)

In this reading, it is gender rather than class that structures women's responses to dispossession.

Another study highlighting this case (Martiniello 2015) seeks from a political economy perspective to illustrate the ways in which ostensibly developmental projects with state backing not only threaten livelihoods, but, crucially, have compelled responses that approximate existing forms of social organisation and social relations of productions of the communities so affected. The Amuru Sugar Works project, initiated in 2007–2008 but stalled at inception, was planned to create employment for 7,000–8,000 people, and to provide livelihoods from sugarcane cultivation to 7,000–10,000 outgrower farmers (Martiniello 2015). The farmers would be housed in labour camps with 10 ha each: 8 ha under sugarcane and 2 ha for food crops. The investor would supply equipment to clear, plough and furrow the land as well as distribute treated cane seeds and give technical advice on agricultural matters. The proposed project would have displaced approximately 20,000 people, almost all family members, around the village of Lakang in this economically depressed region on the periphery, both politically and economically, of Uganda. The overwhelming majority of small-scale rural producers rejected the proposed enclosure of their land, and refused to be incorporated as either outgrower farmers or agricultural labourers (Martiniello 2015: 653–654).

It is, however, the overt response of women to this threat of dispossession that most clearly demonstrated what was at stake with the planned sugar works. To Martiniello (2015), by resisting dispossession and challenging state violence, small-scale poor peasants were reiterating the political salience of rural social struggles and highlighting the significance of land and agrarian questions. The rise in 'rural social protests manifested in both every day, hidden practices of resistance and moments of open, militant contestation are aimed at *(re)establishing and securing access to means of social reproduction*' (Martiniello 2015: 653, emphasis added). The event illuminated crucial aspect of peasants' agency and brought to the fore the present dynamics of national and global political economy (Martiniello 2015). Ultimately, Martiniello (2015) argues that persistent rural struggles in Amuru district embody not only different elements of struggles against dispossession, exploitation, concentration and centralisation, but also struggles for autonomy and sovereignty.

Martiniello's powerful critique nonetheless does not overcome the universalising tendency that necessarily still articulates protest as resistance *to* development. More saliently, the women's protest should be understood through their relationship to the non-capitalist realm of reproduction, which does not so much suggest a critique of modes of women's incorporation into capitalist development, as women's need to protect a realm of social reproduction which they understand as being crucial for the survival of their households and communities. Herein lies the possibility of reading the naked protest in relation to anticapitalist contestations (see Klein and Morreo's Introduction in this volume). This form of resistance led by women is thus both an assertion of women's awareness of the life-centeredness that land portends, and the fact that the preservation of nature is fundamentally driven by acts of care that are embodied, sacred and existential in nature. To cite Kothari, Salleh, Escobar, Demaria and Acosta in this volume (Chapter 6),

> it is most often ordinary care-giving mothers and grandmothers [...] defending and reconstituting communal ways of being and place-based forms of autonomy. In doing so, they, like the Indigenous Others [...] draw on non-patriarchal ways of doing, being, and knowing.

The growing crisis of social reproduction means that women are still expected to play the role of producers and reproducers without recourse to the social, economic and political access to the means of production and reproduction. Women's resistances in this regard show both a recognition of their historical oppression, and assertion of their agencies that stand as critique of the myths of development and illustrate postdevelopment in practice.

Conclusion

This chapter aimed to show the ways in which successive regimes from the colonial to postindependence sought political stabilisation through attempts to resolve the land, food and peasant questions – masked by the language of economic development – on the basis of an inherent but obscured expropriation and exploitation of gendered forms of social organisation and women's reproductive labour economies. Prior to the colonial incursion, societies in Uganda had balanced the demands of conquest, leadership and stability through relations of tribute and reciprocity. In that context, consanguinity and tributary relations, rather than gender, determined modes of access to food and land, and, in turn, political legitimacy of rulers. The gendering of the agrarian economy became pronounced with the colonial capitalist incursion, and with the social conflicts it precipitated through the disruption of the agrarian structure, women found greater inclusion, but on terms that presupposed and exploited their time, labour and resources. Successive postcolonial regimes sought both to manage inherited contradictions and to stabilise the state in the process of its formation through a series of laws and policies that made direct reference to the peasantry and working classes. I have argued that although not overtly the case, a close reading reveals that government and state policies and strategies have also historically assumed an element of social reproduction that, given the agrarian structure of

Uganda, has largely been fulfilled through a stricter definition of gendered roles in both the economic and political terrain. These trends, although located within a discourse of development, do in fact highlight the mythical nature of their aspirations towards development. Social reproduction as such is predicated upon diverse food practices and, significantly, women's unpaid, unrecognised reproductive labour as a condition of possibility; this labour is not fully incorporated into 'development' – neither at its margins nor integrated into its logics. It is driven not purely by capitalistic impulses, but also, significantly, by the need to retain political stability in the face of destabilisation wrought by underdevelopment, neoliberal development and financialisation. In practice, food, land and democratisation in Uganda have been intimately tied to narratives of postdevelopment, illustrated most starkly by the forms of resistance led by women as producers and their role in the matrix of social reproduction. Development, understood as the stabilisation of society and political rule in Uganda, is nuanced by considerations of gendered labour – largely obscured from the existing literature – as emanating from below and instrumentalised from above by successive regimes since the colonial period.

Notes

1 Hanson, H.E. (2003) *Landed Obligation: The Practice of Power in Buganda*.Portsmouth, NH: Heinemann, p 61.
2 The basic unit of the *mailo* system is a square mile, hence the derivation of mailo, which is also equivalent to 640 acres. The term is used in Uganda to describe a land tenure system that came into effect when the kingdom of Buganda signed an agreement with the British-administered Uganda Protectorate there in 1900.
3 For Baganda, the most significant change in this time was the vastly increased amounts of work people had to do. Women had incorporated planting, weeding, harvesting and carrying cotton into their agricultural work calendar. Men had added months of productive work for the Protectorate to months of productive work they had already been doing for chiefs (Hanson 2003: 175).
4 Gukiina (1972); Mamdani (1976); Kabwegyere (1995); Jørgensen (1981).
5 Uganda (1977) *The Action Programme: A Three-Year Economic Rehabilitation Plan, 1977/ 78 – 1979/80*. Entebbe: Government Printer, p 46.
6 *Ibid.*, pp 200–201.

References

Bates, R.H. (1981) *Markets and States in Tropical Africa: The Political Basis of Agricultural Policies*. Berkeley: University of California Press.
Ebila, F. & Tripp, A.M. (2017) 'Naked transgressions: Gendered symbolism in Ugandan land protests'. *Politics, Groups, and Identities*. doi: 10.1080/21565503.2016.1273122.
Gibson-Graham, J.K. (2006) *The End of Capitalism (As We Knew It): A Feminist Critique of Political Economy*. Minneapolis: University of Minnesota Press.
Gukiina, M.P. (1972) *Uganda: A Case Study in African Political Development*. Notre Dame, IN: University of Notre Dame Press.
Hanson, H.E. (2003) *Landed Obligation: The Practice of Power in Buganda*. Portsmouth, NH: Heinemann.

Hyden, G. (1983) *No Shortcuts to Progress*. Berkeley: University of California Press.

Jones, B. (2009) *Beyond the State in Rural Uganda*. Edinburgh: University of Edinburgh Press.

Jørgensen, J.J. (1981) *Uganda: A Modern History*. New York: St. Martin's Press.

Kabwegyere, T.B. (1995) *The Politics of State Formation and Destruction in Uganda*. Kampala: Fountain Publishers.

Kasozi, A.B.K. (2013) *The Bitter Bread of Exile: The Financial Problems of Sir Edward Muteesa II during His Final Exile, 1966–1969*. Kampala: Progressive Publishing House.

Khadiagala, G.M. (1995) 'State collapse and reconstruction in Uganda'. In Zartman, W.I. (ed.), *Collapsed States: The Disintegration and Reconstruction of Legitimate Authority*. Boulder, CO: Lynne Rienner Publishers, pp 33–47.

Leyshon, A. (n.d.) *Book Review: The End of Capitalism (as We Knew It): A Feminist Critique of Political Economy by J.K. Gibson-Graham, 1996*. Oxford: Blackwell.

Luxemburg, R. (1951) *The Accumulation of Capital*. London: Routledge.

Mafeje, A. (2003) 'The agrarian question, access to land, and peasant responses in Sub-Saharan Africa'. *Civil Society and Social Movements Paper No. 6*, United Nations Research Institute for Social Development.

Mamdani, M. (1976) *Politics and Class Formation in Uganda*. London: Heinemann.

Mamdani, M. (1984) *Imperialism and Fascism in Uganda*. Trenton, NJ: Africa World Press.

Mamdani, M. (1987) 'Extreme but not exceptional: towards an analysis of the agrarian question in Uganda'. *Journal of Peasant Studies*, vol 14, no 3, pp 191–225.

Mamdani, M. (1988) 'Uganda in transition: Two years of the NRM/NRA'. *Third World Quarterly*, vol 10, no 3, pp 1155–1181.

Mamdani, M. (1996) *Citizen and Subject: Contemporary Africa and the Legacy of Late Colonialism*. Princeton, NJ: Princeton University Press.

Mamdani, M. (2012) 'The contemporary Ugandan discourse on customary tenure: Some historical and theoretical considerations'. Paper presented to the workshop *The Land Question: Capitalism, Socialism and the Market*, Makerere Institute of Social Research, 9–10 August.

Martiniello, G. (2015) 'Social struggles in Uganda's Acholiland: Understanding responses and resistances to Amuru Sugar Works'. *The Journal of Peasant Studies*, vol 42, nos 3–4, pp 653–669.

Mugyenyi, B.J. (1991) 'IMF conditionality and structural adjustment under the National Resistance Movement'. In Holger, B.H. & Twaddle M. (eds.), *Changing Uganda: The Dilemmas of Structural Adjustment and Revolutionary Change*. Nairobi: EAEP, pp 61–77.

Muhereza, F. (2018), 'The Transformation of Karamoja: Sedentarization of Pastoralists and the Adoption of Settled Crop Farming'. Unpublished PhD thesis, Makerere Institute of Social Research.

Naidu, S.C. & Ossome, L. (2016) 'Social reproduction and the agrarian question of women's labour in India'. *Agrarian South: Journal of Political Economy*, vol 5, no 1, pp 50–76.

Schoenbrun, D.L. (1998) *A Green Place, A Good Place: Agrarian Change, Gender, and Social Identity in the Great Lakes Region to the 15th Century*. Oxford: James Currey.

Tripp, A.M. (2010) *Museveni's Uganda: Paradoxes of Power in a Hybrid Regime*. Boulder, CO: Lynne Rienner Publishers.

Wrigley, C.C. (1959) *Crops and Wealth in Uganda: A Short Agrarian History*. Kampala: East African Institute of Social Research.

15

GREEN AND ANTI-GREEN REVOLUTIONS IN EAST TIMOR AND PERU

Seeds, lies and applied anthropology[1]

Christopher J. Shepherd

Introduction

Ever since the 1950s, international development regimes and client states have pursued the 'development' of agriculture for peasantries and Indigenous peoples of the Global South. Initially unfolded on the stage of Cold War politics by which the West vied to secure geopolitical and economic advantage in the so-called Third World, an expansive network of international and national public research and agricultural extension institutions sought to replace subsistence-oriented food production regimes with market-oriented ones. Operating under the pretext of reducing poverty, they demeaned food production systems centred on agricultural biodiversity while promoting technological packages consisting of improved crop varieties, chemical inputs and irrigation technology (Jennings 1988; Shepherd 2005).

The intervention was popularised as the Green Revolution (GR): the 'green' signified verdant abundance, the 'revolution' underlined the change from extensive, subsistence agriculture to extensive, market agriculture. At the heart of the GR was seed and implicit was the idealisation of a modern, industrial, capitalist society in which a small percentage of people supplied food commercially for a large, non-agricultural sector. The GR quickly revealed its true colours. From Latin America to Africa and Asia, the GR intensified the pace of cultural erosion, environmental degradation, biodiversity loss and dependency on state and markets. Oftentimes, the GR pressured entire peasantries to produce for markets that did not exist. In some places, the capitalisation of agriculture occasioned debt, dispossession of land, social upheaval and widespread violence (Shiva 2016 [1991]). As the nefarious consequences of the GR came to be recognised by development organisations, government bureaucrats, rural peasantries, NGOs, political activists, Third World intellectuals and Western scholars, alternative postdevelopment visions emerged that heralded a return to diversity-based agriculture (Shepherd 2010).

This chapter explores GR practices and counter-practices in Andean Peru and rural East Timor. The GR in Indigenous communities of highland Peru concentrated on tubers, particularly the potato. As the GR faltered, an anti-GR rooted in cultural affirmation gained ground. The GR in East Timor traditionally focused on rice, but also drew in other crops such as maize and cassava. Differently to Indigenous Peru, East Timor's GR still prevails as the dominant development strategy. In exploring this differentiated state of affairs, I tell a personal story about my research experiences in each place. The open debate surrounding the role of Andean culture in development in Peru meant that development institutions were unconcerned as to where I stood in that debate; my access to institutions and projects was a foregone conclusion. This was not the case in East Timor, where my research on GR practices was obstructed by powerful pro-GR actors who were wary of postdevelopment critique. In presenting GR practice and postdevelopment practice as a 'trial of strength' (Latour 1987: 3), I show how in the case of East Timor I became caught up in the very political struggles I sought to observe, particularly given the interference of applied anthropology development consultants. In the conclusion, I propose that the political networks in which ethnographers find themselves need to be analysed as part of the development and postdevelopment landscape, such that they, their locations and approach are treated as agents like any other in the development world.

The Green Revolution in highland Peru

Over millennia, Andean peoples domesticated the potato from its wild progenitors and created an astonishing diversity of varieties for their subsistence. This diversity was embedded in a uniquely Andean form of agriculture that relied upon the management of multiple agroecological levels and diverse and highly evolved crop and plot rotation, tillage, planting, harvesting, seed storage and kin-based labour-exchange systems. The ritual practices that enveloped this farming reminded the people that their relationship with Mother Earth was a reciprocal one; the people nurtured Her, She nurtured them (Revilla Sta. Cruz 2014). The extensive Inca Empire of the 1300s and 1400s, which radiated out from Cusco, was built on the back on this highly productive, diverse Andean agriculture distinguished for the thousands of potato landraces (Zimmerer 1996).

Following the arrival of Europeans (in 1532), Indigenous populations were decimated by disease and the Inca Empire collapsed. Colonials repressed Indigenous spirituality and settlers imposed a feudal system of large *haciendas* that reduced most of the Indigenous highland population to landless serfs, who were pejoratively referred to as Indians (*indios*). This condition continued into the republican era (1826 onwards). Nevertheless, Andean peoples were evidently not fully colonised, for they were still able to continue their Andean diversity-based agriculture on small parcels of land that landowners granted to them to meet their subsistence needs.

Come the twentieth century, the nation-building coastal elites of oligarchic Peru became intent on consolidating central control over the Andean region. Encouraged by developments in the science of agriculture overseas, technocrats from Lima established a Department of Agriculture in 1904 and developed extension services. In the Andean agriculture of diversity, technocrats saw low productivity, poverty and backwardness, which, they thought, did nothing to prosper the nation. That mindset did not change when in the late 1920s visiting Russian geneticist, botanist, and agronomist Nikolai Vavilov flagged the Andean region as one of eight world 'centres of origin' of domesticated plants (Zimmerer 1996). If Vavilov's classification presented an opportunity to link genetic wealth with Andean Indigenous cultural traditions, that opportunity was missed; over coming decades, Andean genetic wealth would be seen as a resource to be extracted from its cultural context and subjected to scientific experimentation and technological innovation.

So it was that after World War II an aggressive international development ideology that had consolidated in the United States Government in conjunction with US research centres, philanthropies and universities descended upon Peru, with agricultural modernisation a principal objective. The United States Government and the Rockefeller Foundation focused on strengthening Peru's national agricultural research capacity. State research bodies organised Andean expeditions to collect hundreds of varieties of potato, deliver them to experimental stations and crossbreed select 'native' varieties to give rise to 'improved' varieties (Shepherd 2005). Around the same time, a US-led cohort of social scientists from Cornell University embarked on an experiment in applied anthropology to determine how best to modernise the rural peasantry. They purchased a large *hacienda* in the central Andes (Ancash) and established the Vicos project (1953–1966), a cornerstone of which was potato extension using the improved varieties (Stein 2004).

The Vicos experiment foreshadowed a state strategy to abolish the hacienda system through an agrarian reform (1969–1974). With support and advice from the USA, non-Indigenous Peruvian bureaucrats were mobilised to organise the peasantry into cooperatives and enterprises. At the same time, new law dictated that 'Indians' be called *campesinos* (peasants). The newly formulated GR, with its knowledge, expertise and extension science, was central to plans to incorporate the peasantry into state-managed structures. The founding of the International Potato Centre (CIP) in 1972 as one in a succession of International Agricultural Research Centres (IARCs) further impelled the taking of germplasm for experimentation. After that, Peru's highland GR began in earnest; state extension agencies and emergent NGOs distributed en masse a relatively small number of improved varieties to replace the innumerable native varieties. As high-yielding varieties of marketable crops were released, native varieties, in particular those of potato, were stamped as inferior, low-yielding, poverty-inducing, inefficient and not worth maintaining in situ; it was sufficient to retain the germplasm in cold storage ex situ. The disintegration of the peasant cooperatives and enterprises (Cleaves & Scurrah 1980) only seemed to harden the resolve of the technocratic state to bring the GR to what were now thousands of autonomous Quechua and Aymara peasant communities. Behind the rhetoric of 'integrated rural development' was the state's determination to fashion from the Indigenous population 'viable' market producers for a country that, thanks to development, had already become highly indebted to foreign banks and was facing a financial and political crisis.

When I first arrived in Peru in 1997 to commence doctoral fieldwork on Indigenous knowledge and rural development, I structured my research around four rural development NGOs working in the provinces around Cusco. Three of the four adhered to the conventional GR model, while the fourth, CESA (Centro de Servicios Agropecuarios), had tried the GR for a decade before abandoning it in 1992 for a postdevelopment strategy known as 'cultural affirmation'. This value-driven pro-Andean affirmation urged a return to diversity agriculture, highlighting reciprocity, community, ecology and spirituality (see Figure 15.1). What I encountered as the local division between conventional anti-Andean GR NGOs and pro-Andean non-GR ones was indicative of the broader situation; all over the southern and central Andes, organisations pushing

FIGURE 15.1 A *campesino* family of the Q'enqomayo Valley, Paucartambo Province, Cusco, in their potato fields observing a ritual tradition at harvest time. Photograph courtesy of CESA (Centro de Servicios Agropecuarios), Cusco. © Luís Revilla Santa Cruz.

GR services greatly outnumbered the dissenting NGOs who had experienced first-hand the clumsy governmental intervention into agrarian structures, appreciated the failings of the GR and sought alternative approaches (Apffel-Marglin 1998; Dueñas, Mendivil, Lovaton & Loaiza 1992).

To find myself poised between two arguing development models was a curious position to be in. Gradually, I took sides. The GR was patently damaging to the agroecosystem. Chemical inputs had damaged soils, and pests had proliferated (Shepherd 2006). In many places, much of the diversity and attendant knowledge had been lost, including the precise phenotypical knowledge of landraces (Dueñas, Mendivil, Lovaton & Loaiza 1992; Ploeg 1993). The economic benefits upon which the GR was premised were concentrated among the few who managed to capitalise their farming. Yet, with higher production, market prices fell and the returns fell short of promises. Nevertheless, extension agents adamantly pressed the GR on peasants; the former presented themselves as superior, all-knowing experts as they disparaged the autochthonous Andean knowledge and spiritual beliefs of the latter. In every human interaction of the development encounter, I saw how old racial prejudices were reconstituted in the routine practice of agricultural promotion. It was often remarked that today's extension agents were yesteryear's *hacendados*. Peasants resented the way the conventional development establishment treated them – and still referred to them, at times, as Indians. Peasants maintained a distrustful distance to agronomy experts. Pragmatically, however, they went along with interventions to the extent that they could acquire materials, incentives and other benefits (Shepherd 2006). I saw for myself how most of the GR interventions failed or floundered, but vested interests kept the GR machinery operative. Proponents generally hid the many failures and dramatised the few successes of 'model communities' and select, upwardly mobile commercial farmers.

Pro-Andean cultural affirmationists such as CESA had a more sensitive approach to the local farmers. To the extent that they validated Andean knowledge, they gave up their own locations as experts. In their work of recuperating diversity, they sought out diversity in the more remote areas and at the higher elevations and then encouraged seed exchange between peasants whose diversity had been eroded and peasants who had retained native varieties (see Figures 15.2 and 15.3). Invigorated seed circulation was the central feature of this recuperative mission, but with seed went the revalorisation and restoration of hundreds of interlocking traditional knowledge elements; women selected the potato seed according to key characteristics, the tweet of a partridge signalled that it was time to sow, ritual offerings to Mother Earth ensured the arrival of the first rains and so on and so forth (Apffel-Marglin 1998; Shepherd 2010).

All of this pro-Andean endeavour might have remained a marginal postdevelopment alternative had agrobiodiversity not become a topic of worldwide importance towards the end of the millennium (Brookfield, Parsons & Brookfield 2003). International organisations (such as the United Nations) sponsoring the in situ conservation of agrobiodiversity drew together a broad sweep of local,

FIGURE 15.2 The director of CESA, Luís Revilla, emphasises the importance of agro-biodiversity conservation in an information session with prospective 'conservationists'. © Luís Revilla Santa Cruz.

FIGURE 15.3 Recuperated diversity. Forty varieties of potato make up this pile. This is about nurturing – not simply cultivating – diversity, which is the patrimony of the family, the community and the Andean cosmos. © Luís Revilla Santa Cruz.

FIGURE 15.4 Each variety has a name, a distinctive taste, a personality and even a story in this all-animate Andean cosmos. Cusco. © Luís Revilla Santa Cruz.

regional and national actors encompassing pro-Andean NGOs, conventional agricultural development NGOs, university-based research institutes, governmental conservation and development bodies and national agricultural research bodies. New impetus was given to both pro-Andean NGOs and to discussions about the significance of Andean culture and the role of traditional farmer knowledge. Reservations about the GR mounted as the Peruvian state humbly looked towards cultural affirmation to work out how to intervene to restore agrobiodiversity.

When I conducted research on the in situ conservation programmes in 2007, the GR was widely viewed as a failed community development model. By the time of my next visit in 2015–2016, the GR no longer existed as a single dominant ideology pitted against a presumed deficient 'Andean agriculture'. Cultural affirmation had moved from being the marginal approach of radical NGOs to one with mainstream legitimacy that eventually even the Peruvian state had come to endorse (Shepherd 2010). Today, it is remarkable to observe how departmental and provincial municipalities across the Peruvian Andes support agricultural fairs which display the rich diversity of potato. Peruvian cultural affirmation can be seen as an archetype of postdevelopment in practice (see Figure 15.4).

The Green Revolution in East Timor

The GR in East Timor dates back to the 1960s, when under the rule of the Portuguese. Colonial agronomists executed a pocketed GR for rice relying on improved varieties from the International Rice Research Institute (IRRI) in the Philippines. In 1975, the Portuguese departed and the Indonesians immediately invaded. Over the next several years, 100,000 East Timorese perished due to direct violence and mass starvation incurred by relocation and disruption to cultivation systems. The Indonesians followed up with an aggressive rice GR just as farmers in other parts of Indonesia began to feel the detrimental ecological effects of the GR imposed upon them (Fox 1991). Indonesia was forced out of East Timor in 1999 and, as the country moved to full independence (2002), the international development industry instituted yet another GR, mainly in rice, but also maize, sweet potato and cassava.

I visited East Timor in January 2003 amidst a veritable invasion of foreign development organisations. Few people there were celebrating traditional agriculture, much less documenting it, as had been done for elsewhere in Austronesia (Fox 1992). One evening in Dili (the capital), I ran into the new country's first representative of the GR. This man took his instructions from the Australian Centre for International Agricultural Research (ACIAR) to trial varieties of rice, maize, cassava and sweet potato under the auspices of a project called Seeds of Life – or perhaps better, Seeds of Lies (henceforth SoL). I accompanied him to various parts of the hinterlands to see his experimental plots. Noticing that the imported varieties of sweet potato hailed from CIP in Peru, I was reminded of the global networks in which both his activities and mine were situated. For their part, the rice came from IRRI, the maize from the International Centre for the Improvement of Maize and Wheat (CIMMYT) in Mexico, and the cassava from the International Centre for Tropical Agriculture (CIAT) in Colombia.

The Australian agronomist's objective appeared to be technical in nature: which varieties could demonstrate the best growth rates and highest yields subject to which conditions (soils and climate) and adversities (pest and diseases). He reiterated the usual story about the pitfalls of a 'primitive' cultivation system whose productivity logic was not empirical but superstitious. I asked him about the potential consequences of another GR on agrobiodiversity. That was irrelevant, he said, because East Timor was not a diversity hotspot. His words spoke to the agroscientific mindset by which only areas super-rich in agrobiodiversity – notably Vavilov's centres of origin – merited protection (see Brookfield, Parsons & Brookfield 2003).

Over the next few years, SoL grew to become a major programme housed within East Timor's Ministry of Agriculture. The Australian bilateral aid body, AusAid, funded the programme, providing several million dollars per funding cycle. A handful of foreign specialists ran the programme, which employed and trained more than 100 Timorese extension workers. The extension workers now brought the varieties that had performed well in off-farm trials to the peasants by way of on-farm demonstration trials. The peasants were invited to plant what was now contrasted as 'local seed' and 'new [or foreign] seed' in contiguous plots under identical conditions (see Figure 15.5). Although many peasants showed little interest in the thousands of on-farm trials, and barely

FIGURE 15.5 A Seeds of Lies research assistant takes data on plant growth at an on-farm demonstration plot while the peasant farmer dreamily looks on. © Christopher J. Shepherd.

attended to the plots, the official logic was as follows: if the peasants saw for themselves that the imported varieties fared better, they would adopt them; if not, they would maintain their own varieties. The reductive, yield-focused method of on-farm demonstration trials was in fact a standard extension strategy that had also been part of Peru's GR campaign.

When in 2005 and 2006 I applied for postdoctoral funding from the Australian Government's research council (ARC) to conduct fieldwork on development in East Timor, I included SoL as one of my case studies. The ARC approved the application. I took up the fellowship in the department of anthropology at the Australian National University (ANU). Two anthropologists there had been involved in SoL for several years, although I was unsure what exactly their contribution was. Seeking their support for my prospective field study of SoL, I met them one afternoon in March 2008 to chat. The first of the two, a prominent anthropologist and mover-and-shaker in the development world, I recall, suggested I study instead a similar seed intervention run by the German Development Agency (GTZ); the other, an applied anthropologist, development consultant and Timor expert underlined how impressive the SoL programme was before complaining that development critique was 'too easy'. 'And what is so hard about what you do?' I might well have asked him. Taken aback at his unsubtle dismissal, I left with the odd impression that this applied anthropologist believed that social scientists should refrain from studying, much less critiquing, development as a sociopolitical phenomenon or, more succinctly, as the cross-cultural exercise of power. I did not grasp at the time how much he would have preferred I steer clear of SoL altogether. Keeping up appearances, however, the applied anthropologist arranged my access to the programme through the in-country programme director. The following month, I went off to Timor unaware that their communications with the director must have included a general caution about the critical nature of my research as well as a specific request that I not be given research access to the concerns of applied anthropology.

The in-country director of SoL was a fast-talking agronomist who swamped listeners in barrages of comparative statistics about yield. His interminable assertions effectively closed off discussion. Being at the receiving end of his monologues was like being swept down a raging river. His non-communicative strategy, I would soon realise, was symptomatic of the way SoL as a whole operated. The director took total control of my research movements by compressing me into a schedule. He bundled me off on a four-week circuit around just as many districts to observe the extension agents' execution of the on-farm demonstration trials. While I enjoyed motor-biking around the stunning countryside with the warm Timorese extension workers, I felt frustrated by the lack of real research autonomy. One day, quite by accident, I heard that the aforementioned applied anthropologist ran a socioeconomic study for SoL, and his team was active in the field as well. However, it became clear to me that when his team were in the east, the director had sent me west; when his team was in the west, I had been sent east.

Over the next couple of months, I came to see that many other SoL spaces were kept out of my range. I never managed to witness the sessions in which farmers compared old and new varieties for their taste. I was never invited to internal SoL meetings, nor to the meetings between SoL and the Ministry of Agriculture. The central office was not somewhere I could freely hang around as I had always been able to do with tens of other institutions in Peru. I was not permitted to browse the shelves, much less open a filing cabinet or peep inside an innocuous box in the corner of the office. I could only enter the office upon the invitation of the director. Absurdly, when I asked to see documents, the director asked me which specific documents I wanted to see, yet I had no way of knowing which documents existed to request them. In effect, I was only ever allowed to see the glossy SoL end-of-year reports which paraded the success of SoL to donors, counterparts and general readers. This was not participant observation; it was institutional dissimulation. If studies in the anthropology of development methodologically exploit the disconnect between development discourse and on-the-ground reality, SoL kept as much of that 'other reality' as possible out of my direct experience. The lack of real access to the programme threw me, but the façade of my being granted access to the programme left me pouting, speechless, bloodthirsty. A friend consoled me insightfully: 'It's all good data!'

A telling moment came when one day I was out to lunch with the SoL director and one of SoL's Australian employees named Bob (pseudonym), who lived in Same and managed a research station on the south coast. Bob invited me to stay in his house in Same, but the director opined I should stay in a guesthouse, a view he kept reiterating. I was puzzled by the director's insistence and struck by his nervous countenance. Bob of lonely Same clearly wanted the company of a compatriot with whom to share beers and so on. One evening, Bob was passed out on the bathroom floor. Still conscious and upright, I happened to peer inside Bob's home office. From the doorway I could see stacks of non-glossy SoL documents. As I stood there contemplating my next step and glancing over my shoulder, I understood why the director had insisted I seek other accommodation.

It was clear to me that the director sought to impede an ethnographic study that could potentially disrupt the credibility of the intervention, critique the input of applied anthropology and, I have every reason to believe, based on my own experience of SoL, show how information and data were twisted to ensure the steady flow of funding. To be fair, SoL's concerns were not ill-founded. Elements within AusAid were known to be apprehensive about funding interventions into agriculture, and it may have been swayed by an independent study that showed the public face of SoL to be highly manipulated. In addition, SoL served the political mileage of politicians keen to showcase their 'humanitarian support' for East Timor against the backdrop of Australia's oil-driven manipulation of sea boundaries (see Shepherd 2014). Applied anthropologists played a special part in the general SoL stage management. In close cooperation with ACIAR, they deployed their expert knowledge of 'Timorese culture' in funding proposals to make good on the expectation that interventions would be culturally appropriate; an inevitable duplicity beset their pose as neutral consultants. To the extent that I was able to learn anything about the input of applied anthropology, it was evident that the 'cultural knowledge' gained and deployed was purely instrumental. Sacred houses and animist ritual, for example, were construed as sites and times to distribute new seed. Applied anthropology's so-called socioeconomic study would have been wide-open to the classic anthropological critique of development in general and of the GR in particular (e.g., Hobart 1993; Ploeg 1993).

I was not SoL's only worry. SoL was also concerned about the strong opposition emanating from Timorese NGOs. Those NGOs questioned SoL's impact on agrobiodiversity. They disputed SoL's spurious claim that the programme would increase diversity; had the enhancement of diversity been SoL's mission, however, it would have introduced new varieties without the systematic problematisation and replacement of local varieties. NGO actors accused SoL of disrespecting Timorese genetic resources. One well-known activist and university lecturer, Ego Lemos, observed that SoL characterised local seeds as 'lacking in quality'. But, he insisted, 'local seeds are local seeds and they should not be compared to foreign seeds' (personal communication, July 2011). NGOs and environmental activists undertook to protect local seeds from SoL's implicitly condescending import of foreign seed, and they compared their mission to the pre-independence resistance struggle, which had worked to protect the country's local populations from outsiders, namely Indonesians (Shepherd 2014).

Indeed, the conspicuous dominance of outside experts in the SoL hierarchy reminded them – and me – of colonialism; a new master had come along in the form of agricultural development experts. NGOs distrusted SoL all the more for its close affiliation with the IARCs and the CGIAR (Consultative Group for International Agricultural Research); they understood that the ACIAR was involved in patenting Timorese seed and conducting research into genetically modified food crops in Indonesia. If SoL tried to prevent its identification with the GR by maintaining that fertilisers and pesticides were not part of its operation, NGOs claimed that it was only a matter of time before SoL would incorporate them. On that count, NGOs turned out to be correct. When I interviewed the new SoL director in 2012, he said that seed had been 'the low-hanging fruit' (personal communication, June 2012).

None of these contentious issues ever made it into SoL's publicly available published materials. The censorship found expression in another telling moment that, to me, pointed to the two-faced involvement of applied anthropology. Loath to be at odds with the applied anthropologist in the same anthropology department, I invited him to be co-author on a number of my papers once I had returned to the ANU after the fieldwork in Timor. One paper was about rice and included a section on SoL (Shepherd & McWilliam 2011 ☺). Ironically, I wrote the section on applied anthropology's socioeconomic study despite my limited knowledge of it, to which the applied anthropologist himself had nothing to contribute. If this development consultant was not one for giving anything away, he was certainly one for erasing things; from one draft he deleted my statements outlining Timorese NGOs' contestations to SoL. This deletion was emblematic of SoL's *modus operandi*. Even as SoL stressed 'the fact' that farmers were happily adopting the new varieties – pathetic images of overjoyed farmers typically filled the end-of-year reports – we can take for granted that this was constructed knowledge built on both calculated deletions and the foregrounding of favourable information and interpretations (Mosse 2005). It was definitely not built on transparency, open evaluation and balanced perspectives. The programme was a beautifully concocted lie.

Conclusion

When one conducts research on foreign development, one is immediately cross-cutting intersecting fields of contested power. In Peru I witnessed a 'trial of strength' (Latour 1987) between the conventional GR model of agricultural modernisation and the alternative postdevelopment cultural affirmation. Because the debate surrounding the positions across the institutional spectrum was relatively open, my research proceeded uninterrupted. It was precisely in this open atmosphere that the postdevelopment alternative of cultural affirmation was able to emerge and flourish, particularly when in situ agrobiodiversity programs forced actors to reassess agrodevelopment orthodoxy and, consequently, shift the balance in favour of in situ conservation. All the while, the GR steadily lost ground as its shortcomings became visible to developers and peasant farmers alike.

In East Timor, I did not so much observe a trial of strength as I did fall into one. For actors pushing the post-independence GR, I was someone who needed to be managed in a context where, unlike in Peru, the debate was less open, more rancorous and emotive. Mainstream development actors in East Timor were distrustful of the more radical NGOs and strategically ignored their vociferous objections. Even now, developmentalist agricultural orthodoxy reigns. No postdevelopment alternative has general legitimacy; there is little common ground, for example, by which to reconcile competing economic and environmental values. Interventions that we might recognise as postdevelopment or cultural affirmation are underfunded, executed only by relatively marginal NGOs through piecemeal initiatives (see Palmer & Amaral de Carvalho 2008); the pragmatic state, meanwhile, adeptly appropriates 'traditions' in the service of the modernising agenda.[2]

In East Timor, therefore, there has been less pressure on the GR to cede ground than in highland Peru. But not only that – the pressure that does exist has been pushed out of discourse; development industry actors everywhere construct images of interventions' successes by averting criticism (Mosse 2005). In respect to diversity agriculture in particular, the general bias towards centres of origin and the low value attached to local landraces in non-origin centres have ensured that East Timor's diversity has not been viewed as an environmental or cultural asset, let alone been subject to serious conservation efforts. In sum, the state and other powerful multi- and bilateral organisations have done little more than mimic the sustainable development narratives of querulous NGOs and affiliated academics (e.g., Palmer 2015); curiously, local seed plays practically no role in this mimicry, for it has been overlooked in favour of more marketable expressions of 'culture' such as animist ritual.

In highland Peru, it eventually became clear where farmers positioned themselves in relation to the GR. No such clarity emerged in East Timor. One of the problems for postdevelopment in East Timor has been the absence of independent studies to assess the real impact of SoL and similar initiatives on farmers' choices and actions. SoL's substantial financial and intellectual resources – including those of applied anthropology – enabled it to forward the most authoritative account of its own intervention. The particular way that I became part of SoL's trial of strength with opposition was in itself illustrative of the way SoL resourcefully quietened critical voices. What Timorese farmer voices were and are in this game of obfuscation remains to be seen now that SoL has metamorphosed into another, similar program. SoL's biggest lie, of course, was that it was ever anything other than a regular GR.

The case study underlines the compromised position of anthropology. Many anthropologists – usually the ones suitably employed in universities – critique the world of development, while others – often those who are underemployed in universities or employed directly in the development industry – profit from it. Anthropology's core disciplinary value is supposed to uphold the protection of 'other cultures', and its abhorrence or at least scepticism surrounding modernisation and development is well established within anthropology's founding theoretical and methodological orientations; cultural relativism seeks a cross-cultural epistemological and ontological equivalence, and participant observation assumes a respectful, sympathetic presence among one's research subjects (Stocking 1992). Anthropology, however, has an 'evil twin' who sells disciplinary expertise to large corporations, PR machinery, military complexes, intelligence agencies and, of course, the development industry (Ferguson 1997). The precise nature of these engagements rarely receives a mention in anthropologists' peer-reviewed publications. One could say that through the strategic foregrounding of the object of anthropological study, high-level mover-and-shaker anthropologists and applied development anthropologists such as those that I encountered at the ANU conceal the questionable politics of their applied trade. Anthropology's evil twin is necessarily anxious about critical studies of development, and so it seeks to side-line them while vainly grasping at moral legitimacy in a disciplinary backyard that balks at the hypocrisy.

My involvement with Seeds of Lies and my inadvertent plunge into the fraught space between anthropology and applied anthropology was a crappy enough experience; little did I know, though, how much worse things could become. When I returned to highland Peru to study a transnational mining project, the area was teeming with applied anthropologists. These 'community relations officers', as they were called, not only impeded my access to research sites but were closely networked with company informants and thugs, who, for their part, repeatedly urged me to leave the area and issued various threats. ('You may find yourself on the riverbank!') From my perspective, the difference between the dissimulating operations of applied anthropologists in Peru and East Timor was only a matter of degree; what in Peru could have easily become physical violence against me manifested in East Timor as an epistemological violence predicated on the imperative to control how much I knew.

I therefore finish with advice for students, particularly ethnographers, of development and postdevelopment. Watch out, first, for development-oriented applied anthropologists or 'consultants', for they understand exactly how *uneasy* this 'too-easy' field of enquiry makes them. Beware, second, of tight communities of social scientists in small countries with vested interests in the development industry; relative anonymity is a great advantage when conducting an ethnographic study of a project that goes beyond the soft-target research site of NGOs. Third, be sure not to give much away in the field. Most people will assume you are interested in culture. But, to be sure, wax lyrical about the interventions you are critiquing and declare your commitment to development by parroting clichés, for example, that you too hope to help make poverty history. Fourth, be aware that occasionally things can get really sticky. Don't react to perceived injustice, crime or lies while still in the field, and if you screw up badly know when it's time to flee the country. Fifth, anything goes; use the investigatory tactics fit for a putrescent industry. 'Development stinks', wrote Gustavo Esteva famously. Forget university ethics and think situated ethics. Sixth, understand that the ethnographer is an actor, not simply an observer, and therefore reflexive topics including easy or problematic access to project sites are important because ethnographers' location and experiences reveal broader developmentalist politics; this is the point at which postdevelopment in practice meets postdevelopmentalist ethnography in practice. Finally, keep the applied anthropologist across the corridor close, if you can. Bide your time, and write a chapter such as this only after weighing the consequences.

Notes

1 The fieldwork in Peru was supported by two Wenner-Gren Foundation postdoctoral fieldwork grants (in 2007 and 2015). I thank Luís Revilla of CESA and all those at PRATEC, APU, AWAY and Chuyma Aru for their support in the field. I am grateful to those at Seeds of Life for allowing me access, albeit restricted, to the programme, which was one of several case studies in a larger research project funded by the Australian Research Council (project number DP0773307).
2 The state's cooptation and distribution of the *tara bandu* tradition for resource management is the notable example (see Shepherd 2014).

References

Apffel-Marglin, F. (1998) 'Introduction: knowledge and life revisited'. In Apffel-Marglin, F. (ed.), *The Spirit of Regeneration: Andean Culture Confronts Western Notions of Development*, pp 1–50. London: Zed Books.
Brookfield, H., Parsons, H. & Brookfield, M. (eds.) (2003) *Agrodiversity: Learning from Farmers across the World*. Tokyo: United Nations University Press.
Cleaves, P.S. & Scurrah, M.J. (1980) *Agriculture, Bureaucracy, and Military Government in Peru*. Ithaca, NY: Cornell University Press.
Dueñas, A., Mendivil, R., Lovaton, G. & Loaiza, A. (1992) '"Campesinos y papas: A propósito de la variabilidad y erosión genética en comunidades campesinas del Cusco'. In Degregori, C.I., Escobal, J. & Marticorena, B. (eds.), *Perú: el Problema Agraria en Debate SEPIA IV, Seminario Permanente de Investigación Agraria (SEPIA)*, pp 287–309. Iquitos, Peru: Universidad Nacional de la Amazonía Peruana (UNAP).
Ferguson, J. (1997) 'Anthropology and its evil twin: "Development" in the constitution of a discipline'. In Cooper, F. & Packard, R. (eds.), *International Development and the Social Sciences: Essays on the History and Politics of Knowledge*, pp 150–175. Berkeley, CA: University of California Press.
Fox, J.J. (1991) 'Managing the ecology of rice production in Indonesia'. In Hardjono, J. (ed.), *Indonesia: Resources, Ecology and Environment*, pp 61–84. Singapore: Oxford University Press.
Fox, J.J. (ed.) (1992) *The Heritage of Traditional Agriculture among the Western Austronesians*. Canberra: Australian National University.
Hobart, M. (ed.) (1993) *An Anthropological Critique of Development: The Growth of Ignorance*. London: Routledge.

Jennings, B.H. (1988) *Foundations of International Agricultural Research: Science and Politics in Mexican Agriculture*. Boulder, CO and London: Westview Press.

Latour, B. (1987) *Science in Action: How to Follow Scientists and Engineers Through Society*. Milton Keynes: Open University Press.

Mosse, D. (2005) *Cultivating Development: An Ethnography of Aid Policy and Practice*. London and Ann Arbor, MI: Pluto Press.

Palmer, L. (2015) *Water Politics and Spiritual Ecology: Custom, Environmental Governance and Development*. London and New York: Routledge.

Palmer, L. & Amaral de Carvalho, D. (2008) 'Nation building and resource management: the politics of "nature" in Timor Leste'. *Geoforum*, vol 39, pp 1321–1332.

Ploeg, J.D. v.d. (1993) 'Potatoes and knowledge'. In Hobart, M. (ed.), *An Anthropological Critique of Development: The Growth of Ignorance*, pp 209–228. London: Routledge.

Revilla Sta. Cruz, L. (2014) *Costumbres de las Papas Nativas*. Cusco, Peru: CESA.

Shepherd, C.J. (2005) 'Imperial science: The Rockefeller Foundation and agriculture in Peru'. *Science as Culture: Special Issue on Postcolonial Technoscience*, vol 13, no 14, pp 113–137.

Shepherd, C.J. (2006) 'From *in vitro* to *in situ*: On the precarious extension of agricultural science in the Indigenous "Third World"'. *Social Studies of Science*, vol 36, no 3, pp 399–427.

Shepherd, C.J. (2010) 'Mobilizing local knowledge and asserting culture: The cultural politics of *in situ* conservation of agricultural biodiversity'. *Current Anthropology* vol 51, no 5, pp 629–654.

Shepherd, C.J. (2014) *Development and Environmental Politics Unmasked: Authority, Participation and Equity in East Timor*. London: Routledge.

Shepherd, C.J. & McWilliam, A. (2011) 'Ethnography, agency, and materiality: Anthropological perspectives on rice development in East Timor'. *East Asian Science, Technology and Society*, vol 5, no 2, pp 189–215.

Shiva, V. (2016 [1991]) *The Violence of the Green Revolution: Third World Agriculture, Ecology and Politics*. Lexington, KY: University Press of Kentucky.

Stein, W. (2004) *Deconstructing Development Discourse in Peru: A Meta-Ethnography of the Modernity Project at Vicos*. New York: University Press of America.

Stocking, G.W. (1992) *The Ethnographer's Magic and Other Essays in the History of Anthropology*. Madison, WI: University of Wisconsin Press.

Zimmerer, K.S. (1996). *Changing Fortunes: Biodiversity and Peasant Livelihood in the Peruvian Andes*. Berkeley, CA: University of California Press.

16
BODY POLITICS AND POSTDEVELOPMENT

Wendy Harcourt

Young women with writing across their stomachs decrying surrogacy; grandmothers dressed in black assembling every week demanding to know about their disappeared children; gay pride events; rap songs that dare to speak of rape and displacement; social media campaigns that call for an end to gender-based violence; YouTube videos by queer Latinas that celebrate sexualities and bodies of all shapes. These are among the myriad examples of body political activism that can be found around the world as part of postdevelopment practice. Body politics refers to the political struggles of people to claim control over their felt and lived biological, social and cultural embodied experiences. Body politics activism aims to transform how bodies are shaped by cultural, economic and social relations and discourses. In these struggles, bodies are sites of cultural and political resistance to the dominant understanding of the 'normal' body as white, male, Western and heterosexual from which all 'other' forms of bodies differ. In its claim to celebrate and reposition otherness, body politics is an essential entry point for postdevelopment discourses. The practices of body politics are important contributions to processes of transformative collective action informing postdevelopment's search for alternatives to development.

Postdevelopment aims to go beyond the metaphors, ideologies, premises of development in its analysis of development as a contested set of cultural, political, economic and historical processes and relations. Postdevelopment scholars engage in both academic and political action and debate which recognises diverse developments and diverse modernities. Postdevelopment questions the core assumptions of the development discourse (e.g., growth, material progress, instrumental rationality, the centrality of markets and economy, universality, modernity and its binaries) and aims to practice a radically different set of ethics and values which promote life-affirming principles such as: diversity, solidarity, commons, oneness with nature, interconnectedness, simplicity, inclusiveness, equity, non-hierarchy, pluriversality and peace. In short, postdevelopment is the unmaking of development through the intervention of new narratives, new ways of thinking and doing (Escobar 1995; Escobar 2008).

In this chapter I explore how body politics is an important feature of postdevelopment actions in the disruptive and critical interventions of feminist activists. In this approach, the body is conceptualised as where 'global capitalism writes its script' and therefore it is also from the body that it is possible to 'demystify capitalism as a system of debilitating sexism and racism, and envision anticapitalistic resistance' (Mohanty 2003: 235). Body politics also builds on the Foucauldian notion of biopolitics. Biopolitics is understood here as the politics of administering and governing of life where the body is measured and analysed in an array of strategies that produces the modern sense of gendered individual and social subjects (Foucault 1976; Harcourt 2009).

In the following, I first situate the discussion on body politics and postdevelopment by examining feminist writings on body politics. I then look at how different forms of body politics are played out in the postdevelopment landscape in three types of activism: 1) reproductive justice, where body politics challenges the intimate and the too-often-unspoken sexism in political and economic spaces of development; 2) racialised bodies in resistance, where body politics confronts Western power expressed in the violence of racism that accompanies colonial undergirding of development practices; 3) reworlding and Indigenous resistances, where body politics is about ways to reimagine and remake the world through pluriversal understandings of life-in-common strategies centred on diverse understandings of wellbeing.

Feminist writings on body politics

The ongoing debates by feminist scholars and activists focus on knowledge production around the body in ways that position the body as the subject, not object, of knowing. In these debates there is a keen awareness of the importance of the writers' positionality and the need to make clear who is speaking for whose bodies, whose knowledge counts about the body and in what ways bodies can know. In the following I summarise three sets of feminist writings about the body which I loosely categorise as Western, postcolonial and decolonial, acknowledging the resonances and overlaps and inevitable gaps in this brief summary.

Western feminism on bodies as sites of meaning

Since the late 1980s and early 1990s, Western feminist writings have analysed bodies as powerful sites of cultural meaning, social experience and political resistance (Grosz 1994; Cornwall, Correa & Jolly 2008; Harcourt 2009; Butler 2003). Western feminist theory has aimed to retell narratives about female embodiment in order to unsettle assumptions about biological sex and gender as natural and unchanging. For example, Judith Butler (1993) challenged dominant views of embodiment in order to unpack how tradition and modernity are played out on the lived body. Inderpal Grewal and Cora Kaplan (1994) critiqued the conceptual frameworks that bind male and female embodied experiences in dominant macro frameworks of politics, economics, culture and society. In these feminist writings aspects of female embodiment (such as pregnancy, rape and ageing) become privileged sites of significance bearing on how female experience is lived (Shildrick 1997; Young 2005)

In these feminist readings of the body, the focus is on how gendered bodies are constructed in Western popular, scientific, economic development discourses (Harcourt 2009). By making visible how these discourses inform embodiment, feminist writings challenge the normative construction of the gendered body in Western discourses around sexual relations, economics, health, medical and biological scientific processes. They reflect on and inform popular activist writing, where feminists reclaim the lived experience of the female body as a vehicle for making and remaking the world.[1] These writings have fed into and reflected on women's rights agendas at national and transnational levels, shaping the 1990s women's-rights-are-human-rights, women's empowerment and reproductive health and sexual rights agendas, now at the basis of critical feminist readings of development programming and policy particularly around gender-based violence and sexuality (Cornwall, Correa & Jolly 2008; Harcourt 2009).

Postcolonial feminism and intersectional analysis

Postcolonial feminism deepens the critique of how the corporeal, fleshly, material existence of bodies is deeply embedded in political relations by looking at body politics from colonialism to population control policies to contemporary biopolitics of migration. The experience of female embodiment is conceptualised as determined by sexism, racism, misogyny and heterosexism (Spivak 1987, 1999; Mohanty 2003; Tamale 2011). In this tradition, feminist writings expose how sexist and racist imperialist structures inform health and population policy and make the fertility of women from the Global South a central 'problem' of development policy. Body politics, then, is at the core of national and international development policy related to gender equality, human rights and public health (Petchesky 2002; Harcourt 2009; Wieringa & Sivori 2013). In the 1990s series of United Nations conferences, feminist advocates brought to the UN arena body political issues such as: domestic violence; rape as a weapon of war; denial of sexual and reproductive rights; sexual oppression of women, children, homosexuals and transgender people; discriminatory practices that stereotype bodies on the basis of age and physical ability.

Body politics in these intersectional struggles make visible previously tabooed issues which condone and institutionalise inequalities based on gender, sexuality identity, age, ability and race in the workplace and social and political life (Petchesky 2002; Harcourt & Escobar 2002; Cornwall, Correa & Jolly 2008). The intersectional analysis of body politics exposes how race and gender interact to shape interlocking matrices of privilege and oppression (Crenshaw 1991; Collins 2000). A postcolonial and intersectional analysis helps to unpack assumptions of development being able to deliver an unproblematised idea of progress by revealing the multiple ways structures such as race, class and gender position different bodies, making them subject to multiple possibilities but also multiple oppressions (McCall 2005; Gopaldas 2013).

Postcolonial feminist analysis and practice illustrates how body politics is interwoven into social, colonial, ethical and economic discourses of development policy and practice, helping to shape the postdevelopment critique of power and knowledge. Body politics challenges contemporary neoliberal political and economic strategies of governmentality as well as the 'politics of subjection and subject-making that continually places in question the political existence of modern human beings' (Ong 2006: 13). These challenges have extended to a reflective internal critique with trans-feminism queering 'cis-heteronormative "whitestream" feminism' of well-funded NGOs and institutes of the Global North and their hegemonic influence over body politics at national and transnational levels (Weerawardhana 2018: 185).

Decolonial writings of the body: beyond gender?

Decolonial scholars have pushed the Western and postcolonial critiques in new directions by looking at embodiment in the historical and contemporary erasures of Indigenous peoples and cultures. According to decolonial feminists, the coloniality of power and knowledge introduced heterosexual gender binary logics into non-Western contexts. They argue that gender logics operate in conjunction with race and class (Lugones 2008). Decolonial writing decentres predominantly white-eurocentric-male analysis in order to open up spaces for other narratives that acknowledge non-eurocentric knowledge production, history and practices around the body. They challenge the whitewash/erasure of non-European/non-white knowledge that reinforces marginalisation, criminalisation and 'memory loss' of racialised peoples (Icaza 2015). As Ochy Curiel states, decolonisation is, 'a political and epistemological position which traverses individual and collective thought and action: our imaginaries, our bodies and sexualities, and our ways of being and doing in the world' (Curiel 2016: 51). Decolonial writings on the body aim to create a differently gendered discourse building from the embodied experiences of the marginalised. For example, Lugones (2010) describes how diverse Indigenous communities in Mesoamerica are marked by the coloniality of capitalism-nation-state-Western knowledge-and gender.

In decolonial analysis, the body is marked by a fluid relation between male-female which is intimately defined and links the material/immaterial, human/non-human beings, the past, the future (Icaza 2015). The 'otherwise' experience of the body unfolds as it is lived in relation to practices of being with the land, the trees, the engagement with others as bodies, while working, eating, breast feeding, birthing, dancing, thinking, praying and resisting. Decolonial feminism challenges the notion of gender as a universalist and ahistorical category and asks that 'feminists writing on the body scrutinize the colonial assumptions and pre-suppositions [...] starting with that of gendered beings' (Harcourt, Icaza & Vargas 2015: 163). An important element of the decolonial feminist strategy is to employ reflexivity mindful of the situated condition of research and who has the right to speak in the name of whom: 'because our work is to look back, forward, and side-ways – we who have the privilege to delve into the wreckage of imperial trauma' (Carrillo Rowe 2013: 114).

In these three strands of feminism, the understanding of the body goes beyond the biological as a natural construct and considers the body through the variables of history, culture, time and place. In the following section, I look at how body politics is lived and experienced in three forms of embodied resistance which illustrate how body politics is postdevelopment in practice through challenging the intimate, confronting racism and learning from reworlding.

Challenging the intimate

By bringing attention to intimate relationships and the lived experiences of the gendered body, feminist activists aim to break taboos and processes that make invisible the importance of the intimacy and stereotyped notions of the female, femininity, non-heterosexual behaviour in economic development discourse. In recent years feminist actions have shifted public political discourse through civic movements and social media as well as through more traditional forms of advocacy. There are many feminist actions where the body is the first entry point into politics and resistance (Cornwall, Correa & Jolly 2008; Harcourt 2009). In the following, I describe how body politics has operated in different contexts in relation to reproductive justice and feminists using their body as intimate weapons of protest to power.

Reproductive justice

Reproductive justice refers to the struggle of women and other genders to gain autonomy over their own bodies in order to be able to exercise their sexuality with pleasure and to be able to decide when to have or not to have children. These struggles have formed the basis of a globally recognised agenda of sexual and reproductive rights. The reproductive justice agenda is the fight for: access to bodily integrity and autonomy; health care; reproductive rights (conception, contraception, abortion, infertility); an end to gender-based violence, domestic violence; and the right to express all forms of sexuality for lesbian, gays, bi and trans people. Importantly, reproductive justice goes beyond matters of individual choice and privacy which was key to the earlier, mostly white feminist middle-class agendas of, for example, the pro-choice movement. Reproductive justice addresses race- and class-based reproductive politics that impact marginalised women and other non-dominant genders. Reproductive justice looks at how race, gender, class, sexuality and (dis)ability come together in daily lives, 'structuring the possibilities for life and death' (Jolly 2016: 167). Today's reproductive justice agenda 'acknowledges that abuses of power affect intimate aspects of all women's lives, especially those who are socially, politically, and economically marginalized and whose bodies remain crucial sites for political battles over health, welfare, and law and order' (Jolly 2016: 166)

From among the many examples of ongoing reproductive justice battles, one new and troubling concern is the practice of transnational surrogacy:

> Surrogacy marks a paradigm shift in the appreciation of the reproductive capacities of poor women in the Global South: for decades in Western discourse, fertility and procreation of subaltern women in the Global South was constructed as backward, passive, subjugated, unruly and unplanned. Now, being placed at the service of pro-natalist policies of the countries of the global North and the global middle class it is gaining unprecedented appreciation.
> (Wichterich 2018)

Modern assisted reproductive technologies bring the intimate biological functions of women to the marketplace and raise the possibilities for (wealthy) infertile, non-cis-women and men to have children. Through this technology and the economic practices that have sprung up around it, birth is commodified through the integration of informatics and biology, raising considerable legal, ethical and policy issues, particularly given it is mostly citizens of rich countries of the Global North who seek the services, and poor subaltern women of the Global South who provide. Called variously reproduction procreative tourism, fertility tourism or reproductive tourism, it is an increasingly common global phenomenon with transnational surrogacy hubs where poor women produce babies for rich couples via private-sector intermediaries. The surrogate women's uteruses are envisaged as places of incubation separate from the emotional and physical markings on the women's bodies. These rapidly growing industries of medical/technological and social interaction erase the embodied experience of surrogates as they follow the market in ways that ethical and legal systems cannot always cover. Governed by a patchwork of laws in 'restrictive' and 'permissive' countries, economic and social inequalities drive procreative tourism. From a postdevelopment perspective, gestational surrogacy reveals deep-seated inequalities sanitised in technology and science that profits from power relationships that unquestioningly treat women who gestate as reproducers with the labour of their wombs able to be sold in ways that deny their social and cultural positioning. These legal provisions are part of the biopolitics of nation-states which control the population, sexuality, health and reproduction. The biopolitical regime fuels deeply troubling practices of fertility tourism as part of the 'transnationalisation of bioeconomic investment and business' (Wichterich 2019). An example of postdevelopment in practice that counters surrogacy can be seen in European feminist movements' campaigns (in Spain, Italy and Sweden) to prevent surrogacy. Feminist groups such as the Italian 'Se Non Ora Quando' (If not now when) campaigns to end surrogacy have successfully prevented surrogacy on the grounds of the reproductive rights of women and as an affirmation of feminine difference (Momigliano 2017).[2]

The power of protesting bodies

An emerging field of body political activism is (young) women taking charge of their exposed or naked bodies as an image of protest. While nudity as protest is not new, what is new in contemporary times is the use of the Internet and social media to create transnational resistance cultures that construct global feminist imaginaries of collective action, solidarity and social justice based on statements made on their body, that challenge 'the patriarchally defined subaltern woman' (Spivak 1999: 68). In these actions the body is seen (and performed) as 'a revolutionary political and expressive medium' (Deb 2016: 177).

For example, the picture of the 'Girl of Enghelab Street', later identified as Vida Movahed, who took off her headscarf on a street in Tehran to protest against the Hijab went viral (Osborne 2018),[3] or during the Arab Spring protests in 2011 in Tahrir Square, images around the world alerting feminists and the public to a high level of sexual violence towards the women protestors. These images of embodied female protest are part of transnational protest where bodies on the streets are connected to those supporters who are virtually engaged in solidarity. Both forms of engagement are needed, in order for women to be safe in the streets during the Arab Spring they required others to be watching and monitoring what was going on. For example, the YouTube clips of Egyptian military police dragging away a woman from Cairo's Tahrir Square, where her vivid blue bra could be seen through her ripped black robe, became a symbol of female bodily protest of the Arab Spring (Deb 2016: 171). Such images picked up by social and mass media make visible violence against women and the ways women are fighting to overcome oppressive patriarchal cultures.

Other examples of transnational body politics that make visible the bodily experiences of sexual violence are campaigns such as '16 Days of Violence Against Women', the 'Billion Rising Campaign', the 'Women Living Under Muslim Law', 'Women Human Rights Defenders' (Harcourt 2013). These protests, on and offline, connect local protests to transnational feminist solidarity in a form of global body politics that challenges patriarchal militarised state structures in political statements that deliberately speak to the performance of power (Butler 2011). Images such as those of the woman removing her headscarf and the woman in a blue bra are able to assert a political vision that challenges stereotypes of the passive inert oppressed subaltern female veiled body.

Another controversial example of women protesters displaying their bodies as a form of political challenge to power in public is the Ukrainian group FEMEN. These young (stereotypically attractive) mostly blonde European women aim to attract media attention by running bare-breasted or naked in front of powerful politicians (such as Putin, Berlusconi etc.). They state they are using their body as their own form of power to confront leaders of patriarchy in a deliberate reversal of how female bodies are usually perceived: 'we're not showing a passive smiling body, we're showing an aggressive, screaming body. My body is always saying something. I use it as a small poster to write my political demand' (Aitken 2013). FEMEN as a form of feminist body politics is contested particularly in relation to its unawareness of intersectionality, racism and colonial imaging of women's bodies. The Tunisian FEMEN member Alia al-Mahdy, who posted a naked picture of herself on her blog in 2011 and subsequently had to leave her country, has been criticised by feminist groups as an unwitting 'handmaiden of the global North' unaware of deeper political economic and social constraints. (Deb 2016: 178). These examples of body politics as postdevelopment practice as they present their bodies as sites of cultural and political resistance to the dominant understanding of the 'normal' body as white, male, Western and heterosexual. Using the Internet and social media these protests open up discussions of otherness determined by the women's own experience and resistance to otherness and as alternatives to mainstream development.

Reverse guerrilla tactics

Other forms of body politics challenge through utilising cultural assumptions around motherhood. The group Women in Black[4] is a global example a network of women who hold vigils in protest against war, militarism and other forms of violence. Mothers of the Plazo de Mayo have held vigils in Buenos Aires for over 40 years in public protest and mourning for their children who have been disappeared by the state (Goni 2017). Further, Italian guerrilla narratives deliberately engage with sanctified images of motherhood in order to interrupt mainstream narratives around health and the ill health of bodies. For example, a campaign sent 150,000 postcards from the region called 'Land of Fires' depicting photographs of mothers who lost their children due to cancer in the provinces of Napoli and Caserta, where illegal dumping of toxic and hazardous waste over decades led to disease and death of both human and non-human life (Iengo & Armiero 2017: 50–51). The postcards were sent to the Italian president and Pope Francis in a strong visual demand for justice. The campaign obtained wide mass media coverage in the fight against the region's 'eco mafia'. The postcards represent practices of resistance which tap into 'social and affective experience' which signal that 'the subaltern body is not an easy subject to be governmentalized' (Iengo & Armiero 2017: 54).

Confronting racism

As discussed above, body politics encompasses not only intimate issues of gender and sexuality but also issues of race and privilege. In the following I look at how body politics around racism challenges the global hegemony of whiteness that inform different social imaginaries and social relationships (Carneiro 2016: 38).

#BlackLivesMatter

One of the most well-known body politics movements that confronts racism and calls for global justice is #BlackLivesMatter, founded by three black queer

US women, in response to the killing of Trayvon Martin (Hall 2016). The US-based movement has inspired people from different historical, cultural, socioeconomic and political identities around the world. It is 'a source of solidarity for the survivors of colonization, exploitation, capitalism and police brutality' (Hall 2016: 94). At the core of #BlackLivesMatter is an understanding of black feminism as: 'an embodied, positioned, ideological standpoint perspective that holds Black women's experiences of simultaneous and multiple oppressions as the epistemological and theoretical basis of a pragmatic activism' (black American activist Irma McClaurin, quoted in Hall 2016: 90).

Intersectional and transnational movements

Afro-Latin American feminist movements are also profound sources of inspiration for body politics in a postdevelopment framework (Laó-Montes 2016). Afro-feminisms bring together decolonial feminist and intersectional analysis in a 'multifaceted politics of liberation, nurturing decolonial Afro-feminism as a robust political-epistemic perspective, as a politics of liberation and a strand of epistemologies of the South' (Laó-Montes 2016: 17). This inspiring confrontation to developmentalism emerges out of black/afrodescendant women's ongoing struggles for access to education, health care and employment, which aim 'to invert the course of the history of marginality and oppression' (Alvarez, Kia, Caldwell & Laó-Montes 2016: v). This sense of common struggles in their encounters with the state, development industries, global markets and transnational forces is evident in transnational black feminist diasporas working with their partners (*mestiza* and white) in the fight against patriarchal, class, heteronormative and racist regimes via networking that engages feminist theories, practices and discourses across localities in the Americas (Alvarez, de Lima Costa, Feliu, Hester, Klahn & Thayer 2014).

Such complex inter-weaving of body political activism at local and global levels is a form of 'justice-focused politics that links patriarchal oppression to capitalist, racial, and imperial domination within a modern/colonial matrix' (Laó-Montes 2016: 8). Latin American-based struggles against racism and patriarchal violence are linked also to the decolonial feminist project, including a vision for the good life (*buen vivir, Suma Kawsai*) which have travelled from Latin American to movements across the world (Escobar 2017; Alvarez, de Lima Costa, Feliu, Hester, Klahn & Thayer 2014). Translocal feminist solidarity and decolonial coalition-building around racism, class, gender and sexuality are a key example of intersectional body politics leading the complex challenge to developmentalism involving multiple translations and negotiations.

The challenge to make visible racialised, gendered and oppressed bodies and their exploitation and instrumentalisation in public politics is supported in important and interesting ways by cultural performances. Chicana feminists, for example, engage in the 'embodied and oral transmission of culture' through popular plays such as *Los Vendidos* (Carrillo Rowe 2013: 114). In dramatising the story of Mexican origins, Chicana feminists reproduce embodied power plays around race and body, leveraging 'history, ancestry, and indigenous spiritual practice' as ways to mobilise contemporary social movements (Carrillo Rowe 2013: 128). In these performances, the erotic and sensual body is seen as a source of power that,

> serves as a source of revision and appropriation for social actors to carve out space for counter-hegemonic subject positions and sexual (be)longings [and to provide] an embodied healing practice through which Chicanas and others move through imperial trauma, mobilizing queer and colored intimacies that alternate temporalities at the edges of nation and empire.
> (Carrillo Rowe 2013: 131)

Reworlding and Indigenous resistances

Following on from the above discussions on decolonial feminism and black feminist challenges to developmentalism, Indigenous resistance is another form of body politics connected to non-Western forms of knowledge. Indigenous resistances are key to postdevelopment's search to reimagine and remake the world through pluriversal understandings of life-in-common strategies centred on alternative non-developmental understandings of wellbeing (Escobar 2017). The postdevelopment strategy of learning to unlearn the legacies of the past and lessons of empire have been inspired by Indigenous scholars such as Linda Tuhiwai Smith (2013) and Leanne Simpson (2011). In learning from Indigenous peoples, there is considerable sensitivity about how to write, mindful of the need to 'push away from western feminist movement's tendency to incorporate indigenous women's lives and bodies into the Western feminist movement' (Mithlo 2009: 7). In the postdevelopment project of reworlding it is important to hear Indigenous voices as 'primary knowledge conveyors, as central subjects rather than objects of study' (Mithlo 2009: 8). In this section I set out how body politics in postdevelopment can move towards negotiation, compromise and balance with indigenous feminisms along side Western feminisms' project to challenge, deconstruct and disrupt normative sexual politics (Mithlo 2009: 11).

Caring for country

As a white Australian (though living and working in Europe), I am specifically drawn to Australian Aboriginal worldviews. The idea of reworlding and caring for country responds to decolonial thinking that points to a different kind of body politics that is not only resisting and challenging the normative eurocentric view of the body but also constructing new ways of seeing body politics in postdevelopment practice. Irene Watson, in her writings on caring for country, argues that these views remain largely homeless because of the failure to recognise Aboriginal sovereignty (Watson 2009: 33).[5] Her analysis of Indigenous struggles around land are interwoven in body politics and with white Australian assumptions about their mission to modernise, protect and 'save' Aboriginal women and children from violence in Aboriginal communities. She counters these racialised stereotypes of vulnerable women and children in her analysis of how white Australian law and policy has, 'pursued the extinction, segregation, protection, and assimilation of the settled native [so that] the unsettled native continued to inhabit fringe spaces that the state would not recognize' (Watson 2009: 34). She repositions Aboriginal laws and cultures which have survived from ancient times as key to otherworlding for native and non-native. Even if white Australian law has tried to extinguish Indigenous laws, these laws and cultures thrive and exist outside of main-stream legal imaginings (Watson 2009: 36). She urges for the erasures to stop:

> Who will be the keeper of the languages of country, its songs, and its laws? Who will remain the unassimilated and unsettled native when the threat of the last song sung lies at our feet? And how might humanity walk the land if the singing stops? Will the possibility of an Aboriginal worldview of the now and the future be extinguished?
>
> *(Watson 2009: 37)*

These profound questions speak to the need to keep the 'good place' full of law and spirit in what is generically referred to as the 'Dreaming'. The imaginary of dreaming understands time and place very differently from modern developmental concepts of territory, progress and history. For the Indigenous peoples of Australia there is an

> ever-present place of before, now, and the future, a place that we are constantly returned to [...] The law-way of nungas is not in the past; it is a way of life that is carried with great struggle into the present *Kaldowinyeri* [dreaming in the ancestral language of Watson], where we are met by the ancestors, to begin all over again. [...] Our laws were born as were the ancestors – out of the land. [...] Aboriginal songs have sung the law, and those laws and stories are held in the land to form the song lines that lie across the entirety of the Australian landscape
>
> *(Watson 2009: 38)*

'Caring for country' is equivalent to caring for one's own body; it is an act of self-preservation and self-protection, and it engages a deep knowledge of interdependency of body and land. In this way of understanding body politics is about both past and present so that the embodied self is part of the history and connections spiritually and physically to country. The mistreatment of First World culture has led to bodily and psychic ill-health which can only be rectified when taking care of country, as practised for thousands of years, is once again allowed (Pascoe 2014). 'The struggle for Aboriginal Australians is that they are unable to care neither for country nor for Aboriginal communities and individuals. They are prevented from experiencing good health and well-being in body and soul and place' (Watson 2009: 41).

Watson describes body politics in her native South Australia where the original owners of the land struggle to undertake their traditional (past, present and future) role as caretakers of country. For example, the campaign by the Kupa Pita Kungka Tjuta senior Aboriginal women of northern South Australia has tried to ensure that the Seven Sisters site remained intact in the Billa Kallina region. The story of the Seven Sisters crosses Australian territories and the traditional storytellers based in those places are responsible for passing on the story and thereby caring for the places where the Seven Sisters travelled. Billa Kallina was selected by the white Australian government to develop a nuclear waste repository site. The Campaign by the Kungkas successfully prevented the development of the site (Watson 2009: 51). In the telling of that story Watson writes of the need to uncover 'a colonial violence that is layered on the broken vertebrae of the past' (Watson 2009: 45).

She depicts these ongoing struggles very powerfully:

> As my ancestors walked over the land, they walked in the law. Today it is difficult to walk that law in a car park that lies on your ancestors' graves or in a derelict and toxic mine site that has replaced ceremonial and gathering places where songs were sung across the land [...] It is the unsettled native that will continue to resist, occupy, and expand fringe spaces
> *(Watson 2009: 44–45)*

Dancing resistance

In looking to understand ways of reworlding by learning from Indigenous imaginaries and ways of being, body politics can also be seen in cultural expressions, particularly in music and rhythm which are practiced and felt differently in terms of time and connection to histories and land, while still engaging in modernity.

In Indigenous Australian practice, set within the political and sacred geography of country, this form of body politics recognises in dancing ceremonies multiple presences and encounters (past, future, present) (Bird Rose 2000: 289). Being in country or in place is part of the politics of the dreaming which includes not only human ancestors but also non-human connections to a vast (past, present, future) knowledge of belonging in country. In the dancing, the concept of place and embodied knowledge of it is not static but is part of a moral connection to country. Bird Rose vividly describes her embodied performance of dancing and engaging in dreaming power and how storytelling and sharing knowledge of country are experienced as ways in which 'place and time pour through the person' (Bird Rose 2000: 290).

The body politics of music and rhythm are expressed in hybrid ways by younger generations of Aboriginal people who sing their country and also their protest interweaving different music traditions. For example, as in other parts of the world, hip hop generates 'provocative discourses on the intricate relationships among race, gender, sexuality, class, and nationality' (Hobson & Bartlow 2008: 1). The songs of award-winning Aboriginal hip hop artist Gina Chrisanthopoulos (Little G), such as 'Hip Hop Invasion Day',[6] confront issues of violence, racism and hope for change through resistance. Her hip hop is combined with her work in the community in Melbourne where she was Koori liaison officer at a Secondary College, where she teaches hip hop in juvenile justice institutions and youth organisations.[7]

These examples from Indigenous Australia indicate different kinds of worlds that can be enacted by breaking down the erasures of traditional knowledge, bodies and place. They indicate the importance of listening to Indigenous knowledge which sets out alternative ways to connect with place and time in order to confront and live well in the face of developmentalist, extractivist and modernising violations.

Conclusion

These forms of body politics and body political activism contribute to the debate on postdevelopment in practice by bringing to the fore the issue of how to restore and listen to the intimate, racialised and erased embodied experiences of many peoples. Body politics and body political activism are about postdevelopment resistance to the mainstream development order, in showing possibilities for regeneration and resurgence. Body politics builds on the lived experiences of people and communities which challenge the modern/capitalist development order through different practices that reshape our understanding of the body away from the norms. Learning and listening to those embodied experiences of marginalised people holds out hope that, despite many violent and painful circumstances, postdevelopment scholars and activists can reimagine and remake the world through pluriversal understandings of life-in-common strategies for our shared wellbeing.

Notes

1 Examples of popular writings on body politics are: the Boston Women's Health Collective's bestselling manual *Our Bodies, Ourselves* (2005) published in 31 languages; see www.ourbodiesourselves.org/global-projects/; Eve Ensler's play *The Vagina Monologues* (1996), which has been shown in over 140 countries and translated into almost 50 languages (Braun-Scherl 2015).
2 See Momigliano, A. (2017) 'When left-wing feminists and conservative Catholics unite'. *The Atlantic*, 28 March.
    www.theatlantic.com/international/archive/2017/03/left-wing-feminists-conservative-catholics-unite/520968/.
3 According to the write-up in *The Independent*: 'Her message is clear, girls and women are fed up with forced [hijab]. Let women decide themselves about their own body' (Osborne 2018).
4 See http://womeninblack.org/.
5 Professor Irene Watson is the Pro Vice Chancellor Aboriginal Leadership and Strategy, and Professor of Law with the School of Law, University of South Australia Business School. Professor Watson belongs to the Tanganekald, Meintangk Boandik First Nations Peoples, of the Coorong and the southeast of South Australia. See https://people.unisa.edu.au/Irene.Watson.

6 See www.youtube.com/watch?v=vSzG1s36my8.
7 See www.multiculturalarts.com.au/events2008/littleg.shtml.

References

Aitken, D. (2013) 'Femen leader Inna Shevchenko: I'm for any form of feminism'. *Guardian*. 8 November 2013. www.theguardian.com/world/2013/nov/08/femen-leader-inna-shevchenko-interview.

Alvarez, S., de Lima Costa, C., Feliu, V., Hester, R.J., Klahn, N. & Thayer, M. (eds.) (2014) *Translocalities/Translocalidades: Feminist Politics of Translation in the Latin/a Américas*. Durham, NC: Duke University Press.

Alvarez, S., Kia, E., Caldwell, L. & Laó-Montes, A. (2016) 'Translations across black feminist diasporas'. *Meridians: Feminism, Race, Transnationalism*, vol 14, no 2, pp v–ix.

Bird Rose, D. (2000) 'To dance with time: A Victoria River Aboriginal study'. *The Australian Journal of Anthropology*, vol 11, no 3, pp 287–296.

Braun-Scherl, R. (2015) 'The dialogue about Vagina Monologues'. *Huffington Post*. The Blog. 6 December 2017. www.huffingtonpost.com/rachel-braun-scherl/the-dialogue-about-vagina-monologues_b_6580394.html?guccounter=1.

Butler, J. (1993) *Bodies That Matter: On the Discursive Limits of Sex*. London: Routledge.

Butler, J. (2003) *Gender Trouble: Feminism and the Subversion of Identity*. London: Routledge.

Butler, J. (2011) 'Bodies in alliance and the politics of the street'. *Transversal - eipcp multilingual webjournal*. www.eipcp.net/transversal/1011/butler/en.

Carneiro, S. (2016) 'Women in movement'. *Meridians: Feminism, Race, Transnationalism*, vol 14, no 1, pp 30–49 (trans. Camargo, R.).

Carrillo Rowe, A. (2013) 'Vendidas y devueltas: Queer times and color lines in Chicana/o performance'. *Meridians: Feminism, Race, Transnationalism*, vol 11, no 2, pp 114–146.

Collins, P.H. (2000) 'Gender, black feminism, and black political economy'. *Annals of the American Academy of Political and Social Science*, vol 568, pp 41–53.

Cornwall, A., Correa, S. & Jolly, S. (2008) *Development with a Body: Sexuality, Human Rights and Development*. London: Zed Books.

Crenshaw, K. (1991) 'Mapping the margins: Intersectionality, identity politics, and violence against women of color'. *Stanford Law Review*, vol 43, pp 1241–1300.

Curiel, O. (2016) 'Rethinking radical anti-racist feminist politics in a global neoliberal context'. *Meridians: Feminism, Race, Transnationalism*, vol 14, no 2, pp 46–55.

Deb, B. (2016) 'Cutting across imperial feminisms toward transnational feminist solidarities'. *Meridians: Feminism, Race, Transnationalism*, vol 13, no 2, pp 164–188.

Escobar, A. (1995) *Encountering Development: The Making and Unmaking of the Third World*. Durham, NC: Duke University Press.

Escobar, A. (2008) *Territories of Difference: Place, Movements, Life, Redes*. Durham, NC: Duke University Press.

Escobar, A. (2017) *Designs for the Pluriverse. Radical Independence, Autonomy and the Making of Worlds*. Durham, NC: Duke University Press.

Foucault, M. (1976) *The History of Sexuality. Volume 1*. Harmondsworth: Penguin.

Goni, U. (2017) '40 years later, the mothers of Argentina's "disappeared" refuse to be silent'. *Guardian*, 28 April 2017. www.theguardian.com/world/2017/apr/28/mothers-plaza-de-mayo-argentina-anniversary.

Gopaldas, A. (2013) 'Intersectionality 101'. *Journal of Public Policy & Marketing*, vol 32, no 5, pp 90–94.

Grewal, I. & Kaplan, C. (1994) *Scattered Hegemonies. Postmodernity and Transnational Feminist Practices*. Minneapolis and London: University of Minnesota Press.

Grosz, L. (1994) *Volatile Bodies. Towards Corporeal Feminism*. Bloomington: Indiana University Press.

Hall, K.M.Q. (2016) 'A transnational black feminist framework: Rooting in feminist scholarship, framing contemporary black activism'. *Meridians: Feminism, Race, Transnationalism*, vol 15, no 1, pp 86–104.

Harcourt, W. (2009) *Body Politics in Development: Critical Debates in Gender and Development*. London: Zed Books.

Harcourt, W. (2013) 'Transnational feminist engagement with activism 2010+: A case study'. *Development and Change*, vol 44, no 3, pp 621–637.

Harcourt, W., Icaza, R. & Vargas, V. (2015) 'Exploring embodiment and intersectionality in transnational feminist activist research'. In K. Biekart, W. Harcourt & P. Knorringa (eds.), *Exploring Civic Innovation for Social and Economic Transformation*. London: Routledge, pp 148–167.

Harcourt, W. & Escobar, A. (2002) 'Women and the politics of place'. *Development*, vol 45, no 1, pp 7–14.

Hobson, J. & Bartlow, R.D. (2008) 'Representin': Women, hip-hop, and popular music'. *Meridians: Feminism, Race, Transnationalism*, vol 8, no 1, pp 1–14.

Icaza, R. (2015) 'Testimony of a pilgrimage. (Un)learning and re-learning with the South'. In Z. Arashiro & M. Barahona (eds.), *Women in Academia Crossing North-South Borders. Gender, Race and Displacement*. Lanham, MD: Lexington Books, pp 1–26.

Iengo, I. & Armiero, M. (2017) 'The politicization of ill bodies in Campania, Italy'. In Connolly, C., Panagiota, K. & D'Alisa, G. (eds.), 'Tracing narratives and perceptions in the political ecology of health and disease'. Special Section. *Journal of Political Ecology*, vol 24, no 1, pp 45–58.

Jolly, J. (2016) 'On forbidden wombs and transnational reproductive justice'. *Meridians: Feminism, Race, Transnationalism*, vol 15, no 1, pp 166–188.

Laó-Montes, A. (2016) 'Afro-Latin American feminisms at the cutting edge of emerging political-epistemic movements'. *Meridians: Feminism, Race, Transnationalism*, vol 14, no 2, pp 1–24.

Lugones, M. (2008) 'The coloniality of gender'. *Worlds & Knowledges Otherwise*, 2, pp 1–17. https://globalstudies.trinity.duke.edu/sites/globalstudies.trinity.duke.edu/files/file-attachments/v2d2_Lugones.pdf.

Lugones, M. (2010) 'Towards a decolonial feminism'. *Hypathia*, vol 25, no 4, pp 1527–2001.

McCall, L. (2005) 'The complexity of intersectionality'. *Journal of Women in Culture and Society*, vol 30, no 3, pp 1771–1800.

Mithlo, M. (2009) 'A real feminine journey: Locating Indigenous feminisms in the arts'. *Meridians: Feminism, Race, Transnationalism*, vol 9, no 2, pp 1–30.

Mohanty, C.T. (2003) *Feminism Without Borders. Decolonizing Theory, Practicing Solidarity*. Durham, NC: Duke University Press.

Momigliano, A. (2017) 'When left-wing feminists and conservative Catholics unite'. *The Atlantic*, 28 March. www.theatlantic.com/international/archive/2017/03/left-wing-feminists-conservative-catholics-unite/520968/<.

Ong, A. 2006. *Neoliberalism as Exception*. Durham, NC: Duke University Press.

Osborne, S. (2018) 'Iranian women protest hijab as defiant headscarf demonstrations spread'. *The Independent*. 30 January 2018. www.independent.co.uk/news/world/asia/iran-women-hijab-protests-arrests-no-headscarf-take-off-girl-of-enghelab-street-vida-movahed-a8185611.html.

Pascoe, B. (2014) *Dark Emu*. Broome: Magabala Books.
Petchesky, R.P. (2002) *Global Prescriptions: Gendering Health and Human Rights*. London: Zed Books.
Shildrick, M. (1997) *Leakey Bodies and Boundaries. Feminism, Postmodernism and (Bio) Ethics*. London: Routledge.
Simpson, L. (2011) *Dancing on our Turtle's Back*. Winnepeg: ARP Publishing.
Spivak, G. (1987) *In Other Worlds: Essays in Cultural Politics*. New York: Methuen.
Spivak, G. (1999) *A Critique of Postcolonial Reason: Toward a History of the Vanishing Present*. Harvard, CT: Harvard University Press.
Tamale, S. (ed.) (2011) *African Sexualities: A Reader*. Oxford: Pambazuka Press.
Tuhiwai Smith, L. (2013) *Decolonizing Methodologies: Research and Indigenous Peoples* (2nd edition). London: Zed Books.
Watson, I. (2009) 'Sovereign spaces, caring for country, and the homeless position of Aboriginal peoples'. *South Atlantic Quarterly*, vol 108, no 1, pp 27–51.
Weerawardhana, C. (2018) 'Profoundly decolonizing? Reflections on a transfeminist perspective of international relations'. *Meridians: Feminism, Race, Transnationalism*, vol 16, no 1, pp 184–213.
Wichterich, C. (2019) 'Transnational reconfigurations of reproduction and the female body: Bioeconomics, motherhoods and the case of surrogacy in India'. In C. Bauhardt & W. Harcourt (eds.), *Feminist Political Ecology and the Economics of Care*. London: Routledge, pp 211–229.
Wieringa, S. & Sivori, H. (eds.) (2013) *The Sexual History of the Global South: Sexual politics in Africa, Asia and Latin America*. London: Zed Books.
Young, I.M. (2005) *On Female Body Experience: 'Throwing Like a Girl' and Other Essays*. New York and Oxford: Oxford University Press.

17

MANOEUVRING POLITICAL REALMS

Alternatives to development in Haiti

Julia Schöneberg

In search of practised alternatives to development

Departing from the claim that development has failed and a different form of engagement is necessary, the postdevelopment school has gained prominence in academic discussions from the early 1990s. Reaching further than previous critiques of development intervention, postdevelopment theorists framed the dominant development paradigm from a post-structuralist perspective differentiating immanent processes of economic progress and power/knowledge divides legitimised by European modernity claims.

Although postdevelopment proponents have by no means been homogeneous in theorising,[1] most generally it can be said that they have formulated a rejection of development. They have claimed that the concept 'stands like a ruin in the intellectual landscape', and the time is 'ripe to write its obituary' (Sachs 1992: 1). Consequently, rather than searching refinements or amendments, like 'alternative development' approaches seek to do, postdevelopment calls for alternatives to development. Despite that many postdevelopment arguments have already been put forward more than 25 years ago, most recently calls to 'rethink' development become vocal again.[2] To attempt a rethinking, or even a formulation of alternatives, it first needs to be defined what we mean when we talk about 'development'.

In doing so, it is useful to differentiate between 'big-D' and 'little-d' development. Hart (2001) describes interventionist and intentional processes of the eurocentric post-World War II development project as belonging to big-D Development. In contrast, little-d development is a 'geographically uneven, profoundly contradictory set of historical processes' (Hart 2001: 650). Escobar (1995) argues that civil society groups, grassroots organisations and all groups subsumed under the term 'social movement' have the greatest potential to shape systemic alternatives to structural injustices. He envisions these groups, in response to the failings of the aid system, to build new social structures through social action. Surveying the alternatives to development put forward by the heterogeneous body of postdevelopment writings, Ziai identifies broad entry points of social restructuring based on different, alternative, conceptions of the 'economy (solidarity and reciprocity instead of Homo Oeconomicus and the world market), of politics (direct democracy instead of centralized authorities) and of knowledge (traditional knowledge systems instead of modern science)' (Ziai 2007: 5).

Postdevelopment propositions have been subject to critique, the most fundamental being that they lack practical concepts for action and the romantisation of poverty. An obvious dilemma is the role of exogenous actors (in most cases: Western development actors and agencies in countries of the Global South), since it is precisely that which postdevelopment rejects. In developing the 'big-D'/'little-d' model further, Bebbington, Hickey and Mitlin (2008) relate it directly to the work of these exogenous actors. INGOs are oftentimes trying to propose alternatives to the 'underlying processes of capitalist development', which 'little-d' describes, while their way of engagement is by means of 'big-D' intervention. Although many INGOs consider themselves as exogenous to this system, they remain an endogenous part of the very same system they seek to revolutionise. In this context, Bebbington, Hickey and Mitlin (2008) argue that meaningful alternatives can only be thought of with reference to the differentiation between 'notions of intervention and of deeper forms of political, economic, structural change' (Bebbington, Hickey & Mitlin 2008: 5). Accordingly, the difference between 'big-D' and 'little-d' 'is between a partial, reformist, intervention-specific alternative, and a structure changing, radical, systemic alternative' (Bebbington, Hickey & Mitlin 2007: 1701). If, as Escobar proposes, these structure-changing, radical and systemic alternatives need to source from within the communities, the question remains which INGOs can play in supporting contestations.

Partnership in development projects, despite decades of critical discussion (Fowler 2000; Lewis 1998; Lister 1999; Maxwell & Ridell 1998), remains a concept of intervention considered to be just. Within these interactions questions of poverty and inequality remain too often reduced to depoliticised framings of problems that can be solved through technological or technocratic intervention, rather than requiring structural and hegemonic contestation. Increasingly, the idea of partnership is 'seen as to misrepresent the power of Northern NGOs' (Pearce 2000: 25). Despite attempts at establishing partnerships on an equal level, relations within development projects too often fall in traps of paternalism and co-optation (Schöneberg 2016).

In this context, McKinnon (2007) proposes engaging with 'development-as-politics'. She envisages local actors as selectively engaging in interactions and political confrontations with institutions of the development 'apparatus' (as coined by Escobar 1995), in particular international non-governmental organisations (INGOs) (McKinnon 2007: 779). The aim is to move beyond depoliticised, technical intervention and interaction within mainstream development projects (Ferguson 2003) and support local actors' struggles for systemic social, political and economic change. In contrast to neopopulist proponents of postdevelopment, the underlying conviction here is that it is not necessary to wholly reject cooperation with international (exogenous) actors, but much more important to question ways and underlying, oftentimes paternalistic, assumptions rooted in Western universalist beliefs of modernisation. It needs to be made clear 'who should be inviting whom to participate' (McGregor 2009: 1697) in processes of change. Edwards (1999) imagines these politicised relationships as profound 'constituencies for change' that would comprise transnational networks of actors and institutions struggling jointly to contest structures and representations that maintain poverty and inequality.

In the following discussion, I focus on possible different or alternative conceptions of the economy, politics and knowledge that may be present in Haitian society and in contestations with endogenous and exogenous actors. To do so, I first bring Haitian solidarity peasant groupings to the focus to explore their resistances and emancipatory potential for alternatives to development. Second, I look at the work of *Kolektif Jistis Min* (KJM), a collective of Haitian civil society actors struggling for voice in civil and political spaces and demanding government accountability. Third, I discuss openings for supporting local resistances and analyse problems and limitations arising from external agents' engagement in local political struggles, before I conclude by proposing possibilities for overcoming dualisms through alliance building.

Discourses of social organisation and civil society

In light of this emphasis of the role of social organisation and solidarity groups, one inevitably needs to look at definitions of civil society and social action. Biekart and Fowler observe that while the insertion of the concept 'civil society' into development discourses initially promised a repoliticisation of depoliticised, technical development framings, in practice, it has been employed as a 'conveniently messy empirical category' that could be adapted to different strategies of aid, development funding and cooperation (Biekart & Fowler 2013: 463). In fact, 'civil society' has no single meaning and has served as a term filled with various, sometimes contradictory subscriptions. Pearce (2000: 34) cautions that we should not confuse a normative subscription with an empirical description. 'Civil society' should not be turned into just another development project. To frame my discussion, I follow Bebbington, Hickey and Mitlin's (2008) understanding of civil society as 'constituting an arena in which hegemonic ideas concerning the organiation of economic and social life are both established and contested' (Bebbington, Hickey & Mitlin 2008: 7). This becomes manifest through social action, which Leitner, Sheppard and Sziarto understand as 'forms of contestation, in which individuals and groups organise and ally, with varying degrees of formality, to push for social change that challenges hegemonic norms' (Leitner, Sheppard & Sziarto 2008: 157–158). Thinking of social action as contestation of and over hegemony this then also leads back to above framings of alternatives, which I will now explore by means of two case studies.

Social organisation in Haiti and the relevance of peasant solidarity groups

The Haitian Revolution is almost invisible in European history books, although Haitians have succeeded in one of the most groundbreaking revolutions in history, with demands reaching much further than those of the French Revolution for the Rights of Man. In August 1791, groups of slaves, *mawons*, in the French protectorate of Saint-Domingue fled the plantations and founded settlements and social communities in the mountains to survive the repressive conditions of colonialism and to organise resistance. The declaration of Haitian independence was sealed in 1804 and Saint-Domingue became the *Repiblik Ayiti*. Sourcing from this history, Haiti has had a long tradition of collective organisation, social action, solidarity and resistances that appears in a variety of different forms both in the countryside (Bell 2013a; Smith 2001) as well as in urban areas such as the capital Port-au-Prince (Schuller 2012). The concept of *mawonaj*, an important emancipatory force of the Haitian Revolution, is considered the historical root of Haitian communal action and provides the basis for collective organisation. The kreyol word *mawonaj* translates as 'breaking free' (Trentmann 2003: 82). This form of resistance continues to serve as an 'expression of popular resistance' (Trentmann 2003) and illustrates the importance of fighting for emancipation today.

A starting point for exploring alternatives to development in Haiti are the various peasant[3] groupings and cooperative community organisations, whose societal relevance and importance needs to be read in a historical context.[4] According to estimates, between 60 and 80 per cent of Haiti's population are peasants (Bell 2013b: 14). Nevertheless, the rural population is largely marginalised and is pejoratively termed as *moun andeyo*, 'outside people' (Bell 2013a: 65–67). Rural areas have been sidelined, particularly after the earthquake in 2010, since many efforts of the international community and the Haitian Government were focused on the capital Port-au-Prince, close to which the epicentre of the quake was. In the 1980s and early 1990s neoliberal structural adjustment programmes had a grave impact on agricultural production in Haiti. International donor institutions exercised considerable pressure on the Haitian Government to promote international investments. Import tariffs were cut and systems of social protection were widely privatised (Pressley-Sannon 2017). The rural population suffered the impact of large-scale food imports and the cheap prices with which local producers were unable to compete (Bell 2013b: 67). Peasant-based movements therefore have been the backbone of popular organisation (Mwasaru 2005: 123).

To illustrate Haitian social organisation, I will give a flashlight view on two distinct yet connected formations of social organisation and resistance. Following Escobar and his call to look for 'alternative practices in the resistance [of] grassroots groups' (Escobar 1995: 222), these two examples seem especially suitable. In both cases resistances to interventions is rooted in a long tradition of social organisation, while one can at the same time detect a hybridisation in their actions. Through hybridisation, so-called traditional cultures transformatively engage with assumptions of development as discourse and modernity (Escobar 1995: 219). The first case looks at peasant solidarity groups, while the second explores social resistance against extractivism. The cases are similar in that sense that both involve a certain degree of INGO involvement, but are distinct in terms of how they formulate resistances and organise them.

As a methodological approach to explore alternatives to development, Escobar (1995) has proposed 'ethnographies of the circulation of discourses and practices of modernity' (Escobar 1995: 222) incorporated in development. To analyse findings collected through participant observation and ethnomethodology, I have therefore drawn upon discourse analysis with the aim to illuminate the '(re-)production of knowledge orders and systems of meaning' (Keller 2011: 7).

Case study: Local self-help and solidarity structures – *Oganisasyon Peyizan* (OP)

From the large variety of local self-help and solidarity structures, I illustrate *Oganisasyon Peyizan* (OP), one of many small peasant organisations in the Gros Morne region. I draw on OP as a case study as it can be considered representative of similar organisations (Trentmann 2003). To protect the people I am accountable to, I have changed both the name of the organisation as well as of individuals.

In contrast to inflationary use of the term 'development' in projects of international aid organisations, this term rarely appears in peasant discourses. OP representatives stress that the main goal of the organisation is to support each other. Instead of *devlopman*, development, in narratives the phrase *fè chanjman*, making change, is often employed. This also becomes apparent in the activities of the organisation, where solidarity is continuously invoked. Using the case of the organisational structure of OP, I will now illustrate possible openings among alternative conceptions of economy, politics and knowledge as suggested by postdevelopment proponents (see, for example, the several contributions in Rahnema & Bawtree 1997; Escobar 1995: 215).

I commence with the sphere of economy. OP was founded in 2001 and currently has 2700 members in close to 28 settlements, which are divided into 226 *gwoupman*. OP representatives formulate as clear objectives of the organisation to 'accompany the peasants in the area with seeds, the cultivation of plantain, manioc and beans as well as with micro credits for women to enable them to engage into trading' (OP representatives, personal interview 2013). They maintain that OP's purpose is to improve the life of peasants in social and economic aspects (OP representatives, personal interview 2013). At the time of the first field research in 2013, the organisation received a small sum of core funding through an INGO, which was ceased in 2014. It should be noted, however, that activities described were carried out before the funding relationship had started and continued after its end. Important cornerstones of economic activities are the *gwoupman peyizan*, literally translated as small groups (Smith 2001), which are actively promoted by the OP board. Their core principle is mutual member support by working the *jaden*, their fields, sharing seeds and discussing plans, activities or solving problems in weekly meetings. *Gwoupman* provide their members with small financial support or credit that is sourced from a shared fund. In regular intervals, the training body of OP organises seminars to train and to inform potentially new *gwoupman* and to branch out of these networks of self-help to eventually cover the whole population in the community. By means of such snowballing of self-help networks, OP reaches out as widely as possible. Another important economic activity is a bakery that is run by reinvesting funds that that OP receives through member contributions. There is formality and bindingness through the structures, but the sense of community, of *mete tèt ansanm* (let's put our heads together), appears to be the driving force of this system. Wilfride Bondieu, a member of the training committee, says: 'It is the sense of solidarity that makes *gwoupman* successful'. However, despite the strong reference to traditionally rooted solidarity economies one can also detect a degree of hybridisation (Escobar 1995: 219). OP members envision the organisation taking over the role of external donors in the long term and being able to provide their own financial means to the smaller organisational units in their community. As a mean of income, they have identified tourism and are currently constructing a guesthouse. OP peasants struggle to become self-sustainable. Nevertheless, although they previously stressed their heritage and peasant identity, there seems to be an understanding that economic self-sustenance can only be reached by copying the role model of external donors and by attracting foreign tourists. This is motivated by the realisation that there are 'not yet enough means for us to move forward' (OP representatives, personal interview 2012). This hybridisation may not necessarily impact negatively, since

> groups with a higher degree of economic autonomy and insertion into the market have at times a better chance of successfully affirming their ways of life than those clinging to signs of identity the social force of which has been greatly diminished by adverse economic conditions.
>
> *(Escobar 1995: 219)*

A second sphere for alternatives to development concerns knowledge. Esteva and Prakash (1998) challenge the assumption of a universal, global knowledge and oppose it with radical pluralism. In non-formalised, Indigenous systems, knowledge becomes manifest (e.g., through language, story-telling, songs and proverbs) in ways that find no or little acknowledgement in eurocentric systems of knowledge production and education (Chilisa 2012). In the Haitian context, proverbs and *chante*, songs, play an important role in everyday life and serve in their poignant symbolism to produce irony and mockery, but also comradeship, motivation and appeal during community work (Smith 2001: 48). Many people in the region are not literate, which means that this is also a way of transmitting knowledge. Knowledge and power are closely related. N'Dione et al. argue that 'dominant beliefs become universal when they are no longer linked to the people who have proclaimed them' (N'Dione et al. 2007: 375). Just alternatives to development therefore require that non-Western knowledges are equally heard and recognised as the 'value of the know-how and the beliefs of the poor [...] [becomes] a political act: it amounts to attacking the bases of legitimacy of the dominant power' (N'Dione et al. 2007: 375).

A third sphere for seeking alternatives to development is the realms of politics. OP structures its coordination on three levels. Structures of decision-making are strictly grassroots democratic. However, meetings are oriented towards very practical decision-making on activities that are aimed at specifically identified problems. Despite a strong critique of the state, there is an absence of political claims or demands. This appears to be quite in contrast to Escobar's propositions, who envisioned political resistance resulting from day-to-day struggles on the grassroots level (Escobar 1995: 215, 222). OP is part of a regional network of peasant organisations in the north of Haiti, but has, as have the other members of this network, little to no connection to the national peasant movements that organise protests and marches and struggle for political voice (Bell 2013b: 68–71). During the 2014 annual meeting of this regional network the individual representatives were asked which benefit they felt participation in the network had, to which they responded in unison: *lajan*, money. The acquisition of financial funds became an end rather than a mean. Rather than building on the potentially emancipative political force of their individual groups, the network was not able to articulate a forceful joint political voice challenging the Haitian Government and the structures of the aid system that are restricting their opportunities.

Organisations such as OP demonstrate that in rural Haiti indeed functional and self-reliant, sustainable structures are existent that are grounded in a strong understanding of community and solidarity. However, a major problem is the limited collaboration and reach of the individual groups among each other. While convictions of solidarity and joined forces are strong within the groups, they do not effectively collaborate among each other. A further limiting factor is the presence of international NGOs that conjure up competition with their promises of project funding (Schöneberg 2016: 167). By failing to recognise the existence of local solidarity groups the INGOs have set up parallel structures in the community, which on first sight may appear more attractive to the population. Goods are given out for free or financial incentives are envisaged. However, project cycles only span a limited period, after which the parallel structure disappears, while the initial structure has been severely undermined or even ceased to exist due to lack of support. The community is left without any sustainable structure at all. Rather than supporting constituencies of change or development-as-politics by engaging with Haitian solidarity groups within realms of the economy, knowledge and politics, INGO involvement merely co-opts and weakens local alternatives.

Case study: The *Kolektif Jistis Min* (KJM)

I will now turn to a second case of social organisation, that seems to have a broader impact towards sociopolitical transformational processes. In recent years a large unexploited mineral wealth, in particular gold resources, was discovered in Haiti (Eurasiaminerals 2015). Community members criticise that permits have been awarded 'behind closed doors, with no independent or community oversight' (Ayiti Kale Je 2013). They fear that the 'government is opening the country up to systematic pillage' (Ayiti Kale Je 2013). As a response to these developments, civil society actors have started to mobilise. The *Kolektif Jistis Min* (KJM – Justice in Mining Collective) is a coalition of several Haitian civil society organisations based in the Haitian capital Port-au-Prince and formed in 2012. The coalition's objective is 'to educate affected communities on the consequences of mining in five sectors: the environment, water, work, agriculture and land, as well as to push for national transparency and a debate on mining' (KJM 2016). An explicit aim is to reach out to local associations within the departments who are affected by mining activities, assist with information and consciousness-raising and ensure compliance with human rights (Ayiti Kale Je 2013). For this reason, the *Kolektif* comprises of a network of community educators and mobilisers (KJM 2016).

Since its foundation in 2012, the KJM has evolved and is recognised as an important actor throughout the country in lobbying for just mining. Activities include participation in conferences and exchanges with activists from other Latin American countries that are impacted by mining activities and have experience of mobilisation. An important pillar of the activities are community meetings, *konferans deba*, that are organised for awareness-raising and education about the effects of mining activities and about rights. Instruments of facilitation are photo exhibitions, community radio stations and workshops.

Two United States NGOs, the Christian Development Committee (CDC) and the American Organization for Ending Poverty (AOEP), have supported the activities of KJM, seeking to engage in alternatives to development beyond apolitical development projects. However, despite the fact that relations and interactions were constructed on a well-intended and openminded level, there has been disenchantment on both sides regarding the realities of interactions.

A respondent of the *Kolektif* described money as the main problem. He said the requirement to write a funding proposal was one of the main points where clashes between the realities of a social movement and those of an actor of the development dispositif became obvious as such a detailed proposal responds to the logic of projects rather than to the realities of a movement. The movement needs to respond flexibly to developments that result from actions of the government or mining companies; the chronology of three distinct project stages was not feasible in practice. Although the local INGO coordinator realised arising problems with regard to the proposal it seemed that he did not have sufficient negotiating space with regard to his own coordinator.

Robenson Louis, member of the *Kolektif*, criticised especially the mechanisms of bureaucracy and technocracy he observed in cooperation with CDC. In his view, CDC repeatedly works according to an

> algorithm the organization has constructed itself, that means they do not view the context and social and political realities in which we live. […] They just repeat what is written in the proposal, but that is not always possible. It is the nature of INGOs, they cannot avoid that, they need to be bureaucratic to be eligible for obtaining funding.

KJM not only encountered difficulties with its funding partners but also within the network. The members of the collective are not homogeneous. While some are operating from an NGO structure with salaried staff, others consist of activists and volunteers. This caused disagreements about time requirements for participation and compensation. It became an issue as soon as there were funds available. In order to balance this, it was decided that an external coordinator should be hired who would be salaried; all other members, however, would not. A member of the *Kolektif* described this as a development mentality, *mantalite developmantis*. Projects always carry the promise of money, an opportunity of generating income, especially in a country where the majority of the population is desperately poor. Money can easily become the main motivation to join a movement and multiply structures in order to generate more opportunities. This was not only a problem with KJM itself, but also with regard to the mobilisation of the population in the departments that is based on conscience and commitment rather than on financial benefit. Social movements have to compete with large INGOs, which has led to an intoxication of social relations in the communities (Robenson Louis, personal interview 2016).

Overcoming dualisms through alliance building

Rather than external actors supporting Haitian social movement groups in struggles of resistance and contestation, as has been imagined by development-as-politics proponents, the above analysis has pointed out that attempts at funding social change are prone to dangers of co-optation and depoliticisation.

Considering the negative effects of external funding described, maybe this leads to the assumption that social change is not as such directly fundable. Or, maybe we need to differentiate more before seeking to support 'the social movement'. What appears to be the most important aspect is the level to which the capacities of the social movement overall and the individual organisations are developed. These capacities include the ability for base building, formulating and following a shared agenda and the capacity to build alliances. In terms of funding it could be differentiated between operational funding, the funding of salaries and the funding of particular activities, some forms of which may bear more unintended side effects than others.

In this regard a model of triple alliance building may prove feasible. KJM's cooperation with the Global Justice Clinic at the University of New York (NYU) can serve as an example of such alliance. NYU supports the *Kolektif* in collecting information and provides legal advice. According to Robenson Louis, a member of the *Kolektif*, this is especially important since the Haitian Government denies access to information to Haitian civil society actors. An outcome of the collaboration is the submission of a formal complaint to the World Bank inspection panel regarding the reformulation of the mining law and the preparation of a hearing in front of the Interamerican Commission of Human Rights. In addition, a study, 'Byen konte, mal kalile', was published that evaluates the impact of mining on the environment and human rights violations. Community members in the departments have received training to be able to monitor the quality and quantity of water in their villages.

Analysing the relationships, the three spheres of economy, knowledge and development can be identified. KJM draws on the spiral method of popular education to include and unite the diverse civil society actors in the affected communities (Happel & Nesner 2018). In consecutive group meetings that sought to include everyone in the community, shared experiences were discussed, space for learning and information gaps were identified and a concrete action plan built on common knowledge was formulated. Efforts and actions to unify resistances are not only important in relation to the Haitian state and the government, but also to companies and international financial institutions (such as the World Bank, mentioned above). KJM facilitators are convinced that community members, through working together 'to articulate common problems and proposing common solutions, meanwhile reifying the local, specific knowledge that rural farmers hold [...] become better equipped to confront injustices' (Happel & Nesner 2018).

An important feature of the NYU-KJM collaboration is the fact that it does not comprise a funding relationship and therefore is not prone to the pitfalls of bureaucracy and technocracy that usually lead to paternalistic and co-opting relations inherent in North-South funding. The relation is based on solidarity and the exchange of knowledge. NYU scholars also have access to further networks for lobbying and influence that the Haitian activists would otherwise not have. Nevertheless, respondents have pointed out that the collaboration would not be as successful if KJM did not have core operational funding provided by AOEP. The relevant aspect here is that AOEP is not directly involved in the agenda and processes of the NYU-KJM collaboration, yet the core funding allows the

KJM to remain autonomous. Without this funding it is questionable whether the KJM would have the capacity to partner with an external body such as the Global Justice Clinic, nor to maintain autonomy and resist processes of co-optation and instrumentalisation.

These insights take us back to the demand for development-as-politics. Indeed, it seems that social change as such is not fundable. Yet, a repoliticisation of the issues of poverty and inequality is desperately needed as a technical framing of inequalites in terms of development projects merely reproduces dependencies rather than questioning the underlying structures producing them. In light of the Sustainable Development Goals Agenda 2030 we are well aware that poverty and inequality are global problems; they are not confined to certain geographic locations. Maybe triple alliances like the one described above can provide a path forward for the future, providing that the focus remains on building knowledge and lobbying networks and not on funding. To be able to engage in funding social change, INGOs must explore paths that undermine the logic of the aid system and reform their internal (bureaucratic and technocratic) logic. AOEP is currently undergoing such a process of reformation. Further research will need to evaluate the outcome of this and analyse spaces available for such liberalisation of established funding logics.

Conclusions

The engagements of Haitian peasant solidarity groups illustrate that on a micro level alternative conceptions of economy, knowledge production and politics exist and are actively practised. Nevertheless, these knowledges and practices either remain marginalised, merely maintaining a status quo rather than challenging global structures producing these injustices, or they become co-opted by (well-intended) external funding. A possible starting point for the resolution of this dilemma and a step towards practised alternatives to development, as pursued by Tèt Kole, KJM and others, is transnationalising social movements, something that Appadurai had framed as 'globalization networks from below' (Appadurai 2002: 23). In these networks, collaborations, building on existent and traditionally rooted alternative conceptions, could work to challenge 'little-d' rather than falling into traps of 'big-D' apoliticised funding dependencies. Esteva and Prakash argue that local initiatives can indeed benefit from alliance building with external actors to forcefully voice opposition (Esteva & Prakash 1998: 281). Alternatives to development in that sense can be imagined as networks of transnational individuals, institutions, activists and academics (Leitner, Sheppard & Sziarto 2008: 162). The collaboration of KJM, AOEP and NYU can serve as an example for such an alliance. International NGOs can support social movements' efforts by providing local activists entry points to global political arenas to which they themselves have easy access and thereby shift local contestations of global inequalities towards a transnational dialogue (Shivji 2007: 44).

Notes

1 See Ziai (2006) for a distinction between neopopulist and skeptical postdevelopment strands.
2 See, for example, the Swedish Development Research Conference on 'Rethinking Development' (22–23 August 2018, Gothenburg, Sweden) or Exceed/DIE Conference 'Rethinking Development Cooperation' (18–19 September 2018, Bonn, Germany).
3 The term 'peasant' is often considered pejorative in English language. However, this a term by which *tipeyizan*, small farmers, in Haiti self-identify (Bell 2013a: 11). It 'accurately describes a socioeconomic position in an intact feudal society in a way that the descriptor "farmer", which names only a profession, does not'. (Bell 2013a: 11). Indeed, the role of peasants in Haitian society and their identity is part of a potential that make Haitian peasants possible agents for change.
4 My observations are based on field research in Haiti between 2012 and 2017. All translations from Haitian kreyol are my own. I used methods of participant observation and ethnography. For the analysis of observations I drew on grounded theory and discourse analysis following Keller (2011).

References

Ayiti Kale Je (2013) 'Haitian grassroots groups wary of "attractive" mining law'. *Haiti Grassroots Watch*. http://haitigrassrootswatch.squarespace.com/haiti-grassroots-watch-engli/2013/8/1/haitian-grassroots-groups-wary-of-attractive-mining-law.html.
Appadurai, A. (2002) 'Deep democracy: urban governmentality and the horizon of politics'. *Public Culture*, vol 14, no 1, pp 21–48.
Bebbington, A., Hickey, S. & Mitlin, D. (2007) 'Reclaiming development? NGOs and the challenge of alternatives'. *World Development*, vol 35, no 10, pp 1699–1720.
Bebbington, A.J., Hickey, S. & Mitlin, D. (2008) *Can NGOs Make a Difference? The Challenge of Development Alternatives*. London: Zed Books.
Bell, B. (2013a) *Fault Lines. Views across Haiti's Divide*. Ithaca, NY: Cornell University Press.
Bell, B. (2013b) *Harvesting Justice. Transforming Food, Land, and Agricultural Systems in the Americas*. New Orleans, LA: Other Worlds.
Biekart, K. & Fowler, A. (2013) 'Relocating civil society in a politics of civic driven change'. *Development Policy Review*, vol 31, no 4, pp 463–483.
Chilisa, B. (2012) *Indigenous Research Methodologies*. London: Sage Publications.
Edwards, M. (1999) *Future Postive: International Cooperation in the Twenty-First Century*. London: Earthscan.
Escobar, A. (1995) *Encountering Development. The Making and Unmaking of the Third World*. Princeton, NJ: Princeton University Press.
Esteva, G. & Prakash, M. (1998) *Grassroots Post-Modernism. Remaking the Soil of Cultures*. London: Zed Books.
Eurasiaminerals (2015) 'Eurasian Minerals homepage'. www.eurasianminerals.com/s/haiti.asp.
Ferguson, J. (2003) *The Anti-politics Machine. "Development", Depoliticization and Bureaucratic Power in Lesotho*. Minneapolis, MN: University of Minnesota Press.
Fowler, A. (2000) 'Beyond partnership: getting real about NGO relationships in the aid system'. *IDS Bulletin*, vol 31, no 3, pp 1–13.
Happel, E. & Nesner, S. (2018) 'In Haiti, legal empowerment is resistance against exploitation'. www.openglobalrights.org/in-haiti-legal-empowerment-is-resistance-against-exploitation.
Hart, G. (2001) 'Development critiques in the 1990s: culs de sac and promising paths'. *Progress in Human Geography*, vol 25, no 4, pp 649–658.

Keller, R. (2011) *Diskursforschung. Eine Einführung für SozialwissenschaftlerInnen*. Wiesbaden: VS Verlag für Sozialwissenschaften.

Leitner, H., Sheppard, E. & Sziarto, K.M. (2008) 'The spatialities of contentious politics'. *Transactions of the Institute of British Geographers*, vol 33, pp 157–172.

Lewis, D. (1998) 'Partnership as process: building an institutional ethnography of an interagency aquaculture project in Bangladesh'. In Mosse, D., Farrington, J., & Rew, A. (eds.), *Development as Process: Concepts and Methods for Working with Complexity*. London: Routledge, pp 94–111.

Lister, S. (1999) 'Power in partnerships? an analysis of an NGO's relationships with its partners'. *CVO International Working Paper 5*. London: Centre for Civil Society, LSE.

Maxwell, S. & Ridell, R. (1998) 'Conditionality or contract: perspectives on partnership for development'. *Journal of International Development*, vol 10, pp 257–268.

McGregor, A. (2009) 'New possibilities? shifts in post-development theory and practice'. *Geography Compass*, vol 3, no 5, pp 1688–1702.

McKinnon, K. (2007) 'Postdevelopment, professionalism, and the politics of participation'. *Annuals of the Association of American Geographers*, vol 97, no 4, pp 772–785.

Kolektif Jistis Min (2016) 'Haiti prepares for another potential disaster'. http://haitimining.weebly.com/.

Mwasaru, M. (2005) 'Beyond approaches and models: reflections on rights and social movements in Kenya, Haiti and the Philippines'. *IDS Bulletin*, vol 35, no 1, pp 120–128.

N'Dione, E. et al. (2007) 'Reinventing the present: The chodak experience in Senegal'. In Rahnema, M. & Bawntree, V. (eds.), *1997 The Post-Development Reader*. London: Zed Books.

Nederveen Pieterse, J. (1998) 'Alternative, post- and reflexive development'. *Development and Change*, vol 29, no 3, pp 43–373.

Pearce, J. (2000) 'Development, NGOs, and civil society: The debate and its future'. In Eade, D. (ed.), *Development, NGOs and Civil Society. Selected Essays from Development in Practice*. Oxford: Oxfam GB, pp 15–44.

Pressley-Sannon, A. (2017) *Many hands: Contemporary Haitian Peasant Struggles and Triumphs* (English edition). n.p.

Rahnema, M. & Bawtree, V. (eds.) (1997) *The Post-Development Reader*. London: Zed Books.

Sachs, W. (ed.) (1992) *The Development Dictionary. A Guide to Knowledge as Power*. London: Zed Books.

Schöneberg, J. (2016) *Making Development Political. NGOs as Agents for Alternatives to Development*. Baden-Baden: Nomos.

Schuller, M. (2012) 'Genetically modified organizations? understanding & supporting civil society in urban Haiti'. *The Journal of Haitian Studies*, vol 18, no 1, pp 50–73.

Shivji, Issa G. (2007) *The Silences in the NGO Discourse. The Role and Future of NGOs in Africa*. Oxford: Fahamu.

Smith, J.M. (2001) *When the Hands Are Many: Community Organization and Social Change in Rural Haiti*. Ithaca, NY: Cornell University Press.

Trentmann, C. (2003) 'Mète Tèt Ansanm. Sozialkapital in ländlichen Gebieten Haitis'. Dissertation am Fachbereich Sozial- und Kulturwissenschaften, Universität Gießen.

Ziai, A. (2006). 'Post-development: Ideologiekritik in der Entwicklungstheorie'. *Politische Vierteljahresschrift*, 47 Jg., Heft 2, pp 193–218.

Ziai, A. (2007) 'Development discourse and its critics: An introduction to post-development'. In Ziai, A. (ed.), *Exploring Post-development. Theory and Practice, Problems and Perspectives*. New York: Routledge, pp 3–17.

18

TECHNOAFFECTIVE REINSCRIPTIONS

Networks of care and critique 'inside' and 'outside' of Europe in the age of precarity

Anyely Marín Cisneros and Rebecca Close

From the position of the reconstruction and disaster economy, an image of destruction is the perfect trick. First, it intensifies speculation over new markets for development (an image of destruction in Syria hikes the potential value of reconstruction contracts, while an image of death in the Mediterranean inflates the income of privatised border control surveillance agencies). Then as the image circulates through the global news track it repeats a racist fixing of certain bodies to certain contexts, cultivating in the spectator an indifference routed in seeing (and not seeing). How can we, as expert and amateur spectators, account for what engineers participating in current machine learning and algorithmic vision experiments perhaps already know: that the gaze is codified through technoscientific intervention?

Observing the relationship between seeing and not seeing and racism as an affectivity might be one way to comprehend and resist the link between image technologies and financial speculation. This is a link that underlies the transformation of twentieth-century development as the project of moral and economic progress to the twenty-first-century development industry's approximation to disaster as a (private security or NGO) business opportunity. We are drawn to the question of scale that characterises the interventions that resist the temporal and spatial coordinates of twentieth- and twenty-first-century development – highlighted by this publication's review of *postdevelopment in practice*.

Over the last few years we've been working to sustain the question of what strategies are useful for intervening in the context of digital (data) financial capitalism – a regime characterised by the hyper-circulation of images, unprecedented affective indifference, the making redundant of human labour forces (creating what Achille Mbembe (2016) calls 'superfluous populations') and the hyper-financialisation of war. We have come across a wealth of experiences of resistance emerging from across the academic, artistic and activist practices of the feminisms,[1] decolonial studies and the anti-racisms. We would like to take the opportunity to consider how these diverse perspectives and activities have forged *networks of critique and care* that actively respond to the technologies and infrastructures of twentieth- and twenty-first-century development.

The scale of our work is rooted by the lesbian-feminist figure of the *amateur-amante*, a term that names a process of research but also a system of self- and collective production that operates at the very margins of the fields of technoscience and art knowledge production. The *amateur-amante* moves between formalised institutions and informal networks, sensitive to the distinct hierarchies and forms of production of each. The *amateur-amante* acts to visibilise the routes of transmission of ideas and knowledge that travel between us and other networks of care and critique, distributing and diffusing the traditional direction of knowledge transmission (from scientist to academy; from teacher to class; from artist to public). We might also talk about this scaling down from 'infrastructures' to 'interventions' as a question of resistance, or, as Berthold Brecht (2000) writes, the production of an agent 'listener';

> The increasing concentration of mechanical means and the increasingly specialised education – trends that should be accelerated – call for a kind of rebellion by the listener, for [her] mobilisation and redeployment as a producer.
>
> *(Brecht 2000)*

'The mechanizing of education' has been accelerated, intensified and rationalised in the age of 'machine learning' and calling on Brecht's rebel listener is as urgent as ever. The rebel listener answers to the (impossible) scale of financial capitalism by guaranteeing the (possible) exercise of situating oneself within and among its (infra)structures and economies. Rebel listening thus operates for us in relation to notions of 'location', 'context' and 'situatedness', anchoring the intentions and structuring the methodologies of our work.

One central methodology, for example, is inhabiting the distance between the space of the workshop and other processes of production such as collective performance or reading, screening and audio composition. In a recent article (Close & Marín 2018) we explored the workshop as a space in which the distinction between the pedagogical and the performative exercise can be productively interrupted – where the listening, reading and voice techniques rehearsed in the workshop contribute to the actual fortifying and strengthening of collective alliances and collective voices within the group. We take advantage of the workshop as a site of production of dialogue (but also conflict), spontaneity (and structure), experimentation (and rehearsal) in order to, on one hand, collectively construct questions that may be marginalised in academic or arts spaces and, on the other hand, test strategies for intervening in the local context. The space of the workshop is above all a space of listening: listening to the context as the participants, who often bring with them particular questions and struggles, define it. The questions we have co-constructed across the various projects in collaboration with other collectives, associations, artists, precarious workers and poets are, for example: what is the connection between gentrification and coloniality? What is the material of inscription of the coloniality of time? How do the anti-colonial and anti-racist activisms and artistic practices contribute to the invention of decolonising technologies? What technologies of silence can be named? How does the codified gaze structure our capacity to respond to each other and to political crisis? What is the precise history of the codified gaze (here and now)? What technologies of seeing can be named? Do the global mappings of migration include 'sexiles'? Is coloniality a sensibility? How can a sensibility be dismantled?

Precisely because the workshop is both performative and pedagogical – both a temporary structure and sensitive to context – we see it as a possible site for practising rebel listening. In this chapter we reflect on a number of recent projects as strategies for intervening in a technoaffectivity governed by visual and aural (technological and infrastructural) excess, arguing that technoaffective reinscriptions activated from the position of the rebel listener may be one way to 'practise postdevelopment'.[2]

Technologies of silence, archival power and the sonic action

Radio Europe (2015) was a performance consisting of a composition of audio fragments, music and live reading, enacted for a conference held at the University of Rennes II, France in April 2015. The work departs from the premise that especially in the context of the European Union, where censorship is itself banned – according to Article 11 of the EU Charter of Fundamental Rights on 'freedom of expression' – the silencing of critical voices operates in different ways, finding alternative logics. The conference happened to coincide with the mediatised political crisis in France surrounding the murder of workers and associates of the French journal *Charlie Hebdo* in Paris. In a context in which public mourning was being transformed into a nation-wide performance of racialised belonging, *Radio Europe* aimed to strengthen alliances between poets, activists, academics and artists at the conference and raise awareness of the subtlety and complexity of diverse forms of censorship.

The title of the work references Frantz Fanon's (1963) critique of the CIA-funded radio network 'Radio Free Europe'. Its transmissions were present across Europe and North Africa throughout the postwar period. Radio Free Europe has since been recognised for its imperial role in dismantling communist institutions. As Fanon's critique of radio as a powerful affective tool highlights, in some cases censorship operates not through techniques of prohibition but through amplification. We were further inspired by the questions posed by US poet and critic Adrienne Rich (1978), who writes in a poem entitled 'Cartographies of Silence',

Silence can be a plan/rigorously executed/the blueprint to a life/It is a presence/it has a history a form/Do not confuse it/with any kind of absence.

(1978: 17)

Rich's thesis that silence is produced and that the forms of production can be traced and named informed our selection of archival material that was either inscribed with the 'noise' of official national memory or by practices that speak rather to and from feminist and decolonial critiques of nationalisms.

The performance gathered a number of live and pre-recorded voices around the questions 'what is the sound of censorship' and 'how loud is silence', among them poets and musicians who have been imprisoned in France for critiquing nationalist discourses in their music. Included among the audiovisual material selected were fragments from the soundtrack to Jean Luc Godard's 1993 *Ici et ailleurs* (*Here and Elsewhere*) and Michael Powell and Emeric Pressburger's 1946

FIGURE 18.1 *Radio Europe*, performance, Rennes, April 2015. Gabrielle Leroux, Johanna Renard and Anyely Marín Cisneros reading the performance script.
Photo credit: Richard Guilbert. Image courtesy the artists.

film *A Matter of Life and Death* – a British Technicolor fantasy film about a British pilot who survives a plane crash and falls in love with a North American radio operator. While the former problematises notions of image and noise – nation and official systems of representation – the latter takes them for granted in its hyperbolic repetition of dominant postwar narratives around European-North American, Anglo-American relations. A presenter figure (a role read by the conference's organiser, Johanna Renard) led the audience through these sonic fragments, interspersed with spoken quotes from a range of poetic-political texts including poems by Audre Lorde and Adrienne Rich. The format of *Radio Europe*, whereby invitations to read fragments of manifestos and poetic texts were extended to conference participants, sought to create complicity through simple exercises in reading and listening.

Also key for the development of this work was Dutch theorist Fatima El-Tayeb's analysis of poetry, sound, music and discursive or theoretical production across European hip hop and Black feminist practices during the 1980s and 1990s (2006). Studying such transatlantic dialogues between, for example, US poet Audre Lorde and Afro-German poet May Ayim, as well as the appropriation of US-rooted musical techniques on the part of European hip hop artists such as La Rumeur in France, Black Tiger in Switzerland or Italian-Egyptian rapper Amir Issa, El-Tayeb argues that these transnational and translocal informal networks operated a powerful critique of the European nation-state's official discourses (on migration, race, belonging, history) as well as providing support in the face of the violence of racialisation and sexualisation at the level of everyday life. Writing on the sonic in relation to Haitian anthropologist Michel-Rolph Trouillot's notion of 'archival power', El-Tayeb writes:

> The lack of attention to the sonic as opposed to the visual in analysis of twentieth and twenty-first century mass technologies partially explains the persistent exclusion of African diaspora populations from the histories of technological progress.
>
> *(2006: 56)*

El-Tayeb's work advanced our approach to notions of sonic critique in the context of Europe, and influenced our decision to frame this work as a sound- or voice-based action. These referents continue to inspire a resistance to visual or overly transparent forms of representation in the projects that deal specifically with notions of archive, memory and the (racialised and sexualised) body. Because of the linguistic make-up of the readers (which included native Castellano, French and English speakers), we used a blank video with subtitles that translated the material into either English or French, depending on the source. We decided to read the script from behind this video projection. Many in the audience thought that the work was a video work and were surprised to see the readers walk out from behind the screen after the performance finished. This incorporation of moments of hiding and showing processes of production (visibilising or obscuring the 'liveness' of the reading and sound composition) is key in relation to the Brechtian notion of rebel listening. We hoped this testing of the audience's mechanisms of recognition of visual and sonic formats would highlight the role of the senses in processes of consumption and production of official (national) memory.

Radio Europe as a *performance* (and not a broadcast) aimed to reinscribe and scale down the radio technique of amplification to serve the strengthening of a small network of critical voices, contained within the architecture of the space. To the extent that the exercise cannot be repeated in the same way with the same materials in a different context, we hope that this methodology was successful in enacting a situated poetics-politics – an exercise in rebel listening.

Transmission, networks of care and critique and the cannibal fugue

Exilio Tropical (2016–2018) – a video trilogy composed of fragments of live and pre-recorded performance and narrations of processes of archival research – intensifies the question around amplification as a technology of silence, extending it towards an analysis of 'the tropics' and 'the tropical' as a technique of hyper-production of subjectivity regulated by an aesthetics of *alegria*, musical rhythms and geopolitical sexual fictions. *Exilio Tropical*'s first chapter, *How to Write a Tropical Disease/How to Write a Manifesto* (2016–2017), is situated in the early years of the formation of the field of tropical medicine from the perspective of inhabitants of the city of Guayaquil, Ecuador, where we lived and worked for nearly two years. The work narrates the process of researching how the yellow fever prevention campaigns, directed between 1880 and 1919 across Central and South America and Asia with resources from the Rockefeller Institute for Medical Research and the London School of Hygiene and Tropical Medicine, crossed with the more ideological projects of 'moral regeneration' in urban centres.

In 2016, we invited local poets and activists from Guayaquil to perform a script consisting of quotes from documents pertaining to the hygiene and tropical medicine discourses and responded to through a 'counter-archive of contagion' – poetry and manifestos written throughout the twentieth century that name the pathologising tendencies of the hygiene movement. These fragments evidence the moment in which the model of the 'hygienic' (European) city was being imported and imposed as part of a wider neocolonial restructuring of resources across the North/South divide. The hygiene movement would of course later deeply inform the official discourses of development after the 1940s. By focusing on the ways in which the Rockefeller Institute actually intervened in the daily life of the inhabitants of the city in Guayaquil, mixing irreverently yellow fever disease prevention techniques with social cleansing (handing out hygiene pamphlets, transforming domestic practices of water collection and use but also informing legislation to prohibit sex work and *vendedores ambulantes*), the

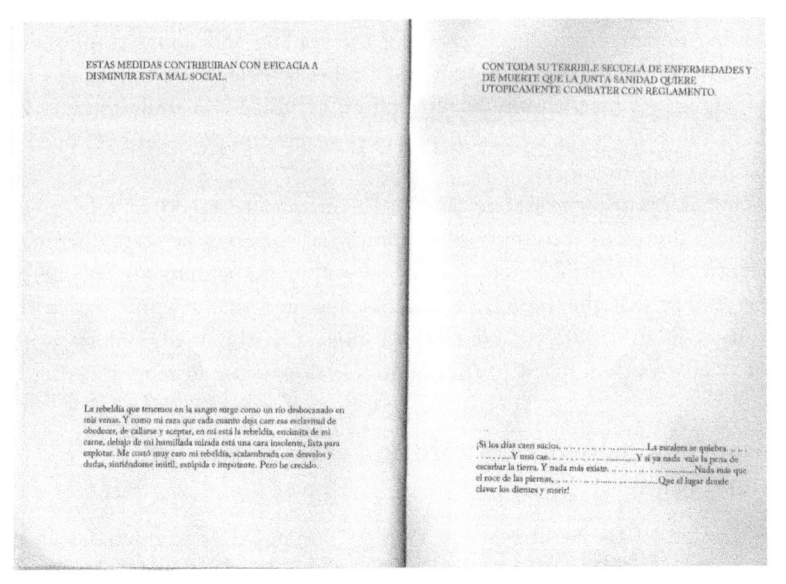

FIGURE 18.2 *How to Write a Tropical Disease/How to Write a Manifesto*, performance, 2016. Scan of a page of the performance script. Image courtesy the artists.

work tries to visibilise how erroneous medical theories worked to validate new forms of racial and sexual surveillance.

The performance, held in a domestic setting in Guayaquil, was, like *Radio Europe*, an exercise in activating a counter-archive. It was also intended as a homage to the many theorists, critics, poets, artists and activists who have resisted multiple forms of pathologisation, reinscribed and intensified in times of public health crisis from the nineteenth century onwards. As well as forwarding a critique of the management of disease as a capitalist method for regulating markets (controlling port commerce and informal economies such as sex work and street selling), the work attempts to etch in the memory of the city a vulnerable but strong network of care and critique. The script connected the pro-sex manifestos of Ecuador-based organisation *la Marcha de las Putas* to a set of manifestos written in the 1960s and 1970s by sex workers across the USA and Europe. The script also aimed to connect the writings of Guayaquileñan poet David Ledesma, Chilean poet Francisco Casas, US poet Essex Hemphill and Chicana writer Gloria Anzaldúa with the work of writers and activists currently working in Guayaquil, such as Maria Auxiliadora Balladares and Francisco Santana, who both participated in the performance as readers of the script. Both writers have produced poetic-political work that challenges the pathologising of dissident sexualities and critical voices in the context of the city of Guayaquil itself.[3]

It was important to account for the technological and representational differences between the management of yellow fever in the nineteenth century and the management of HIV and Aids in the twentieth and twenty-first – the latter characterised by a

FIGURE 18.3 *How to Write a Tropical Disease/How to Write a Manifesto*, performance, Guayaquil, 9 September 2016. María Auxiliadora Balladares and Francisco Santana reading a text of various fragments of manifestos and archival documents.

globalised hyper-visuality and the development of the pharmaceutical industry. However, it was also important to open a space to reflect on the need to experiment with diverse strategies of resistance to multiple forms of pathologisation – especially with the view towards the formation of unlikely alliances. In this sense our approach to disease, urbanity, medical practice, capitalism and its resistances is deeply informed by Paul B. Preciado's (2013) work on the Aids crisis as a key moment in the development of neoliberalism. Particularly important is Preciado's critical rereading of Aids activism as a means of intervening in new popular authoritarian forms of representation and new forms of racial and sexual surveillance – a transformed politics of the body the author names the 'pharmacopornographic regime'. Similar to *Radio Europe*, we were interested in *scaling down* the transmission – from the hysteria, paranoia and obsession that characterises mass-mediatised narratives of contagion to the careful exchanges of advice or poetry that constitute feminist and decolonial networks of care and critique.

Entitled *Llamando al mago* (*Calling the Magician*) (2017), the second chapter departs from a text by Aìme Césaire of the same name in which the artist critiques the exoticising gaze of the surrealist movement and particularly Andre Breton's fascination with the tropics as a site of the primitive and the unconscious. The immediate context of the work is the Venezuelan passport crisis (affecting Venezuelans since 2016), which also effectively interrupted our working process, as we were not able to take up an invitation to travel to North America and present work there together.[4] The global migratory control system and the Venezuelan passport crisis thus became a protagonist in the work, informing the format of presentation as we composed a series of 'video posters' and sent them to each other in response to the impossibility of being present in the same place.

Llamando al mago is conceived to be a live performance in which one of us sits before an audience and opens and plays a number of videos while generating other videos live, such as skype calls or 'image sonifications' (images turned into sound using sketch code in processing). The work was first performed at a dance studio in New York with the participation of artists and performers Damali Abrams, Dalida Maria Benfield and Naomi Elena Ramirez – all engaged in arts practices that explore and resist dominant forms of racialisation and sexualisation, as well as experiences of migration and border-crossing. The audience members, around 15 artists, activists, teachers and students, had all participated in a one-hour workshop before the performance in which we shared and

FIGURE 18.4 *Llamando al mago*, video performance, 2017. Film still. Image courtesy the artists.

FIGURE 18.5 *Llamando al mago*, video performance, 2017. Film still. Image courtesy the artists.

discussed some of the texts used in the performance script, including Aime Cesaire's *Calling the Magician*. The work was performed for a second time at an event in Barcelona entitled 'Selfcare is Warfare', curated by Julia Morandeira, a Madrid-based writer and curator whose research into artistic practices that enact an 'affective exchange' has nurtured our own.

Llamando al mago is a 'sketch' in the sense of being 'rough'; there is an intention to share the process of generating and stitching audio-visual material together. The video does not represent us but rather speaks back to us as we traversed a moment structured by a series of contradictions: travel versus travel restrictions; the capacity to 'represent' versus the incapacity to 'present'; conversations versus interruptions; hyper-translatability (of digital modes of production) versus a commitment to opacity.

FIGURE 18.6 *Llamando al mago*, video performance, 'Selfcare is Warfare', Bar Ocaña Barcelona, 2017.

Photo credit: Marc Serra. Image courtesy Sant Andreu Contemporani.[5]

As well as referencing the work of Césaire, the format – a composition of material culled from the media and fragments of pre-recorded poetry and music – borrows much from UK filmmakers such as Pratibha Parmar and Isaac Julien. *Llamando al mago* in fact quotes a scene from Parmar's experimental documentary film *Reframing Aids* (1989) – an ensemble of interviews with a number of British artists and activists (including Julien, Stuart Marshall and Sunil Gupta) about the Aids crisis as a crisis not only in public health provision, but in national narratives around race and sex. Parmar's *Reframing Aids* is a powerful document evidencing the personal and collective experiences of the changes to immigration legislation and police practices put in practice in the UK as a result of the Aids media hysteria. By intervening into the visual syntax of the crisis with a chorus of 'talking heads' from among the artist, activist and Black British communities, Parmar (1989) fragments the dominant subject of the epidemic and successfully explores the wider implications of the crisis in terms of what David Harvey has called, 'the increasingly contested politics of daily life' (2012).

While television and televisual discourses are the immediate context of intervention, the work is concerned above all with resisting intensified police surveillance and violence at the level of the street and daily life. The work's affirmation of collectivity and its focus on alliances between diverse communities can be seen as strategy for resisting the neoliberal stratification of identities, heightened during the 1980s and 1990s. We would argue that Parmar's video work from the 1980s until present is dedicated to representing and strengthening what we have been calling networks of care and critique.

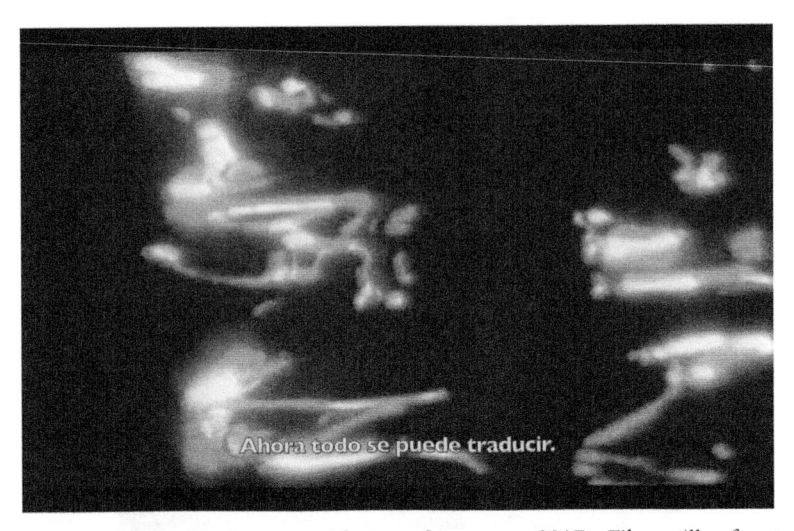

FIGURE 18.7 *Llamando al mago*, video performance, 2017. Film still of extract from Pratibha Parmar's *Reframing Aids* (1989), which uses an extract of Isaac Julien's *This is Not An AIDS Advertisement* (1987). Image courtesy the artists.

This interruption to the seamless flow of neoliberalised identity is underscored by a scene in Parmar's *Reframing Aids* in which the director uses a particular scene from Isaac Julien's *This is Not an AIDS Advertisement* (1988), a work that consists of video-manipulated Super 8 sequences of the Grand Canal in Venice footage of Julien with his lover and images of the work's title flashing in neon lights – all set to a soundtrack that repeats the lyrics 'feel no guilt in your desire'. *Llamando al mago* quotes Parmar's quoting of Julien's river scene as a means of referencing the proposal we understand to be at the centre of both Julien and Parmar's work: if identity becomes the site of production of desire – that is, if it were put in continuous movement like a river or video syntax itself – it would be more difficult to capture, exclude, silence or amplify.

In our work we are interested, above all, in bringing the engagements with other thinkers and makers to the centre of the work. This becomes a method for our own process of self- and collective production, essentially the work of assemblage that is not only in progress but *in motion*. We thus understand the feminisms not as identities but as a methodology that allows autonomy over what is consumed and produced.

In *Exilio Tropical*'s third chapter, titled *Fuga Caníbal* (2017), we developed these questions around movement, consuming and producing through the enactment of a literal (and metaphorical) musical 'fugue' – the moment in which the orchestra's diverse instruments 'exit' the performance. Here a number of lines of research are superimposed. The title cites Viveiros de Castro's (2010) metaphysics of the cannibal, in which the author articulates the possibility of 'betraying those who have betrayed you' – a strategy for responding to systems

FIGURE 18.8 *Fuga Caníbal*, video, 2017. Film still.

of representation that claim to speak for or on one's behalf. *Fuga Caníbal* departs from the representational gap that exists between the (lack of) history of 'lesbian art' in the 'tropics' and the hyper-representation of the 'sensual tropical woman'. The voice of *Fuga Caníbal* references the voice of the 'sexile', an inscription of experiences of exile and immigration across South and Central America during the decades of dictatorships and the Aids crisis – exemplified in the writings of Marsha P. Johnson in the USA, Nestor Perlongher in Argentina and Pedro Lemebel in Chile. *Fuga Caníbal* consumes the work of the trans-sexile poets and activists as a tactic for reinscribing a Caribbean lesbian sexuality in a space defined by intense erasure of histories and practices of lesbian critique and dissidence.

For *Fuga Caníbal*, the sexile also functions as a technology of seeing. From this perspective, which takes into account the effects of absence and excess (silence and amplification) as a mode of production of subjectivity, the forms of sexualisation of the Bolivarian socialist woman in Venezuela appear as a variation in a wider genealogy of exoticised sexual and racial fictions that reach back to nineteenth century visuality, evidenced in the work of Paul Gauguin and, later, the surrealist movement's artists and poets. Pointing to this fact that de-Westernising revolutionary projects have appropriated European forms of visuality, helps us to problematise reductive readings of what it means to be either 'inside' or 'outside' of a country or continent. Here exile and migration are explored rather as conditions that regulate and produce intimacy or alienation, exclusion or belonging, affective reinscription or disaffectedness. *Fuga Caníbal* constructs a flight from both absence and presence, from the lack of lesbian (art) history and the over-representation of the tropical woman (worker). The cannibal devours and eats everything in her path, to the extent that consuming allows for the (self- and collective) production of a desiring subject.

Technoaffective reinscriptions

Our more recent work, *Reinscriptions* (2018), is a publication that collects a series of 'annotations' in the form of essays, poems and fictional narratives. The work departs from the popular mediatised debates around machine learning and computer vision. *Reinscriptions*, as with all our projects, was developed through constant engagement with colleagues, students, activists and interlocutors – the space of the workshop was, as ever, a key space of commitment and complicity. A series of workshops, entitled 'Reinscriptions' and 'Algorithms of Race' respectively, sought to connect questions relating to the technoscience of seeing with previous research around European racial laws (the Black Codes) and the history of the management of illness in urban centres as it crosses with the history of the tradition of data visualisation. In the *Reinscriptions* workshop, given as part of the 'Escuelita' programme at CA2M in Madrid – a pedagogical 'art school' experiment – 2017, we annotated a set of extremely diverse images: nineteenth-century 'data' visualisations or information maps, excerpts from the Black Codes, images culled from the media and finally microscopic sketches produced by seventeenth-century scientists as they experimented for the first time with the technology of the microscope. This space of collective and performative annotation was fundamental for the development of the structure of the publication. Parallel to this, Anyely Marín activated the workshop 'Algorithms of Race', which was offered twice in the self-organised autonomous activist space T.I.C. T.A.C – run by a collective of migrant and sex-worker activists and artists in Barcelona. In this workshop participants studied in more detail the Spanish and French Black Codes and reflected on present notions of the 'codified' gaze.

Reinscriptions (2018) the publication develops the questions explored in both workshops around codified vision by focusing on two particular technologies of seeing and two moments in a possible history of the codified gaze. The first is the transformation of the White population into a surveillance camera through the European Black Codes. The essay 'Algorithms of Race' explores in detail how, from 1607 onwards, the White population comes to be defined by their role in maintaining public space (roads, squares etc.) as White. This segregation was intensified by formal apartheid laws, such as the prohibition of inter-racial marriage and the excessive control over the children and sexual reproduction of the racialised and enslaved. A separate fictional text, entitled 'My Difference/My Indifference', departs from research around the first scientific engagements with

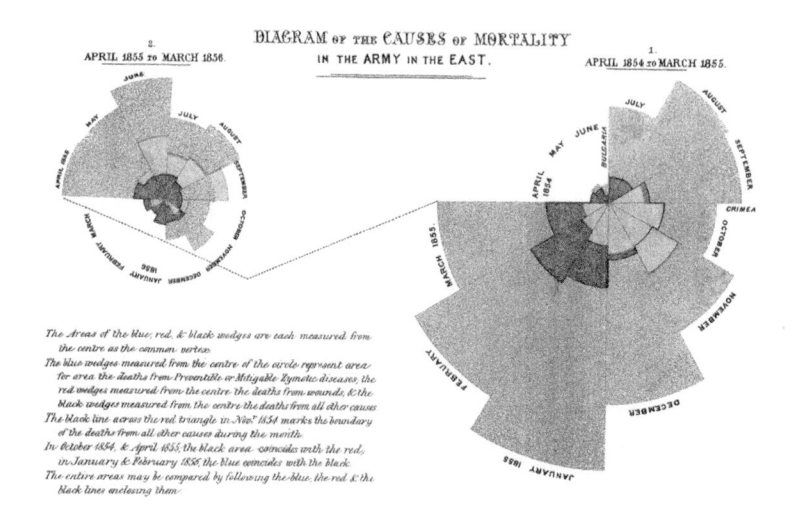

FIGURE 18.9 'Diagram of the causes of mortality in the army in the East' by Florence Nightingale was published in *Notes on Matters Affecting the Health, Efficiency and Hospital Administration of the British Army*, sent to Queen Victoria in 1858.

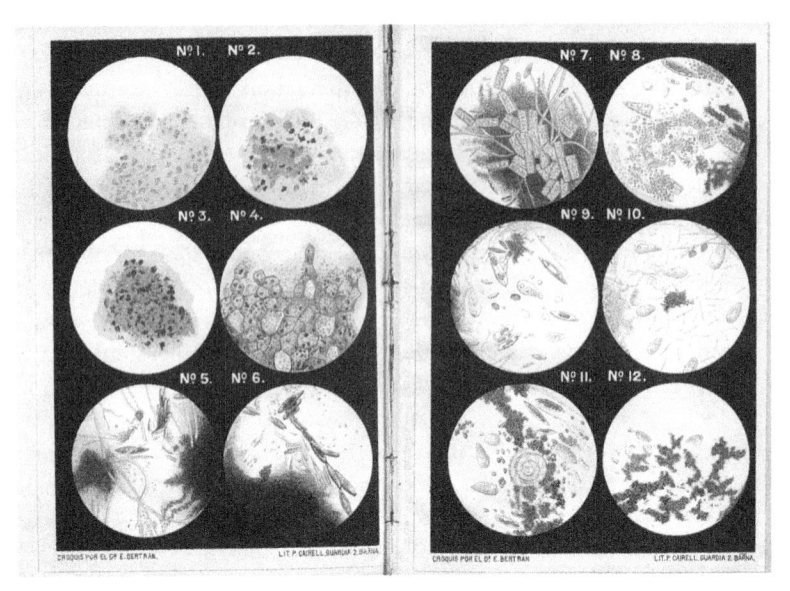

FIGURE 18.10 Chromolithographs (produced in Catalonia during the 1872 yellow fever epidemic). Sourced in the Cataluña Biblioteca Nacional. Image courtesy the artists.

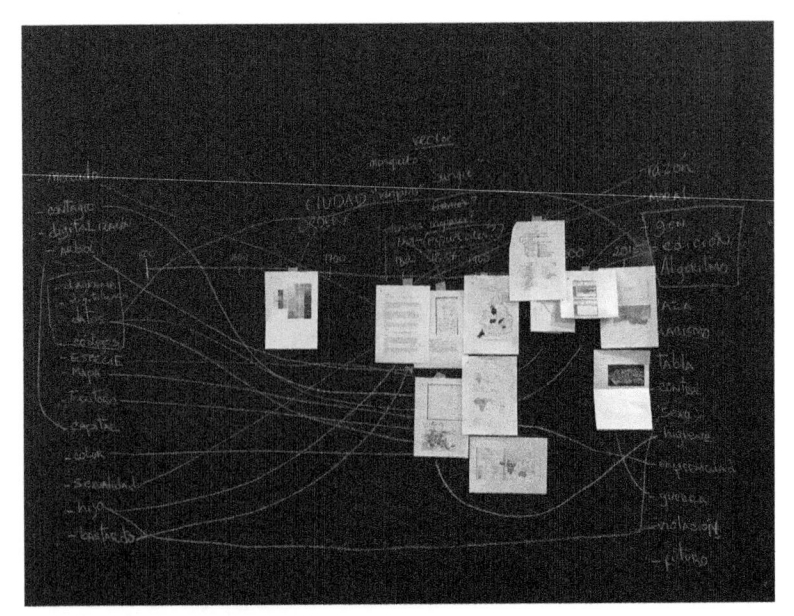

FIGURE 18.11 Photo taken during the workshop 'Reinscripciones', part of the 'Escuelita' public programme at CA2M, Madrid, curated by Julia Morandeira. Here, a group of participants named and ordered a corpus of images from the history of data visualisation (from maps to phylogenetic trees) on a timeline and connected them to keywords. Photo credit: Julia Morandeira. Image courtesy CA2M.

the technology of the microscope, as a parallel (seventeenth-century) technology of seeing. This was the moment of the 'amateur scientist' – 'amateur' to the extent that the sciences and scientific research, while key in validated colonialism and coloniality, were not yet directly plugged into capitalist forms of production as they would be from the nineteenth century onwards.

Distinct from previous projects that dialogue with a particular located space and context, *Reinscriptions* was conceived as a dispersed action; it is not clear in the presentation of the texts in the book who is writing, when, for whom and where. In this sense the context of intervention of the work is the delirious multiplication of forms of representation and the condition of dislocation and fragmentation of work that characterises data capitalism. Similarly experimenting with the representational method of 'flight' or 'fugue', the work proposes a continuous movement through and between diverse languages, vocabularies and practices of high- and low-tech: from dream maps to data visualisations, from algorithms to race laws, from the human eye to the surveillance camera.

With *Reinscriptions* – the workshops and the publication – we were interested in pinpointing, discussing and attempting to invert not only the technologies of seeing but the affectivities associated with them, both of which are palpable today – first a modern paranoid obsession with the surveillance of race across public space and second a kind of innocent curiosity in relation to technological and scientific experiment.

The terms *amateur-amante* and *disobedient observation* are proposals for future interventions into these particular technoaffectivities, which we see as being reinscribed in current debates around machine learning and surveillance technologies. Later we reflected on how the workshops in this project were an important space to resist the (dominant seventeenth-century) technologies of seeing that the publication would later name and study. We saw that the workshop could be seen as a form of intervention into a technoaffectivity characterised by the amateur scientist's 'innocent curiosity' to the extent that it directed this curiosity towards the 'codes' of data capitalism itself (the phylogenetic tree and the neurotic studies of virus, colonial maps and the production of data, the politics of the body and the silencing of the voice in urban centres). This point about the collective and temporarily contained space of the workshop emphasises the defining feature of the figure of the *amateur-amante* and the technoaffective practices of *disobedient observation, fuga caníbalismo* and *rebel listening*: they operate in collaboration with other collectives, artists, poets, activists, teachers and students – past and present – who are working from decolonial, feminist, anti-racist and anti-colonial perspectives. It is these networks of care and critique (that we nurture and that nurture us), which we argue present a systematic response to the infrastructural and subjective violence of twentieth- and twenty-first-century development.

It is clearly not possible to conceive of the project of *amateur-amantes* without taking into account the fact that as artists we are working in a context structured by the precarisation and fragmentation of work; local and global art systems rely on the contributions of vulnerable underpaid workers and communities while artist salaries are minimised through highly competitive and short-term project grants, presenting considerable class boundaries in terms of access to art making. While the questions contemporary arts institutions pose are critical in their formulation, they lack criticality in terms of how they relate to artists as workers, as well as art as *practice*. The actions of urban artists living in the context of the European Union, wanting to activate projects from decolonial, feminist and postdevelopment perspectives, are forced into a dialogue with an arts infrastructure whose linguistic content is often very politicised but whose forms actively work to fragment networks of care and critique. The capacity to reinscribe technoaffectivty is thus necessarily (but not out of choice) informed by an immediate context, characterised by shifting economic systems of racialised and sexualised inclusion and exclusion. Upheld by informal and formalised networks of care and critique, as *amateur-amantes* we will continue to move between the official and unofficial infrastructures of technoscience and art.

Notes

1 We have chosen to use the term 'the feminisms' as a means of recognising the diversity of feminist practices, as well as referencing the various anti-colonial, anti-racist, Black feminist and decolonial critique of universal 'Equality Feminism' motivated by defending and reproducing a universal woman subject.
2 Our notion of technoaffective reinscriptions and the production of indifference references the work of Achille Mbembe (2016) and his research around 'the empire of disaster and reconstruction' (27).
3 See Santana, F. (2015) *Historia sucia de Guayaquil*. Guayaquil: Cadaver Esquisito; Balladares, M.A. (2017) *Guayaquil*. Premio Pichincha de Poesía, Quito.
4 Since 2016, Venezuelans have faced multiple difficulties when trying to obtain or renew a passport. The process implies economic challenges and a long and complicated procedure, which in some cases takes over two years.
5 See Morandeira Arrizabalaga, J. (2017) *Be Careful With Each Other, So We Can Be Dangerous Together*. Barcelona: San Andreu Contemporani.

References

Balladares, M.A. (2017) *Guayaquil*. Quito: Premio Pichincha de Poesía.
Brecht, B. (2000) 'Explanations [about the flight of the Lindberghs]'. In Silberman, M. (trans.), *Brecht on Film and Radio*. London: Methuen, p 135.
Close, R. (2017) 'Videos for post-truth times: Revisiting the AIDS-related work of Pratibha Parmar and Isaac Julien'. *ArtAsiaPacific*, September/October, vol 10, no 105, pp 65–66.
Close, R. & Marín, A. (2018) 'Contagion as method: Generating stages of enunciation'. In *Performance Research, On Generosity*, vol 23, no 5, pp 90–92.
El-Tayeb, F. (2006) *European Others: Queering Ethnicity In Postnational Europe*. Minneapolis: University of Minnesota Press.
Fanon, F. (1963) *The Wretched Of The Earth*. New York: Grove Press.
Harvey, D. (2012) 'Neoliberalism is a political project'. *Jacobin* magazine. www.jacobinmag.com/2016/07/david-harvey-neoliberalism-capitalism-labor-crisis-resistance/.

Mbembe, A. (2016) *Crítica de la razon negra. Ensayo sobre le racism contemporáneo*. Barcelona: Ediciones NED y Futuro anterior.

Morandeira Arrizabalaga, J. (2017) *Be Careful with Each Other, So We Can Be Dangerous Together*. Barcelona: San Andreu Contemporani.

Preciado, P. (2013) *Testo Junkie: Sex, Drugs and Biopolitics*. New York: Feminist Press.

Rich, A. (1978) 'The cartographies of silence'. In *The Dream of a Common Language: Poems 1974–1977*. New York: W.W. Norton & Company, p 17.

Santana, F. (2015) *Historia sucia de Guayaquil*. Guayaquil: Cadaver Esquisito.

Viveiros de Castro, E. (2010) *Metafísicas canibales. Líneas de antropología postestructural*. Buenos Aires: Katz Editores.

19
DESIGN FUTURING IN A BORDERLAND OF POSTDEVELOPMENT

Tony Fry

While there is a substantial literature on the relation between technoscience and development, design has had little mention until recently.[1] This is surprising when one considers that development has been *de facto* the imposition of a design paradigm of earlier and late modernity by the West on 'the underdeveloped' rest, thus designating the form of its future. The ambition of development has been to configure the underdeveloped (recoded as 'developing' or the 'newly industrialising') nation's industries, institutions, infrastructure and a plethora of economic, legal, social and political systems within a eurocentrically conceptualised design matrix as the new or as the to-be-'retrofitted'. A major reason for the absence of design in critiques of development has been the inward-looking character of design scholarship and practice, while critiques of development simply have not grasped design's agency in the making of worlds within the world.

Design so situated has to be confronted and contested. Design practices need to be redirected away from technical and aesthetic service provision to the economic status quo and towards transformative engagements with the historically inscribed and present consequences of 'development'. Notwithstanding having to overcome major challenges, design can be seen as an imminent contributor to the advancement of postdevelopment as praxis.

...

The case for design so positioned will be presented in two parts. Design will first be placed in relation to development as it has been implicated in the 'darker side' of modernity (Mignolo 2011), and as an agent of 'defuturing' and the defutured (Fry 1999). Part two will outline design as ontologically prefigurative of futures, and then introduce the emergence of design in the context of (the post-geographic and geographic) Global South. Finally, design will be linked to the formation of a postdevelopment 'borderland' wherein Western and Indigenous knowledge, border thinking, design and the Global South are brought together to establish the proto-conditions of 'being in the world otherwise'. So positioned, the borderland is the locus and condition of in-betweenness where negotiation becomes possible.

Part one

Development was integral to the logic of Western modernity long before it became a specific discourse of applied modernisation policy. Throughout this history, one consequence, in various modalities, has travelled from the distant past into the present: defuturing – the negation of cultural and environmental futures. At its most general, defuturing can be understood as an imposed process of world-making that effectively enviro-culturally unmakes a world, and in so doing displaces the prior temporal conditions of 'being-in-the-world'.

Modernity, in its founding moment, especially as marked by the 'discovery' of the New World, attempted by design to make the world at large in its own theologically constituted image of 'the civilised'.[2] Two defuturing actions were employed in this endeavour and, while undergoing transformation over time, the basic intent of both has remained the same: the destruction of the difference of the Other; and, the expropriation of the land, resources and labour-power of the Other. Historically, genocide, ethnocide and ecocide connected in this defuturing moment of environmental and cultural destruction – one that established structural conditions of unsustainability.

While this condition is now increasingly evident in the enviro-climatic impacts of industrial society, what is less recognised in the Global North is the elimination of modest and sustainable ways of life of so many of the planets 'undeveloped' peoples. This has been a de-worlding of the ways of life of Indigenous cultures: an erasure of so much of peoples' knowledge, and modes of being that sustained them for millennia. Three qualifications of this process of negation immediately need to be made.

First, the level of destruction of Indigenous peoples over more than 400 years of Western colonialism was unevenly distributed in time and space between the 'ravages of the conquistadors in Spanish America' through to the nineteenth-century 'carve-up of Africa'. Certainly, violence and destruction have not ceased post the decolonisation wars of the mid-twentieth century. While retaining its old forms, new ones arrived. For example, the designation of the undeveloped peoples as underdeveloped by development theory was in actuality an act of ethnocidal violence. Frank, Johnson and Cockcroft (1970) made this clear when underdevelopment theory was in full ascent in the 1950s and 1960s – 'Even a modest acquaintance with history shows that underdevelopment is not original or traditional and that neither the past nor the present of the underdeveloped countries resembles in any important respect the past of the now developed countries' (Frank, Johnson & Cockcroft 1970: 3). As will be shown later, this observation has salience for how postdevelopment is advanced by design.

Third, unsustainability as linked to colonialism and development reveals differential chronologies of defuturing. The defuturing and de-worlding of the colonised Other was in its initial moment rapid, but its afterlife is slow and relentless. It converges with the structural unsustainability of contemporary global industrial/post-industrial societies, where the ongoing defuturing trajectory is protracted and is putting our being, and the being of much else, at risk, not least from climate change. So said, those disadvantaged populations of former colonised nations, who live across the equatorial belt, are of greatest and most immediate risk.

The relational complexity of what constitutes unsustainability encompasses risk from: the consequences of ever-present major conflicts; the increasing and now unstoppable impacts of climate change destined to exist for at least several centuries as layered onto other and ongoing forms of damage to the natural environment; and population and resource pressures. A clear example here is between climate change and conflict; this as displaced people cross borders *en masse* looking for food, water and shelter (Dyer 2008). The scale and duration of these convergent risks, as they extend out into the distant future, mostly goes by without address. The announcement that the world is at the commencement of a sixth extinction event (Kolbert 2014) is met with silence. Life is always at risk.

In sum, what development, from arrival out of industrial society to late modernity, and post-industrial globalisation have helped develop is universal unsustainability. From this perspective postdevelopment cannot be contemplated without being directly linked to 'sustainment' (Fry 2009: 197–207).[3] One can view sustainment's significance in relation to the Enlightenment, which in the company of modernity brought the modern world into being. So characterised, what sustainment names is the futural task of dealing with this world so that life as we know and value it has a future. As such it names a project of a scale of modernity, but the obverse of its violence.

Such action is not just political, economic and technical, but also psychological. In its inequity, what drives the propensity of 'humanity' toward unsustainability in large part has been the universalisation of the designing of desire, materialised in the actuality of hyper-consumption as the front end of consumer-led economic development. Desire-driven capitalism was prefigured by design in the 1930s and by the design industries service to global corporate capitalism. Crucial here was the arrival, in the USA in the 1930s, of streamlining, an aesthetic of product styling (applied to everything from cars and aircraft to toasters and ashtrays). The technology remained the same, but appearances were transformed, and thus became far more desired. Along with the F.D. Roosevelt 'New Deal' programme and the introduction of hire purchase, streamlining was a key factor in the nation's overcoming of the Depression by 1939. Besides marking the arrival of the modern industrial design profession, streamlining was also the launch pad of mass-marketed consumerism (Meikle 1979).

The creation of the unsustainable drive for development to deliver the benefits of the modern world was an amplification of a desire that had arrived earlier, one that was more grounded, and political and economically complex. This desire to be modern, as it was instilled by colonialism, on adoption equally could create recoil against the prospect and divide the nation. In all cases the modern arrived by combinations of imported knowledge, expertise, goods and technoscience transfer, as well as by the creation of an internal Global North educated elite. Rather than the modern being a means of postcolonial liberation, what was emplaced was a continuity of the erasure of difference and cognitive colonisation via what is now understood as 'epistemological colonialism' (de Sousa Santos 2014). Because it played such a crucial but mostly silent role in the advancement of development it is worth looking at it in some detail.

As we know, the conditions of domination created by European colonialism meant the destruction of Indigenous knowledge, the establishment of a regime of order and the imposition of Western knowledge and practices. By the early to mid-nineteenth century this process had become incorporated into the transfer of technologies to both colonised and undeveloped non-colonised nations. The claim was basic: superior technology equalled superior knowledge and modes of organisation. China and Japan and their establishment of respective British and French arms industries powerfully illustrate the point (Fry 2014: 12–36). Both these nations imported exemplary samples of well-designed manufactured produces, machine tools, manufacturing methods, plus technicians to set up production systems as well as the means to translate large numbers of instruction manuals. The old order was devalued as the new started to become established, and with it the grounds of epistemological colonialism, mostly unknowingly and ambiguously, despite claims by cultural theorists that the creation of a local modernity wherein cultural traditions survived in hybrid forms (Bhabha 1994); but they are not surviving. Notwithstanding retained appearances of difference, the generational erasure of fundamental local knowledge and values is ongoing as ethnocidal practices encroach (Clastres 1994) and take on remade forms (Casula 2015: 700–718).

In the contradictory nature of its modernisation, China is perhaps the most overt example of this ambiguity as a nation futurally marked by colonising modernity without ever being occupied by a colonial power. As China's modern history evidences, importing technology and the appropriation of technological knowledge via translation provides a clear example of a nexus between colonising modernity, technology and the agency of epistemological colonialism (Zhong 2003).

As a result of the loss of face due to the national defeat by Britain and France in two Opium Wars, together with decades of rebellions directly connected to clashes between defenders of Confucian traditionalism and forces of modernisation, the national government decided to embark on establishing a modern arms industry. It did this with the support of a campaigning organisation the 'Self-Strengthening Movement'. Thus began the import of technology and expertise, together with translation of technical and scientific literature.[4] While the initial intent was to arm the nation's armies with modern weapons, the result was to create a much wider environment of modernisation based upon the designing power of Western technology and knowledge.

Epistemological colonialism is not the end of the story of the relation between modernity, subjectivity and mind in China or globally. While it continues there is a transmogrification of colonialism that is moving it to another level, wherein there is a fundamental change in the colonising agent. Put succinctly: what is in progress is a move from technology deployed as an instrument of colonial power *to it becoming an independent ontological agent of colonisation* (producing a posthuman technoid lacking a critical perspective) which *overrides* the ongoing geometry of neo-colonialism as it enfolds epistemological colonialism. Thus techno-colonised subjects facing technology do so without recourse to a 'saving power', for they are completely within its metaphysical gathering. Essentially, what can still be tentatively called technological colonialism has no exteriority. It makes no distinction between the coloniser and the colonised, natural and artificial environments, and in so doing brings the adequacy of conventional thinking about contemporary colonialism, its sources and effects into question.

Techno-colonialism

Effectively, instrumental reason has become disembodied and, as technology, is acting back to colonise its source of creation. Disarticulated from any geopolitical and identifiable familiar source of power, the forces of the digital corporate empire have unwittingly – via ubiquitous computing, social media and machine learning, all within the constantly expanding domain of artificial intelligence – created consciousness-colonising psychotechnologies.[5] These empires are starting to mobilise their power without comprehending its ontological nature or futural consequences. Instrumental reason as disembodied and directed by unreflective design is reaching the apotheosis of its developmental flaw – evident in the ability to bring amazing technologies into being 'because we can', but without the slightest idea of their resulting independent designing and colonising agency.

Philosopher of technology Bernard Stiegler (2012) has drawn attention to the 'entropic tendency of digital technology' and its place in expanding all domains of logical and computational technology 'that impose calculation on everything that constitutes the movement of life' (Stiegler 2012: 197). Stiegler understands psychopower as a new kind of power that expresses and exercises the political agency of digital technologies as they are used to colonise the collective consciousness of societies, their sumptuary conduct and the life of the mind of individuals. Psychopower is delivered by psychotechnologies as they act upon those neural-informational circuits that influence human behaviour (Grincheva 2013: 16–22).[6] The mental ability to attend and remember in an age of the industrialisation of memory are two related cognitive changes. Psychopower does this in the service of the corporations of the digital empire and associated culture industries (Ronfeldt & Arquilla 2008).[7] What is unfolding is the psycho-affects of psychopower as they directly correlate to the scale, uptake and spread of digital technologies with, at the extreme, the consequential ontological designing of fully instrumentalised individuals within particular social groupings.

To emphasise: psychotechnologies are effectively creating and extending neo-colonial occupation of consciousness unevenly across colonised time and space without regard for the past geometry of power of colonialism (Jandrić &

Kuzmanić 2015: 13).[8] Currently the impact is partial, but it will increase. What is resulting is a new kind of digital divide and the 'rise' of a data-captured psychotechnological (systems compliant) class, while at the same time there is an abandonment of the data poor (another new class). This transforming of the hominoid/technology relation supports the view that our species no longer has a teleological evolutionary pathway of biological adapting to varied environments, while generative of difference of the same essential being, but exposure to the cognitive/psychotechnologies has very different consequences. What it produces are ontologies disassociated from beings of the same biology. This difference is un-bridgeable. Thus 'our' species mode of being-in-the-world is fragmenting, and so becoming plural at a fundamental level beyond cultural difference. At one pole there is a being wholly technologically (instrumentally) colonised, an actual 'post-human' non-human. Technology as such a setting is not just the sum of individual technological tools, instruments, processes and systems but a metaphysical and *psychological* domain. Now at the other pole there is the utterly abandoned bio-politically managed dehumanised being of abandonment and displacement. Clearly, us, the rest, are between these poles, but without a security of position.

Placed in the context of the technological encroachment into how colonisation is currently defined, 'the human' and development are understood, postdevelopment cannot be seen as a counter-direction and discourse. The binary logic of development has fallen, yet its illusory presence persists. And along with development our understandings of the political, the relations of and to technology – and power is also dissolving and reforming: such a process will continue for some time. Conceiving the project, practices and politics of postdevelopment, it is suggested, can no longer just be framed by its socio-political attachments or in familiar geopolitical, economic and humanitarian terms. What has to be developed after development, and how it is done, has to radically change. Obviously the question is, how? What follows is a contribution towards the answer to this question.

Part two

Postdevelopment as futuring can be considered as a counter-discourse and a practice of making sustain-able futures against the defuturing consequences of forms of action negating the conditions that sustain life – this includes the propensity of development and psychopower to defuture. In the face of the complexity outlined there are no immediate solutions to hand. There is much to understand, practices to create and politico-cultural spaces in which to work to create. So what follows are places to begin in the recognition of two framings: our species fragmentation and where and how as critical post-humanists we situate ourselves – and the absolute importance of the defence of memory when dealing with psychotechnologies, or, as Stiegler puts it, advancing 'the politics of memory' (Stiegler 1998: 276).

As futuring, postdevelopment can be considered as an extension of design futuring and, specifically situated within 'design and/in the Global South' and in relation to 'design in the borderland' (Kalantidou & Fry 2014: 1–12), such design can be understood as a path to autonomous practices directed at sustainment. To make the implication of these summary remarks clear, each of the key concepts and critical relations will be explicated.

Futuring and design futures

Design futuring (Fry 2009), as ontological design is an ethos. At an individual and basic level, futuring means action that gives the self (as a unity of body, mind and spirit) a 'future with a future' (Fry 2009: 182–196).[9] Such action turns in two directions, the first towards care of the self physically and mentally, the second towards care for the natural and constructed environment upon which selves depend. These two domains of care are understood as indivisibly elemental from the ontological care-structure that Heidegger (1988: 237/193–238/194) presents as intrinsic to the fundamental ontology of 'our' 'being-in-the-world', for we are, as the philosopher Maurice Merleau-Ponty put it, part of 'the flesh of the world' (Merleau-Ponty 1968: 248–251).

Viewed collectively, futuring extends care of the self to care of the Other and the environment, for, if not damaged beyond its ability to renew itself, it cares for us. Care so understood, as Heidegger (1988: 225–235) explains, is a fundamental material process and imperative lodged in our being rather than an emotional disposition or a moral action. Bringing design to futuring implies prefiguring the agency of things material and immaterial that have been performatively given the ability to deliver care. As agency and condition, care is thus the means by which something is sustained and therefore futured. So posed, care can, and does, come from an act of design, positing care as an ontologically inscribed performative quality of some designed and created thing.

In some respects, design for care is not new. Road signs are designed to care, as obviously are seatbelts in cars and aircraft; likewise, so are numerous electrical safety devices and a vast array of health and safety industrial process protective clothing and equipment and so on. But such care is functionally circumscribed; for example, a fighter aircraft is designed to care for its pilot and those who maintain it, but it is not designed to care for others (especially hostiles) or the natural environment. Where design futuring differs is when something brought into being with care, posited with caring, ontologically active performative features, is enabled to care for selves and others; it aims to do so without producing environmental damage either in its production, use or disposal. What this focus on care illustrates is that nothing is without ethical implications. For while many things can be given futuring caring qualities, most lack them. Even things, material and immaterial, designed and made with care are often uncaring in their use and disposal. The decision is thus often not a simple choice between that which futures or defutures but rather one of a materialist ethical recognising performatively that requires an assessment between the degree of caring versus uncaring, futuring versus defuturing, creation versus destruction. Such an ethics is grounded in the dialectical nature of the creation of 'things', for the act of creation is indivisible from one of destruction and therefore an empirical (rather than moral) judgement of material effect.

Design and/in the Global South

As is hopefully now clear, design was and still is a silent and powerful force of (neo-)colonialism. The ordering of the spaces of colonisation – the colonial city, the plantation, mines and more – were ontologically designing spaces of power and control that directed conduct and ruptured the colonised subjects from their prior ways of life and thereafter imposed a mode of being and acting in place (Legg 2007). As subjects were inducted into the educational institutions that naturalised eurocentric epistemological sensibilities across generations, thinking and values so established, continued post the withdrawal of the colonial power normative. Design theory, education and practices in the Global South were constituted in this context.

Design in the 'Global South' (not just a geography but also its dispersed populations) is arriving as part of an emergent liberation from the history of institutionally established universalised eurocentrism. There can be no design *for it*, only design *within it*. As such, it is an example of resistance, in a particular sphere of knowledge and practice, to what Boaventura de Sousa Santos (2014) calls epistemicide. Such design is informed by border thinking, as constituted in an epistemological borderland between a selective appropriation of received and Indigenous knowledge (Mignolo 2011: 206–207). In essence this dialogical process means design thinkers/designers selectively create a bricolage that is embraced in situated contexts of *a recovered and remade culture of memory* – as a negation of psychopower.

The aim of design in the Global South is to constitute an appropriately situated synthesis of knowledge and practice that is from and for the South, which in its active political and creative autonomy transforms relations with the North. While not easy, and slow, the process has begun. The scale of the difficulty arrives once it is understood that what is required is far more than just a welding together of ways of knowing and acting in relation to two worlds and the ways they understand and employ design. The actual hybridisation of design demands a *careful* critically reflective process of considered selection and exchange from different 'socially constructed realities' – there can be no appeal to a common world (Berger & Luckmann 1966).[10] Moreover, comprehending these realities/worlds cannot be done via a universal model of the human – another imposition on Indigenous cultures that, within their cosmologies, form their own understanding of being and beings. The inability to recognise this difference, and the values upon which this understanding rests, was a primary feature of the defuturing violence of colonial formalism and development.

Working across cultures epistemologically, to create affirmative transformations that enable the South to design its future requires collectives based on a 'commonality in difference', created in the in-between conditions of the borderland formed by a situated imperative of sustainment. Here is the locus in which a mode of futural designing can be constituted. This means forming a designing community of internal integrity (or what Arturo Escobar (2018) has called 'autonomous design', a concept he has addressed as a major theme in his exposition of *Designs for the Pluriverse*).

What begs emphasis is that the convergence of design for the Global South and autonomous design exists within a condition of possibility. This is illustrated in the recent and still emergent uptake of these ideas and practices in Latin America and globally elsewhere. There are two clear longstanding reasons that they are now beginning to be responded to. The first is the economic, social and community need for postdevelopmental sustain-able futures that counter those offered, desired, appropriated from and imposed by the Global North. The second is that the numbers of commercial design practices in nations of the Global South are limited, but design education is, in some of these nations, increasing. The obvious implication is that the supply of designers already does (or will soon) exceed the market demand. This means that new counter-practices have the potential to become alternative careers. What encouragingly is worth noting, although again variable, is that these practices, in the company of design futuring, are starting to be taken up by design educators and design education institutions in the Global South. Last, the economics of disadvantage can perhaps be regarded, for the time being, as potentially advantageous, as this situation is currently unconducive to an unrestrained encroachment of psychopower.

Although the developments just indicated are encouraging, the challenges faced by futural design practitioners disengaging from, but aware of, globalised design education and practice are substantial. For 'designers' to work in the condition outlined requires they gain critical acumen and find other and localised ways to think, acting to establish conditions that care for their selves and others. Critical and effective design practices, in association with postdevelopment, have to be formed by embracing problems that are relationality defined and engaged – which implies an unavoidable engagement with defuturing and unsustainability. To do this requires overcoming current disciplinary divisions of knowledge (development economics being an obvious example) that so often have created the thinking and practices that have created the problems. Correspondingly it also means adopting and employing a transdisciplinary mode of thinking and working, and then understanding that unsustainability has been, and remains, a structural feature of the capitalist economy – including for design practices. Both design in the Global South and autonomous design, as indicated, as situated within communities and as working outside market provision, represent practices that need to be seen as working against the dominant condition of limitation and towards 'acting in time'. What this means is acting in the medium of time with a sense of urgency, but equally recognising progress will be incremental and take time.

Finally, what such approaches to design mean is that unless a solution can be concretised, it is not actually a solution (a lesson that theory steeped in idealism eternally refuses to learn), and likewise neither is utopianism; it is an ever-diminishing currency – to illustrate the point: Enrique Dussel's idea of 'transmodernity' (Dussel 1999) is a rich and interesting idea of new formations of modernity liberated from, and transcending, its eurocentrality, but it was acknowledged to be utopian in its inception. However, now, over twenty years later, after the geopolitical, technoscientific and enviro-climatic changes in the world, transmodernity is an even more remote prospect. In a world of fragmenting humanity, with a fragmented world order, talk of global solutions and of universal universals has no purchase (Jullien 2014). Action towards praxis has to be grounded and conjuncturally situated.

The overarching point to be deduced from these remarks is that doing postdevelopment is not just about finding a way to accommodate difference in the shadow of global capitalism, but in common with design to begin to constitute and ground a designing environment in which non-utopian formative concrete practices can be brought into constructive convergence. In both cases, isn't the potential for a postdevelopment and contra-design practice not just to seek to be insinuated into capitalism, but rather to present capitalism with practices it would have to contend with as operationally critical agents of the status quo?

Notes

1 Design is not simply the product of industrial culture, although the design professions are. Understood fundamentally, design is intrinsic to the evolution of hominoids, thus all members of our species act prefiguratively whereby an object of intent is envisaged, imagined or visualised before the act of its materialised creation. The earliest of all tools (selected and fashioned stones), the first images on cave walls, the original objects made by craft all evidence the anthropological presence of design. Thus, design is a structural feature of our being and all cultures.
2 While modernity has been subjected to critical address for many decades, a consensual understanding has not arrived, and now is even less likely to arrive. But what is clear is that the world never was made modern and the project of making it so can never be completed. While our planet is *singular*, the world is a unifiable *plurality* now being widely referred to as a pluriverse by theorists like Walter Mignolo and Arturo Escobar.
3 The terms sustainment and sustain-ability are used in place of the overused and ambiguous term sustainability. See Fry, T. (2009) *Design Futuring: Sustainability, Ethics and New Practice*. Sydney: UNSW Press, pp 197–207.
4 John Fryer (1839–1928), the son of an English Protestant minister, was perhaps the most prolific translator of technical and scientific literature (Bennett 1967). He translated seventy-seven books that were published by the Kiangnan Arsenal, for whom he worked. These scientific textbooks also influenced men like Yan Fu (1853–1921), who trained at the Fuzhow Shipyard and Kiangnan Arsenal (Elman 2001: 130) and became widely regarded as the most significant translator of his age and 'the first Chinese literatus who related himself seriously, rigorously, and in a sustained fashion to modern Western thought' (Schwartz 1964: 3).
5 Bernard Stiegler defines pyschopower as 'the technological, industrial, systematic capture of attention' that has been called cognitive capitalism, which has been made possible by the emergence of psychotechnologies (Stiegler n.d.a; see also Stiegler n.d.b).
6 What psychotechnologies do is to act upon those neural-informational circuits that influence 'human' behaviour in the service of the corporation of the digital empire and the culture industries of cultural capitalism.

7 These circuits are defined as constituting de Chardin's notion of the *noosphere* (the ecology of the informational network of conscious thought).
8 This divide is illustrated at its extremes: as of 2015 the Netherlands has 92.9% of its population online while Ethiopia has 1.1%.
9 Design futuring's theoretical foundation, methods and strategies are influencing design education and professional practice, albeit more slowly. Presented as a 'redirective practice', it is underscored by a sustain-ability agenda that goes beyond a business-as-usual model of sustainability to centre on the concept and imperative of sustainment.
10 The concept of the 'social construction of reality' was first outlined in Berger and Luckmann's seminal text of 1966.

References

Bennett, A. (1967) *John Fryer, The Introduction of Western Science and Technology into Nineteenth-Century China*. Cambridge, MA: East Asian Research Center, Harvard.
Berger, P.L. & Luckmann, T. (1966) *The Social Construction of Reality*. New York: Random House.
Bhabha, H.K. (1994) *The Location of Culture*. London: Routledge.
Casula, P. (2015) 'Between "ethnocide" and "genocide": Violence and otherness in the coverage of the Afghanistan and Chechnya wars'. *Nationalities Papers*, vol 43, no 5, pp 700–718.
Clastres, P. (1994) *Archeology of Violence*, trans. Herman, J. New York: Semuiotext(e).
de Sousa Santos, B. (2014) *Epistemologies of the South: Justice Against Epistemicide*. Bolder, CO: Paradigm Publishers.
Dussel, E. (1999) *Postmodernidad, y Transmodernidad*. Puebla: Universidad Iberoamericana.
Dyer, G. (2008) *Climate Wars*. Melbourne: Scribe.
Elman, B. (2001) *New Terms, New Ideas (Review)*. Leiden: E. J. Brill.
Escobar, A. (2018) *Design for the Pluriverse: Radical Interdependence, Autonomy, and the Making of Worlds*. Durham, NC: Duke University Press.
Frank, A.G., Johnson, D.L. & Cockcroft, J.D. (1970) *Dependence and Underdevelopment*. New York: Doubleday & Co.
Fry, T. (1999) *A New Design Philosophy: An Introduction to Defuturing*. Sydney: UNSW Press.
Fry, T. (2009) *Design Futuring: Sustainability, Ethics and New Practice*. Oxford: Berg.
Fry, T. (2014) 'China vs China'. In Kalantidou, E. & Fry, T. (eds.), *Design in the Borderlands*. London: Routledge.
Grincheva, N. (2013) *Psychopower of Culture Diplomacy in the Information Age*. Los Angeles, CA: Figero Press.
Heidegger, M. (1977) *The Question Concerning Technology and Other Essays*, trans. Lovitt, W. New York: Harper & Row.
Heidegger, M. (1988) *Being and Time*, trans. Macquarrie, J. & Robinson, E. Oxford: Blackwell.
Jandrić, P. & Kuzmanić, A. (2015) 'Digital postcolonialism'. *IADIS International Journal on WWW/Internet*, vol 13, no 2.
Jullien, F. (2014) *On the Universal: The Uniform, the Common and Dialogue between Cultures*. Cambridge: Polity Press.
Kalantidou, E. & Fry, T. (eds.) (2014) *Design in the Borderlands*. London: Routledge.
Kennedy, T.L. (1978) *The Arms of the Kiangnan Arsenal*. Bolder, CO: Westview Press.
Kolbert, E. (2014) *The Sixth Extinction: An Unnatural History*. New York: Henry Holt.
Legg, S. (2007) *Spaces of Colonialism*. Oxford: Blackwell.

Meikle, J. (1979) *Twentieth Century Limited*. Philadelphia, PA: Temple University Press.
Merleau-Ponty, M. (1968) *The Visible and the Invisible*, trans. Lingis, A. Evanstone: Northwestern University Press.
Mignolo, W.D. (2011) *The Darker Side of Western Modernity: Global Futures, Decolonial Options*. Dutham, NC: Duke University Press.
Ronfeldt, D. & Arquilla, J. (2008) 'A new paradigm for public diplomacy'. In *Routledge Handbook of Public Diplomacy*. London: Routledge.
Schwartz, B.J. (1964) *The World of Thought in Ancient China*. Cambridge, MA: Harvard University Press.
Stiegler, B. (1998) *Technics and Time 1*, trans. Beardsworth, R. & Collins, G. Stanford, CA: Stanford University Press.
Stiegler, B. (2012) 'Theatre of individuation'. In de Boever, A., Murrey, A., Roffe, J. & Woodward, A. (eds.), *Gilbert Simondon, Being and Technology*. Edinburgh: Edinburgh University Press.
Stiegler, B. () 'Biopower, psychopower and the logic of the scapegoat'. *Ars Industralis*. www.arsindustrialis.org/node/.
Stiegler, B. () 'Within the limits of capitalism: Economizing means taking care'. *Ars Industrialis*, http://arsindustrialis.org/mode/2922.
Zhong, W. (2003) 'An overview of translation in China'. *Translation Journal*, vol 7, no 2. https://translationjournal.net/journal/24china.htm.

20
IS CONTEMPORARY ART POSTDEVELOPMENTAL?

A study of 'art as NGO'

Verónica Tello

Contemporary art doesn't engage with the discourse of postdevelopment in any explicit form. A quick Google search and a search on my university library database confirms this. It's also worth adding that, as the author of this chapter, I am new to postdevelopment. I'm an amateur, trained as an art historian, specialising in contemporary art and working across border politics and decolonial theory, not postdevelopment. But even from this perspective, I can see that there are postdevelopmental tendencies in contemporary art, or, more specifically, a dialectic of development/postdevelopment.

I am thinking of the art of the Danish collective Superflex, for example. For *Supergas* (1997), Superflex collaborated with European and African engineers to develop an alternative, cheap energy source for farmers and families living 'in rural areas of the Global South' (Superflex 1998) – the biogas system converts human and animal stool into a gas fuel source. Superflex also worked with the African organisation SURUDE (Sustainable Rural Development) to trial the biogas system on a small farm in central Tanzania in 1997.

While the trial was funded by the esteemed Louisiana Museum of Art, Denmark, in order to further develop the biogas system prototype, the collective initiated the shareholding company *Supergas A/S* in 1998. The company closed due to lack of investors in 2005. In turn, Superflex turned their attention once more to European art institutions, extracting further funds to advance the prototype. Crucially, they also worked with the Grameen Foundation so that, through its micro-financing system, it could offer small loans to farmers to purchase the technology.

A slogan of the Grameen Foundation is, 'All humans are potential entrepreneurs' (in Kester 2011: 131), suggesting that becoming indebted – and participating in neoliberal systems – is a means to circumvent systemic geoeconomics inequity. This is completely simpatico with Superflex's own thinking. A key motivation for *Supergas* was to, in Superflex's mind, critique and circumvent the 'dependent' relations between 'marginalised' Africans and NGOs while also allowing such people to tap into their entrepreneurial potential and become 'independent' (Superflex in Kester 2011: 126–127). As Grant Kester argues (2011: 127), Superflex seem to be unaware of the extent to which NGOs have produced similar projects to *Supergas*, and also caricatures NGOs – rendering them as non-self-reflexive participants in development.

They do so, however, to position their project as not-another-NGO, but rather as something like 'art as NGO'. By this I mean that they leverage the performative, and representational, capacities of art – so that the artwork (*Supergas*) *appears* as something (an NGO), and thus undeniably *refers* to it, but at the same time it is *not quite the thing* which is being referred to. This aesthetic effect, theoretically, allows for a critical distance, and difference, between the artwork and the thing that is being referred to. Or, put more concretely, it creates a critical distance/difference between the artwork (*Supergas*) and the NGO.

Superflex are highly critical of the role of NGOs in development, and position projects such as *Superflex* as critiques of development and alternatives to it. But they are not quite postdevelopmental, for their critiques of the development industry are nullified by their methods: extracting funds from European art institutions via their art projects and rerouting them to developing countries in order to liberate Africans. In other words, perhaps they are not quite NGOs, and neither are they embedded in development policy or legacies, but they nonetheless generate similar social relations (they just do so through other capitalist circuits).

Having said that, it's best not to throw out the baby with the bathwater; if I am asking, 'is contemporary art postdevelopmental?', Superflex still offer an important means through which to answer this question. Their artworks, such as *Supergas*, remain strong signifiers of an emergent impulse in contemporary art – characterised by a desire to critique NGOs, generate 'art as NGO' and provide alternatives to normative development practice via art. There are a number of projects that represent such an impulse, some of which I will analyse below, including the *Institute for Human Activities* (*IHA*, 2012–) and *The Silent University* (*SU*, 2012–). But first, it is crucial to note, all of them emerge out of a particular strand of contemporary art: social practice.

Since the late 1990s, the field of contemporary art has witnessed the proliferation of what is variously termed social practice (my preference), relational aesthetics and socially engaged art.[1] While such terms arise out of the writings of different, albeit interconnected, theorists (Claire Bishop, Nicolas Bourriaud, Grant Kester), they share much in common. They describe a mode of art born out of the legacies of 1960s/1970s conceptual art, especially performance art and its privileging of the body as material. In seeking to extend its focus beyond the artist's body as material, as was common for conceptual/performance artists in the postwar period, social practice includes other bodies, the bodies of art's audiences. Social practice is fundamentally participatory; the social relations that unfold within are not just a process or method; rather, the act of audience participation fundamentally constitutes, and completes, the artwork.

With the increasingly extra-disciplinary nature of art, which engages fields historically extraneous to art, such as economics or development, the audience of art has also expanded. Social practice artists work across a number of social, cultural, political, economic phenomena – engaging with housing, welfare, ageing, disability, migration and countless other crises, and heterogeneous publics and communities, which have historically been the concern of governments and NGOs, and correlative biopolitical policy. Social practice is defined by its intimacy with crisis, as well as its dependency on publics and participation.

As a field, social practice has catalysed the development of what I am terming 'art as NGO', which is evident in *Supergas*. But since 1997, and the initiation of *Supergas*, the nature by which this mode of art has unfolded has changed. Art as NGO now appears far more sophisticated, more self-reflexive and more firmly aligned with social justice movements, decolonial politics and discourse. It appears, *but perhaps only appears*, more postdevelopmental – for it is still in many ways embroiled in the legacies of development.

I offer a recent example of art as NGO. *The Institute for Human Activities* is an ongoing project, initiated in 2012 in response to the exploitative labour market in the Democratic Republic of Congo by the Dutch contemporary artist Renzo Martens (with the support of the Berlin Biennial, De Hallen Haarlem, Kunstenfestivaldesarts and the Van Abbemuseum). The *IHA* began on a former Unilever plantation site. After the multinational corporation vacated its premises, workers were left without access to water, sanitation and electricity. In collaboration with the workers, Martens began what he termed the 'Gentrification Program' via the *IHA*, as a means to create infrastructure for improving access to collective goods, and a space to critically analyse the politics of labour, urbanisation, wealth and self-determination. A key role of the *IHA*'s Gentrification Program has been to set up an arts research centre (in collaboration with Yale University and Ghent University), through which the project attracts international visitors to the Congo in order to research art's capacity to intervene in global crises. The art research centre, formally known as the 'Critical Curriculum' (Figure

FIG 20.1 *Institute for Human Activities*, Critical Curriculum programme, initiated by Renzo Martens. Image courtesy of the *Institute for Human Activities*.

20.1), is crucial to the *IHA*'s philosophy and finances. Art attracts capital, argues Martens — in turn, one of the key drivers of the *Institute* is to exploit capital attached to art which visualises and thematises global inequality, including inequality in the Congo (think of Steve Mcqueen's *Gravesend* of 2007). Marten's argument is that such art almost always benefits and accumulates capital in European and American cultural centres — the sites where art is exhibited and sold; in contrast, the *IHA* attempts to accumulate capital, via its art programme focused on global inequality, to improve access to collective goods and human rights in the Congo. It is an experimental infrastructure that acts as a means to enable access to collective goods/rights through art. It is a contemporary example of art as NGO.

As the *IHA* hints, art as NGO has changed somewhat since the late 1990s. It still appears in sites of crisis — emergent or ongoing, in both the Global South and North. In the north, however, art as NGOs increasingly work with subjects/migrants from the Global South — or what Ramaswami Harindranath (2017) has termed the 'mobile global south'. It is thus, in one way or another, shaped by the geoeconomics of the South, and seeks to tap into and expand the potentiality of Southern energies. It does so by manifesting infrastructure or 'alter-institutions' (after Lambert Beatty 2009; Galleria 2016). Leasing real estate or establishing temporary sites, bearing logos and generating websites and social media presence, art as NGO adopts the aesthetics of mimicry (see 'mockstitutions'; Sholette 2011: 152), to generate experimental educational, cultural, housing and other services. Initiated by artists, sometimes artists living in and from the North, art as NGO is, like all social practice, participatory, but crucially, it is so to make a case that while conceptualised by artists, these infrastructures will eventually become self-determined by the communities they work with. 'Initiation' of infrastructures by the artists, rather than long-term ownership over them, is key. Art as NGO is a collaborative endeavour, involving communities, cultural institutions and aligned with social movements with the aim of locating ways of living together otherwise (drawing on Sheikh 2016). The rhetoric of art as NGO is aspirational, anticipatory even. It adopts experimental 'adhocratic structures' (Ögüt 2013) and/or practices of 'commoning' that aspire to make manifest decolonial, anti-capitalist worlds, and worlds within worlds (Tan 2014). Such worlds, art as NGO posits, are defined by the social relations permitted by the infrastructures that shape/govern lives.

From the above, it is possible to see that by now, in 2018, the impulse to generate art as NGO is closer to postdevelopmental than it was in the 1990s. Indeed, like postdevelopment it drives a critique of Western hegemony — and correlative geo-economics — while simultaneously locating alternatives to Western modernity *with* rather than *for* subjects of the Global South. However, as the editors of this book argue, postdevelopmental practice is not simply 'post'-development, that is, connoting a clean teleological-like temporal break with 'development'. Rather, postdevelopmental practice unfolds through and in a tension with the vocabularies, values and traditions of development, and the geopolitical (and cultural) phenomena support it. Postdevelopmental practice, then, is a messy practice. It is located in an in-between space, where the legacies of modernity and modernism require constant negotiation in constructing a postdevelopmental option in contemporaneity.

Thus, for the remainder of the chapter I will argue that art as NGO is a tentatively postdevelopmental practice, seeking to make manifest anti-colonial, anti-capitalist alternatives and structures through which to live and organise life (via mimicry, critical distance). It is tentative because it does not easily forego the value systems and logic of Western culture which creates hierarchies and divisions between subjects of the Global North and South. And crucially, as I will argue, it is dependent on, exploitative of, even, the international division of labour which sustains geo-economic inequity. There are limits to which art as NGO is 'post'-developmental, yet, as a suggestive, anticipatory concept, it is still able to engage with the speculative, futural horizon of postdevelopmental practice, so long as it becomes more robust in the ways it negotiates and disrupts capital's/modernity's/coloniality's social structures.

To advance my argument, I take as my case study one particular example of art as NGO, the *Silent University*, initiated by the Kurdish artist Ahmet Öğüt in 2012. I focus on the *SU* because I am very familiar with it, visiting it and participating in some of its activities over the last few years. I have gained an insight into how both it operates as a fairly large-scale and ambitious operation, and the social relations that unfold therein. But I also choose to focus on the *SU* because it represents a robust example of as art as NGO, allowing an advanced theorisation of this artform/artistic impulse and its relationship with the dialectics of development/postdevelopment.

Art as NGO: *The Silent University*

First, some background information on the *Silent University*, and an overview on how it self-represents. The *Silent University* self-represents as an experimental education platform initiated in London in 2012 by the Turkish, Amsterdam-based artist Ahmet Öğüt. As its website details, it was developed in partnership with the Tate Modern's Education department and the Delfina Foundation – a philanthropic programme with a historical commitment to artists living in the Middle East and North Africa, though today it has a broader international focus (I discuss the *University*'s relationship to such old capital elite further below. For now, I want to offer more background information). The *University* was conceived by Öğüt as a means to contest the various ways that immigration and education policies mute and disregard migrant/Southern knowledge and qualifications. It recognises the academic qualifications of refugees, asylum seekers, migrants – fleeing the conflict, economic and ecological crises in the Global South – appointing them as 'faculty.' After six years in operation, the *Silent University* has campuses in many European cities including Athens, Hamburg, Mulheim/Ruhr, Copenhagen and Stockholm. Most recently it has been established in the Middle East, in the Jordanian city of Amman. By now, these campuses are supported by a large number of institutions, Delfina and the Tate, but also Tensta

Konsthall, Curating the City Hamburg, Impulse Theatre Festival, Ringlokschuppen, Spring Sessions and State of Concept in Athens. While receiving support from these institutions in terms of space – and some funding – the *University* mostly operates through volunteer labour. As the *Silent University* website states: 'alternative currencies' in the form of 'free voluntary service' allow the *University* to, purportedly, operate outside capitalist markets – I say purportedly because, as noted above, it was founded using old philanthropic money via the Delfina Foundation and funds from the Tate, which is sponsored by BP and BMW amongst other global corporations. While I discuss the *Silent University*'s relationship to capital in more detail below, for now, it suffices to say that it sees its relationship with capital as strategic. By this I mean that it aims to develop 'alternative currencies', using volunteer labour, for example, but simultaneously, when it does engage with capital, it (claims Ögüt) does so to strategically exploit art market resources so as to advance the decolonial, social justice movements that it aligns itself with (building on Sheikh 2016). It does so, the *University* claims, to construct anti-capitalist, experimental social spaces that contest the erasure of Southern knowledge by Western neoliberal universities and immigrant policies (Ögüt & Malzacher 2016).

Engaging with the *University*'s discourse on retooling art world resources, collaboration and time and skills sharing, critics have broadly argued that it engages with the radical 'politics of commoning' (Tan 2014; Bağcıoğlu 2016). As art historian Neylen Bağcıoğlu (2016) argues in the *Silent University*, 'commoning' is enabled by the artist's decision to circumvent normative modes of art production. That is, rather than producing an object – by a single author – artistic labour is instead invested into dematerialised, inclusive collaborative processes. Bağcıoğlu states, '[b]y utilising [his] artistic labour as a tool, [Ögüt has] essentially shown that there can be a common ground between artists and non-artists [migrants] outside of the […] neoliberal system' (2016: 125). Similarly, art historian Pelin Tan argues, in the *University*, the 'commons' is not simply ' […] the way in which resources [knowledge, skills, expertise] are pooled and made available to a group of individuals', but also how this process allows participants the chance to 'rediscover a sense of community' (2014: n.p.). So, we have the *University* enabling the rediscovery of a sense of community and returning to Bağcıoğlu, opening up a space for 'ethical social relations to perform "a new, possible world"' (118). The *Silent University* is commonly seen as embodying a radical mode of commoning – where the act of sharing resources and ideas opens up a new way of co-existing; where collaborative practice ruptures the individualising effects of neoliberalism and the divisiveness of border politics; and where an experimental knowledge platform imagines and forges an alternative space to organise bodies. Underpinning existing discourses on the *University* is not only the value of collaborative practice – that is, the labour of co-production – but also the valuing of collectivity – the act of co-existing and creating spaces constituted by an inclusive 'we' – comprised of disparate subjects working together to construct alternative socialities.

These discourses ignore the nuances of the socio-political context out of which art as NGO emerges – and erase the complexities of the labour of postdevelopmental practice. First, art as NGO emerges out of increasingly widespread cultural policy and cultural discourse which expects art projects, especially those that are socially engaged, to be able to promise and bring to bear demonstrable social justice impact (Bishop 2012: 14). There exists, as EC Feiss (2015: 70) argues, 'a structural relationship between dominant policy regimes which mandate artistic social outcomes and justice-oriented critical practices'. Art as NGO may very well be embedded in anti-colonial, anti-capitalist discourse, but it also a by-product of neoliberalism. It creates a space for highly ambitious individuals, including artists, to simultaneously engage with radical, de- and anti- colonial impulses and exploit precarity (including their own) to generate speculative infrastructures, such as the *Silent University* or the *IHA*. In other words, communities affected by crisis – austerity, poverty and statelessness – attract sub-contractors or freelancers, including artists, to come and propel 'recovery' or elicit 'empowerment'. As Marina Vishmidt (2013) has argued, the community is put to work in a kind of 'non-politics of inclusion' where art, in lock step with business, gives the impression of empowerment but which actually inhibits the capacity to question systemic structures that maintain inequity.

Here, the solidarity required to organise effectively against exploitation or marginalisation is difficult to locate as the discourse around recovery and crisis becomes one about exploiting market resources to address the crisis but never to protest the ongoingness – that is, the making and perpetuating – of crisis. When Vishmidt (2013: n.p.) is describing such art, she has in mind the work of the celebrated artist Theaster Gates, who is well known for 'adding value' to derelict African-American areas in Chicago through his practice, including by putting the affected, or target, community to work on urban regeneration. In a (reasonably) cynical analysis, Vishmidt (2013) argues that Gates uses his projects to celebrate the capacity for collective 'labour' to elicit social change; but to be frank, the labour that Gates devotes himself to is centred around negotiating with NGOs, real-estate developers and circulating objects based on his socially engaged projects in the art market, under his *authorship*. Similarly, I argue that the *Silent University* is founded on the preservation of the Western subject – via the figure of the author – (and) the denegation of the mobile Global South which is relegated to the 'exploited' side of the international division of labour (after Spivak 1988). Such a dynamic emerges because contemporary art discourse overvalues the Western figure of the artist/author and its labour over that of others. The discourses around art as NGO reflect institutionalised formulas of artistic value: the promise of the artist – an expression of an inner world that is not yet a reality – and the fetishisation of what this will bring forth, a utopia, an ultimate alternative, an innovation that can't be supplanted, a totalising paradigm.

Art labour

The division of labour in industrialised society is characterised by the breaking down of specific tasks to be performed by individuals working together as part of a larger system for maximum efficiency. In art, the division of labour is contingent on something else. As Marx and Engels (1932) argue, the artist's distinct social position presupposes that their mental work (genius) is differentiated from that of the masses (and presumably the uneven social relations that underpin capital). This differentiation is in fact nothing more than the division of labour, which places the 'exclusive concentration of artistic talent in individuals and the suppression of it in the greater masses' (Marx & Engels 1932).

Since the 1960s, with the advent of conceptual art, de-skilling and dematerialisation, the distinct 'mental labour' of artists, as divorced from other kinds of labour, has only intensified (Lippard 1997). Delegated labour or outsourcing and contracting work out to others, in the name of conceptual art, is by now a relatively common occurrence (Bishop 2012). Within such an aesthetic regime, the artist's mental (and not physical) labour is the basis by which art accrues its value, symbolic or otherwise. Collaborators labour to produce objects which gain their exchange-value, and symbolic-value, through the artist's name, reflecting and instituting a division of labour which ensures that the intellectual labour of the artist is inalienable from the object, even if the object is the labour of others.

Art as NGO and the politics of labour

Within the *Silent University* and the *Institute for Human Activities* one method to attempt to critique the category of the 'author' – and the division of labour it institutes – has been to deploy the term 'initiator' instead.[2] Such a term is meant to connote 'founding' an institution/organisation/art-as-NGO that may have been conceptualised by an artist but which ultimately operates and is maintained as a collaborative entity – with the *Silent University*'s faculty and the coordinators. This is an attempt to open up an aesthetic of participation not defined by the 'author' but by those who enter into the project, however intermittently, to support the durational work. Following André Lepecki (2013), 'initiation' can be read as an attempt to energise, to set in motion, movements that elicit social ruptures – it could be a 'verb-event' which opens up space for responsive, dynamic movement between different subjects, rejecting both tokenistic participation *and* 'authoritative authorship' for the purposes of forming political assemblages and structures. In this light, the act of initiation and, more specifically, initiating long-term projects might be read as a radical move – one that is attuned to expanding the boundaries of art and its institutions for collaborating with social movements and subjects outside its usual purview (which is arguably the bourgeois public).

Yet, while promoted as a self-determined migrant social movement, there is a clear division of labour in the *SU*. It designates specific tasks and fixed roles for its members – 'artist as initiator'/Ögüt, the 'faculty'/migrants and, last but not least, a category I have not yet clearly articulated, the female volunteers who perform the bulk of the administrative and affective labour to maintain 'the university'. They are called the 'coordinators' therein. Following the patterns of humanitarian volunteerism, and unpaid work, in the *Silent University*, the

FIG 20.2 Daniela Ortiz, *97 empleadas domésticas* (*97 House Maids*), 2016. Creative Commons.

affective labour of coordinating – of organising lectures, forming support networks with/for the faculty, running social media for events – is performed by mostly white European women: students, activists, curators without or with little pay, or social workers doing extra time. They represent what feminist Marxist theorists Andrea Francke and Ross Jardine (2017) have termed the 'administrator as infrastructure', allowing the 'hero/author' to maintain the semblance of working as a sole operator (a process contingent on concealing labour) while the administrator's labour is devalued, considered un-authored and un-skilled. If they appear, it is on the margins – much like the women in Daniela Ortiz' *97 House Maids* of 2016, a work comprised of found photos posted by wealthy Peruvian families on Facebook (Figure 20.2). In the photos, housemaids appear in the background, peripheries. While there are clearly distinctions between the housemaids and the coordinators, nonetheless they represent what Franke and Jardine have termed 'service or administrator as infrastructure' – commonly perceived as un-skilled, de-valued labour that art institutions – or domestic spaces – rely upon. Coordinators are highly aware of the gendered division of labour within the *Silent University*. As one coordinator observed in conversation with me: 'The artist performs the artist, the refugee performs the refugee, the coordinator the coordinator. The question is, can we transcend these normative roles and put them into question as well?'

If the coordinators' labour is rendered invisible, the faculty performing in front of a lectern or on a stage, usually accompanied with the *Silent University* logo, act as the key public interface of the *SU*. In turn, images of such events are heavily disseminated in the *SU*'s online communications. Such events and images work to evidence that the *University* is performing its task of circumventing the racialised division of labour that mutes the knowledge of migrants once they cross the border. Yet, such events and images are also constituted by the labour conditions of the *SU*. In an act of what Claire Bishop (2012) has termed 'delegated performance', migrants are paid to perform themselves within the artwork. Their presence offers the work a level of authenticity – and symbolic capital – that is otherwise unavailable through the body of the artist or coordinators. Yet, most are only offered the chance to give a lecture once or twice, subjecting them to the norms of precarious, casual academic labour which only values bodies and knowledge in fragments, leaving them without support in the 'in-between' temporalities of the *Silent University*'s public programmes. Moreover, as some faculty members have expressed (in conversation with the author), there is little or no opportunity to align the *University* with their own self-determined migrant social movements, such as Lampedusa in Hamburg, or the African Women's United Organisation in Athens.

The artist delegates the authenticity of the work to the faculty of migrants, while still remaining the 'artist', which gives the work its symbolic value. It's worth dwelling on the fact that in spite of being a self-proclaimed 'adhocratic' organisation, at every mention of the *Silent University*, the artist's name – as 'initiator' – is uttered on promotional material, in art publications, or lectures and public programmes – across *Frieze*, *e-flux*, Tensta Konsthall or the *SU*'s website. In a way, this reflects art business as usual. In today's art economy, the artist's persona is called upon, valued and extended in multiple ways – not just by having shows or selling works on the art market, but also by posting on social media, or appearing in video interviews, in symposia, or publishing essays in art magazines. The artist as persona can and needs to perform all the time. As Sven Lütticken (2012) argues:

> [a]s an artist or writer or curator, you perform when you do your job, but your job also includes giving talks, going to openings, being in the right place at the right time. Transcending the limits of the specific domain of performance art, then, is what I would call general performance as the basis of the new labor.

This new labour – or general performance – is seen as necessary to obtain resources for the *SU* to develop its symbolic value and keep the work going (Ögüt & Malzacher 2016). However, this labour/performance also leaves us with an inevitable outcome: everything that the *SU* does, or however it is described and narrated in discourse, is another means to extend not only the artist's persona, but also the artist's unshakeable relationship with, and ownership over, the artwork/art as NGO. The artist's persona (Ögüt) becomes a means to value the art as NGO (*SU*).

Indeed, critics invariably turn to the interviews and other statements uttered by the artist as initiator, including the *SU*'s manifesto (2012), in their analysis of the project. Statements (from the manifesto), such as, 'We act in solidarity with other refugee struggles and collectives around the world', or 'Decentralised, participatory, horizontal and autonomous modality of education, instead of centralized, authoritarian, oppressive, and compulsory education', reflect the general tone and register in which the *University* self-articulates. With the forceful polemical affect, these texts come to stand in as the art 'work'. They are the signifiers of authorship, which (for critics) point to the conceptual scaffold – the mental work – of the *SU*. By repeatedly valuing these signifiers, *attribution*, by which I mean the process of individualising the creator of the work and locating signs of an author (a unique idea), is at play. Within the discourse of the *SU*, the reiteration of the artist as initiator works to constantly contain the project within the borders of artistic, singular models of authorship.

While the term 'initiator' suggests a desire to abandon capitalist forms of art production under the banner of progressive politics – to form a new community – I posit this: the role of the artist here is closer to one of management (including delegation and negotiation), than to initiation. While not producing anything tangible themselves, artists are nonetheless unable to be alienated from the work of art. The artist delegates the role of operating the *SU* to others, but the artist's autonomy, and ownership over the work, is nevertheless maintained because the artist's role has (through dematerialised conceptual art practice) expanded to the task of being a (de-skilled) 'service worker' or 'curator of social creativity' (Vishmidt n.d.). Their task is to initiate and manage social practice projects – intended to advance social justice – but this is difficult to do when the values of neoliberal entrepreneurship override those of collaboration.

Social practice: the value of collaboration/collectivity

The exploitative conditions of social practice, and collaborative art forms, are not new. As Stephen Wright argued (2004: 534–535):

> artists make forays into the outside world, [and] 'propose' (as artworlders like to say) usually very contrived services to people who never asked for them, or rope them into some frivolous interaction, then expropriate as the material for their work whatever minimal labour they have managed to extract from these more or less unwitting participants (whom they sometimes have the gall to describe as 'co-authors'). In so doing, they end up reproducing within the symbolic economy of art the sort of class-based relations of expropriation that Marx saw at work in the general economy: on the one hand, those who hold the symbolic capital (the artists), and on the other, those whose labour (such as it is) is used to foster the accumulation of more capital. And this is precisely what is usually passed off as 'collaboration' – making cynical mockery of the term – not just by such artists as Rirkrit Tiravanija, Maurizio Cattelan and all those whose names figure in all the almanacs of relational aesthetics, but by countless others besides.

In the years since Wright wrote the above apt, and still resonating, passage, discourse on social practice has tended to forego materialist analysis of the social relations that ensue therein. In fact, the most prominent analyses of social practice (Bishop 2012; Thompson 2011) have preferred to focus their energies on the *potentiality* for such practice to offer a space for robust collectivity, or to think through the challenges and limits of collectivity, without expecting much in terms of material manifestations of non-hierarchical modes of being and working together.

Perhaps the strangest manifestation of such discourse has been Bishop's concept of 'delegated performance', briefly mentioned above. As Bishop (2012: 219) argues, delegated performance is characterised by the act of the artist hiring people to 'perform their own socio-economic category' (e.g., migrant or refugee) and, in turn, delegating the 'authenticity' of performance to subjects other than the artist. The category of delegated performance marks a shift between artists using their own bodies and identities as signs of authenticity in performance-based works from the 1970s, toward artists hiring others (including migrants) to perform themselves within the logic of the work that they conceptualise (note, the division between mental and banal labour remains). Overall, Bishop is overly keen to praise the way in which such practices offer a 'self-reflexive', 'paradoxical' means to think through the politics of collaboration by deploying exploitative labour practices (2012). In other words, the use of exploitative practices in such works are valued by Bishop for the ability to critically *thematise* exploitation. For Bishop, the rules of capitalism are suspended therein for the sake of enabling a critical *reflection* of capitalism. Bishop has been quick to dismiss Marxist and post- and de-colonial interpretations of delegated performance, which would, as she says, attempt to think delegated performance in relation to other historical instances where 'third world' subjects have been asked to perform themselves in global exhibitions. While offering no substantive critique or citations, such approaches, she argues, reduce delegated performance to 'standard-issue questions of political correctness', condemning it as a 'reiteration of capitalist exploitation' in a 'seamless continuum with contemporary labour' rather than the more 'complicated' interpretation (hers) of 'offering a specific space of experience where those norms are suspended' (2012). Bishop, in other words, promotes delegated performance as an aesthetic experience that offers a means to think through the limits of collaboration amongst geo-economically disparate subjects within capitalism, without giving much credence to the global art industry's exploitation of uneven social relations in its pursuit to create images of conviviality, community and collectivity. But the question remains: what are often highly precarious subjects from the Global South being 'initiated' into via delegated performance or art as NGO, if not the fully functioning economy of contemporary global art markets?

As Peter Osborne (2013) argues, as a form of capital, contemporary art projects 'the utopian horizon of global social interconnectedness, in the ultimately dystopian form of the market' (115). Explorations of the unity of geopolitically diverse subjects are increasingly common in global art circuits. In the Central Pavilion of the 57th Venice Biennale (2017), Olafur Eliasson organised an iteration of his workshop series *Green Light* (2016–) through which asylum seekers and refugees collaborate on constructing lamps made from recycled materials;

the lamps are sold for a minimum of 250 euros, the proceeds of which support NGOs that work with refugees. In Athens, Rick Lowe set up the *Victoria Square Project* (2017–2018), a short-term community space hosting dialogues and skill-based workshops for/by refugees and migrants in collaboration with dozens of Greek NGOs and small businesses as part of *documenta 14*. Such artworks – also examples of art as NGO – offer gestures toward global conviviality while being cultural representations of globalisation. They are symbols of capital's ease in crossing borders *and* celebrations of cultural differences. Capital here is embodied in the itinerant artist – enabling articulations of being and working together in time across the spaces of global art. But this vision, is bound to collaborations that depend on the mobile, often illegalised labour power embodied in migrants, and the free labour of volunteers.

I'd like to propose that works like the *Silent University* represent what I term 'necro-art': art production underpinned by the exploitation and labour power of precarious subjects. In other words, art is in a position to extract capital (symbolic or actual) from those subjected to what Mbembé (2003) terms 'death-worlds'. Necropolitics creates markets for art works that offer images of solidarity and collectivity while being dependent on the exploitation and alienation of the labour of both volunteers (coordinators) and those subjected to and attempting to flee death-worlds. Necro-art is dependent on the autonomy of the artist in the most traditional sense, a division between their labour and capacity to 'extract' artworld resources through their persona and the performance of volunteer and/or precarious subjects as willing participants in the development of a 'new world' and absolute alternatives.

Is contemporary art postdevelopmental?

One could argue that postdevelopmental practice via art as NGO is speculative, or futural – not empirical – it remains on the horizon as something to aspire to. As Osborne (2013) argues, contemporary art is a privileged catalyst for exploring the 'geopolitically diverse forms of social experience that have only recently begun to be represented within the parameters of the common world' (27). Its imaginative capacities enable it to produce prototypes, prototypical infrastructures to experiment with sociality, collectivity and postdevelopmental alternatives. Though it is simultaneously working through the global art system which privileges subjects of the Global North (it advances a dystopian market form which, to my mind, stubbornly holds onto the regime of modernity and authorship).

The question thus remains: how can art as NGO produce a space comprised of disjunctive subjects, without foregoing the potentiality of the collective 'we' (and refuse to default to the individualism of the neoliberal 'I')? It may be less a matter of 'initiating' projects which pursue normative concepts of artistic authorship, even if done so in the name of collaboration, and more a matter of creating a space through which both the 'author' is rigorously deconstructed and the *interdependencies* (rather than *division*) of labours are embraced as core to the advancement of postdevelopmental, collective practices (even if such collective practice is never constituted by equivalent subjects).

Art must register and critically engage with its relation to global capital – including its relations to 'collectivity' as a commodity niche – and forge a path that maintains the radical aspects and potentiality of art as a site of resistance, while refusing to insist on the West's avant-gardist notion of the hero/author. This will remain critical for further locating and advancing the full postdevelopmental potential of art as NGO. It will be central for how art as NGO can unfold with the incommensurable subject positions and voices that define the global era, rather than opt for defaulting to structures that maintain Western paradigms – of authorship, sociality and claims on the future.

Notes

1 Google trends.
2 The term is also used in the abovementioned projects, *Immigrant Movement International*, *New World Summit* and the *Victoria Square Project*.

References

Bağcıoğlu, N. (2016) 'Artistic labour: Seeking a utopian dimension'. *Cadernos De Arte E Antropologia*, vol 5, no 1, pp 117–133.
Bishop, C. (2012) *Artificial Hells: Participatory Art and the Politics of Spectatorship*. London and New York: Verso, pp 219–240.
Feiss, E.C. (2015) 'Autonomy for a "New World"?' *Radical Philosophy*, no 189, p 72.
Francke, A. & Jardine, R. (2017) 'Bureaucracy's labour: The administrator as subject', *Parse*, no 5, pp 24–33.
Galleria, I. (2016) 'Self-institutionalizing as political agency'. *ArtMargins*, vol 5, no 2, pp 50–73.
Harindranath, R. (2017) Conversation with the author. The concept of the 'Mobile Global South' is being developed in Harindranath's forthcoming book, *Southern Discomfort*.
Kester, G. (2011) *The One and The Many: Contemporary Collaborative Art in a Global Context*. Durham, NC: Duke University Press.
Lambert Beatty, C. (2009) 'Make-believe: Parafiction and plausibility'. *October*, no 129, pp 51–84.
Lepecki, A. (2013) 'From partaking to initiating: Leading following as dance's (a-personal) political singularity'. In Siegmund, G. & Hölscher, S. (eds.), *Dance, Politics & Co-Immunity: Current Perspectives on Politics and Communities in the Arts*. Zurich: Diaphanes, pp 21–38.
Lippard, L. (1997) *Six Years: The Dematerialization of the Art Object from 1966 to 1972*. Chicago, IL: University of Chicago Press.
Lütticken, S. (2012) 'General performance'. *E-Flux Journal*, no 31. www.e-flux.com/journal/31/68212/general-performance.
Marx, K. & Engels, F. (1932) 'Saint Max'. In *The German Ideology [1845-6]*. Amherst, NY: Prometheus Press.
Mbembé, A. (2003) 'Necropolitics'. *Public Culture*, vol 15, no 1, pp 11–40.
Öğüt, A. (2013) 'The pitfalls of institutional pedagogy'. *World Policy*. http://worldpolicy.org/blog/2013/06/12/pitfalls-institutional-pedagogy.

Ögüt, A. & Malzacher, F. (2016) 'How can we imagine a school culture based on solidarity?' In Ögüt, A., Malzacher, F. & Tan, P. (eds.), *The Silent University: Transversal Pedagogy*. Berlin: Sternberg Press, pp 12–23.

Osborne, P. (2013) *Anywhere or Not at All*. London and New York: Verso.

Sheikh, S. (2016) 'Art after Trump'. *e-Flux Conversations*. https://conversations.e-flux.com/t/simon-sheikh-art-after-trump/5325.

Sholette, G. (2011) *Dark Matter: Art and Politics in the Age of Enterprise Culture*. London: Pluto Press.

Spivak, G. (1988) 'Can the subaltern speak?' In Nelson, C. & Grossberg, L. (eds.), *Marxism and the Interpretation of Culture*. Urbana, IL: University of Illinois Press, pp 271–313.

Superflex (1998) *Supergas*. www.superflex.net/tools/supergas/image/10.

Tan, P. (2014) 'The Silent University: Alternative pedagogy as our commons'. *Migrazine*. www.migrazine.at/artikel/silent-university-alternative-pedagogy-our-commons-english.

Thompson, N. (2011) *Seeing Power: Art and Activism in the Twenty-First Century*. Cambridge, MA: MIT Press.

Vishmidt, M. (2013) '"Mimesis of the hardened and alienated": Social practice as business model'. *E-Flux Journal*, no 43. www.e-flux.com/journal/43/60197/mimesis-of-the-hardened-and-alienated-social-practice-as-business-model.

Vishmidt, M. (n.d.) 'The politics of speculative labour'. *Transformative Art Production*. http://transformativeartproduction.net/the-politics-of-speculative-labour/.

Wright, S. (2004) 'The delicate essence of artistic collaboration'. *Third Text*, vol 18, no 6, pp 533–545.

CONCLUDING REMARKS AND AN INVITATION

Elise Klein and Carlos Eduardo Morreo

Writing a conclusion to our edited collection seems premature – one gets the sense this collection is only getting started. The authors within these pages have shown through rich analysis and theoretical reflections how postdevelopment in practice is already underway in both the Global South and North. In their contributions, authors have also traced areas of postdevelopment practice requiring further reflection and analysis, of which there are many. Throughout these pages, we see how postdevelopment is a continual struggle to shake off development. At the same time, postdevelopment names the provincialisation of development by embracing the world of the third, the realities of hybrid economies, the pluriversal and the multiple ways peoples, places and ecologies have made and retained other worlds. Just getting started also means that there is still much to think through.

Postdevelopment in practice confronts the difficulty of overcoming development's hold amid a series of (postdevelopment) practices. A poignant example of this is offered in Tello's powerful study of postdevelopment art – not the usual place scholars go searching for a critique of development or postdevelopment practice. But Tello presents a careful study of the difficulties and limitations encountered by art projects and interventions seeking to value Southern knowledges and to highlight the struggles of refugees in Europe. Tello's critique, advanced through the suggestive formula of 'art as NGO', makes a compelling case. The entangled relations sustaining these interventions are simultaneously reproducing certain forms of exclusion and modernist frames. That this is so reveals the need to further reflect upon and to have postdevelopment art practice link up with other social movements and political organisations. Within postdevelopment practice, the decolonial art intervention seeking to value Southern knowledges now needs to engage with the study of its diverse economy, both allowing for the intervention, while blocking its decolonial thrust. Postdevelopment names this complexity and the careful commitment to working it through.

This means that whilst we are moving towards the end of development, we are also amidst transition. And in transition we are searching out these horizons of difference, care, critique and hope. As Katharine McKinnon, Stephen Healy and Kelly Dombroski put it in their chapter: 'what postdevelopment scholars are exploring is how to move ahead uneasily – without confidence that any particular approach is the "right" one, and with the knowledge that any development work is always already embedded in politics'. For us, a commitment to staying with the trouble does not mean giving up on 'doing something', but committing to a path that questions and transforms not only development but the project of postdevelopment as we knew it. As Donna Haraway has put it, 'staying with the trouble' is something important for scholars and activists to do; it allows us to sketch out the messy and uncomfortable areas of being complicit, whilst trying to deconstruct amid practice. The difficulty is itself part of working within the transition. Still, it should be of comfort for the many within the development machine that your concerns and critiques of the defuturing of development should not be confined any longer to corridor whispers – it's time for futuring, as Tony Fry might put it.

Similarly, there are chapters within the collection that map out the 'world of the third', as Dhar and Chakrabarti call it – sites that are not capitalist, nor pre-capitalist. This is not just sanguine and hopeful, but a crucial point, in that postdevelopment is not always just emerging from cracks in the machine, but is the world for many. Here is a reminder to parochialise the West and its development, even within the North, as Bendix, Müller and Ziai show us.

The volume's invitation to have emerging and prominent scholars and activists engage with postdevelopment practice repeatedly raised the question of 'practice' and 'praxis'. The latter is, of course, a complex notion most powerfully developed by the Marxian tradition, whereby practice is recursively informed by theory. The current project, premised on the coupling of 'postdevelopment and practice', and therefore highlighting already existing work within a world of many worlds as knowledges and practices seeking to render these diverse ontologies stronger, immediately calls forth the notion of praxis, though without privileging a Marxian register.

The focus on practice within these pages has led to ways of worlding, of doing economies and futuring, that matter to many, yet we have been reminded that postdevelopment theory is crucial in guiding and reflecting upon practice. Postdevelopment theory assists us from not getting lost in the thick of it – it is the line leading us through the woods. Theory helps critically consider events and processes as postdevelopment, helping us also to assess claims and to rethink how something may or may not be postdevelopment in practice. Here, we see how recovering and thinking with other theoretical traditions remains central. In the volume we are fortunate to have several genealogies of postdevelopmental critique and practice presented. Along with Marxian and poststructural genealogies, Caria and Domínguez show how what came to be known as postdevelopment had also been informed by other strands of sociological critique and ecological thinking about economy. Similarly, Nakano discusses the earlier work of Yoshirou Tamanoi on regionalism as a form of postdevelopmental critique developed in Japan, which in turn informed diverse environmental and regional projects. Also, Dhar and Charkabarti's work on the world of the third points to yet another series of worlding postdevelopment alternatives. The futures of postdevelopment are being informed by these and other experiences and genealogies of critique, theory and practice. Postdevelopment as practice, reproducing worlds, making worlds and defending worlds, will be informed by dialogues crossing these multiple genealogies.

Sites of postdevelopment in practice also challenge a set of sad and old, but enduring, views. As the volume has emphasised, postdevelopment in practice is not simply a project of the Global South, but also one very much being advanced in the Global North. Sites are bodies – and, as Harcourt so skilfully shows us, flesh may become a site of resistance, resurgence and renewal. Sites of postdevelopment in practice are multiple, art work and stories, not just what the (sometimes) harsh pen of the academic presents. This practice expands and ignites imaginaries – it affects practice, providing atmospheres of possibility.

Crucially, we must continually reflect on who are the actors of postdevelopment. Who is telling the story, who gets to define worlds? In this volume, our authors are academics, artists and activists who have presented the worlds of people – many writing together with those that are the focus of their chapters. Many of these are communities, as shown in Pattnaik and Balaton-Chrimes, Curchin, and Chitranshi's chapters. Others are people coming from NGOs, such as the work of Schöneberg. There is a lot to learn from this careful work. At the very least, their considerations have to be central to any future project of postdevelopment in practice, to learn from listening – as a *rebel listener* described by Cisneros and Close. They remind us that a rebel listener engages in a politics of care and critique – moving between worlds and tracing the contours and cracks that allow for the possibility of solidarity, collaboration and learning. The rebel listener is just as much about scaling down and focusing in to censor and silence racism, as much as amplifying out – in order to remind, to project and to interrupt. This work can be doubling down on development research itself – the hard work of holding ourselves and colleagues to account – Christopher Shepherd's warning is raw and serves as a reminder of the ways in which universities have been complicit and have capitalised on development's lie – the many consultancies undertaken and the investments made in training the next generation in Western-oriented technocratic expertise, firmly set on voiding the pluriverse.

Chapters in this collection have also helped us think about the role of the state in postdevelopment in practice. How does a state *do* postdevelopment? Can it? We have seen how this question fares differently in the settler-colonial context to the postcolonial context. Lang's discussion, for instance, foregrounded how the Ecuadorean state has played an ambivalent role as regards *buen vivir*, both promoting it in official documents and seeking to tame its transformational potential, while at the same time enabling local governments to pursue *buen vivir* in complex ways. Yet Spencer, in her work with First Nations groups in the

Northern Territory in Australia, has shown the difficulties and limited ability of a settler state to engage postdevelopmentally, while also illuminating the limits of research in trying to facilitate this process.

We also cannot forget the technological shifts and functionalities globalising particular worlds. Fry shows how technology has changed everything so that even if 'the binary logic of development has fallen, [development's] illusory presence persists, and along with it our understanding of the political'. Given the transformations wrought by what Fry discusses as 'techno-power', the practices and politics of postdevelopment must address the agencies of technology, such that the futuring of postdevelopment can no longer be framed in familiar geopolitical, economic or humanitarian terms.

Overall, though, we see how affirming and rediscovering pluriversality is intimately linked to the efforts of postdevelopment in practice, as is a greater concern with our everyday ontologies and their ways of worlding. The chapter by Ashish Kothari, Ariel Salleh, Arturo Escobar, Federico Demaria and Alberto Acosta points to their important project exploring more widely the pluriverse in the *Postdevelopment Dictionary*. A revival is underway.

Postdevelopment in practice: an invitation

In just getting started, this collection makes one wonder what else and who else has something to say about postdevelopment in practice? These final passages, then, must be an invitation to you, the reader, the writer, the activist and the artist, to find ways to also think and communicate moments and experiences of postdevelopment already in train within and towards the pluriverse.

It may be then appropriate to consider this volume as a call to continue sharing already existing postdevelopment practice, to work up this diversity as worlding alternatives already under way. Indeed, all the contributions share such a commitment. But an edited volume can only go so far, and much more can be done. The task of sharing projects, of reading their difference, of engaging with their particular histories and struggles, of appreciating the ontologies at stake and the vital 'cosmopolitical' challenges, of dialogue and discussion, of forming solidarities in light of pluriversal understandings – all of this points to a postdevelopmental path. If development has no 'place', as a reading of Dhar and Chakrabarti's contribution to this volume may lead us to argue, in documenting this diversity, we seek to facilitate its displacement, though documenting already existing postdevelopment is insufficient on its own. A pluriversal solidarity, in light of postdevelopment practice, is necessary.

INDEX

Page numbers: Figures given in *italics;* Tables in **bold;** Notes as: [page number] n [note number].

Aboriginal Australians 163–175, 203–216, 256–259
absence 193–194
action research 85–86, 88, 91, 196, 200n1
actor-network theory (ANT) 6
adivasi 119–132
affective labour 313–314
affectivity 276–293
Afro-feminism 255
agriculture: alternative models 135–138, 143; applied anthropology 231–246; collective processes 127; CSA participation 144; development thinking 119–120; feminist practice 122; gendered subsidies 217–230; labouring activities 124, 128–129; of solidarity 133–137; state policy 152; wage labour 157, *see also* farming
agrobiodiversity 235, *236*, 238, 242–243
aid approaches 27, 29, 192
AIDS crisis 282–284, 286–287
alliance building 271–273
alterity, development 163–175
'alternative forms of development' 90–91
'alternatives to development' 31, 40, 48, 86, 90–91, 97n6, 106–107, 134, 263–275
Althusser, Louis 90
Altman, Jon 163–175
amateur-amante figure 277, 291–292

Amin, Idi 218, 224
AMP *see* Asiatic Mode of Production
Andean GR practices 232–233, 235, 237, *237, see also* Ecuador; Peru
Anderson, Elizabeth 166
ANT (actor-network theory) 6
anthropocentrism 101
anthropological studies 231–246
'anti'-movements 155, 159, 231–246
applied anthropology 231–246
Arab Spring 253
archival power 278–281
art 292, 306–320, 321
art labour 312–313
Asiatic Mode of Production (AMP) 70, 73
Australia 163–175, 203–216, 238–239, 241–242, 256–258
authenticity 315, 317
authorship 312–313, 316, 318
autonomia 33
autonomous design 302
autonomy 26–27, 33

Babones, Salvatore 22, 24
Bağcioğlu, Neylen 311
balanda people 205, 215n4
Balaton-Chrimes, Samantha 11
Balladares, Maria Auxiliadora 282
barefoot economics 55–57, 63n5

basic needs 23, 56, 59–60, 186
Bebbington, A.J. 264, 265
Bendix, Daniel 11
Benjamin, Walter 25
Bharatiya Janata Party (BJP) 159n1
big-D Development 263–264
biocentric perspectives 58
biomedical practice 195–196
biopolitics 248, 252
Bird Rose, D. 258
Bishop, C. 317
BJP (Bharatiya Janata Party) 159n1
#BlackLivesMatter movement 254–255
bodies/the body 226–227, 248–249, 253–254, 307, 323
'the body multiple' 194–199
body politics 247–262
Bondieu, Wilfride 268
'borderland' 294–305
breastfeeding practices 194–197
Breton, André 284
budgeting 184, 212
buen gobierno concept 182
buen vivir concept 52, 54–62, 106, 109, 143–144, 176–189, 323
Buganda kingdom 220–221, 223
Butler, Judith 248–249

campesinos (peasants) 233, *234*
cannibal fugue 281–288
capital–art relationship 309, 311, 318
capital circuits, class 94, 97
capitalism 30, 35, 69, 219–220, 276; defining 77; delegated performance 317; design futuring 303; desire-driven 296; development forms 91; economic precarity 2; green model 104; Indigenous Australia 170, 172; industrialised 150, 157–159; operational analysis 67–68; resiliency 9
capitalocentrism 68, 86, 91, 94, 97
care: for country 256–258; networks of 276–293; of the self 300
Caria, Sara 10–11, 322–323
Cattaneo, C. 138
Cayambe, Ecuador 179–183, 186
CDU *see* Charles Darwin University
censorship 278–279
centralisation projects 39, 222
Césaire, Aimé 284–286
Chakrabarti, Anjan 11
Charles Darwin University (CDU) 203, 213, 215n2
Charusheela, S. 10, 78

Chaudhury, Ajit 78
Cheah, P. 204
Chicana feminists 255–256
China 194–197, 297
Chitranshi, Bhavya 11
Chrisanthopoulos, Gina 259
Christie, M. 208
Churuchumbi, Guillermo 179, 181–183
civil society 168, 265–266
civilisational transitions 27, 31
class/class processes 68, 70–78, 92–97, **93**, **95–96**, 124–126, 219
climate justice movement 141–143
Close, Rebecca 12, 287
cocooned space 92, 94
cognitive justice 193, 197
collaborative practice 311, 316–318
collective farming 119–132
collective housing 140, 143
collective 'labour' 312
collectivity 18–185, 311, 316–318
colonial legacies 144, 220–224, 232–233, 237–238
colonialism/coloniality 5, 131n7, 137, 295–299, 301
commodification processes 136, 166–167, 171–172
'commodities consensus' 7–8
commodity production 157–158
'commoning', politics of 311
the commons 34, 41–45, 136–137, 143–144, 182–185
communitarian logics 180–183
the community 25–26, 109–110; decline of 41–42; labour 312; modernity 26, 28; peasantry 225; as people-places 206; well-being 190–202
community-supported agriculture (CSA) 135–138, 143–144
constitutionalization, *buen vivir* 177–178
consumerism 172
contemporary art 306–320
cooperation, forms of 26–27, 29
cooperative movements 131n6
coordination, labour as 313–314
Corbridge, S. 156
Coronil, Fernando 9
Correa, Rafael 176, 178–179, 182–183
cosmopolitics 203–216
crisis debate 100–116, 312
critique 276–293, 307, 308–309
crypted space 92, 94
CSA *see* community-supported agriculture
Cubillo-Guevara, A.P. 54

cultural affirmation 234–235, 237, 242–243
cultural diversity 108
cultural relativism 244
culture–class typology 75–76
Curchin, Katherine 11
Curiel, Ochy 250
customary sector 165, 167–168, 170

Danby, Colin 72
dancing resistance 258–259
D'Costa, Anthony 2
de la Cadena, Marisol 120
de Sousa Santos, Boaventura 47–48, 49n5, 151, 193–194, 197
decolonial writings 250–251, 255
deconstructive project *see* genealogical intervention
deficit discourse 168
defuturing process 295–296, 301
degrowth movement 141–142
delegated democracy 107
delegated performance 315, 317
Deleuze, G. 123
democracy 60, 100, 107–109
democratic dividends 217–230
design 214, 215n7, 300–303, 303n1
design futuring 294–305
desire 27, 28, 296
'developed' societies discourse 133
development: adaptation 3–4; beliefs 35; current state 30; defining 263; discourses of 133; failures 1, 24; forms of 90–91, 94, 97; impossibility 23; measures of 101; myths of 217–230; paradigm of 38; as reconstruction 91–97; resistance to 227–228, *see also* 'alternative…
development aid *see* aid approaches
development alterity 163–175
The Development Dictionary 21–22
development studies 84–99, 135
development thought 52–65, 119–120, 122–130
developmentalism/developmentality 100–101, 103
Dhamarrandji, Stephen 205–206, 210–211
Dhar, Anup 11
Dietrich, Wolfgang 33
diplomacy 212–214
discourse, performativity of 192
disobedient observation 291
diverse economies framework 66, 68, 70–73, 75–77, 79n2, 80n5
diversity-based agriculture 232–233, 235, 236, 243

division of labour 310, 312–314
Dodson Gray, Elizabeth 109
Dombroski, Kelly 194–197
Domínguez, Rafael 10–11, 322–323
dreaming, Aboriginal 257–258
dualisms, overcoming 271–273
Dulaldeb, Mr. 127
Dussel, Enrique 10, 303

East Timor 232, 237–244
Ebila, F. 226–227
ecological development 54–57
ecological values 107
ecology of knowledges 47–48
economic democratization 107–108
economic growth/development 52–53, 103–104, 151, 193–194, 224
economic hybridity 163–175
economic organisations 267–268, 272
economic precarity 2
economic relations, sets of 9–10
economics: of the commons 43; development thinking 125; poverty and 152; social world 68, 71–72
economy: basic needs and 59–60; centralisation 222; conceptions of 4; discourses 42; of living system 39–40, 43
Ecuador 52, 54, 57–62, 143, 176–189, 281–282, 323
education system, communitarian 180–181
EJ (*The Environmental Justice*) *Atlas* 102, 112n9
El-Tayeb, Fatima 280
Elder advisors, Aboriginal 205, 210–211, 213–214
electoral processes, Ecuador 178, 185
Eliasson, Olafur 317–318
Emaliguda village, Odisha 119–132
embodiment *see* bodies/the body
'Ende Gelände' initiative 134, 141–144
energy practices 134, 141–143
engaged care practices 194–195
engaged government practices 207, 209–211, 213–214
Engels, Friedrich 312–313
entropy 39–40, 43
The Environmental Justice Atlas (EJ Atlas) 102, 112n9
epistemo-political practices 204
epistemological colonialism 297–298
epistemologies of the South 45–48
equity, ontologies 193–194
Escobar, Arturo 4, 7, 10, 52, 66–68, 71–72, 263–264, 267, 269
Esteva, Gustavo 10, 155, 157

ethics 44–45, 77, 124–125, 300–301
ethnography practice 245
eurocentrism 67–69, 72
European networks/practices 138, 276–293
Eversberg, D. 142
Exilio Tropical performance 281, *282–286*, 287–288
exogenous actors, role of 264
exploitation systems 137
exploitative class process 72–75, 77–78, 93
exploitative labour 317
extension strategy, GR 233, 235, 238–240
extractivism activities 109
extractivismo concept 30

Fanon, Frantz 278
farming, collective 119–132, *see also* agriculture
Feiss, E.C. 312
female embodiment *see* bodies/the body
FEMEN group 253–254
'feminisms' 277, 287, 292n1
feminist approaches 5, 108, 197–199, 248–262
feminist praxis 119–132
feudalism 73–77
fieldwork 86–87, 234, 245n1
finances *see* funding issues
fishing industry 166–167
food systems 133–138
Foucault, Michel 34, 248
Fraad, H. 73–75
Frank, A.G. 295
Frankfurt School 97n4
Fry, Tony 12, 324
Fryer, John 303n4
Fuga Caníbal video 287–288, *287*
fuga caníbalismo 291
fugue moment, music 287
funding issues 203–216, 269–273
future: ethics of 44–45; transition 322
futuring by design 294–305

Gago, Verónica 26
Galiwin'ku, Australia 205–206, 209–213
Gandhi, Mohandas 103
Gates, Theaster 312
GDP measure *see* gross domestic product measure
gender 5, 43, 122–123, 126, 131n2, 131n7, 250–251, *see also* women
gender equity, ontologies 193–194
Gender (Illich) 48n4
gendered bodies discourse 249

gendered subsidies 217–230
genealogical intervention 66–67
Germany 133–135, 137–143
Gibson-Graham, J.K. 68, 91, 140, 192, 194, 219–220
global capital circuits 94, 97
Global North: contemporary art 318; developmentalism 100–101, *see also* the North
Global South: design and/in 301–303; developmentalism 100–101; epistemologies 46–47; NGOs working with 309, *see also* the South
global–local contexts 85–86
global–local markets 98n7
good life concept 150
government engagement, Australia 207, 209–211, 213–214
GR *see* Green Revolution
gram panchayats 153, 156
gram sabhas 155–156
Gramsci, Antonio 102
grassroots people 22, 25, 29
'the Great Singularity' 193
green economy concept 104
green growth concept 105
Green Revolution (GR) 231–246
Grewal, Inderpal 249
gross domestic product (GDP) measure 53, 55, 101
'Ground Up' project 203, 205, 207–208, 214, 215n1
Guattari, F. 123
guerrilla tactics, protests 254
gwoupman, Haiti 267–268

haciendas system, Peru 232–233, 235
Haiti 263–275
Haraway, Donna 197, 322
Harcourt, Wendy 5, 12
Harindranath, Ramaswami 309
harmony with nature 58–59
Harris-White, Barbara 2
Hart, G. 263
Harvey, David 136
health networks 180–181
hegemony concepts 78
hegemonic forms, development 90–91
Heidegger, M. 88–89, 300
Heidegger's school 97n4
Heller, Agnes 28
highland Peru 232–237, 243–244
Hildalgo-Capitán, A.L. 54
Hinkson, M. 168

history: of ideas 52, 62; theory of 70
HIV/AIDS epidemic 282–283
households, class process 73–75, 219
housing practices 134, 138–141, 143
human-scale development 54–57, 61
human-scale lifeworld 43–44
hunting activities 169
hybrid economies 163–175
hybridisation, solidarity groups 267–268
hyper-separation, theory/practice 88

ideas 52, 62, 85
identification, subjectivity 44–45
identity, neoliberal 286–287
IHA see Institute for Human Activities
Illich, Ivan 21, 24–25, 27–28, 41, 43, 47, 48n3–4
income sources, Aboriginal 168
India 2, 119–132, 149–162
Indian Modes of Production debate 76–77
Indigenous justice 182–183
Indigenous people-places 204, 209–211
Indigenous peoples/practices: decolonial feminism 250; defuturing 301; economic hybridity 163–175; GR practices 232–234; pluriversality 110–111; political movements 178–179; underdevelopment theory 295, *see also* Aboriginal Australians
Indigenous resistances 256–259
Indonesian agriculture 238, 242
industrialisation 103, 151–153
industrialised capitalism 150, 157–159
inequality–politics relationship 273
INGOs *see* international NGOs
'initiator' term 313, 315–316
'inside' Europe, care/critique 276–293
Institute for Human Activities (IHA) 307–309, *308*, 312–313
institutional development 176–189
instrumental reason 298
insurrectionary politics 35n2
interculturality principle 180
interdependencies of labour 318–319
international NGOs (INGOs) 264–265, 267–271
intersectional analysis, body politics 249–250
intersectional movements 255–256
intimacy 251–254
Ireland, Phil 192

Jagatsinghpur, India 149–162
Japan 37–51
Julien, Isaac 286–287

Kabwegyere, T.B. 222
Kant, Immanuel 204
Kaplan, Cora 249
Karamojong society, Uganda 217–218
Kayatekin, Serap 78
Kester, Grant 307
KJM *see Kolektif Jistis Min*
knowledge democracy 108
knowledge/know-how: *amateur-amante* figure 277; body politics 248; commons movement 34; development alternatives 268–269, 272; ecology of 47–48; local knowledge 137; place-based 46; praxis acquiring 89; slaves 87–88; world of the third 85
Kolektif Jistis Min (KJM) 270–273
Kondh society 119–132
Kuninjku people, Australia 163–165, 169–173

labour 124, 128–319
Lacan, J. 87–88, 90
'lacking Other' 125
land 152, 183, 217–230
landless people 158–159
Lang, Miriam 11
Laos 197–199
Latin America 7–8, 33, 52–65
Latour, Bruno 6
Left ideology 7, 102, 155, 222, 224
legal provisions 252, 257
Lemos, Ego 241
Lenin, Vladimir 78–79
Leopold, Also 106
Lepecki, André 313
lesbian critique 288
liberal ideology 113n41
listening practices 277–278, 323
little-d development 263–264
livelihood of man principles 41
livelihood practices 134, 136–137, 142–143, 157–158, 168–170
living system 39–40, 43, 45
Llamando al mago text 284, *284–285*, 285–287
the local: centralisation projects 39; global–local contexts 85–86; regionalism and 40; world of the third 94–95, 97
local–global markets 98n7
local knowledge 137, 144
local self-help structures 267–270
local state institutions 176–189
'located micro-political' praxis 86
Louis, Robenson 271–272

Lowe, Rick 318
Lugones, María 5
Lütticken, Sven 315
Luxemburg, R. 219

McKinnon, Katharine 11, 192, 264–265, 322
mailo land, Uganda 221, 229n2
Mamdani, M. 218, 222, 225–226
Marín Cisneros, Anyely 12, 289
market-imposed needs 28–29
market sector, interactions 165–167, 170–172
market system 41, 98n7, 143, 157, 192–193
Martens, Renzo 308–309
Marxism 66–71, 73, 76–78, 102–103, 312–313, 322
masculinity 108
maternity care 190–202
mawonaj concept 266
Max-Neef, Manfred 53, 55–56, 58–60
MDGs *see* Millennium Development Goals
meaning, sites of 248–249, 323
medicine 195–196, 281
Meiji Restoration, Japan 38, 48n1
'mental labour' 313
Merleau-Ponty, Maurice 300
'Mietshäusersyndikat' association 134, 138–141
migrant social movements 313, 315
migrants 310, 314–315, 318
Millennium Development Goals (MDGs) 52–53
mingas, Ecuador 182
'modern' paradigm 33
modern political theory 43–44
modernisation: China 297; Japan 38–39
modernism 69, 72, 90–91, 94, 97
modernity: communities 26, 28; conception of 101–102; definition problem 303n2; design futuring 294–297, 303; disillusionment with 31, 33; Japan 41–42; the West 32
modes of production 69–70, 76–77
monetary benefits 269–271
Morandeira, Julia 285
Muhereza, F. 217
multiple ontologies 193–194
multiple worlds, the body in 194–195
Mumeka, Australia 165
Muniesa, F. 192
Museveni, Yoweri 223
music 258–259, 287

Nabón, Ecuador 179–181, 183–186
Naht Hanh, Thich 31
Nakamura, Yujirou 45–48, 49n5
Nakano, Yoshihiro 10
Nandy, Ashis 31
National Resistance Army/Movement (NRA/M), Uganda 224–225
National Resistance Movement (NRM), Uganda 217, 223–226
nationalisation 222–223
nature 58–59, 61, 111
N'Dione, E. 269
'necro-art' 318
needs 23–25, 27–28, 56, 59–60, *see also* basic needs
neoliberal identity 286–287
networks of care/critique 276–293
new commons 136–137, 143–144
new social movements 90
NGOs *see* non-governmental organizations
non-capitalist class processes 94, 125
non-capitalist formations 219–220
non-exploitative class process 72, 93–94
non-governmental organizations (NGOs) 234–235, 237, 242, 270–271, 306–321
non-market sector 171–172
noosphere notion 304n7
the North, alternatives 133–148, *see also* Global North
northern Australia 203–216
Nost, E. 136
NRA/M *see* National Resistance Army/Movement
NRM *see* National Resistance Movement
nudity as protest 253–254
Nyikamula, Djankirrawuy 205

Obote, Milton 221–223, 224
Odisha, India 119–132, 149–162
Ögüt, Ahmet 310
Okinawa Self-Governance Constitution (Tamanoi) 42–43
on-farm demonstration trials 238–239
ontological colonial agents 298–299
ontological pluralism 190–202
ontological turn 6–7
'ontology of design' 215n7, 300
oppositional politics 151–155
ordinary justice 182–183
orientalism 70–71, 91, 94, 97
Ortiz, Daniela 314, *314*

Osborne, Peter 317
Ossome, Lyn 11
the Other/otherness 125, 247, 295
'outside' Europe, care/critique 276–293

panchayati raj system 156, 160n6
páramos, Ecuador 183–184, 187n8
Parmar, Pratibha 286–287
partial commodification concept 166, 171
participatory budgeting 184
participatory social practice 307, 309
partnerships 264
patriarchal order 109–110
Pattnaik, Sandeep 11
Pearce, J. 265
'peasant' term 274n3
peasant solidarity groups 266–271, 273
peasantry 218–219, 224–228, 233–235, 238–239
Peck, J. 168
Pedanti, Daima 128, 129
Pedenti, Aiya 123–124
Pedenti, Debi 122
people-places 204, 206, 209–211
performance art 307, 315, 317
performativity of discourse 192
person-based development 56
Peru 232–237, 243–244
Peterson, Nicolas 169
phronesis–praxis 87–88, 97n5
place 84–85, 92, 97, 97n2
place-based knowledge 46
pluralistic ontology 190–202
plurinationality 176–189
pluriversality 7, 32, 100–116, 159, 324
poiesis 88–90
Polanyi, K. 41
political movements 178–179
political ontology 6
political relations 180–183
political theory 43–44
politics: of the common good 42; of commoning 311; of labour 313–316; of ontological pluralism 190–202; oppositional 151–155; of place 92; postfeudal 76–79; realms of 263–275; state-funded services 203–216
POSCO Pratirodh Sangram Samiti (PPSS) 149–151, 153–154, 156–159
POSCO project 149–150, 153–154, 156
postcapitalist–feminist practice 122–130
postcapitalist praxis 119–132
postcolonial feminism 249–250
postcolonial theory 4–5

postcolonialism, defining 9
postdevelopment: alternatives to 133–148; defining 191–193; emergence 3–4; theoretical links 4–8
postfeudal politics 76–79
postneoliberalism 7–8, 12n2
potato farming 232–237, *236–237*
poverty 103, 152, 185–186, 273
power: archival 278–281; of colonialism 298–299; economic growth 224; knowledge relationship 269; of protesting bodies 253–254; of the state 222; of technology 324; theories of 159
PPSS *see* POSCO Pratirodh Sangram Samiti
'practical' behaviour 88–90
practice–praxis question 322
Prakash, M. 155
praxis, world of the third 84–99, 322
precarity, age of 276–293
Preciado, Paul B. 283–284
production, modes of 69–70, 76–77
productivity concept 171
progress system 4
prosperity discourse 169–170
protesting bodies 253–254
psychological limits/harmonies 54–57
psychopower 298, 299, 301–302, 303n5
psychotechnologies 298–299, 303n6
public-communitarian partnerships 183
public policy goals 57–60
public works 182
'pure technique/theory' 90

Quezada, Magali 181

racism 254–256, 276
radical subaltern consciousness 78–79
Radio Europe performance 278, *279*, 280–282, 284
Ramírez, René 57
Rayagada district, Odisha 119–132
re-constitutive project 66
'rearguard theory' 151
rebel listening 277–278, 281, 291, 323
reconstruction, development as 91–97
RECS *see* Remote Engagement and Coordination Strategy
Reframing Aids (Parmar) 286–287
refugees 140–141, 317–318
regime changes, Uganda 220–224
regional economies 164
regionalism 37–51, 323
Reinscriptions publication 288–289, *290*, 291
relationality approaches 5

religion 106
Remote Engagement and Coordination Strategy (RECS) 207, 212–213
representation systems, lesbian critique 288
reproductive justice 251–252
research projects, state-funded 207–209, 214–215
resignification 177
resistance 154, 224–225, 227–228, 256–259, 266–267, 276–277
Resnick, S. 71
reverse guerrilla tactics 254
Revilla, Luís *236*
reworlding, body politics 256–259
rice agriculture 237–242
Rich, Adrienne 278–279
Right ideology 102
rights 58–59, 61, 111
risk 168, 296
Rivera Cusicanqui, Silvia 26
Robbins, B. 204
romanticism 25, 134
Rudra, Ashok 77
rulership, Uganda 220–224
rural livelihoods 136–137

sabka sath strategy 120, 130n1
sabka vikas strategy 120, 130n1
Sachses development approach 22
Sahoo, Abhay 154
Said, Edward 32
Sampedro, José Luis 53–55, 57–58, 61
Sanghathan farming 120–124, 126–130
Santana, Francisco 282
satisfiers–needs distinction 56
scaling down 284
Schmelzer, M. 142
Schöneberg, Julia 12
science and technology studies (STS) 6–7
scientific knowledge 144
SDGs *see* Sustainable Development Goals
Seeds of Lies (SoL) project 238–241, *239*, 243–244
seeing, technology of 288, 291
Seers, Dudley 53, 56
self care 300
self-governance 155–157
self-help 154, 267–270
Sen, Amartya 3, 55
sensitivity, cosmopolitics 214–215
sensus communis concept 46
services delivery 203–216
sex–gender oppression 109
sexual rights agenda 251

sexual violence 253
Shafiee, Katayoun 6
Shelley, Mary 103
Shepherd, Christopher 11
Shiva, Vandana 156–157
signifiers of authorship 316
silence, technology of 278–281
The Silent University (SU) project 307, 310–313, 315, 318
singleness, women 121, 123, 125
sites of meaning 248–249, 323
slaves/slavery 74, 87–88
small-scale industrialised capitalism 150, 157–159
social action discourses 265–266
social justice 27, 60, 107
social movements 263–264, 272, 273, 313, 315
social organisation 265–271
social practice 307–309, 316–318
social processes 68, 71–72, 76
social reproduction 217–230
socialism 60
'socio–economic dualism' 91
socioeconomic studies 240–241
sociology of absence 193–194
SoL project *see* Seeds of Lies project
Solawi 135–138
'Solidarische Landwirtschaft' groups 133–134, 135–136
solidarity 55, 133–141, 143
solidarity groups 266–271, 273
sonic action 278–281
the South: 'art as NGO' 321; 'development' in 134–135; epistemologies 45–48, *see also* Global South
space 84–85, 88, 92, 94
Spain 52–65, 138
Spencer, Michaela 11
Spivak, G.C. 70
squatting practices 138–141
Sriniketan institution 86–87
'standard of living' notion 27
standardized development narratives 185–186
the state: industrialised capitalism 157–159; oppositional politics 151–152; power of 222; role of 323–324; self-governance and 155–157; women/peasantry incorporation 226
state-centric *buen vivir* 60, 62
state-funded services 203–216
state-imposed needs 28–29

state institutions 176–189
state sector, interactions 165, 167–168
state subsidisation 167, 172
'staying with the trouble' process 197, 322
Stengers, Isabelle 204
Stiegler, Bernard 298
streamlining technology 296
STS *see* science and technology studies
SU project *see The Silent University* project
subaltern consciousness 78–79
subaltern imagination 119–120
subaltern know-how 88
Subaltern Studies 69, 79n3
subaltern subjectivity 70–71, 76
subjectivity 44–45, 70–71, 75–76, 78
subsidisation practices 167, 172, 217–230
sumak kawsay concept 59–60
Superflex collective 306–308
surplus appropriation 76, 129–130
surplus labour 92–93, **93**, 124, 169
surrogacy practices 252
'surviving well together' approach 190–202
sustainability 103–105, 299–300
Sustainable Development Goals (SDGs) 3, 63n1, 104–105
Svampa, Maristella 7
swaraj concept 106, 109, 155

Tagore, Rabindranath 86–88
Tamanoi, Yoshirou 37–51
Tan, Pelin 311
TCM *see* Traditional Chinese Medicine
techne reasoning 89
techno-colonialism 298–299
technoaffective reinscriptions 276–293, 292n2
technology 28–29, 158, 278–281, 288, 291, 298–299, 324
techno-power 324
Tello, Verónica 12, 321
tenement trust 143–144
territorial practice 178–180
theoria 87–89
third worldism 84–99
Thomassin, Annick 166–167
Timor *see* East Timor
tipeyizan term 274n3
Torres Strait 166–167
tourism 252, 268
Traditional Chinese Medicine (TCM) 195–196
transformative strategies 106–107, 176–189

transitions 66–83, 111–112, 322
transmissions 281–288
'transmodernity' idea 303
transnational body politics 253, 255–256
transnational social movements 273
transnational surrogacy 252
triple alliance building 272–273
Tripp, A.M. 223–224, 226–227

ubuntu concept 106, 109
Uganda 217–230
underdevelopment 133, 295
Underhill-Sem, Yvonne 192
United States (US), agriculture 135–138
universality concept 110
The *University see The Silent University* project
university studies 86–87
unsustainability 295–296
US *see* United States

Vavilov, Nikolai 233, 238
Venezuelan passport crisis 284, 292n4
vernacular gender 43
Verran, Helen. 208
Vicos project, Peru 233
Vikalp Sangam values 107–108, 110, 113n32
Vishmidt, M. 312
Viveiros de Castro, Eduardo 287–288
volunteer labour 311

wage labour 113n35, 157–159, 171–172
Walsh, Catherine 5
water management 181, 183–184
Watson, Irene 256–258, 259n5
well-being 107, 183–186, 190–202
the West: alternative postdevelopment 133; modernity 32
Western art 312, 319
Western feminism 248–249, 256
'Western medicine' 195
WHO *see* World Health Organization
Wolf, R.D. 71
women: collective farming 119–132; coordinating labour 314; dispossession of 227; land control 221; liberal ideology 113n41; maternity care 190–202; peasant struggles 225–226; pluriversality 108, 111; protesting bodies 253–254; reproductive justice 251–252; rights of 249; wage labour 113n35, 158–159, *see also* gender
'working-in-the-fields' 86–87

workshop space 277–278, 288, 291
World Health Organization (WHO) 194–195
world of the third 84–99, 127, 322–323
Wright, Stephen 316

Xining, China 195–197

Yalu' organization 205, 212–213, 215n3
Yasuní-ITT Initiative 61, 111, 143–144
yellow fever epidemic 281, *290*
Yolŋu Aboriginals 204–206, 209–214

Zapatistas 28–30, 33
Ziai, A. 152–153, 157, 264